(left) **Insectarium p99**

(above) **Beignets, Café du Monde p63**

(right) **Rainbow flags, French Quarter p48**

Mid-City, Bayou St John & City Park p139

Tremé-Lafitte p151

Faubourg Marigny & Bywater p82

French Quarter p48

CBD & Warehouse District p95

Uptown & Riverbend p125

Garden, Lower Garden & Central City p112

Welcome to New Orleans

The things that make life worth living – eating, drinking and merrymaking – are the air that New Orleans breathes.

Epicurean Appetite

We hope you're not reading this at home. We hope you're *in* New Orleans, because you're about to eat better than most others. When it comes to food, New Orleans does not fool around. Well, OK, it does: its playful attitude to ingredients and recipes mixes (for example) alligator sausage and cheesecake into a dessert fit for the gods. This sense of gastronomic play is rooted in both deep traditions – truly, this city has one of the few indigenous cuisines in the country – and, increasingly, a willingness to accommodate outside influences, both in terms of technique and ethnicity.

Celebration Seasons

We're not exaggerating when we say there is either a festival or a parade every week of the year in New Orleans. Sometimes, such as during Mardi Gras or Jazz Fest, it feels like there's a new party for every hour of the day. At almost any celebration in town, people engage in masking – donning a new appearance via some form of costuming – while acting out the boisterous side of human behavior. But the celebrations and rituals of New Orleans are as much about history as hedonism, and every dance is as much an expression of tradition and community spirit as it is of joy.

Unceasing Song

New Orleans is the hometown of jazz, but neither the city nor the genre she birthed are musical museum pieces. Jazz is the root of American popular music, the daddy of rock, brother of the blues and not too distant ancestor of hip-hop – all styles of music that have defined the beat of global pop for decades. All these varieties of music, plus a few you may never have heard of, are practiced and played here on every corner, in any bar, every night of the week. Live music isn't an event: it's as crucial to the city soundscape as streetcar bells.

Candid Culture

There aren't many places in the USA that wear their history as openly on their sleeves as New Orleans. This city's very facade is an architectural study par excellence. And while cities like Boston and Charleston can boast beautiful buildings, New Orleans has an added lived-in grittiness that either feels intimidating or easily accessible. As a result of its visible history you'll find a constant, often painful, dialogue with the past, stretching back hundreds of years. It's a history that for all its controversy has produced a street culture that can be observed and grasped in a very visceral way.

Why I Love New Orleans

By Adam Karlin

On those days when I can relax, New Orleans is there to ease me into the experience. I can have a few day drinks at a favorite bar, eat a meal at a corner restaurant, watch a parade or theater or music unfold in the street itself, and all the while be ensconced in an architectural pastiche that is simply heart-rending. Down here there's beauty, for all the senses, all the time – but it's a *lived-in* beauty, and it sets my heart right.

For more about our writers, see p256

Top: Daniel Farrow performing at Preservation Hall (p68) in the French Quarter

New Orleans'
Top 10

Loving Live Music *(p39)*

1 Music flows deep in the soul of New Orleans. Every beat, be it Cajun fiddle or brass-band drumline, measures out the rhythm of the cultures that came together to create this startlingly unique city. Frenchmen Street is packed with joints playing rock, metal, hip-hop, folk and, of course, jazz. If you can walk its few small blocks without hearing something you like, you may as well keep walking out of New Orleans, because the sound and the soul of this city are inextricably married.

☆ *Entertainment*

Creole Architecture *(p48)*

2 Looks aren't always skin deep. In New Orleans the architectural skin is integral to the city's spirit – and gives an undeniably distinctive sense of place. What immediately sets New Orleans apart from the USA is the architecture of the Creole *faubourgs* ('fo-burgs'), or neighborhoods. This includes the shaded porches of the French Quarter, of course, but also filigreed Marigny homes, candy-colored Bywater cottages and the grand manses of Esplanade Ave (pictured). Look down streets in these areas and you'll know, intuitively and intensely, that you are in New Orleans.

◉ *French Quarter; Faubourg Marigny & Bywater*

CHUCK WAGNER/SHUTTERSTOCK ©

FOTOLUMINATE LLC/SHUTTERSTOCK ©

Mardi Gras (p74)

3 There's spectacle, and then there's Mardi Gras. On Fat Tuesday, the most fantastic costumes, the weirdest pageantry, West African rituals, Catholic liturgy, homegrown traditions, massive parade floats, and a veritable river of booze all culminate in the single most exhausting and exhilarating day of your life. At all times of year, New Orleans is a feast for the senses, but she becomes a veritable all-you-can-eat banquet during Carnival time, and achieves a sort of apotheosis of hedonism come Mardi Gras day.

🎭 *Mardi Gras & Jazz Fest*

Eating a Po'boy (p29)

4 If by 'sandwich' we mean a portable meal that contains vegetable and meat enclosed by starch, the po'boy is perfection, the Platonic ideal of sandwiches. But let's get to the detail: its fresh filling (roast beef or fried seafood are the most common, but the possibilities are endless), tomatoes, lettuce, onion, mayo, pickles and a perfect loaf of not-quite-French bread. The ideal po'boy is elusive: try Mahony's on Magazine St, Domilise's Po-boys Uptown or Parkway in Mid-City. Bottom left: Oyster po'boy

🍴 *Eating*

Drinking Classic Cocktails (p32)

5 A significant case could be made that the cocktail, a blend of spirits mixed into something delicious and dangerous, was invented in New Orleans. Bitters, long considered a crucial component of any cocktail, is the homegrown creation of a French Quarter pharmacy. When someone calls a drink a 'classic cocktail,' it's because local bartenders have been making it here for centuries. The ultimate New Orleans drink is the Sazerac (pictured above); it can be enjoyed at any time of day, but always adds a touch of class.

🍷 *Drinking & Nightlife*

Second Lines (p158)

6 New Orleans is a city that loves to celebrate, but you don't have to wait for a specific day on the calendar to throw down. Second Lines – neighborhood parades thrown by African American civic organizations known as Social Aid and Pleasure Clubs – are weekly parades that kick off every Sunday outside of summer. Folks gather somewhere in the city (often in Tremé); a band leads the way, dancers parade in their finest clothes, and the Second Line – a following crowd, which should include you – high steps behind.

◉ *Tremé-Lafitte*

Crescent Park (p84)

7 The Mississippi River has long been the defining geographic feature of New Orleans, but for years, it lacked a park that truly allowed for quiet enjoyment of the waterfront (the path that edges the French Quarter has always been too busy for contemplation). No longer. Crescent Park not only links the Marigny to Bywater; it showcases, via a mix of green landscaping and austere metallic installations, both the watery might of the Mississippi and the gothic edges of old riverfront industrial facilities.

◉ *Faubourg Marigny & Bywater*

6

8

St Charles Avenue Streetcar *(p129)*

8 Some of the grandest homes in the USA line St Charles Ave, shaded by enormous live oak trees that glitter with the tossed beads of hundreds of Mardi Gras floats. Underneath in the shade, joggers pace themselves along the grassy 'neutral ground' (median) while Tulane kids flirt with Loyola friends. Clanging through this bucolic corridor comes the St Charles Avenue Streetcar, a mobile bit of urban transportation history, bearing tourists and commuters along a street as important to American architecture as Frank Lloyd Wright.

👁 *Uptown & Riverbend*

Shopping on Magazine Street *(p40)*

9 Forget Fifth Ave. Erase Oxford Street. So long, Rue Saint-Honoré. Magazine Street – specifically the 3-mile stretch of it that smiles along the bottom bend of New Orleans' Uptown – may be the world's best shopping street. Sure, there's an absence of big names, but you'll uncover a glut of indie boutiques; tons of vintage; po'boys for the hungry; antiques warehouses galore; art galleries in profusion; big shady trees; and architecture that will charm your toes off.

Right: Funky Monkey (p123), Magazine Street

🛍 *Shopping*

Bayou St John *(p143)*

10 The Mississippi River is nice and all, but it's big and busy and, to be frank, it doesn't always smell great. Bayou St John, on the other hand, is a quiet, rustic, yet aquatic escape located smack in the middle of the city. This winding waterway once served as a riverine highway across the swamps, but today it's a spot to walk your dog, take a romantic stroll, have a breeze-blown picnic and just generally escape from the urban jungle.

◉ *Mid-City, Bayou St John & City Park*

What's New

Lafitte Greenway

It's been years in the making, but this walking and cycling path has finally opened, connecting the Tremé all the way to City Park. (p154)

Catahoula Hotel

Fine new contemporary hotels are popping up across the New Orleans CBD, but the Catahoula deserves a shout for being a homegrown addition to the boutique property game. (p183)

Passions

If we told you there was a vampire bar in New Orleans, would you believe us? Well, you've got to find the password first... (p66)

Marjie's Grill

Lots of restaurants try to re-invent Southeast Asian cuisine, but the brilliant cooks at Marjie's have learned to simply adhere to the best traditions of that region, adding minor twists. (p146)

Audubon Louisiana Nature Center

Head out to New Orleans East to this center, and you can explore the hardwood forest and dark water wetlands of the South Louisiana wilderness without leaving the city.

French Library

It's not just an impossibly adorable bookstore – it's an impossibly adorable bookstore where the books are all in French. (p137)

Broad Theater

Cinema lovers will enjoy reveling in this new movie hall, which shows everything from art-house indie to the most explosive Hollywood blockbusters.

Seaworthy

This seafood restaurant is, more than any other place in town, pushing the boundaries of what can be done with the fresh bounty of the Gulf of Mexico. (p102)

Poke Poke

This city loves to fry its seafood, but new restaurants like Poke-chan (p86) and Poke Loa (p116) are bringing *poke* – Hawaiian seafood salad, a thing of beauty – to the city of New Orleans.

Compère Lapin

Chef Nina Compton's restaurant has added a new dimension to New Orleans Creole cuisine, throwing in the roots of the Caribbean to this northernmost Caribbean city. (p104)

For more recommendations and reviews, see **lonelyplanet. com/usa/new-orleans**

Need to Know

For more information, see Survival Guide (p213)

Currency
US dollars ($)

Languages
English, Spanish

Visas
Visas are required for most foreign visitors unless eligible for the Visa Waiver Program (VWP).

Money
ATMs are widely available.

Cell Phones
Local SIM cards can be used in European and Australian phones. Other phones must be set to roaming.

Time
Central Time (GMT/UTC minus six hours)

Tourist Information
The New Orleans Welcome Center (☎504-568-5661; www.crt. state.la.us/tourism; 529 St Ann St; ⊗8:30am-5pm) in the lower Pontalba Building offers maps, listings of upcoming events and a variety of brochures for sights, restaurants and hotels. You can also order or download a Louisiana-wide travel guide online from the **Louisiana Office of Tourism** (www.louisianatravel.com).

Daily Costs

Budget: Less than $150
➡ Dorm bed: $30
➡ Self-cater or cheap takeout meal: $10
➡ Beer at local bar: $3–5
➡ Bicycle rental: $20
➡ All-day streetcar pass: $3

Midrange: $150–250
➡ Guesthouse or B&B double room: $100–150
➡ Neighborhood restaurant meal for two: $50–70
➡ Bicycle rental or split taxi fares: $20–40

Top End: More than $250
➡ Fine dining for two, plus wine: $150–200
➡ Four-star double hotel rooms: from $200
➡ Taxis or car rental: $40–60

Advance Planning

Three months before Check if any festivals are going down; book hotel rooms if you're arriving during Mardi Gras or Jazz Fest.

One month before Organize car rental. Make bookings at high-end restaurants you don't want to miss.

One week before Read *Gambit* (www.bestofneworleans.com) and check www.neworleansonline.com to see what's going on in the way of live music during your visit.

Useful Websites

Gambit (www.bestof neworleans.com) Arts and entertainment listings.

New Orleans Online (www. neworleansonline.com) Official tourism website.

WWOZ radio (www.wwoz.org) Firm finger on the cultural pulse.

Times-Picayune (www.nola. com) Three-times-a-week newspaper.

Lonely Planet (www.lonely planet.com/usa/new-orleans) Your trusted traveler website.

WHEN TO GO

In Mid-March to late May the weather is pleasant for shorts and shirt sleeves. By October, the weather begins to cool off from the long, long summer.

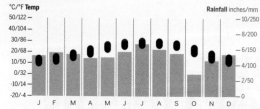

New Orleans

°C/°F Temp

Rainfall inches/mm

Arriving in New Orleans

Louis Armstrong New Orleans International Airport (MSY) Located 13 miles west of New Orleans. A taxi to the CBD costs $36, or $15 per passenger for three or more passengers. Shuttles to the CBD cost $24/44 per person one way/return.

Amtrak & Greyhound Located adjacent to each other downtown on Loyola Ave. A taxi from here to the French Quarter should cost around $10; further afield you'll be pressed to spend more than $20.

For much more on **arrival** see p214

Getting Around

Streetcar Service on the charming streetcars is limited. One-way fares cost $1.25, and multitrip passes are available.

Bus Services are OK, but try not to time your trip around them. Fares won't run more than $2.

Walk If you're just exploring the French Quarter, your feet will serve just fine.

Bicycle Flat New Orleans is easy to cycle – you can cross the entirety of town in 45 minutes.

Car This is the easiest way to access outer neighborhoods such as Mid-City. Parking is problematic in the French Quarter and CBD.

For much more on **getting around** see p215

Sleeping

Local accommodations are generally of a high standard. Hotels are found in the French Quarter and CBD. These are large, mul-tistory affairs kitted out with amenities; hotels in the French Quarter tend to have a more boutique, historical feel, while CBD properties are more modern. More intimate (and quirky) guesthouses and B&Bs are the norm in the Garden District, Uptown, Faubourg Marigny and the Bywater. There is one hostel in Mid-City.

Useful Websites

➡ **New Orleans Online** (www. neworleansonline.com/book) Official tourism website.

➡ **Louisiana Bed & Breakfast Association** (www.louisianabandb.com) Directory of local B&Bs and guesthouses.

➡ **New Orleans Hotels** (www. bestneworleanshotels.com) Has some links to private home rentals and national chains.

➡ **Lonely Planet** (http:// www.lonelyplanet.com/ usa/new-orleans/hotels) A comprehensive, curated list of properties.

For much more on **sleeping** see p161

THE NEW ORLEANS COMPASS

North, south, east and west? Not in New Orleans. This city's directions are determined by bodies of water and how they flow, not by a compass. Here folks say Lake, River, Up and Down. 'Lake' is Lake Pontchartrain, north of the city. 'River,' of course, is the Mississippi. 'Up' and 'down' refer to the flow of the river, which heads 'down' towards the Gulf of Mexico. So 'Down' basically means 'east,' and 'Up' basically means west. Confused? It makes more sense when you're here, honest.

First Time New Orleans

For more information, see Survival Guide (p213)

Checklist

➡ Make sure your passport is valid for at least six months past your arrival date.

➡ Check airline baggage restrictions.

➡ Inform your debit-/credit-card company.

➡ Reserve dinner at higher-end spots.

➡ Check what festivals are occurring (there will be at least one).

➡ Organize your rental car (p216).

➡ Confirm dates with your lodging.

➡ Check WWOZ for Second Line (p158) information.

What to Pack

➡ Rain gear.

➡ Comfortable walking shoes or sandals.

➡ A nice shirt or dress for a potential night out.

➡ Something that could work as a costume – a feather boa, silly hat etc.

➡ A form of identification besides your passport; New Orleans bouncers are getting strict about IDs.

Top Tips for Your Trip

➡ The French Quarter is one of the most beautiful slices of preserved architecture in North America, and it's home to many of the city's great restaurants, bars and music venues. With that said, many tourists never leave the Quarter. That's a shame, as much of the city's local life occurs outside of its confines.

➡ From May until as late as October, New Orleans can be hot. Face-melting hot. Make sure to hydrate often.

➡ If you're going to be driving, avoid trying to park in the French Quarter and the CBD, unless you're OK with paying a lot fee. Street parking is tight and subject to residential restrictions.

What to Wear

New Orleanians are pretty casual about fashion, but some of the city's nicer restaurants have a jackets-only policy for men. Usually a jacket will be provided by the restaurant in question (call ahead to check), but gents will still want to bring a collared shirt and slacks. Ladies can get by with a dress or nice set of slacks and shirt.

Be Forewarned

New Orleans has a high crime rate, but most violent crime occurs between parties that already know each other.

➡ Muggings do occur. Solo travelers are targeted more often; avoid entering secluded areas alone.

➡ The French Quarter is safe around the clock for the visitor.

➡ The CBD and Warehouse District are busy on weekdays, but relatively deserted at night and on weekends.

➡ The B&Bs along Esplanade Ridge are close enough to troubled neighborhoods to require caution at night.

➡ Some areas of Central City can feel lonely after dark. At night, park close to your destination on a well-traveled street.

➡ Be wary before entering an intersection: local drivers are notorious for running yellow and even red lights.

➡ Drink spikings do occur.

Money

ATMs are widely available.

Tipping

Hotels A dollar or two per bag carried to your room.

Restaurants Mandatory. Standard 18% for good service, 20% for exceptional service.

Music Kick in a few bucks when the band passes around a bucket or hat.

Bars Leave a dollar every time you order – more for a large round.

Taxi Tip 10% or round up the fare.

Taxes & Refunds

A 10% sales tax is tacked onto virtually everything, including meals, groceries and car rentals. For accommodations, room and occupancy taxes, add an extra 13% to your bill plus $1 to $3 per person, depending on the size of the hotel.

For foreign visitors, some merchants in Louisiana participate in a program called Louisiana Tax Free Shopping (www.louisianataxfree. com). Look for the snazzy red-and-blue 'Tax Free' logo in the window or on the sign of the store. Usually these stores specialize in the kinds of impulse purchases people are likely to make while on vacation. In these stores, present a passport to verify you are not a US citizen, and request a voucher as you make your purchase. Reimbursement centers are located in the Downtown Refund Center (p221) and the Airport Refund Center (p221) in the main ticket lobby in Terminal C at the airport.

Live music on Royal Street (p54)

Etiquette

New Orleanians tend to be a casual bunch, but good manners go a long way here, as is the case in much of the rest of the American South.

Greetings It's bad form to just dive into the business at hand in New Orleans. Greet someone, ask how they're doing, and expect an honest answer in return; this city has a good attitude, but it also has an honest one.

Conversation In a similar vein: New Orleanians like to chat. Be it small talk or rambling on a topic at hand, the citizens of this city are not, on balance, a reserved people. Don't be surprised if you hear a few uncomfortably long anecdotes or life stories within minutes of meeting someone.

Katrina

Hurricane Katrina irrevocably changed New Orleans, and discussions about it can be charged. If you deem it a natural disaster, realize that many people here consider it (with some justification) more of a failure of human-made institutions. Some New Orleanians didn't even live here during the storm; some did and want to forget about it; and some will open their hearts to you. Judge your conversation carefully.

Top Itineraries

Day One

French Quarter (p48)

 Wake up and smell the coffee (and enjoy a croissant) at Croissant D'Or Patisserie (p63). Afterwards, take a stroll around the streets as they wake up (or shake off last night), and then sign up for the Friends of the Cabildo walking tour (p73), our favorite introduction to the architectural wonders of the French Quarter.

 Lunch Mister Gregory's (p63): French baguettes with truly innovative fillings.

French Quarter (p48)

Wander through Jackson Square (p52), the green heart of the neighborhood, and explore the Quarter's museums, such as the Cabildo (p50) and Presbytère (p53), where you can learn more about the history of New Orleans and Louisiana. Afterwards, enjoy a free afternoon concert at the Old US Mint (p57).

Dinner Modern Louisianan at Bayona (p60), base of local hero Susan Spicer.

French Quarter (p48)

Relax with a drink at Bar Tonique (p64) or French 75 (p66), two of the finest cocktail bars in a city that invented the cocktail. Take in a show at Preservation Hall (p68) or One Eyed Jacks (p69), and when the music is over, have a 3am breakfast at the Clover Grill (p63).

Day Two

CBD & Warehouse District (p95)

 Spend a morning visiting the Ogden Museum of Southern Art (p98). Once you've immersed yourself in the aesthetics of the region, consider immersing yourself in the contemporary art scene at the appropriately dubbed Contemporary Arts Center (p99), and maybe catch a gallery on Julia St while you're at it.

 Lunch Cochon Butcher (p101) for artisan meats with a Cajun twist.

Garden, Lower Garden & Central City (p112)

Stroll along pretty Magazine St in a state of shopping nirvana. Then walk north, pop into Lafayette Cemetery No 1 (p114) and hop onto the St Charles Avenue Streetcar (p129), heading west toward Audubon Park (p128). Along the way, you'll soak up the lovely architecture and the shade of live oak trees that runs along all of St Charles Ave. Afterwards, continue along in the streetcar towards the Riverbend.

Dinner Creative Vietnamese at Ba Chi Canteen (p129).

Uptown & Riverbend (p125)

Have a boozy night perusing the excellent beer menu at Cooter Brown's Tavern & Oyster Bar (p135) and consider having an oyster or ten on the side. Then finish it off by heading to the Maple Leaf Bar (p136) or Tipitina's (p136) and rocking out to whoever is playing.

Day Three

Faubourg Marigny & Bywater (p82)

 Get the day going with oysters and grits at Cake Café & Bakery (p86). Eat early so you can join the morning Creole Neighborhoods cycle tour with Confederacy of Cruisers (p94). If you don't fancy traveling on two wheels, walk past Washington Square Park (p85) and Elysian Fields Ave into the residential portion of the Marigny and just lose yourself amidst all of the candy-colored houses.

Lunch Lost Love (p87) dive bar has a surprise Vietnamese kitchen.

Faubourg Marigny & Bywater (p82)

Walk east (or 'down' in New Orleans directional-speak) along Royal or Congress Sts and check out the riot of rainbow residences; on the way, you'll pass the Press Street Gardens (p84). Once you pass Press St, you're in the Bywater; look for Dr Bob's Studio (p93). Then take a walk into the Crescent Park (p84), where you can enjoy great views of the Mississippi.

Dinner Bacchanal (p88) for wine and cheese in a musical garden.

Faubourg Marigny & Bywater (p82)

 Head back into Faubourg Marigny to listen to live music on St Claude Ave or on Frenchmen Street (p84).

Day Four

Tremé-Lafitte (p151)

 Consider renting a bicycle and riding around the Tremé; Governor Nicholls St is particularly attractive. Driving is also an option. While in the neighborhood, don't miss the Backstreet Cultural Museum (p154); from here, it's an easy walk into Louis Armstrong Park. (p154)

Lunch Willie Mae's Scotch House (p158) Get the fried chicken. Just do it.

Tremé-Lafitte (p151)

Head up Esplanade Avenue (p143) and gawk at all the gorgeous Creole mansions sitting prettily under live oaks. Take Esplanade Ave all the way to City Park (p141) and wander around the New Orleans Museum of Art (p143). Afterwards, you can relax for a spell under the trees or along the banks of bucolic Bayou St John.

Dinner Café Degas (p147) for fabulously romantic French fine dining.

Mid-City, Bayou St John & City Park (p139)

 Have a well-mixed drink at friendly Twelve Mile Limit (p148); it also serves barbecue, in case you feel peckish again. Now that the night is ending, consider catching some more live music (this is New Orleans, folks) at a favorite venue you've discovered during your trip.

If You Like...

Architecture

The urban 'skin' of New Orleans – her buildings and streetscape – is the most distinctive in the USA.

Royal Street This is quintessential French Quarter: stroll past fine Creole town houses and wonderful iron balconies. (p54)

St Charles Avenue Live oak trees shade some of the most beautiful plantation-style mansions in the South, best viewed by streetcar. (p129)

Esplanade Avenue Another shady street where the villas are French Caribbean inspired; Degas once lived here. (p143)

Coliseum Square Lovely multilevel historical homes from this pretty little park. (p115)

Faubourg Marigny & Bywater Lovely, colorful Creole cottages are scattered over this area like candy. (p82)

Preservation Resource Center Your one-stop shop, as it were, for learning about the city's architecture. (p101)

Creole Cuisine

The flavors may stem from France, Africa and the Americas, but New Orleans has developed her own cuisine.

Commander's Palace One of New Orleans' most legendary restaurants, a proving ground for many a young local chef. (p119)

Patois Excellent French cuisine given a New Orleans twist, housed in a wonderfully atmospheric historic home. (p134)

Historic Southern-style home, Faubourg Marigny (p82)

FOTOLUMINATE LLC/SHUTTERSTOCK©

Galatoire's Where the New Orleans elite still gathers every Friday; a restaurant and experience of another era. (p60)

Dooky Chase The grand dame of African American New Orleans Creole cooking. (p159)

Jacques-Imo's Café An eclectic twist on Creole traditions. (p132)

Free Stuff

You don't have to spend a lot (to soak up the magic of this enchanting city.

Jackson Square One of America's great town greens and the heart of the Quarter. (p52)

Frenchmen Street A ton of fun, especially on weekdays, when the crowds thin out but music still plays. (p84)

Mardi Gras No introduction necessary. (p90)

New Orleans Jazz National Historic Park Soak up the rich history of jazz here. (p58)

Preservation Resource Center Can provide all you need for a self-guided architecture tour. (p101)

Sydney & Walda Besthoff Sculpture Garden Take a pleasant stroll around 60-odd sculptures. (p143)

Green Spaces

Semi-tropical New Orleans fairly bursts with greenery; these are some of the public places where her nature is preserved.

City Park The largest, most beautiful green space in the city of New Orleans. (p141)

Bayou St John This waterway is one of the nicest places for a stroll in the city. (p145)

Audubon Park A great green lawn overhung by live oak trees in Uptown. (p128)

Lafitte Greenway A pedestrian and cycling path that connects some of the city's most iconic neighborhoods. (p154)

The Fly Stroll along the riverside while kids play and pets poke around the trees. (p129)

Live Music

No city in the country can match New Orleans for its history and depth of live-music venues.

Tipitina's Legendary live music in Uptown; heaps of character and atmosphere. (p136)

d.b.a. Hosts local legends and international acts of acclaim throughout the week. (p91)

Spotted Cat One of the great smoky jazz bars of New Orleans. (p90)

Preservation Hall Find wonderful old-school jazz in the heart of the French Quarter. (p68)

Hi Ho Lounge Shows range from bluegrass to punk to hip-hop to electronic dance music at this eclectic venue. (p91)

AllWays Lounge Come for frontier-pushing music, experimental stuff and damn good dance parties. (p90)

Museums

This city is unafraid to have fun, but it's also unafraid to learn about itself and the world around it.

New Orleans Museum of Art Features both contemporary work and a large archaeological section, plus a gorgeous sculpture garden. (p143)

Ogden Museum of Southern Art A mesmerizing peek into the aesthetic of America's most distinctive geographic region. (p98)

Backstreet Cultural Museum Enthralling journey into the

For more top New Orleans spots, see the following:
→ Eating (p28)
→ Drinking & Nightlife (p32)
→ Entertainment (p37)
→ Shopping (p40)

street culture of African American New Orleans. (p154)

Insectarium Bugs! Fun for kids, but also accessible to adults, especially those with an interest in the animal kingdom. (p99)

Le Musée de f.p.c. Learn about the city's unique demographic, the free people of color. (p155)

National WWII Museum This enormous institution provides fascinating insights into the largest armed conflict in history. (p97)

The Arts

The arts have always held a deep influence over this unabashedly creative city.

Contemporary Arts Center Regular rotating installations feature at this excellent arts museum. (p99)

Royal Street Packed with galleries that showcase the many iterations of local art. (p54)

New Orleans Museum of Art Classic landscapes share gallery space with ancient archaeology. (p143)

Palace Market A regular showcasing of some of the city's most creative minds. (p84)

Marigny Opera House A funky little performance venue located in an old church. (p91)

Saenger Theatre Beautifully restored performance space for all manner of shows. (p159)

PLAN YOUR TRIP IF YOU LIKE...

Month By Month

January

Contrary to popular belief, New Orleans gets cold, and January is pretty nippy. Sports events and tourism-oriented New Year's debauchery give way to the professional partying of Carnival Season by month's end.

Joan of Arc Parade

On January 6, New Orleans celebrates the birthday of the Maid of Orleans – Joan of Arc – with a family-friendly parade (www.joanofarcparade.com) that runs through the French Quarter. Parade-goers dress in meticulously detailed historical costume.

Martin Luther King Jr Day

On the third Monday in January, a charming mid-day parade, replete with brass bands, makes its way from the Bywater to the Tremé, down St Claude Ave.

February

It's Carnival time! In the weeks preceding Mardi Gras the madness in the city builds to a fever pitch, culminating in the main event, the party to end all parties.

Carnival Season

During the three weeks before Mardi Gras, parades kick off with more frequency each day. Large 'krewes' (parade marching clubs) stage massive affairs, with elaborate floats and marching bands, that run along St Charles Ave and Canal St.

Mardi Gras Day

In February or early March, the outrageous Carnival activity reaches a crescendo as the city nearly bursts with costumed celebrants on Mardi Gras (p74). It all ends at midnight with the beginning of Lent.

Tet

Folks of all backgrounds like to show up at Mary Queen of Vietnam Church in New Orleans East for firecrackers, loud music and great food during the Vietnamese New Year (www.mqvncdc.org).

March

The city has barely nursed its Mardi Gras hangover when the fun starts again. Locals call this Festival Season, as small concerts and free music events kick off every weekend.

BUKU

In a city of old-school music and traditional jazz, BUKU (p210) is an unapologetically contemporary music festival that brims with EDM (electronic dance music), hip-hop and installation art.

Congo Square Rhythms Festival

This huge world-music festival (www.jazzandheritage.org/congo-square) rocks into Congo Sq in mid- to late March; expect drumming, dancing, indigenous crafts and delicious food.

Louisiana Crawfish Festival

This huge crawfish feed (www.louisianacrawfishfestival.com) qualifies as the epitome of southern Louisiana culture. It's fun for the family, with rides, games and Cajun music. Held in nearby Chalmette in late March/ early April.

St Patrick's Day

The party picks up the weekend of Paddy's Day (www.stpatricks dayneworleans.com) with the Jim Monaghan/Molly's at the Market parade, which rolls through the French Quarter; and the Uptown/ Irish Channel parade, where the float riders toss cabbages and potatoes.

Super Sunday

St Joseph's Night, March 19, is a big masking event for black Indian gangs, who march after sunset around St Claude Ave and LaSalle St. The following Sunday, known as Super Sunday (p157), tribes gather for a huge procession.

Tennessee Williams Literary Festival

The last weekend of March features a four-day fete (p93) in honor of Tennessee Williams. The playwright called New Orleans his 'spiritual home.' There's a 'Stell-a-a-a!' shouting contest, walking tours, theater events, film screenings, readings and the usual food and alcohol.

April

Festival season continues. Concerts and crawfish boils pick up in frequency as the weather turns a balmy shade of amazing.

French Quarter Festival

One of New Orleans' finest events, the French Quarter Festival (www. fqfi.org) rocks the Vieux Carre in mid-April with stages featuring jazz, funk, Latin rhythms, Cajun, brass bands and R&B, plus food stalls operated by the city's most popular restaurants.

Gay Easter Parade

On Easter Sunday, (p42) the LGBT+ population of New Orleans (and their straight friends) dress up in their hyperbolic, frilliest Sunday best, then march or ride in horse-drawn carriages past the gay bars of the French Quarter. Fabulous fun.

Jazz Fest

The Fair Grounds Race Course – and, at night, the whole town – reverberates with good sounds, plus food and crafts, over the last weekend in April and first weekend of May for Jazz Fest (p74).

May

There's another month or two before the weather starts to get soupy and, to be honest, the days are already fairly hot. So too is the ongoing music, the food and the parties.

Bayou Boogaloo

Mid-City gets to shine with this wonderful outdoor festival (p27), held on the banks of pretty Bayou St John in mid-May. Expect the usual: food stalls, lots of bands and general good times.

New Orleans Wine & Food Experience

This being a culinary town, the local food and wine fest (www.nowfe.com) is quite the affair. Join to attend various tastings, seminars and meal 'experiences' that push gastronomic frontiers. Late May.

July

There's a sultry romance to summer that makes you want to sit in a sweat-stained tank top or summer dress and do nothing but drink iced tea. Don't rest. The New Orleans calendar doesn't let up.

Essence Music Festival

Essence magazine sponsors a star-studded lineup for the largest celebration (www.essence.com) of African American culture in the country. Expect an absolutely devastating series of performances at the Superdome on the July 4 weekend.

Running of the Bulls

In mid-July the Big Easy Rollergirls dress up as bulls and chase crowds (www. nolabulls.com) dressed in Pamplona-style white outfits with red scarves. The 'bulls' run through the Warehouse District and CBD – trust us, this one's lots of fun.

Tales of the Cocktail

Sure, New Orleans is a 24/7 festival, but this three-day event (www.talesofthe-cocktail.com) sets its sights high. Appreciating the art of 'mixology' is the main point, and getting lit up is only an incidental part of the fun.

August

Damn. It's hot. So very, very hot. And there may be hurricanes on the horizon. Who cares? The eating, drinking and merry-making continue, and hotel rates are bottoming out.

🏃 Red Dress Run

The Nola Hash House Harriers lead this charity run (www.noh3.com) through the Quarter and Downtown. It's a 3- to 4-mile run with one rule: wear a red dress. Or less. Open to both men and women, so there's lots of crimson dressing up afoot.

☆ Satchmo SummerFest

Louis Armstrong's birthday (August 4) is celebrated with four days of music and food in the French Quarter. Three stages present local talents in 'trad' jazz, contemporary jazz and brass bands.

🎊 Southern Decadence

Billing itself as 'Gay Mardi Gras,' this five-day Labor Day weekend festival (www.southerndecadence. net) kicks off in the Lower Quarter. Expect music, masking, cross-dressing, dancing in the streets and a Sunday parade that's everything you'd expect from a city with a vital gay community.

(Top) Southern Decadence (p43)
(Bottom) Red Dress Run

SUZANNE C. GRIM/SHUTTERSTOCK ©

SUZANNE C. GRIM/SHUTTERSTOCK ©

☆ White Linen Night

Get decked out in your coolest white duds and wander about the Warehouse District on the first Saturday in August. Galleries throw open their doors to art appreciators and there are lots of free-flowing drinks.

September

The heat doesn't let up and the threat of hurricanes gets even worse, but the music certainly doesn't take a break.

NOLA on Tap

The beer scene in New Orleans has been overflowing (as it were) with good talent – microbreweries and nanobreweries crop up all the time. This festival (http://nolaontap.org) celebrates said suds in all their variety.

October

Locals love dressing up, costumes, ghost stories and the supernatural, so October is a pretty big month in these parts.

☆ New Orleans Film Festival

Theaters around the city screen the work of both local and internationally renowned filmmakers for one week in mid-October (www.neworleansfilmsociety.org/festival).

☆ Voodoo Music & Arts Experience

If you thought New Orleans was all jazz and no rock, visit during Halloween weekend. Past acts at Voodoo (p210) have included the Foo Fighters and the Flaming Lips; these days, the festival is incorporating more hip-hop and dance music.

November

The weather is cooling down and winter is arriving. Arts and entertainment events, plus some of the best sandwiches you'll ever eat, fill up the calendar.

✶ All Saints Day

Cemeteries fill with crowds who pay their respects to ancestors on November 1. It is by no means morbid or sad, as many people have picnics and parties. It wouldn't be out of line for families to serve gumbo beside the family crypt.

✖ Po-Boy Festival

Fifty thousand sandwich-lovers descend on Riverbend in November to sample po'boys from New Orleans' best restaurants (www.poboyfest.com) – the sandwiches are good, but the crowds are intense.

✖ Tremé Creole Gumbo Festival

At this family friendly festival (www.jazzandheritage.org/treme-gumbo), the iconic New Orleans dish and the iconic New Orleans neighborhood are united and celebrated during a weekend long party.

December

Christmas brings flickering torch lights, chilly winds, gray skies and a festive atmosphere to this city of festivals.

✶ Celebration in the Oaks

This City Park celebration (p142) is New Orleans' take on Christmas in America, with 2 miles of oak trees providing the lit-up superstructure. You can view it in its entirety from your car or in a horse-drawn carriage.

✶ Feux de Joie

'Fires of joy' light the way along the Mississippi River levees above Orleans Parish and below Baton Rouge in December and on Christmas Eve (December 24).

With Kids

New Orleans is a fairy-tale city, with its colorful beads, weekly costume parties and daily music wafting through the air. The same flights of fancy and whimsy that give this city such appeal for poets and artists also make it an imaginative wonderland for children, especially creative ones.

MICHA WEBER/SHUTTERSTOCK ©

Best Animal Encounters

Exploring the Audubon Zoo

There's wildlife from around the world in this attractive zoo (p127), but the main attraction is the excellent showcasing of local critters in the form of the Louisiana Swamp. Out in this cleverly landscaped wetland, your kids will get a chance to mug next to a genuine albino alligator, as pretty as freshly fallen snow in a bayou.

Undersea Adventures at Aquarium of the Americas

Dip a toe into the waters of marine biology at this excellent aquarium (p99), where the aquatic habitats range from the Mississippi Delta to the Amazon River Basin. Kids and adults will marvel at rainbow clouds of tropical fish, and guess what? There's a white alligator – 'Spots' – living here, too.

Bug Out in the Insectarium

You've got to love a museum dedicated to New Orleans' insects (p99), where one display focuses on cockroaches, and another is sponsored by the pest-control business. Yet this isn't a museum that focuses on the 'ick' factor. Rather, you'll get a sense of the beauty and diversity of the entomological world, from gem-colored-beetle displays to the serenity of the Butterfly Garden.

History & Culture for Kids

Under the City's Skin

The Louisiana Children's Museum (p99) is a good intro to the region for toddlers, while older children and teenagers may appreciate the Ogden Museum (p98), Cabildo (p50) and Presbytère (p53). Little ones often take a shine to the candy-colored houses in the French Quarter, Faubourg Marigny and Uptown. The Latter Library (p128) on St Charles Ave has a good selection of children's literature and is located in a pretty historical mansion. The city's cemeteries, especially Lafayette Cemetery No 1 (p114) in the Garden District, are authentic slices of the past and enjoyably spooky to boot.

Festival Fun

The many street parties and outdoor festivals of New Orleans bring food stalls and, of course, great music. Children will love dancing to the beat. Seek out festivals held during the day, such as Bayou Boogaloo (www.thebayouboogaloo.com).

Mardi Gras for Families

Mardi Gras and the Carnival Season are surprisingly family-friendly affairs outside of the well-known boozy debauch in the French Quarter. St Charles Ave hosts many day parades with lots of krewes roll and families set up grilling posts and tents – drinking revelers aren't welcome. Kids are set up on 'ladder seats' (www.momsminivan.com/extras/ladderseat.html) so they can get an adult-height view of the proceedings and catch throws from the floats. The crazy costumes add to the child-friendly feel of the whole affair. See www.neworleansonline.com/neworleans/mardigras/mgfamilies.html.

Outdoor Adventures

Wander Through City Park

The largest green space in New Orleans is undoubtedly also its most attractive. City Park (p141) has plenty of big trees for shade, lazy waterways filled with fish (and sometimes small alligators!), a model train diagram of the city built entirely of biological materials, and a wonderful carousel and sculpture garden that will be of interest to older kids. Plus Storyland – a nostalgic minipark with more than two-dozen storybook scenes reproduced on a life-size scale.

Barataria Preserve

This green gem (p163) in the national-park crown is located just south of the city. Toddlers to teenagers will enjoy walking along the flat boardwalk, which traverses the gamut of Louisiana wetlands, from bayous to marsh prairie.

Let's Go Ride a Bike

Cycling in New Orleans is pretty easy for fit kids. Younger ones can be taken on short rides through the French Quarter or the Garden District. Older kids should

be able to swing bike tours like the ones offered by Confederacy of Cruisers (p94), which take in the city's older Creole neighborhoods on big, tough, comfortable cruiser-style bicycles. Avoid riding through the traffic-congested CBD.

Crescent Park

Need to run off some energy? Might as well do it with a front-row view of the greatest river in North America. The Crescent Park (p84) runs through the Marigny and Bywater, and follows the bend – or crescent – of the Mississippi. Watch ships ply their way up and down the mother of waters, and grab a picnic lunch from Pizza Delicious (p86) while you're out here.

Jackson Square & the River

Jackson Sq (p52) is essentially a constant carnival. Any time of day you may encounter street artists, fortune-tellers, buskers, brass bands and similar folks all engaged in producing the sensory overload New Orleans is famous for (and kids go crazy over). The square is framed by a fairytale cathedral and two excellent museums, and nearby are steps leading up to the Mississippi River, where long barges evoke *Huckleberry Finn* and the Mississippi of Mark Twain. Drop by Café du Monde (p63) for some powdered-sugar treats.

Louisiana crawfish boil

Eating

In what other American city do people celebrate the harvest season of sewage-dwelling crustaceans? The crawfish boil exemplifies New Orleans' relationship with food: unconditional love. This city finds itself in its food; meals are both expressions of identity and bridges between the city's many divisions.

The Native Example

Settlers who arrived in Louisiana had to work with the ingredients of the bayous, woods and prairies, and so developed one of America's only true native-born cuisines. As a result, some say the New Orleans palette is limited to its own specialties, that this is a town of 'a thousand restaurants and three dishes.'

That cliché is a bit tired. First, lots of restaurants are serving what we would deem Nouveau New Orleans cuisine – native classics influenced by global flavors and tech-

niques. And second, international options are popping up more frequently in this town.

Still, this is a place where the homegrown recipes are the best stuff on the menu. As such, we present a rundown of New Orleans and Louisiana specialties.

ROUX

Very few meals begin life in Louisiana without a roux (pronounced 'roo'): flour slowly cooked with oil or butter. Over time, the product evolves from a light-colored 'white' roux into a smokier 'dark' roux. The final product is used as a thickening and flavoring agent. While deceptively simple, local cooks insist their dishes live or die based on the foundation roux.

GUMBO

No cook is without a personal recipe for this spicy, full-bodied soup or stew, which is a bit like Louisiana itself: food-ified. Ingredients vary from chef to chef, but gumbo is almost always served over starchy steamed rice. Coastal gumbo teems with oysters, jumbo shrimp and crabs, while prairie-bred Cajuns turn to their barnyards and smoke-houses.

PO'BOY

Maybe you call it a submarine, a grinder or a hoagie. You are wrong. Simply put, a po'boy is an overstuffed sandwich served on local French bread (more chewy, less crispy) and dripping with fillings; the most popular are roast beef, fried shrimp and/or fried oysters, and 'debris' (the bits of roast beef that fall into the gravy). When you order, your server will ask if you want it 'dressed,' meaning with mayonnaise, shredded lettuce and tomato. Say yes.

RED BEANS & RICE

A poor man's meal rich in flavor, this is a lunch custom associated with Mondays. Monday was traditionally wash day and, in the past, a pot of red beans would go on the stove along with the ham bone from Sunday dinner. By the time the washing was finished, supper was ready.

JAMBALAYA

Hearty, rice-based jambalaya (johm-buh-lie-uh) can include just about any combination of fowl, shellfish or meat, but usually includes ham, hence the name (derived from the French *jambon* or the Spanish *jamón*). The meaty ingredients are sautéed with onions, pepper and celery, and cooked with raw rice and water into a flavorful mix of textures.

MUFFULETTAS

It's only a slight exaggeration to say that New Orleans *muffulettas* are the size of manhole covers. Named for a round sesame-crusted loaf, *muffulettas* are layered with various selections from the local Sicilian deli tradition, including Genoa salami, shaved ham, mortadella and sliced provolone cheese. The signature spread – a salty olive salad with pickled vegetables, herbs, garlic and olive oil – is what defines the sandwich.

NEED TO KNOW

Price Ranges

In our listings we use the following price ranges to indicate the cost of a main course.

$ less than $15

$$ $15 to $29

$$$ more than $30

Opening Hours

➡ Restaurants generally open from 11am to 11pm, with last seatings around 10:30pm.

➡ Breakfast usually starts around 7am.

➡ Many restaurants close Sunday, Monday or both.

Reservations

➡ Where reservations are necessary, we say so in our reviews. Sometimes, you can't book ahead – if you want to attend the famous Galatoire's (p60) day-long brunch, for example, you have to wait in line on the sidewalk. Some local elites even pay people to wait in line for them, a practice that is simultaneously charming and feudal all at once.

➡ There are lots of small family-run places in New Orleans. Call ahead to these places if you're in a large group.

Tipping

Tipping is not optional. A good tip is 18%, but folks tend to be munificent here; 20% is almost standard. If service is only adequate, 15% is fine. Some places will charge an automatic 18% gratuity for large groups (usually six or more people).

Courses

The New Orleans School of Cooking (p73) is a popular and pretty awesome way to learn the ins and outs of one of this city's great exports – its culinary tradition. Both open demonstrations and hands-on cooking courses are available.

TASSO

This highly prized butcher-shop specialty is basically a lean chunk of ham, cured with *filé* (crushed sassafras leaves) and other seasonings, and then smoked until it reaches the tough consistency of beef jerky.

Eating by Neighborhood

Faubourg Marigny & Bywater
Innovative eats attracting discerning diners (p86)

Tremé-Lafitte
Old-school family restaurants dominate the local dining scene (p156)

Mid-City, Bayou St John & City Park
Locals' spots, neighborhood diners and a few cutting-edge restaurants pushing boundaries (p145)

French Quarter
High-end restaurants and tourist traps (p59)

CBD & Warehouse District
The city's fanciest fine dining (p101)

Uptown & Riverbend
Cozy fine dining and student cafes (p129)

Garden, Lower Garden & Central City
Romantic neighborhood restaurants and local diners (p116)

Mississippi River

BOUDIN
A tasty Cajun sausage made with pork, pork liver, cooked rice and spices. A popular quick bite, especially in Cajun country.

SNOWBALLS
Shaved ice in a paper cup doused liberally with flavored syrup, snowballs are blasts of winter on a steamy midsummer's afternoon.

BEIGNETS
Not so much a dessert as a round-the-clock breakfast specialty akin to the common doughnut, *beignets* are flat squares of dough flash-fried to a golden, puffy glory, dusted liberally with powdered (confectioner's or icing) sugar, and served scorching hot.

BREAD PUDDING
A specialty in New Orleans and Acadiana, this custardy creation is a good use for leftover bread. Local variations involve copious amounts of butter, eggs and cream, and will usually come topped with a bourbon-spiked sugar sauce.

Lonely Planet's Top Choices

Marjie's Grill (p146) Southeast Asian street food done with care and attention.

Bacchanal (p88) Wine, cheese, bread and a magically lit garden.

Seaworthy (p102) Incredibly fresh seafood, prepared with care and expertise.

Boucherie (p132) Southern cuisine prepared with fascinating new twists.

DTB (p133) Oak Street's contender in the 'great food, great drinks' department.

Surrey's Juice Bar (p116) Best breakfast in the city.

Romantic Meals

Café Degas (p147) Candlelight and French cuisine on a beautiful stretch of Esplanade Ave.

Adolfo's (p88) An intimate Italian eatery sitting over a live-music mecca.

Bacchanal (p88) Outdoor dining, plentiful wine, good cheese and a band on the side.

Lilette (p134) Take your date out for French fare at this lovely, porch-fronted bistro.

Po'boys

Mahony's Po-Boy Shop (p132) A perennial po'boy favorite with innovative sandwiches and awesome ingredients.

Domilise's Po-Boys (p132) This down-home shack is the Platonic ideal of a New Orleans sandwich shop.

Parkway Tavern (p145) Grab a po'boy and enjoy a picnic on the banks of Bayou St John.

Guy's (p131) Uptown joint where the sandwiches are made to order every time.

Classic Creole Cuisine

Commander's Palace (p119) This Garden District institution is the grande dame of classic Creole cuisine.

Gautreau's (p134) A lovely Uptown establishment that nails the New Orleans approach to food.

Jacques-Imo's Café (p132) Savory takes on New Orleans' classics. Don't plan on losing any weight.

'Nouveau' New Orleans Cuisine

Peche Seafood Grill (p102) One of the most highly regarded seafood restaurants in the USA.

SoBou (p60) Funky French Quarter restaurant that's decadent and playful with New Orleans recipes.

Bayona (p60) Local ingredients are buttressed by an international approach to cooking techniques.

Herbsaint (p103) Old-school New Orleans food gets a dash of haute technique and execution.

For Vegetarians

Carmo (p101) Creative cuisine and innovative recipes shine at this CBD restaurant.

Sneaky Pickle (p86) A no-frills yet delicious vegan diner located in Bywater.

Seed (p118) Comfort food, contemporary design and vegan cuisine come together here

Poke Loa (p116) Hawaiian bowls can be catered to vegetarian tastes.

Satsuma (p88) Hip cafe has plenty of vegetarian options.

Best by Budget: $

Pizza Delicious (p86) It's pizza. It's seriously delicious. Just trust us.

Stein's Deli (p116) A glorious homage to the deli and sandwich making arts.

Ba Chi Canteen (p129) Delicious Bahn Mi 'baco's' are well worth the detour.

Buttermilk Drops (p156) These 'drops' are baked goods tossed down from heaven.

Best by Budget: $$

Peche Seafood Grill (p102) It's amazing what a deal this fine dining spot is.

Red's Chinese (p86) New ground in Southern-Chinese fusion is being broken here.

1000 Figs (p146) A fantastic neighborhood hideaway for Middle Eastern fare.

Coquette (p119) Friendly service and gorgeous food in this elegant restaurant.

Avo (p132) Italian fare both reimagined and true to its delicious roots.

Best by Budget: $$$

Compère Lapin (p104) The gastronomy here merges Louisiana and the Caribbean, a marriage made in foodie heaven.

Gautreau's (p134) Fancy dining doesn't come cheap, but it comes delicious.

Bayona (p60) Breaking new ground in Creole cuisine ever since it opened.

Clancy's (p133) Simply one of the city's outstanding Creole restaurants.

La Boca (p104) This Argentine steakhouse is the place for red meat.

KRIS DAVIDSON/LONELY PLANET ©

Cure bar (p134)

Drinking & Nightlife

New Orleans doesn't rest for much. But the city isn't just an alcoholic lush. A typical New Orleans night out features just as much food and music as booze. Here, all your senses are appealed to: your ear for a brass band, your taste for rich food, your sensing of heat on your skin, your observing the visual composition of a streetcar line running past historic homes, as well as your whetted thirst for another beer or shot.

Classic New Orleans Cocktails

The argument can well be made that New Orleans invented the cocktail, and while mixing spirits properly was once a lost art, today a generation of dedicated mixers are out there prepping some mean classics.

➡ **Sazerac** A potent whiskey drink that uses either rye or bourbon as its primary ingredient, with aromatic bitters (including the locally produced Peychaud's), a bit of sugar and a swish of Herbsaint. The Sazerac is the emblematic drink of the city, and you shouldn't leave town without trying one.

Ramos Gin Fizz Named for 19th-century New Orleans bartender Henry Ramos, this is a rich, frothy blend of gin, cream, egg whites, extra-fine sugar, fizzy water and a splash of orange-flower water. The drink was invented as a hangover cure, and old-school bartenders still like making them prior to noon. Pro tip: this is a notoriously difficult drink to make. If you order it while a bartender is busy, don't be surprised if you get some stink eye.

Aviation Try it on a hot day: gin, maraschino (cherry) liqueur and lemon juice, plus some other trade secrets depending on which bar is mixing it. Very refreshing.

Pimm's Cup A summer tipple traditionally associated with the infamous French Quarter bar Napoleon House. It's a simple mix of the British gin-based liqueur Pimm's No 1, topped with soda or ginger ale.

Café Brûlot A drink that is as much about visual spectacle as imbibing, the Café Brûlot requires specialized equipment and training – you can only order these at old-line Creole restaurants, where it is served as the ultimate after-dinner drink for an entire table. A Café Brûlot is, effectively, black coffee, sugar, spice, orange peel, lemon peel, plus brandy or cognac. The whole affair is mixed tableside by talented waiters who then set everything on fire. The resulting drink is hot, sweet, spirited, and will likely knock you the heck out.

Beer

Across the city, one of the newest bar 'types' are microbreweries like Wayward Owl and Second Line that feature either outdoor play areas or beer-hall atmosphere. As an added bonus, they brew really fine beer.

Abita, based in St Tammany Parish, is the most-well known local brewery outside of New Orleans, although NOLA Brewing is starting to pop up far outside of Orleans parish. Regional Louisiana breweries like Bayou Teche, Chafunkta, and Tin Roof are also widely distributed in the city.

Founded in 1907, Dixie Beer used to be the beer everyone associated with New Orleans, but since Katrina operations have been shipped north to Wisconsin. You can still get a Dixie here, but it's no longer a locally produced drink.

Wine

Wine is and always has been popular in Louisiana thanks to a strong French cultural influence, but the homegrown industry is small; this state is too humid for viticulture.

Tourist Drinks

The bars on Bourbon St feature neon, sugary beverages that will melt your face and give you an awful hangover. Still interested? OK. The Hurricane, made famous by Pat O'Brien's, is a towering rum drink that gets its bright-pink hue from the healthy portion of passion-fruit juice. The Hand Grenade, sold at Tropical Isle, is a mix of melon liqueur, grain alcohol, rum, vodka and who knows what else. Frozen daiquiris, by New Orleans' definition, are a class of alcoholic Slurpees that come in all the brightest colors of the rainbow. You can pick them

up, sometimes by the gallon from, yes, drive-through takeouts.

Nonalcoholic Drinks
COFFEE & CHICORY

Coffee here is traditionally mixed with chicory, a roasted herb root. Originally used to 'extend' scarce coffee beans during hard times, chicory continues to be added for its full-bodied flavor, which gives local coffee a slightly bitter twist. We like it served best as

NEED TO KNOW

Opening Hours

Most dedicated bars open around 5pm, although some places serve drinks during lunch, and some are open 24 hours. Closing time is an ill-defined thing; officially it's around 2am or 3am, but sometimes it's whenever the last customer stumbles out the door. Cafes open early and closing times vary from lunch to late evening (around 9pm).

Prices

This is, by and large, still a cheap town for nighthawks, although prices in the French Quarter and CBD are starting to balance out with the rest of the country. In other neighborhoods, you'll rarely pay more than $5 for a beer. Sometimes domestics will go for under $3. Cocktails can get into the double digits at higher-end bars, but at plenty of places they rarely top $8. Shots of hard spirits go for around $3 to $5 (more for top-shelf stuff), and everything is cheaper during happy hour. Wine can be expensive at wine bars, but is generally of very high quality.

Tipping

It's common to leave a dollar or more for your bartender, even if they just pop the cap off a bottle of beer. You don't have to tip for every drink, but the general rule is to leave a couple of bucks extra for every hour spent at the bar.

Bars vs Lounge vs Clubs

Many bars in New Orleans pull triple duty as live-music venues and restaurants. In our reviews, we try to categorize places based on their primary 'function' – eating, drinking or music.

Drinking by Neighborhood

Tremé-Lafitte
Local bars that often have
live music (p159)

Faubourg Marigny & Bywater
A huge concentration
of live music (p88)

Mid-City, Bayou St John & City Park
Neighborhood watering holes,
hip live music (p148)

French Quarter
Rowdy music, stiff cocktails,
gay clubs (p64)

CBD & Warehouse District
Fancy hotel bars, big concert venues (p104)

Uptown & Riverbend
Small venues, friendly local bars (p134)

Garden, Lower Garden & Central City
Student pubs and corner dives (p120)

Mississippi River

café au lait – coffee mixed with scalded (not steamed) milk poured from two cups.

ICED TEA
In hot and humid Louisiana, iced tea is more than just a drink – it's a form of air-con in a tall, sweaty glass. 'Sweet tea' is served with enough sugar to keep an army of dentists employed. If you want a proper English cuppa, specify 'hot tea.'

Bars
In general, bars in New Orleans would often be considered 'dives' elsewhere. That's not to say bars here are grotty (although some certainly are); rather, there are many neighborhood joints in New Orleans that are unpretentious spots catering to those looking to drink, as opposed to those who want to meet and chat someone up. If you're in the latter category, head to lounges, which tend to be newer, more brightly

lit and possessed of a general modern sensibility. That said, some bars, such as Mimi's in the Marigny (p89), are good spots for both a beer after work and a bit of random flirtation.

Clubs
New Orleans isn't much of a nightclub city. There's a general lack of the large spaces nightclubs like to utilize, particularly in tourist-magnet neighborhoods that have a glut of historical housing. And nightclubs aren't really to most folks' speed. If people want to drink, they tend to head to bars; if they want to dance, they opt for live music; and in general locals reject the whole red rope concept. The closest thing the city has to a clubbing scene takes up parts of the Warehouse District, CBD and some of the lounges in swisher hotels.

Lonely Planet's Top Choices

Buffa's (p89) It's divey, the music is great, the drinks are strong, and it never closes.

Bar Tonique (p64) A bartenders' bar with great cocktails.

Tiki Tolteca (p66) Crazy mixed tropical drinks in a gloriously kitsch atmosphere.

Mimi's in the Marigny (p89) Mixed drinks, cold beer, great music.

Twelve Mile Limit (p148) Casual neighborhood vibe, great spirits and drinks.

Cane & Table (p66) Expert mixed drinks and a courtyard plucked from tropical fantasies.

Best Beer

Avenue Pub (p120) A balcony tops a carefully curated beer menu and talented pub-grub kitchen.

NOLA Brewing (p120) This brewery's own very fine bar and tasting room.

Bulldog (p120) How much do they love beer? Check out the outdoor keg-handle fountain.

Second Line Brewing (p148) A brewery that has created a courtyard with food trucks and a play area for kids.

Urban South (p120) Another contender in the family-friendly brewery competition, in which everyone wins.

Best Cocktails

Cane & Table (p66) Tropical drinks mixed with a ton of attention and skill.

Bar Tonique (p64) Worth the wait for the expertly mixed drinks at this little bar.

French 75 (p66) A bar so dedicated to cocktails it was named for one.

Cure (p134) The bar that gentrified Freret St on the strength of its cocktail menu.

Twelve Mile Limit (p148) A stupendous, complex cocktail menu in a laid-back neighborhood bar.

Treo (p148) The mixed drinks are as creative as the artwork in the on-site gallery.

Best Coffee

Fair Grinds (p149) Great coffee, tasty baked goods, friendly staff and an artsy cafe atmosphere.

Station (p148) Strong coffee and handmade pastries in Mid-City.

Spitfire Coffee (p67) French Quarter cafe dishing out potent drip coffee a step below rocket fuel.

Solo Espresso (p89) Artsy little Bywater cafe that sources coffee from around the world.

Best For Jukebox

St Joe's (p135) An Uptown, student-centric crowd jams out to oldies and '90s/'00s rock.

Markey's (p90) A neighborhood jukebox selection that could have been plucked from the 1960s.

Pal's (p148) Music flits between eclectic quirks and classical soul.

Twelve Mile Limit (p148) Great bars deserve great music, in the form of oldies, newbies and everything between.

Best For Solo Travelers

Mimi's in the Marigny (p89) Someone always seems ready to strike up friendly conversation.

St Joe's (p135) The long bar and friendly clientele makes for an engaging solo stop.

BJ's (p89) Enter solo, leave with new friends. Or drink alone – no one minds.

Verret's Lounge (p120) Laid-back dive where folks can be as sociable or isolated as they like.

Bar Tonique (p64) The small space invites easy mingling.

Pal's (p148) A super-friendly bar where anyone can do their own thing.

Best For Students

F&M's Patio Bar (p136) Watch the collective tuition of hundreds of students get blown on cheap beer.

Bulldog (p120) Med students, young lawyers and older undergrads clink mugs at this Garden District spot.

Handsome Willy's (p105) Besides the great name, this bar has regular DJ nights.

Snake & Jakes (p135) Students pack one of the craziest late-night bars in New Orleans.

Best Historical Bars

French 75 (p66) This bar drips history, from the attached Arnaud's restaurant to the suited staff.

Napoleon House (p67) Peeling paint, crumbling walls and a general sense of timeless debauchery.

Lafitte's Blacksmith Shop bar (p67)

Carousel Bar (p66) Baroque lights spin at the vintage eponymous carousel in this hotel bar.

Lafitte's Blacksmith Shop (p67) It may be the oldest continuously operated bar in the USA – 'nuff said.

Chart Room (p67) Grotty French Quarter dive that feels to us like a relic of a bygone drinking age.

Best Neighborhood Bars

Pal's (p148) No trip to Bayou St John is complete without a gingerita at Pal's.

Twelve Mile Limit (p148) Great drinks, good pub food and a local vibe that can't be beat.

BJ's (p89) The epitome of a dirty, dingy and utterly irreplaceable Bywater dive.

Finn McCool's (p148) Mid-City residents cluster at this fantastic sports bar seven nights a week.

Mimi's in the Marigny (p89) Good music and creative cuisine at marvelous Mimi's.

Ms Mae's (p135) A legendary dive of which many an Uptown youth has fun, fuzzy memories.

Preservation Hall (p68)

☆ Entertainment

Be it live music, the visual arts, dance, film or theater, New Orleans knows how to entertain guests. The city is one great stage, and visitors need not just watch the show but participate as costumed players.

Live Music

There is great live music happening every night of the week in New Orleans, which makes a strong claim to being the best live-music city in the nation. Jazz is definitely not the only genre on offer: R&B, rock, country, Cajun, zydeco (p209), funk, soul, hip-hop and genre-defying experimentation are all the norm.

The Arts

The city of New Orleans has been actively using the arts as a means of revitalizing neighborhoods and building cachet with 'creative class' travelers – the ones who come to a destination looking for a local aesthetic. In many ways, the city has always been a bit of an arts colony, and creativity comes naturally to its citizens.

Many New Orleanians came here as aspiring artists, attracted by a low cost of living vis a vis cities like New York and Los Angeles. But climbing rents and low job prospects – not just art jobs, but the day jobs that put a roof over one's head – have combined to make conditions not as welcoming as they once were for the artistically inclined.

NEED TO KNOW

Price Ranges

➡ Standard cover for shows is $5 to $10.

➡ During events like Jazz Fest, however, seeing local celebrities like Kermit Ruffins may run to $15 or even $20.

THEATER

New Orleans has a strong theatrical bent; numerous local theater companies and a few large theatrical venues for touring productions frequently stage shows. Broadway blockbusters cross the boards at the Mahalia Jackson Theater (p159). Student plays are often performed at the **University of New Orleans** (☑504-280-7469; www.uno.edu; 2000 Lakeshore Dr) and Tulane University's Lupin Theatre (p136).

In Faubourg Marigny, improv comedy can be found at the New Movement Theater (p92), while Cafe Istanbul (p92) in the Healing Center hosts performances ranging from indie to classics. The Mudlark Theater (p93) in the Bywater hosts performance art, fringe shows and, occasionally, giant puppet extravaganzas.

FILM

New Orleans has a few quality cinemas scattered about; our favorites are Prytania Theatre (p136) and the Broad Theater (p159). Indie films are sporadically screened in some bars and clubs; check www.bestofneworleans.com for the latest events.

CLASSICAL MUSIC

The Louisiana Philharmonic Orchestra (p107) is a respected, musician-owned and operated symphony based out of the Orpheum Theater (p107). In the spring, the Birdfoot Festival (p210) is a lovely little party that celebrates chamber music in small venues across town.

DANCE

The **New Orleans Ballet Association** (NOBA; ☑504-522-0996; www.nobadance.com; tickets $30-75) usually runs a few productions annually. The season is short and fleshed out with presentations by visiting dance companies from around the world. Performances are primarily held at the Mahalia Jackson Theater and Nocca (New Orleans Center for Creative Arts; www.nocca.com). For contemporary dance, see what's on at Nocca.

OPERA

The **New Orleans Opera** (☑504-529-2278; www.neworleansopera.org; tickets $30-125) remains an important part of local culture. Productions are held at the Mahalia Jackson Theater.

Entertainment by Neighborhood

French Quarter Tourist-oriented entertainment, with a smattering of venues that have genuine local flavor.

Faubourg Marigny and Bywater Fantastic concentration of live music, plus avant-garde galleries and theater.

CBD & Warehouse District A few large concert halls and a handful of mid- or small-sized gig spots.

Garden, Lower Garden and Central City Neighborhood bars and corner dives occasionally feature live music acts.

Uptown and Riverbend University-oriented arts scene and a few music spots and bars-cum-venues, many with a student vibe.

Mid-City, Bayou St John and City Park Again, neighborhood bars that often have live music at least a few nights a week.

Tremé-Lafitte Locals-oriented options and bars that feature live music and dancing.

Lonely Planet's Top Choices

d.b.a. (p91) Consistently great live music nightly.

Hi Ho Lounge (p91) Eclectic schedule, funky shows.

AllWays Lounge (p90) Oddball shows and friendly bartenders.

Maple Leaf Bar (p136) Student-y spot for Uptown's best shows.

Marigny Opera House (p91) Live dance and eclectic performance art.

Tipitina's (p136) Legendary spot for a live show Uptown.

Best for Free Entertainment

Mardi Gras (p74) The party more than earns its reputation as the best free show on Earth.

Frenchmen Street (p84) The city's most concentrated live-music strip is a show unto itself.

Bayou Boogaloo (p23) A bucolic Bayou St John setting girded by a fantastic music lineup.

Barkus Parade (p77) It's a parade of dogs in cute costumes! What more do you need?

Second Lines (p158) These brass-band-led neighborhood parades are a peek into New Orleans backstreet culture.

Best for Hip-Hop & Bounce

Blue Nile (p92) Hip-hop and dance-hall acts regularly take the stage at the Nile.

Siberia (p91) Bounce shows and serious booty-shaking are a regular occurrence.

Maison (p92) Younger hip-hop acts attract the college crowd at this Frenchmen venue.

Dragon's Den (p92) A wide mix of genres and talent, but hip-hop often features.

Best for Jazz

Spotted Cat (p90) A cozy dive bar that hosts some of the funkiest jazz acts in the city.

Snug Harbor (p91) Elegant bar with cocktail attire–style service and classy acts.

Fritzel's European Jazz Pub (p68) Live jazz in a tiny venue where you're never more than ten feet from the performers.

Three Muses (p92) Dinner and jazz come together at this intimate Frenchmen St venue.

Preservation Hall (p68) The guardians of the classic New Orleans jazz sound.

Chickie Wah Wah (p149) A locals' spot that features great music in the heart of Mid-City.

Best for Live Music

d.b.a. (p91) Live music pops off all the time, and the beer menu is extensive to boot.

Spotted Cat (p90) A fantastically dingy Frenchmen St dive for the quintessential New Orleans jazz show.

Tipitina's (p136) One of the city's most storied concert halls.

Hi Ho Lounge (p91) An edgy little spot for a wide variety of music.

AllWays Lounge (p90) The place to go for an eclectic mix of genres and dance parties.

Best for Rock Music

Siberia (p91) Heavy metal, punk and singer-songwriter nights keep Siberia red hot.

One Eyed Jacks (p69) One of the best live performance venues in the French Quarter.

Checkpoint Charlie (p92) A little bar that hosts some big noise on its dark, intimate stage.

Saturn Bar (p92) Wild acts tear down the roof in this oddball, artsy venue.

Banks Street Bar (p149) A neighborhood bar that isn't afraid to bring the rock.

Best for Zydeco

Rock 'N' Bowl (p136) A zydeco dance party tears up this bowling alley on Thursday nights.

Jazz Fest (p78) Hit up the *fais-do-do* tent for a foot-stomping Cajun dance party.

French Quarter Festival (p23) Zydeco acts are a regular feature of this free music festival.

Bayou Boogaloo (p23) Nothing like some Cajun dance tunes to accompany a perfect day on the water.

Maple Leaf Bar (p136) Get funky with the student crowd at the Leaf's famous zydeco parties.

PLAN YOUR TRIP ENTERTAINMENT

Shopping

Too many travelers assume shopping in New Orleans equals unspeakable T-shirts from the French Quarter. Wrong! New Orleans is a creative town that attracts innovative entrepreneurs and, as such, features all sorts of lovely vintage antiques, cutting-edge boutiques, functional art and amusing kitsch – and generally lacks the worst chain-store blah.

Magazine Street

For the true-blue shopper, New Orleans doesn't get much better than Magazine St. For some 6 miles the street courses through the Warehouse District and along the riverside edge of the Garden District and Uptown, lined nearly the entire way with small shops selling antiques, art, contemporary fashions, vintage clothing, and other odds and ends. The street hits its peak in the Lower Garden District (near Jackson Ave), the Garden District (between 1st and 7th Sts) and Uptown (from Antonine St to Napoleon Ave). No car? Take bus 11.

Souvenirs

There are some really great awful souvenirs out there: T-shirts, foodstuffs (you're in hot-sauce heaven, here), Mardi Gras masks, stripper outfits, voodoo paraphernalia, French Quarter–style street signs and, of course, beads, beads, beads. Besides the unintentional kitsch there's quite a bit of intentional tackiness – this city seems to know how to mock itself.

Arts

Music makes New Orleans go round, and this is a fantastic town for buying original CDs, vinyl and the like, plus very high-quality instruments. A large literary scene has resulted in a good number of independent bookshops, some of which have evolved into unofficial anchors of their respective communities. And visual artists will find no shortage of stores selling supplies for their work.

Antiques

Antiques are big business here, and sometimes it feels like you can't walk past parts of Royal, Chartres, lower Decatur and Magazine Streets without tripping on some backyard, warehouse or studio space exhibiting beautiful examples of found furniture. Pieces tend to be relatively cheap compared to the antiques action in similarly sized metropolises, and the genre goes beyond chairs and armoires to lots of old maps, watches, prints, books and similar doodads.

Shopping by Neighborhood

French Quarter Antiques shops, souvenir stalls and art galleries.

Faubourg Marigny and Bywater Arty, eclectic emporiums and vintage.

CBD & Warehouse District Art galleries, clothing and shopping malls.

Garden, Lower Garden and Central City Boutiques, antiques and vintage.

Uptown & Riverbend More boutiques, plus student stores.

Mid-City, Bayou St John and City Park Some neat boutiques and specialty stores.

Tremé-Lafitte Light on shopping; check out the Quarter or Mid-City.

Lonely Planet's Top Choices

Euclid Records (p93) Awesome vinyl and old posters; knowledgeable staff.

Potsalot (p137) Get a mug, plate, vase or sink that you'll treasure a lifetime.

Kitchen Witch (p160) It's a bookstore – dedicated to cooking books! Brilliant.

Fifi Mahony's (p70) Wild wigs and costuming craziness.

Tchoup Industries (p122) Handmade bags and accessories made from local materials.

SecondLine Art & Antiques (p70) Great chance to meet and mingle with the artists, and support local talent.

Best Antiques

Bywater Bargain Center (p93) An endless emporium of found treasures and bric-a-brac from around the world.

James H Cohen & Sons (p72) Holds an enormous vault of coins, swords, maps and other objects culled from the past.

Moss Antiques (p72) Decorative arts, historic furniture and other home accoutrements.

Magazine Antique Mall (p124) Never-ending rows of trinkets that seem to have been culled from a collective city attic.

Le Garage (p73) Just what it sounds like: an endless supply of odd antiques.

Best Book Stores

Faulkner House Books (p71) The former home of the great Southern writer is now an iconic indie bookstore.

Crescent City Comics (p138) A great comic and graphic-novel store with friendly staff who know their geeky trade.

Kitchen Witch (p160) Vintage and first-edition cookbooks are the stock in trade at this speciality shop.

Tubby & Coos (p150) Every city deserves a bookshop dedicated to science fiction, fantasy and children's books.

Best Music Stores

Euclid Records (p93) This Bywater shop is one of the iconic local record shops of the South.

Disko Obscura (p123) Funky niche shop specializing in underground synth.

Louisiana Music Factory (p93) The shop that sets the standard in collecting and selling local music.

Peaches Records & Tapes (p137) A French Quarter record shop that loves to introduce tourists to local artists.

Best Souvenirs

Palace Market (p84) A boutique art market for those seeking a unique gift from New Orleans.

Simon of New Orleans (p123) Bright and beautiful hand-painted signs with cheeky messages.

Louisiana Music Factory (p93) If you need some local music, you've come to the right store.

Home Malone (p150) Filled to the brim with New Orleans–inspired gifts and goodness.

NEED TO KNOW

Opening Hours

Hours vary, but as a rule of thumb, shops are open from 9am or 10am to 7pm Monday to Friday, and 10am to 2pm Saturday and Sunday. Some stores are shut on Sunday or Monday, and sometimes both.

Buy Local

Even before Hurricane Katrina, and particularly after the storm, there was a big push in the city to promote local businesses and commerce. To keep abreast of the 'buy local' movement, visit http://staylocal.org.

5 Press Gallery (p94) Original art by students and alumni of a local arts-magnet school.

I.J. Reilly's (p93) Awesome gifts and objects d'art with an identifiable New Orleans twist.

Best Vintage Stores

Funky Monkey (p123) Cool, college-age-oriented clothing in the heart of Magazine St.

Trashy Diva (p122) Vintage dresses with a '40s and '50s feel and lots of attitude.

Bloomin' Deals (p138) This store, run by the Junior League, offers genuine cut-rate prices for used clothes.

LA46 (p94) Funky vintage deals at the edge of Faubourg Marigny.

LGBT+
New Orleans

Louisiana is a culturally conservative state, but its largest city bucks that trend. New Orleans has always had a reputation for tolerance and it remains one of the oldest gay-friendly cities in the Western hemisphere, marketing itself as the 'Gay Capital of the South.' Neighborhoods such as the French Quarter and Marigny are major destinations on the LGBT+ travel circuit.

The Vibe

New Orleans is a pretty integrated city. Except for the lower part of Bourbon St, few areas or businesses feel exclusively gay. Rather, the queer vibe in the city seems to be strongest during major festivals such as the Gay Easter Parade and Southern Decadence.

History

New Orleans has always had a reputation as a city for outcasts, which for much of history has included the gay and lesbian population. Even today, in conservative states such as Alabama and Mississippi, gay and lesbian youth feel the pull of the Big Easy, where acceptance of their sexuality isn't hard to find.

Artists such as Tennessee Williams, Truman Capote and Lyle Saxon, among many others, found acceptance and purpose here; Williams went so far as to dub New Orleans his 'spiritual home.' Gay Civil Rights battles were fought in New Orleans by groups such as the Gertrude Stein Society. In 1997 Mayor Marc Morial extended domestic-partner benefits to gay and lesbian couples who were city employees; in the same year, Louisiana became the first state in the Deep South to pass hate crimes legislation that covered sexual orientation. One year later, New Orleans pushed new boundaries by being one of the first American cities to list gender identity as protected from discrimination.

Fabulous Festival Fun

On **Easter Sunday**, the LGBT+ population of the city (and their straight friends) dress up in their fanciest, frilliest Sunday best, then march or ride in horse-drawn carriages past the gay hangouts of the French Quarter. Great fun.

LGBT+ by Neighborhood

French Quarter The Lower Quarter, from St Philips St to Esplande Ave, is a lively gay party.

Faubourg Marigny and Bywater Quieter gay scene largely made up of established couples.

Uptown and Riverbend An out student scene concentrated near Tulane and Loyola.

Garden, Lower Garden and Central City While there are few dedicated LGBT+ hangouts, all of Magazine St is gay friendly.

CBD and Warehouse District A mix of professional and artsy LGBT+ folks hang out at hotels like the Ace and Catahoula.

For LGBT+ Travelers

Faubourg Marigny Book Store (p93) This bookstore is also a cornerstone of the gay community.

Country Club (p89) Clothing-optional heated pool? Sounds good.

Café Lafitte in Exile (p67) Oldest gay bar in the South.

Southern Decadence (p24) One of the craziest parties in town.

Bourbon Pub & Parade (p68) It's 24-hour madness on Bourbon St.

LGBT+ Bars

Country Club (p89) Good drinks and food, and a pool in a tropical courtyard.

Bourbon Pub & Parade (p68) A big, over-the-top gay bar that anchors the Quarter's LGBT+ scene.

AllWays Lounge (p90) Frequently puts on cabaret and drag shows.

Big Daddy's Bar (p90) Laid-back 'gayborhood' bar with a down-to-earth vibe.

Café Lafitte in Exile (p67) Six decades running and going strong; this is a bedrock of the Quarter gay scene.

Dance Floors

Oz (p68) A nonstop dance floor that brings out all of the beautiful boys.

Bourbon Pub & Parade (p68) Throws big parties that cater to an all-ages crowd of travelers and locals.

Café Lafitte in Exile (p67) Has been hosting awesome dance parties for years, and shows no signs of stopping.

Festivals

Southern Decadence (p24) The biggest LGBT+ event in New Orleans is always a party for the record books.

Gay Easter Parade (p42) Bunny costumes, tea parties, dainty dresses and lots of fun.

Mardi Gras (p74) Carnival's enormous arts and DIY scene features a strong LGBT+ presence.

Halloween Many of the city's best costuming and masking events have overlap with the gay community.

Gay Pride New Orleans Catch the parade and the spectacle, but note this event is decently family friendly.

Gay Stays

Green House Inn (p184) Adults-only accommodations close to a glut of fine bars and restaurants.

Lamothe House (p181) Gay-friendly accommodations on the attractive end of Esplanade Ave.

Lions Inn B&B (p180) Located in the cozy center of the Marigny; a locus for the gay community.

W French Quarter (p179) Hip decor, fantastic on-site eating and the nightlife of the Quarter at your fingertips.

NEED TO KNOW

Gay Bars Never Close

OK, that's not entirely true, but it's safe to say that if you want a 24-hour party, the gay bars on Bourbon St (especially Bourbon Pub) are the place to be. Even the bars that aren't technically open 24 hours are often still kicking around 5am, so it's not like they attract the shrinking-violet crowd.

Best Gay Online Resources

Check out these websites for information on queer travel in New Orleans:

Gay New Orleans Online (www.neworleansonline.com/neworleans/lgbt) Probably the most comprehensive collection of queer listings online.

Gay Cities (http://neworleans.gaycities.com) Listings, user reviews and LGBT-related content.

Ambush Magazine (www.ambushmag.com) Local take on queer news and issues.

Purple Roofs (www.purpleroofs.com/usa/louisiana.html) Reliable gay-travel resource.

Explore New Orleans

NEW ORLEAN'S
TOP SIGHTS

Neighborhoods at a Glance

❶ French Quarter p48

Also known as Vieux Carré ('voo car-*ray*'; Old Quarter) and 'the Quarter', the French Quarter is the original city as planned by the French in the 1800s. Here lies the infamous Bourbon St, but of more interest is an elegantly aged grid of shopfronts, iron lamps and courtyard gardens. Most visitors begin exploring the city here and some never leave the area. That's not to say the Quarter isn't

lovely, but it's a bit like a theme park: heavy on tourist traffic and light on locals.

❷ Faubourg Marigny & Bywater p82

Just downriver from the French Quarter, the Marigny and Bywater are both Creole *faubourgs* (literally 'suburbs,' although 'neighborhoods' is more accurate in spirit).

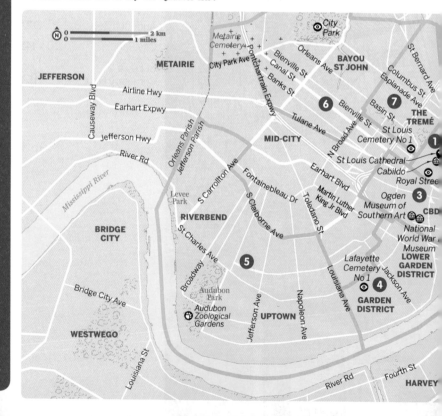

They once stood at the edge of gentrification, and attracted a glut of artists and creative types, as such areas are wont to do. While gentrification has firmly set in, these remain fascinating, beautiful neighborhoods – the homes are bright, painted like so many rows of pastel fruit, and plenty of oddballs still call this home.

❸ CBD & Warehouse District p95

The Central Business District (CBD) and Warehouse District have long been a membrane between downriver Creole *faubourgs* like the French Quarter and the large leafy lots of the Garden District and Uptown. This is an area that has always been in search of an identity, in a city with a distinct sense of place. Between offices and forgettable municipal buildings lie some of the city's best museums, as well as posh restaurants, art galleries and converted condos.

❹ Garden, Lower Garden & Central City p112

As one proceeds south along the curve of the Mississippi River, the streets become tree-lined and the houses considerably grander. When you tire of craning back to take in multiwing mansions, you're in the Garden and Lower Garden Districts, the beginning of New Orleans' 'American Sector' (so named because it was settled after the Louisiana Purchase). Nearby Central City's main thoroughfare, Oretha Castle Haley Blvd, is undergoing a fitful but steady renaissance following years of neglect.

❺ Uptown & Riverbend p125

In Uptown, the views of mansion after mansion on St Charles Ave are worth checking out even if you're not an architecture fan.

Magazine St is one of the coolest strips of restaurants and shopping outlets in town. Eventually the 'U' curves north again along the river's bend into Riverbend, popular with the university crowd.

❻ Mid-City, Bayou St John & City Park p139

Back in the day, this was the back of beyond: the bottom of the depression that is the New Orleans geographic bowl, an area of swampy lowlands and hidden gambler dens. Today? This lovely district includes long lanes of shotgun houses, bike lanes, the gorgeous green spaces of City Park, the elegant mansions of Esplanade Ave and the slow, lovely laze of Bayou St John.

❼ Tremé-Lafitte p151

Few neighborhoods hold their finger on the city's cultural pulse like the Tremé. This handful of square blocks has had a disproportionate impact on world music. This is where jazz was invented, by free people of color and the descendants of slaves, who mixed African rhythms with European syncopation and homegrown improvisation. When you consider jazz led to rock led to hip hop led to modern pop, just remember, the roots of that musical tree find their soil here.

French Quarter

Neighborhood Top Five

1 Riverfront (p59) Walking up and down the Mississippi River, watching crowds disembarking from ferries, listening to music and watching buskers along the way.

2 New Orleans Jazz Museum (p57) Catching a concert and seeing living local culture playing its Dixieland heart out.

3 Bar Tonique (p64) Slow-sipping a marvelous cocktail in a busy spot often frequented by bartenders.

4 Fifi Mahony's (p70) Fitting yourself out for the perfect wig at this treasure trove of hairpieces.

5 Cabildo (p50) Grounding yourself in the history of Louisiana at this museum in the elegant former seat of the state's colonial government.

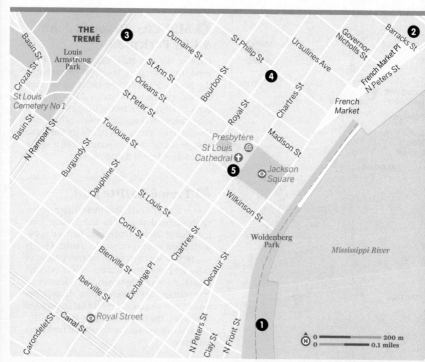

For more detail of this area see Map p234 ➡

Explore the French Quarter

Many visitors treat the French Quarter as a sort of adult playground, with Bourbon St serving as a neon heart of bad behavior, where the drinks are as fluorescent as the lights. Skip this side and you'll find a compact neighborhood where historical preservation, incredible dining and great nightlife intersect like nowhere else in the USA.

Start your first day with the morning walking tour run by Friends of the Cabildo. It's an excellent introduction to both the architecture and history of the area. After the tour, take a walk along the river and consider catching a concert sponsored by the National Park Service at the New Orleans Jazz Museum. Finish the evening with dinner at either Coop's Place or Galatoire's, and drinks at French 75.

Next day, walk up and down Royal Street and lounge alongside the river. If you feel inclined, rent a bicycle; you can cover lots more ground that way. Go shopping or peruse some galleries, and get yourself to Preservation Hall early enough in the evening to see the show. As night well and truly falls, have dinner at Meauxbar, and then hop over for drinks at Bar Tonique or meander back to the river for a late-night bite at St Lawrence – perhaps with a wander (eyes wide shut) along crazy Bourbon St to vicariously take in the drunkenness and debauchery.

Local Life

History History seeps though the brick walls of the French Quarter. Locals love the concentration of museums, historical homes and tours that take in this city's colorful (and often criminal) past.

Music While many locals tend to skirt the Quarter, others love to wander down Royal Street and listen to the buskers doing their musical thing. Jackson Square is another great spot.

Food Some of the city's best restaurants are found in the French Quarter, and many New Orleanians splurge on a romantic night out here.

Getting There & Away

Streetcar The Canal, Rampart and Riverfront Streetcars all skirt the edges of the French Quarter.

Bus The 91 bus runs up Rampart St and Esplanade Ave, which are both boundary roads of the Quarter.

Car Parking is a hassle in the Quarter; don't bother driving here. If you do, be prepared to park in a garage or bring lots of moolah for the meters.

Ferry A ferry (p216) connects Canal St with Algiers Point (one-way $2), running most days from 6:15am to 9:45pm. This can be a nice way to cheaply see the city from the Mississippi.

Lonely Planet's Top Tip

Many of the finest restaurants have hefty price tags to match, but on weekdays they often have super-reasonable prix-fixe menus.

 FRENCH QUARTER

 ## Best Places to Eat

➡ Arnaud's (p60)

➡ Meauxbar (p62)

➡ Coop's Place (p61)

For reviews, see p59 ➡

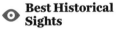 ## Best Places to Shop

➡ Boutique du Vampyre (p70)

➡ Little Toy Shop (p70)

➡ Hové Parfumeur (p71)

For reviews, see p70 ➡

Best Historical Sights

➡ Cabildo (p50)

➡ Presbytère (p53)

➡ Ursuline Convent (p56)

For reviews, see p50 ➡

 ## Best Places to Sleep

➡ Saint (p178)

➡ Audubon Cottages (p177)

➡ City House Hostel New Orleans (p176)

For reviews, see p176 ➡

 ## Best Nightlife

➡ Bar Tonique (p64)

➡ French 75 (p66)

➡ Cane & Table (p66)

➡ Deja Vu (p67)

For reviews, see p64 ➡

TOP SIGHT
CABILDO

The former seat of power in colonial Louisiana serves as the gateway for exploring the history of the state, and New Orleans in particular. The Cabildo, a Spanish term for a city council, leads visitors into airy halls reminiscent of Spanish Colonial design, and features a mansard roof (the narrow, steep-sided roofs commonly found in Europe) added in French style.

History

Fire has played an important role in this building's story, both in its 1795 construction (after the Great New Orleans Fire of 1788, which tore through much of the Quarter, cleared this site of its existing structure) and two centuries later, when the Cabildo was burned in 1988. Painstakingly restored, and returned to its original glory, the building is a treasure in its own right – not to mention the treasures that are on display inside its halls.

Exhibits

The exhibits, from Native American tools on the 1st floor to 'Wanted' posters for escaped slaves on the 3rd, do a good job of reaffirming the role the building and the surrounding region have played in history. Highlights include an entire section dedicated to the Battle of New Orleans, anchored by an enormous oil painting by 19th-century French artist Eugene Louis Lami; a historical *Plan de la Nouvelle Orléans* from 1744, showing a four-block-deep city; and the death mask of Napoleon Bonaparte. Give yourself at least two hours to explore.

DON'T MISS

➡ Native American exhibition hall
➡ Reconstruction exhibits
➡ Death mask of Napoleon Bonaparte
➡ Sala Capitular

PRACTICALITIES

➡ Map p234
➡ ☎504-568-6985
➡ http://louisianastate-museum.org
➡ 701 Chartres St
➡ adult/student/child under 6yr $6/5/free
➡ ⊙10am-4:30pm Tue-Sun

Sala Capitular

The magnificent Sala Capitular (Capitol Room), a council room fronted by enormous windows giving sweeping views onto Jackson Sq, was the most important room in Louisiana for decades. Civic functions and legal action were conducted here; this was the courtroom where *Plessy v Ferguson*, the 1896 case that legalized segregation under the 'separate but equal' doctrine, was tried. The Sala now includes a comprehensive exhibition dedicated to the Louisiana Purchase.

Reconstruction

American author William Faulkner wrote, 'The past is never dead. It's not even past.' That quote only begins to hint at the troubled history of race relations in the South. The wing of the Cabildo dedicated to post–Civil War Reconstruction is as even-handed and thorough an attempt at explaining this difficult period and its consequences as we've seen, and should be of interest to both history enthusiasts and casual visitors alike.

FEELING PECKISH

Make a day of it and have brunch at Court of the Two Sisters (p60), a few blocks away on Royal St. A little further on, grab a well-earned drink at Toulouse Dive Bar (p59) and shoot a game of pool.

Although the Cabildo is closed on Mondays, Friends of the Cabildo still offers walking tours, which are excellent.

SNEAK A PEEK

Be sure to take a peek at Jackson Square out of the large windows on the 2nd floor.

Check http://louisianastate museum.org/events for current listings of events including concerts, yoga and more.

TOP SIGHT
JACKSON SQUARE

Whatever happens in the Quarter usually begins here. Sprinkled with lazing loungers, surrounded by fortune tellers, sketch artists and traveling performers, and overlooked by cathedrals, offices and shops plucked from a Paris-meets-the-Caribbean fantasy, Jackson Square is one of America's great town squares. It both anchors the French Quarter and is the beating heart of this corner of town.

The square was part of Adrien de Pauger's original city plan and began life as a military parade ground called Place d'Armes (Place of Weapons). Madame Micaëla Pontalba, a 19th-century aristocrat, transformed the muddy marching grounds into a trimmed garden and renamed the square to honor Andrew Jackson, the president who saved New Orleans from the British during the War of 1812. Today, along the edges of that garden you'll see street performers, artists, bands and tourists taking in the atmosphere. It's a gentle, carnivalesque scene, invariably lovely at sunset, which belies a bloody history: during the 1811 German Coast Slave Uprising, three leaders of the rebellion were hung here.

DON'T MISS

➡ Street performers
➡ Artists
➡ The Andrew Jackson statue

PRACTICALITIES

➡ Map p234
➡ Decatur & St Peter Sts

TOP SIGHT
PRESBYTÈRE

Pay a visit to the Presbytère, a museum dedicated to contemporary Louisiana, to learn about the state's present as one of the most dynamic regional cultures in the USA. The structure is as elegantly crafted as the Cabildo, the Presbytère's twin building dedicated to the history of the state; the siblings are separated by St Louis Cathedral overlooking Jackson Sq.

History
The Presbytère was originally designed in 1791 as a place of residence (also known as a rectory, or *presbytère*) for Capuchin monks. That function never panned out, and the building switched between commercial and civic use for decades, finally becoming a museum in 1911.

Exhibits
The museum features rotating special exhibits on local life, documenting everything from fashion to art to music, plus two noteworthy permanent exhibitions.

Mardi Gras
The wonderful permanent exhibit on Mardi Gras exhaustively explores the city's most famous holiday. Here you'll find there's more to Fat Tuesday than wanton debauchery, through an encyclopedia's worth of material on the krewes (parade marching clubs), secret societies, costumes and racial histories that are the threads of the complex Mardi Gras tapestry. It's got some tongue-in-cheek humor too, such as the steel NOPD fencing barriers used to hold back the crowds. We particularly like the exhibit on the 'Courir' Cajun Mardi Gras, held in rural Louisiana, and the bathrooms – modeled after the porta-potties that are as rare as spun gold on Mardi Gras day.

Living with Hurricanes
The 'Living with Hurricanes: Katrina & Beyond' exhibit is the best of the many spaces in New Orleans dedicated to explaining the impact of Katrina. It tackles the issue of how the city survives (and thrives) within the hurricane zone. Multimedia displays, stark photography, several attics' worth (literally) of found objects and a thoughtful layout combine to create a powerful experience.

DON'T MISS

➡ Special exhibits
➡ 'Mardi Gras: it's Carnival Time in Louisiana' exhibit
➡ 'Living with Hurricanes: Katrina & Beyond' exhibit

PRACTICALITIES

➡ Map p234
➡ ☎504-568-6962
➡ http://louisianastatemuseum.org
➡ 751 Chartres St
➡ adult/student $6/5
➡ ⊙10am-4:30pm Tue-Sun

TOP SIGHT
ROYAL STREET

Royal St, with its antiques shops, galleries, and potted ferns hanging from cast-iron balconies, is the elegant yin to well-known Bourbon St's debauched yang. Head here to engage in the acceptable vacation behavior of culinary and consumer indulgence, rather than party-till-unconscious excess. Stroll or bicycle past and get a sense of the bygone ambience of the Vieux Carré.

DON'T MISS

➡ Antiques stores
➡ Architecture
➡ Art galleries
➡ Restaurants
➡ Music and buskers

Outdoor Arcade

Royal St is one of the places where soul still exists in New Orleans. Blocks and blocks of the strip are dedicated to antiques stores and art galleries, making Royal a sort of elegant 19th-century (and very long) outdoor shopping arcade. But there's no getting around the fact that far more visitors have heard of, and spend time on, Bourbon St than Royal St. And to be fair, Royal St is, in a sense, as artificial and manufactured as Bourbon St.

PRACTICALITIES

➡ Map p234

Pedestrian Performances

The blocks of Royal St between St Ann St and St Louis are closed to vehicle traffic during the afternoon. Musicians, performers and other buskers set up shop; you may see some teenagers shill for pennies, or accomplished blues musicians jam on their Fenders. Either way, the show is almost always entertaining.

TOP SIGHT
ST LOUIS CATHEDRAL

One of the best examples of French architecture in the country is the triple-spire Cathedral of St Louis, named for the French king sainted in 1297. It's an attractive bit of Gallic heritage in the heart of old New Orleans. Still used for services, the structure is one of the most important (and beautiful) churches serving Catholics in the USA.

History

In 1722, a hurricane destroyed the first of three churches built here by the St Louis Parish. The second was destroyed in the Great New Orleans Fire. Architect Don Gilberto Guillemard dedicated the present cathedral on Christmas Eve in 1794. Pope Paul VI awarded it the rank of minor basilica in 1964.

Besides hosting African American, white and Creole congregants, St Louis has attracted those who, in the best New Orleanian tradition, mix their influences. Voodoo queen Marie Laveau worshiped here during the height of her prominence in the mid-19th century.

DON'T MISS

➡ Ornate decorations
➡ Stained glass
➡ Christmas services
➡ Ash Wednesday service

PRACTICALITIES

➡ Map p234
➡ ☎504-525-9585
➡ www.stlouiscathedral.org
➡ Jackson Sq
➡ donations accepted, audio guide $8
➡ ⊙8am-4pm, Mass 12:05pm Mon-Fri, 5pm Sat, 9am & 11am Sun

Services

Throughout the year, St Louis hosts events that are at the core of New Orleans' Catholic community. If you're in town during any of the following holidays, try to attend. Christmas services are packed, including a 5pm vigil on December 24 and midnight Mass on December 25 (doors open at 11:15pm). On Palm Sunday (the Sunday before Easter), the transfixing Blessing of the Palms ceremony begins at 10:50am. If you can drag yourself out of bed, come on Ash Wednesday, the day after Mardi Gras; ashes, a symbol of mourning and penitence, are distributed at 7:30am, noon and 5pm.

 SIGHTS

The French Quarter is full of incredible museums, historic buildings, unique views, and other fun attractions. Even better, a lot of it (such as walking Bourbon or Royal St) is completely free.

JACKSON SQUARE   SQUARE
See p52.

CABILDO   MUSEUM
See p50.

ROYAL STREET   STREET
See p54.

ST LOUIS CATHEDRAL   CATHEDRAL
See p55.

**THE HISTORIC
NEW ORLEANS COLLECTION**   MUSEUM
Map p234 (THNOC; ☑504-523-4662; www.
hnoc.org; 533 Royal St; admission free, tours $5;
☺9:30am-4:30pm Tue-Sat, from 10:30am Sun,
tours 10am, 11am, 2pm & 3pm Tue-Sat) A combination of preserved buildings, museums
and research centers all rolled into one, The
Historic New Orleans Collection is a good
introduction to the history of the city. The
complex is anchored by its Royal St campus,
which presents a series of regularly rotating
exhibits and occasional temporary exhibits.
Some of the artifacts on display include an
original Jazz Fest poster, transfer documents of the Louisiana Purchase, and utterly disturbing slave advertisements.

The Williams family was always considered eccentric, and the museum's Williams
Residence – purchased by the family in
1938, in what was then considered a dowdy
neighborhood – is stuffed full of art and
furniture collected on the Williams' world
travels. As entertaining as the tour is, even
better is the introductory video, although it
glosses over the source of their fortune (ie
harvesting out the old-growth cypress of
the Louisiana wetlands).

**NEW ORLEANS
PHARMACY MUSEUM**   MUSEUM
Map p234 (☑504-565-8027; www.pharmacy-
museum.org; 514 Chartres St; adult/student/
child under 10yr $5/4/free; ☺10am-4pm Tue-
Sat) ✐ This beautifully preserved shop,
groaning with ancient display cases filled
with intriguing little bottles, was established in 1823 by Louis J Dufilho, at a time
when the pharmaceutical arts were – shall

we say – in their infancy. The museum
suggests Dufilho was the nation's first
licensed pharmacist, although today his
practices would be suspect (gold-coated
pills for the wealthy; opium, alcohol and
cannabis for those with less cash).

UPPER BOURBON STREET   AREA
Map p234 (btwn Canal & Dumaine Sts) Like
Vegas and Cancun, the main stretch of
Bourbon St is where the great id of the re-
pressed American psyche is let loose into
a seething mass of karaoke, strip clubs
and bachelorette parties. It's one of the
tackiest experiences in the world, but it
can be fun for an evening. As one T-shirt
here says, 'I'm more wasted than a liberal
arts degree.'

PRESBYTÈRE   MUSEUM
See p53.

URSULINE CONVENT   HISTORIC BUILDING
Map p234 (☑504-529-3040; www.stlouis
cathedral.org/convent-museum; 1112 Chartres St;
adult/student $8/6; ☺10am-4pm Mon-Fri, 9am-
3pm Sat) One of the few surviving French Colonial buildings in New Orleans, this lovely
convent is worth a tour for its architectural
virtues and its small museum of Catholic bric-a-brac. After a five-month voyage
from Rouen, France, 12 Ursuline nuns arrived in New Orleans in 1727. The Ursuline
had a missionary bent, but achieved their
goals through advancing the literacy rate of
women of all races and social levels; their
school admitted French, Native American
and African American girls.

LOWER BOURBON STREET   AREA
Map p234 (btwn St Philip St & Esplanade Ave) At
St Philip St, Bourbon shifts from a Dante's
Inferno–style circle of neon-lit hell into an
altogether more agreeable stretch of historical houses, diners and bars, many of which
cater to the gay community. In fact, said gay
bars are the loudest residents on this, the
quieter, more classically New Orleans end
of the street.

HAROUNI GALLERY   GALLERY
Map p234 (☑504-299-4393; www.harouni.
com; 933 Royal St; ☺11am-5pm) Artist David
Harouni, a native of Iran, has lived and
worked in New Orleans for several decades. He creates works of absorbing depth
by painting and scraping multiple layers of
medium; the finished product has a surreal,
eerie beauty.

NEW ORLEANS JAZZ MUSEUM
AT THE OLD US MINT   MUSEUM
Map p234 (504-568-6993; www.nolajazzmuseum.org; 400 Esplanade Ave; adult/child $6/5; 10am-4:30pm Tue-Sun) The Mint, a blocky Greek Revival structure, is the only building of its kind to have printed both US and Confederate currency. Today it is home to the New Orleans Jazz Museum, with rotating exhibits on local jazz history and culture. It also contains the Louisiana Historical Center, an archive of manuscripts, microfiche and records related to the state. New Orleans Jazz National Historic Park (p58) hosts concerts here on weekday afternoons; check in at its office to see who is playing or visit the museum's website.

FRENCH MARKET   MARKET
Map p234 (504-636-6400; www.frenchmarket.org; 1008 N Peters St; 9am-6pm) This long shopping arcade was once the great bazaar and pulsing commercial heart for much of New Orleans. Today the French Market is a bustling tourist jungle of curios, flea markets, food stalls and artist kiosks, some of which sell genuinely fascinating, memorable souvenirs, and some of which sell alligator heads, belt buckles and sunglasses. Whether it's kitch or catch, you can find it here, often with live musical accompaniment. Events sometimes keep the market open later in the evenings.

Following cycles of fire and storm, the market has been built and rebuilt by the Spanish, French and Works Progress Administration (WPA). These days it's a large, several-block-long area, some of it tented, some of it covered by a permanent shelter. A new stairway leads down to the riverfront.

BEAUREGARD-KEYES
HOUSE   HISTORIC BUILDING
Map p234 (504-523-7257; www.bkhouse.org; 1113 Chartres St; tours adult/student/child $10/4/9; tours hourly 10am-3pm Mon-Sat) This 1826 Greek Revival house is named for its two most famous former inhabitants. Confederate General Pierre Gustave Toutant Beauregard commanded the artillery battery that fired the first shots at Fort Sumter in Charleston, SC, starting the Civil War. Frances Parkinson Keyes wrote 51 novels, many set in New Orleans (and many that had, let's say, not the most sympathetic depictions of African Americans, Jews, Italians and the Irish). Her collection of some 200 dolls and folk costumes are on display.

The home itself is drop-dead gorgeous – a classic French Quarter center-hall mansion that drips with historic beauty. Frequent events such as weddings are held here.

GALLIER HOUSE
MUSEUM   HISTORIC BUILDING
Map p234 (504-274-0746; www.hgghh.org; 1132 Royal St; adult/student & senior $15/12, combined with Hermann-Grima House $25/20; tours hourly 10am-3pm Mon, Tue, Thu & Fri, noon-3pm Sat) Many New Orleans buildings owe their existence, either directly or by design, to James Gallier Sr and Jr, who added Greek Revivalist, British and American accents to the Quarter's French, Spanish and Creole architectural mélange. In 1857, Gallier Jr began work on this town house, which incorporates all of the above elements. The period furniture is lovely; not so much are the intact slave quarters out back – once you see these, you'll recognize them throughout the French Quarter.

HERMANN-GRIMA HOUSE   HISTORIC BUILDING
Map p234 (504-274-0746; www.hgghh.org; 820 St Louis St; tours adult/student & senior $15/12, combined with Gallier House Museum $25/20; tours hourly 10am-3pm Mon, Tue, Thu & Fri, noon-3pm Sat) Samuel Hermann, a Jewish merchant who married a Catholic woman, introduced the American-style Federal design to the Quarter in 1831. Hermann sold the house in 1844 to slaveholder Judge Grima after Hermann reportedly lost $2 million during the national financial panic of 1837. Cooking demonstrations in the open-hearth kitchen are a special treat on alternate Thursdays from October to May.

1850 HOUSE MUSEUM   HISTORIC BUILDING
Map p234 (504-568-6968; http://louisianastatemuseum.org; 523 St Ann St; adult/child $3/free, senior & student $2; 10am-4:30pm Tue-Sun) The 1850 House is one of the apartments in the lower Pontalba Building. Madame Micaëla Pontalba, aristocratic daughter of Don Andrés Almonaster y Roxas, built these long rows of red-brick apartments flanking the upper and lower portions of Jackson Sq. Today, volunteers from the Friends of the Cabildo (p73) give tours of the apartment (every 45 minutes or so, assuming docents are available), which includes the central court and servants' quarters. There are period furnishings throughout. A self-guided tour is fine too.

HEMMERLING GALLERY
OF SOUTHERN ART
GALLERY

Map p234 (📞504-524-0909; 733 Royal St; ⏰11am-6pm Mon-Sat, noon-5pm Sun) William 'Bill' Hemmerling was a self-taught folk artist who incorporated wood, debris and found objects into a powerfully vital body of work. This gallery displays his originals, as well as art by other folk painters and sculptors whose work demonstrates much of the same raw energy.

MUSEUM OF DEATH
MUSEUM

Map p234 (📞504-593-3968; http://museumofdeath.net; 227 Dauphine St; cash/credit card $15/16; ⏰10am-7pm) If death is your thing, or you have an interest in serial killers, the Museum of Death will not disappoint. Starting with skulls (both animal and human) and moving on to various death-related topics, such as cannibalism, shrunken heads, morticians' instruments, disastrous events (the massacre in El Salvador etc), and even a how-to autopsy video, this is a smorgasbord of any and all things related to kicking the bucket.

HISTORIC VOODOO MUSEUM
MUSEUM

Map p234 (📞504-680-0128; www.voodoomuseum.com; 724 Dumaine St; $7; ⏰10am-6pm) Of the (many) voodoo-themed spots in the French Quarter, this one is a favorite. The narrow corridors and dark rooms, stuffed with statues, dolls and paintings, are something approaching spooky, and the information placards (seemingly written by anthropology dissertation students with too much time on their hands) are genuinely informative.

MICHALOPOULOS GALLERY
GALLERY

Map p234 (📞504-558-0505; www.michalopoulos.com; 617 Bienville St; ⏰10am-6pm Mon-Sat, from 11am Sun) Michalopoulos has become one of New Orleans' most popular painters in recent years, in part on the strength of his best-selling Jazz Fest posters. His shop showcases his colorful and expressive architectural studies and paintings that look like Van Gogh meets the Vieux Carré. Visit the website or call ahead to confirm hours and check on upcoming events.

A GALLERY FOR
FINE PHOTOGRAPHY
GALLERY

Map p234 (📞504-568-1313; www.agallery.com; 241 Chartres St; ⏰10:30am-5:30pm Mon & Thu-Sat, noon-5pm Sun, by appointment Tue & Wed) This impressive gallery usually has prints such as William Henry Jackson's early-20th-century views of New Orleans and EJ Bellocq's rare images of Storyville prostitutes, made from the photographers' original glass plates. The gallery also regularly features Herman Leonard's shots of Duke Ellington and other jazz legends, as well as the occasional Cartier-Bresson enlargement (available at second-mortgage prices).

LUCKY ROSE
GALLERY

Map p234 (📞504-309-8000; http://cathyrose.com; 840 Royal St; ⏰11am-5pm Thu-Mon) Cathy Rose blends wonder, whimsy and ethereal aesthetics; her art has whiffs of Chagall, if you can picture him on the Mississippi. Rose uses mixed media in her sculpture, often making wooden dolls, twisted wire, or reimagining scrap items.

RODRIGUE STUDIO
GALLERY

Map p234 (📞504-581-4244; www.georgerodrigue.com; 730 Royal St; ⏰10am-6pm Mon-Sat, noon-5pm Sun) The late Cajun artist George Rodrigue's gallery is the place to see examples of his unbelievably popular 'Blue Dog' paintings. The iconic dog became his signature, and why not: it was working for him. Look for topical works, displayed in rotating exhibits that showcase the artist – and, most often, the dog.

NEW ORLEANS JAZZ
NATIONAL HISTORIC PARK
CULTURAL CENTER

Map p234 (📞504-589-4841; www.nps.gov/jazz; 916 N Peters St; ⏰9am-4:30pm Tue-Thu, to 4pm Fri & Sat) FREE The headquarters of the Jazz National Historic Park has educational music programs on most days. Many rangers are musicians and knowledgeable lecturers, and their presentations discuss musical developments, cultural changes and musical techniques in relation to the broad subject of jazz. Live music happens Tuesdays through Saturdays. You can pick up a self-guided walking tour map of jazz sites from this office – the tour can also be downloaded from their website.

GALLERY BURGUIERES
GALLERY

Map p234 (📞504-301-1119; www.galleryburguieres.com; 736 Royal St; ⏰10am-7pm) Ally Burguieres' artwork demonstrates plenty of technical skill, but there's also a lot of heart in her paintings and sketches, which focus on animals and fairy-tale scenes. There are lots of prints available if you're looking for affordable artwork for your home.

SECRET, SPOOKY & MACABRE

There's no question that for all the boisterous partying and the fine dining, there's something a little bit spooky here in the French Quarter too. Voodoo got its continental start here, nearly every building has a ghost story or two, and if you talk to residents long enough, some will even come clean about hearing an unexplained bump in the night.

Whether you believe in all that or not, you can have a lot of fun at the following spots, all of which feature something quirky, spooky or just plain dead.

Passions (p66) This hidden, locked speakeasy above a popular Bourbon St bar is password-protected better than most computers, by a secret phrase that you can only find out by visiting the lovely clerks at Boutique du Vampyre (p70). Be nice to them. If they deem you and your compatriots worthy, they'll let you know where the bar is, and what magic password will get you in.

Toulouse Dive Bar Map p234 (☎504-522-2260; 738 Toulouse St; ◉2pm-6am Mon-Thu, 11am-7am Fri-Sun) Yes, in most respects this is exactly what it appears to be: a dive bar on Toulouse St. But try to find the bathroom and you'll see why we've included it here.

Muriel's (p60) What's not to like about a place that sets a table (even pours a glass of wine!) for their resident ghost? You don't have to dine here to get a view of that (it's visible from the street), but don't miss out on visiting the upstairs **Seance Lounge**, a plush, curtained, dimly lit red room guarded by two Egyptian-style sarcophagi.

Museum of Death Nothing secret or hidden about this museum, and it's not for the queasy: see letters written by serial killers, skulls, even shrunken heads. If you need a macabre reminder of what's in store for all of us, this is your place. Afterwards, sufficiently depressed and reminded that you do indeed only live once, head to Bourbon St and live the rest of the day as if it were your last.

MOONWALK PARK
Map p234 (off Decatur St; ◉24hr) Named for former mayor and politician Maurice 'Moon' Landrieu, this riverside promenade offers great Mississippi views.

RIVERFRONT PARK
Map p234 (from Bienville to St Philip St) It's supremely pleasant to stroll up to the Mississippi River as it runs by the Quarter. The entire riverfront area has been landscaped with pedestrian paths, public arts projects and small green spaces such as the **Woldenberg Park**. Sunset is the best time to come up here: couples walk around in love; container ships and ferries ply the water; and all feels bucolic. Nearby is the Jackson (Jax) Brewery, a mediocre shopping mall that *does* have free public restrooms.

MUSICAL LEGENDS PARK PARK
Map p234 (www.neworleansmusicallegends.com; 311 Bourbon St; ◉8am-midnight Sun-Thu, to 1am Fri & Sat) This pleasant little public square is peppered with statues of some of New Orleans' great musical heroes: Louis Prima, Chris Owens, Pete Fountain, Al Hirt, Fats Domino and Ronnie Kole. Musicians play live jazz within the park from 10am until it closes.

WILLIAMS RESEARCH CENTER RESEARCH CENTER
Map p234 (☎504-523-4662; www.hnoc.org; 410 Chartres St; ◉9:30am-4:30pm Tue-Sat) Dedicated travelers and history heads should pop into the Williams Research Center; if you have specific queries about almost anything to do with New Orleans, the staff can help. The archives contain more than 350,000 images and some 2 miles of manuscripts.

✕ EATING

The French Quarter has its share of top-notch restaurants, so good that, by the time you leave, you may need to let your belt out a notch or two. Even the cheap eats are awesome, with incredible po'boys, decent dive fare and cheap-yet-tasty ethnic restaurants. The mid- and top-range categories are where the Quarter really shines, with haughty dress-code-enforced establishments

side by side with newcomers, making this area a feast (literally). Many of the fancy dinner places have great deals during lunch, too. Also look for excellent brunches on weekends.

BAYONA — LOUISIANAN $$$

Map p234 (✆504-525-4455; www.bayona.com; 430 Dauphine St; mains $28-33; ⊘11:30am-1:30pm Wed-Sat, plus 6-9pm Mon-Thu, 5:30-10pm Fri & Sat; ⚲) Bayona is one of our favorite splurges in the Quarter, and a pioneer of the slow-food movement. It's classy but unpretentious, an all-round fine spot for a meal. The menu changes regularly, but expect fresh fish, fowl and game, prepared in a way that comes off as elegant and deeply cozy at the same time.

★GALATOIRE'S — CREOLE $$$

Map p234 (✆504-525-2021; www.galatoires.com; 209 Bourbon St; mains $20-44; ⊘11:30am-10pm Tue-Sat, from noon Sun) Friday lunchtime is the best time to visit this revered institution for its traditional Creole cuisine. That's when local ladies in big hats and gloves and men wearing bowties (without irony) buy copious bottles of champagne, gossip to high hell and have eight-hour boozy lunches that, in their way, have been going on forever. Dress the part; jackets are a must for men.

Galatoire's is a special place. Its interior has been frozen in time for over a century, and some families still run tabs here, a sure sign that your name rings out in the right New Orleanian social circles.

If you're looking to dine on a dime (er, make that a Jackson or two) then come for lunch, when they offer – like many fine spots in the Quarter – a very nice prix-fixe special from Tuesday to Thursday. Expect to dine on old-line masterpieces and mainstays: pompano meunière (seasoned white fish), liver with bacon and onions, and the signature chicken Clemenceau.

Be sure to wander around after you finish eating, as some of the back rooms here have a near-museum-like quality, offering a fascinating glimpse back into the past.

SOBOU — AMERICAN $$$

Map p234 (✆504-552-4095; www.sobounola.com; 310 Chartres St; mains $17-52; ⊘7am-10pm) The name means 'South of Bourbon'. And the food? Hard to pin down, but uniformly excellent. The chefs play with a concept that mixes Louisiana indulgence with eccentricities: sweet-potato beignets slathered

with duck gravy and chicory-coffee glaze – mmmm! The menu changes seasonally, but it's always solid, as is the innovative cocktail bar.

ARNAUD'S — CREOLE $$$

Map p234 (✆504-523-5433; www.arnauds.com; 813 Bienville St; mains $26-42; ⊘6-10pm Mon-Sat, 10am-2:30pm & 6-10pm Sun) Back in 1918, 'Count' Arnaud Cazenave turned roughly a whole city block into a restaurant that's served upscale Creole cuisine ever since. The menu includes shrimp Arnaud (shrimp in a rémoulade sauce), and oysters Bienville (an original dish with mushrooms and a white-wine sauce). Show up early for a French 75 at, hey, French 75 (p66). And men, bring a jacket.

BOURBON HOUSE — CREOLE $$$

Map p234 (✆504-522-0111; 144 Bourbon St; mains $21-42; ⊘6:30am-10pm Sun-Thu, to 11pm Fri & Sat) The Bourbon House is an outpost of the Brennan restaurant empire. While you'll find a nice steak and pulled pork on the menu, seafood is the specialty here. Catfish is served crusted with pecans in a rich butter sauce, while the barbecued shrimp, heavily laced with rosemary and black pepper, is absolute magic. Not surprisingly, plenty of bourbons as well.

MURIEL'S — CAJUN $$$

Map p234 (✆504-568-1885; www.muriels.com; 801 Chartres St; mains $21-39; ⊘11:30am-2:30pm & 5:30-10pm Mon-Fri, from 10:30am Sat & Sun) Muriel's has a ghost (they set a table nightly for him!), a fascinating history, and it's one of the main stops on the Haunted History (p73) tours. The food is fine, and – if it's not rented for a private event – you can bring your drinks to the dimly lit, blood-red Seance Lounge and sip them side by side with two sarcophagi.

COURT OF THE TWO SISTERS — CREOLE $$$

Map p234 (✆504-522-7261; www.courtoftwosisters.com; 613 Royal St; mains $18-37, brunch $32; ⊘9am-3pm & 5:30-10pm) The Court regularly ranks in 'best place for brunch in New Orleans' lists, a standing that can be attributed to its setting as much as its food. The latter is a circus of Creole omelets, Cajun pasta salads, grillades, fruits, meats and fruity cocktails; the former is an enchanting Creole garden filled with sugar-scented warm air with soft jazz playing.

Reservations are recommended.

DICKIE BRENNAN'S
STEAKHOUSE   STEAK $$$

Map p234 (☎504-522-2467; www.dickiebren-nanssteakhouse.com; 716 Iberville St; mains $26-85; ⊗5:30-10pm Sat-Thu, 11:30am-2:30pm & 5:30-10pm Fri) New Orleans, a city of seafood and swamp ingredients, isn't known as a steak town. Yet this steakhouse is consid-ered one of the greatest in the South. This place does steak, and it does it right. For a side, try the Pontalba potatoes, done up with garlic, mushrooms and ham.

ANTOINE'S   CREOLE $$$

Map p234 (☎504-581-4422; www.antoines.com; 713 St Louis St; dinner mains $27-48; ⊗11:30am-2pm & 5:30-9:30pm Mon-Sat, 11am-2pm Sun) Established in 1840, Antoine's is the oldest of old-line New Orleans restaurants. The dining rooms look like first-class lounges on the *Orient Express* and are named for Mar-di Gras krewes. This restaurant invented dishes such as oysters Rockefeller, and com-ing here means eating history in a space that feels like it should host Jay Gatsby.

BROUSSARD'S   CREOLE $$$

Map p234 (☎504-581-3866; www.broussards.com; 819 Conti St; mains $18-40; ⊗5:30-10pm) Broussard's has been around since 1920, of-fering tasty executions of Creole standbys such as veal and crawfish in a béchamel sauce, and redfish stuffed with shrimp, crabmeat and oysters, as well as bottomless mimosas. The on-site Empire Bar does for classic cocktails what the restaurant does for old-line Creole cuisine. No T-shirts, ripped jeans, flip-flops, tank tops or shorts, folks.

BRENNAN'S RESTAURANT   CREOLE $$$

Map p234 (☎504-525-9711; www.brennansne-worleans.com; 417 Royal St; mains $20-40; ⊗9am-2pm & 6-10pm Mon-Fri, from 8am Sat & Sun) One of the grande dames of Creole din-ing, Brennan's has undergone an enormous overhaul. It still offers decadent breakfasts and cocktail 'eye-openers' to start the day. But the cuisine has gotten a little more in-ternational, even as it remains old-school rich: roasted pork tenderloin ($28) and lump crab ($34) to name a few. Live music makes it even better.

K-PAUL'S LOUISIANA KITCHEN   CAJUN $$$

Map p234 (☎504-596-2530; www.kpauls.com; 416 Chartres St; mains $33-37; ⊗5:30-10pm Mon-Sat, 11am-2pm Thu-Sat) This was the home base of late chef Paul Prudhomme, who was essentially responsible for putting modern Louisiana cooking on the culinary map. The kitchen's still cranking out qual-ity: blackened twin beef tenders ($37) come with an incredibly rich 'debris' gravy that's been slowly cooked over a two-day period.

GW FINS   SEAFOOD $$$

Map p234 (☎504-581-3467; www.gwfins.com; 808 Bienville St; mains $28-46; ⊗5-10pm Sun-Thu, to 10:30pm Fri & Sat) Fins focuses, almost en-tirely, on fish: freshly caught and prepped so that the flavor of the sea is always accented and never overwhelmed. For New Orleans this is light, almost delicate dining – you'll still find crabmeat stuffing and tasso top-pings, but Fins also knows how to serve a rare yellowfin tuna with fine sticky rice.

★COOP'S PLACE   CAJUN $$

Map p234 (☎504-525-9053; www.coopsplace.net; 1109 Decatur St; mains $10-20; ⊗11am-midnight Sun-Thu, to 1am Fri & Sat) Coop's is an authentic Cajun dive, but more rocked out. Make no mistake: it can be grotty and chaotic, the servers have attitude and the layout is annoying. But it's worth it for the food: rabbit jambalaya or chicken with shrimp and tasso (smoked ham) in a cream sauce – there's no such thing as 'too heavy' here. No patrons under 21.

EAT NEW ORLEANS   CREOLE $$

Map p234 (☎504-522-7222; http://eatnola.com; 900 Dumaine St; mains $13-27; ⊗11am-2pm Tue-Fri, 5:30-10pm Tue-Sat, brunch 9am-2pm Sat & Sun; ☑) Eat dishes out neo-Creole cuisine that has become immensely popular with locals; when a New Orleanian is willing to brave French Quarter parking for pork and mustard greens or stuffed peppers, you know something good's going on. Brunch is special, with highlights such as fried chick-en and gravy with eggs. Rare as the unicorn in NOLA, this spot allows BYOB.

SYLVAIN   LOUISIANAN $$

Map p234 (☎504-265-8123; www.sylvainnola.com; 625 Chartres St; mains $14-29; ⊗5:30-11pm Sun-Thu, to midnight Fri & Sat, 11:30am-2:30pm Fri-Sun) This rustic yet elegant gas-tropub draws inspiration from the dedi-cation to local ingredients demonstrated by expert chefs. The menu changes often, but the focus is Southern haute cuisine, burgers, fish, ribs and the like – combined with craft cocktails with inventive names such as 'Bang for the Buck' and 'Alexander Hamilton'.

IRENE'S CUISINE
ITALIAN $$

Map p234 (☎504-529-8811; 529 Bienville St; mains $20-29; ⏰5:30-10pm Mon-Sat) Irene's is a romantic gem, tucked in a corner that's generally missed by travelers. Not that it's easy to miss, given the lovely scent of garlic emanating from this intimate Italian cavern. Irene's is Italian–French, really: pick from rosemary chicken, seared chops, pan-sautéed fish fillets and great pasta. Reservations aren't accepted and long waits are the norm.

NOLA
AMERICAN $$

Map p234 (☎504-522-6652; www.emerilsrestaurants.com/nola-restaurant; 534 St Louis St; mains $14-29; ⏰11:30am-10pm Sun-Thu, to 11pm Fri & Sat) TV chef Emeril Lagasse's French Quarter outpost is pretty damn good. Emeril himself isn't in the kitchen 'Bam!'-ing up your food, but whoever is does a great job with the fare. Following a major menu change and renovation in 2017, Nola still serves that famous Emeril's Barbecued Shrimp, which keeps 'em coming back time after time.

GREEN GODDESS
FUSION $$

Map p234 (☎504-301-3347; www.greengoddessrestaurant.com; 307 Exchange Pl; mains $12-20; ⏰11am-9pm Wed-Sun; ✍) Who serves South Indian pancakes and tamarind shrimp? Alongside smoked duck and (oh, man) truffle grits? Green Goddess, that's who. The Goddess combines a playful attitude to preparation with a world traveler's perspective on ingredient sourcing and a workman's ethic when it comes to actually cooking the stuff. No reservations accepted.

MEAUXBAR
FUSION $$

Map p234 (☎504-569-9979; www.meauxbar.com; 942 N Rampart St; mains $17-43; ⏰5-10pm Mon-Thu, to midnight Fri, 10am-2pm & 5pm-midnight Sat, 10am-2pm & 5-10pm Sun) Meauxbar sounds French, but there's a strong Louisiana influence running through the kitchen, as is good and proper. So think along the lines of American-French, with a menu that includes mussels, roasted beets, sweetbreads and Gruyère cheese. The seared scallops are cooked to perfection, even better with a cocktail or two. The dark setting is romantic; dress smart casual.

PORT OF CALL
BURGERS $$

Map p234 (☎504-523-0120; http://portofcall-nola.com; 838 Esplanade Ave; mains $12-25; ⏰11am-midnight Sun-Thu, to 1am Fri & Sat) As one (albeit inebriated) local raved, 'You come here, you get the burger.' But it's true:

the meat is like umami condensed into a patty. Then there's the baked potato on the side, buckling under the weight of sour cream, butter and bacon bits, all served in a 1960s-ish Polynesian tiki-bar setting. Expect a wait; no reservations are accepted.

ST LAWRENCE
GASTROPUB $$

Map p234 (☎504-525-4111; www.saintlawrencenola.com; 219 N Peters St; mains $15-24; ⏰11am-2am) So you're dying for a late-night meal but don't feel like pizza or bar nuts? Look no further. In a near-saintly move, these guys keep their kitchen open until 2am, and among other great options, offer a rice-and-beans-and-sausage plate that will stop you in your tracks (it could feed a small army).

CAFÉ AMELIE
FRENCH $$

Map p234 (☎504-412-8965; www.cafeamelie.com; 912 Royal St; mains $15-29; ⏰11am-3pm Wed-Sun, 5-9pm Wed, Thu & Sun, to 10pm Fri & Sat) We wax rhapsodic over the Quarter's beautiful backyard gardens, and Amelie's, much beloved by locals, takes the cake. An alfresco restaurant tucked behind an old carriage house and surrounded by high brick walls and shady trees, this is a supremely romantic dining spot. Fresh seafood and local produce are the basis of a modest, ever-changing menu.

DEANIE'S SEAFOOD
SEAFOOD $$

Map p234 (☎504-581-1316; www.deanies.com; 841 Iberville St; mains $16-32; ⏰11am-10pm Sun-Thu, to 11pm Fri & Sat) Charbroiled oysters are a key reason to come here – they're done perfectly, with garlic and butter and cheese. This large, 'proper attire required' restaurant gets packed at peak times, but can be walk-in friendly during its off hours. They have a variety of other 'Nawleans' seafood specials, too. Grab a table, order some charbroiled bits of heaven, and enjoy!

ACME OYSTER & SEAFOOD HOUSE
SEAFOOD $$

Map p234 (☎504-522-5973; www.acmeoyster.com; 724 Iberville St; mains $11-24; ⏰10:30am-10pm Sun-Thu, to 11pm Fri & Sat) They still shuck oysters to order here, which is a beautiful thing, but they also serve gumbo in a 'poopa' (bread bowl). It's a good spot for fresh oysters close to the Bourbon St craziness.

FIORELLA'S
ITALIAN $$

Map p234 (☎504-605-4816; www.fiorellasnola.com; 1136 Decatur St; mains $16-28; ⏰11am-10pm

Mon-Wed, to midnight Thu & Sun, to 2am Fri & Sat) Tasty sangria specials and sweet, friendly servers make Fiorella's a nice stop for an afternoon tipple. While the food is good, that doesn't quite cut it in the gourmand's paradise of the French Quarter; if you come, don't plan on ordering anything other than the unexpectedly tasty fried chicken.

BENNACHIN
AFRICAN $$

Map p234 (☑504-522-1230; 1212 Royal; St; mains $16-18; ⏱11am-9pm Sun-Thu, to 10pm Fri & Sat; ☑) West African cuisine (specifically Cameroonian and Gambian) doesn't pose too many challenges to the conservative palate. It's basically meat and potatoes, with a main, such as beef in peanut stew or spinach and plantains, served with some kind of starch used as a scooping accompaniment. The heavy use of okra reminds you how much this cuisine has influenced Louisiana. And BYOB!

★MISTER GREGORY'S
FRENCH $

Map p234 (☑504-407-3780; www.mistergregorys.com; 806 N Rampart St; mains $5-13; ⏱9am-4pm; ☑) That the French expat community of New Orleans regularly makes its way to Mister Gregory's should tell you something about the quality of this bistro's baguettes and sandwiches. This no-frills lunch and breakfast spot specializes in deli baguettes, plus it does a mean line of croque-style sandwiches (ie with melted cheese and béchamel on top), salads and waffles.

CROISSANT D'OR PATISSERIE
BAKERY $

Map p234 (☑504-524-4663; www.croissantdornola.com; 615-617 Ursulines Ave; mains $3-7; ⏱6:30am-3pm Wed-Mon) Bring a paper, order coffee and a croissant – or a tart, quiche or sandwich topped with béchamel sauce – and bliss out. Check out the tiled sign on the threshold that says 'ladies entrance' – a holdover from earlier days. While the coffee is bland, the pastries are perfect, and the shop is well-lit, friendly and clean.

CAFÉ BEIGNET
CAFE $

Map p234 (☑504-524-5530; www.cafebeignet. com; 334 Royal St; mains $6-8; ⏱7am-10pm) In a shaded patio setting with a view of Royal St, this intimate cafe serves omelets, Belgian waffles, quiches and beignets. There's a low-level war among foodies over who does the better beignet – this place or Café du Monde – with the general consensus being that this spot uses less powdered sugar.

STANLEY
CREOLE $

Map p234 (☑504-587-0093; www.stanleyrestaurant.com; 547 St Ann St; mains $10-16; ⏱7am-7pm) While sandwiches and other lunchy things are available at Stanley, we're all about the breakfast. Bananas Foster French toast and fluffy pancakes provide the sweet, while a Breaux Bridge Benedict with boudin (Cajun sausage) and local hollandaise does up the savory side. Either option is delicious.

CAFÉ DU MONDE
CAFE $

Map p234 (☑504-525-4544; www.cafedumonde. com; 800 Decatur St; beignets $3; ⏱24hr) Café du Monde is the most popular destination in New Orleans and, unfortunately, it often feels that way. But once you do get seated, the beignets (square, sugar-coated fritters) and chicory café au lait, served here since 1862, are decadent and delicious. Open 24 hours a day, seven days a week – the cafe only closes for Christmas Day.

CENTRAL GROCERY
DELI $

Map p234 (☑504-523-1620; 923 Decatur St; sandwiches $12-23; ⏱9am-5pm) There are a few New Orleans names inextricably linked to a certain dish, and Central Grocery is the word-association winner for the *muffuletta*. That's pronounced 'muffa-lotta', and the name about sums it up: your mouth will be muffled by a hell of a lotta sandwich, stuffed with meat, cheese and sharp olive salad.

This is a real grocery, by the way – one of the last neighborhood vestiges of the New Orleans Sicilian community, and the fresh Italian produce is a draw on its own.

MONA LISA
ITALIAN $

Map p234 (☑504-522-6746; 1212 Royal St; mains $10-17; ⏱5-10pm Wed-Mon) An informal and quiet local spot in the Lower Quarter, Mona Lisa is dim, dark and candlelight-romantic in its own quirky way. Kooky renditions of Da Vinci's familiar subject hang on the walls. Wearing hair curlers, looking 50lb heavier or appearing in the form of a cow, she stares impassively at diners munching on pizzas, pastas and spinach salads.

CLOVER GRILL
DINER $

Map p234 (☑504-598-1010; 900 Bourbon St; mains $4-10; ⏱24hr) This spot near the gay end of Bourbon St resembles an Edward Hopper painting, in which the clientele consists of an out-of-makeup drag queen and a drunk club kid arguing to a background of blaring disco.

MISSISSIPPI RIVERBOATS

New Orleans' current fleet of steamboats are theme-park copies of the old glories that plied the Mississippi River in Mark Twain's day. Gone are the hoop-skirted ladies, wax-mustachioed gents, round-the-clock crap games and the bawdy tinkling on off-tune pianos. Instead the steamboats offer urbane (but sterile) evening jazz cruises, and while the calliope organ survives, it's hard not to feel like the tour is a bit over-the-top, especially given the hefty price tag.

Still, few visitors to New Orleans can resist the opportunity to get out on the Mississippi and watch the old paddle wheel propel them up the river and back down again for a spell. It's a relaxing pastime that the entire family can enjoy.

Creole Queen Map p242 (☑800-445-4109, 504-529-4567; www.creolequeen.com) Runs a two-hour dinner-and-jazz cruise (adult/child six to 12 years/child three to five years $79/36/12, without dinner $48/24/free), featuring a live Dixieland jazz combo, boarding nightly at 6:30pm from the Riverwalk on Canal St. A historical river cruise leaves from the Chalmette Battlefield at 1:30pm daily (adult/child six to 12 years/child under six years $34/14/free).

Steamboat Natchez Map p234 (☑504-589-1401; www.steamboatnatchez.com; 600 Decatur St) The closest thing to an authentic steamboat running out of New Orleans today, the Natchez is both steam-powered and has a bona-fide calliope on board. The evening dinner-and-jazz cruise (adult/teenager/child $81/37/18, without dinner $48/24/free) departs at 7pm nightly. There are also brunch-and-jazz cruises at 11:30am and 2:30pm (adult/teenager/child $44/22/9, without brunch $32/13/free).

The food is dependable diner fare: good for a hangover.

JOHNNY'S PO-BOYS
SANDWICHES $

Map p234 (☑504-524-8129; http://johnnyspoboy.com; 511 St Louis St; dishes $7-16; ⊙8am-4:30pm) A local favorite since 1950, Johnny's is the only traditional po'boy joint around. It's all checkered tablecloths, hustle, bustle and good food served by good folks. Breakfast is simple and delicious. Cash only.

VERTI MARTE
DELI $

Map p234 (☑504-525-4767; 1201 Royal St; sandwiches $7-15; ⊙24hr) Sometimes you just wanna wander the Quarter with a tasty sandwich in hand. If that's the case, get to Verti, a reliable deli with a take-out stand offering a menu as long as a hot New Orleans summer day. Try the 'All that Jazz', a ridiculously scrumptious blend of turkey, shrimp, 'wow sauce', ham, cheese and who knows what else.

🍷 DRINKING & NIGHTLIFE

The French Quarter, with its 24-hour bars and open-carry alcohol policy (where you can drink openly in public), is a fantastic spot for a drink. Whether it's at a raging Bourbon St bar or a quiet dive-bar on a secluded corner, if ethanol is your thing, it's here.

The Upper Quarter gets most tourist traffic, but don't miss the quieter spots, such as Pirate Alley. Alternatively, head down to lower Decatur St for a collection of interesting dives and locals' pubs, or just follow Royal, Bourbon or Decatur to Esplanade, drinking as you go, then finish the night on Frenchmen.

⭐ BAR TONIQUE
COCKTAIL BAR

Map p234 (☑504-324-6045; www.bartonique.com; 820 N Rampart St; ⊙noon-2am) 'Providing shelter from sobriety since 08/08/08', Tonique is a bartender's bar. Seriously, on a Sunday night, when the weekend rush is over, we've seen no fewer than three of the city's top bartenders arrive here to unwind. This gem mixes some of the best drinks in the city, offering a spirits menu as long as a Tolstoy novel.

The one drawback: if Tonique is crowded, it can take awhile to get your drink. Deep breaths. These cocktails are made with love and care, and deserve a little patience. If it's too crowded, they may not even make you that Ramos Gin Fizz you're craving. If you

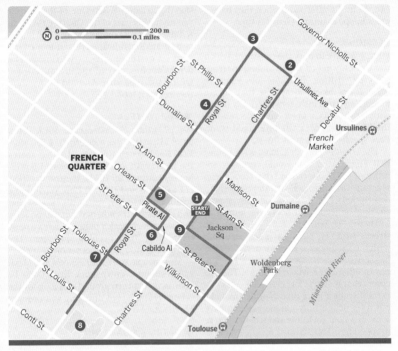

Neighborhood Walk
A Stroll in the Vieux Carré

START JACKSON SQ
END JACKSON SQ
LENGTH 1.1 MILES; 1½ HOURS

Begin your walk at the **1 Presbytère** (p53) on Jackson Sq and head down Chartres St to the corner of Ursulines Ave. Directly across Chartres St, at No 1113, the 1826 **2 Beauregard-Keyes House** (p57) combines Creole and American styles of design. Walk along Ursulines Ave to Royal St – the soda fountain at the **3 Royal Pharmacy** is a preserved relic.

When it comes to quintessential New Orleans postcard images, Royal St takes the prize. Cast-iron galleries grace the buildings and a profusion of flowers garland the facades, while buoyant buskers blare their tunes from practically every street corner.

At No 915 Royal, the **4 Cornstalk Hotel** (p179) stands behind one of the most frequently photographed fences anywhere. At Orleans Ave, stately magnolia trees and lush tropical plants fill **5 St Anthony's Garden** (tough to see beyond the rows of street art) behind St Louis Cathedral.

Next to the garden, take the inviting Pirate Alley and turn right down Cabildo Alley and then right up St Peter St toward Royal St. Tennessee Williams lived at No 632 St Peter, the **6 Avart-Peretti House**, in 1946–47 while he wrote *A Streetcar Named Desire*.

Turn left on Royal St. At the corner of Royal and Toulouse Sts stands a pair of houses built by Jean François Merieult in the 1790s. The building known as the **7 Court of Two Lions** (now a gallery), at 541 Royal St, opens onto Toulouse St and next door is The Historic New Orleans Collection museum.

On the next block, the massive 1909 **8 State Supreme Court Building** was the setting for many scenes in director Oliver Stone's movie *JFK*.

Turn around and go right on Toulouse St to Decatur St and turn left. Cut across the road and walk the last stretch of this tour along the river. As Jackson Sq comes into view, cross back over to the Presbytère's near-identical twin, the **9 Cabildo** (p50).

can, go in the afternoon, when they have a great happy hour and plenty of time.

PASSIONS
COCKTAIL BAR

First, you have to have the password, which you can only get (if you're among the 'chosen') by visiting Boutique du Vampyre (p70), a few blocks away. Use that phrase for entrance to a lush, sensual, dimly lit bar with plush sofas, a great bartender, and all the black and red a vampire could want. Pure speakeasy fun at its finest.

The cocktails are delicious, with names that Edgar Allan Poe would certainly approve of – 'The Black Cat,' the 'Blood Drop Martini' – and fun spell- or vampire-themed descriptions, such as 'good for shapeshifting' or 'feeds your nocturnal hunger.'

There's a balcony for watching the street's insanity, but best is just chatting with the bartender, a local for decades, who has seen just about everything New Orleans has to offer and a whole lot more. The $10 cover charge isn't for everyone, and it's certainly not a local dive or watering hole, but it's a delightfully unique place to have some excellent cocktails and feel like you've dropped into Transylvania for the evening.

CAROUSEL BAR
BAR

Map p234 (☑504-523-3341; http://hotelmonteleone.com/entertainment; 214 Royal St; ⓘ11am-midnight Sun-Thu, to 1am Fri & Sat) At this smart-looking spot inside the historic Hotel Monteleone, you'll find a revolving circular bar, canopied by the top hat of the 1904 World's Fair carousel, adorned with running lights, hand-painted figures and gilded mirrors. In 15 minutes the 25-seat bar completes a full revolution. A top spot for a tipple you'll remember for a while. Careful on your way out.

★FRENCH 75
BAR

Map p234 (☑504-523-5433; www.arnaudsrestaurant.com/bars/french-75; 813 Bienville St; ⓘ5:30-11:30pm Sun-Thu, to 12:30am Fri & Sat) This spot is all wood and patrician accents, but the staff is friendly and down to earth. They'll mix high-quality drinks that will make you feel (a) like the star of your own Tennessee Williams play about decadent Southern aristocracy and (b) blissfully drunk. Definitely dress up for this ritzy place, which is perfect after a dinner at Arnaud's (p60).

★CANE & TABLE
COCKTAIL BAR

Map p234 (☑504-581-1112; www.caneandtablenola.com; 1113 Decatur St; ⓘ3pm-midnight

Mon-Thu, to 1am Fri & Sat) One of the classier venues in this part of the Quarter, the Cane & Table – with its romantically faded interior and Mediterranean-style outdoor courtyard – is so stunning it's hard to knock. The drinks are fun, playful and inventive, some with a tiki-type vibe. And did we mention they're tasty, too?

★TIKI TOLTECA
BAR

Map p234 (http://tikitolteca.com; 301 N Peters St; ⓘ5-11pm Mon-Thu, noon-2am Fri & Sat, noon-11pm Sun) Though this great tiki bar shares the block with another tiki-themed powerhouse, Latitude 29 (p67), they're as different as Tahiti and Hawaii. Here you'll find a small, intimate bar, where it's easy to chat and make new friends, and some impressive drinks – which pack a punch. There's a daily happy hour (from opening until 7pm). The entrance is around the corner on Bienville.

Most people walk into Felipe's, the Mexican restaurant downstairs, first. Don't be confused, just turn around and look for the relatively small sign directing you upstairs via the stairwell.

★PATRICK'S BAR VIN
WINE BAR

Map p234 (☑504-200-3180; http://patricksbarvin.com; 730 Bienville St; ⓘ4pm-midnight Mon-Thu, noon-1am Fri, 2pm-1am Sat, 2pm-midnight Sun) With its carpets, plush chairs, nooks and shelves upon shelves of wine, you'll feel like you're visiting a rich friend's house when you have a glass or two here. Along with its own extensive collection, Patrick's Bar Vin offers a limited number of personal, temperature-controlled wine lockers to keep your precious bottles safely stored.

BLACK PENNY
BAR

Map p234 (☑504-304-4779; www.facebook.com/BlackPennyNola; 700 N Rampart St; ⓘnoon-4am) Run by the folks from nearby Bar Tonique (p64), this spot focuses on great brews, though you can get a fine cocktail if you so desire. Even folks without much taste for traditional beer can find a tipple they might like (such as fruit or ginger beers), and the comfy booths make it easier to talk with friends.

MOLLY'S AT THE MARKET
IRISH PUB

Map p234 (☑504-525-5169; www.mollysatthemarket.net; 1107 Decatur St; ⓘ10am-6am) A cop, a reporter and a tourist walk into a bar. That's not a joke, just a good description of the eclectic clientele you get at this excellent neighborhood bar. It's also the home of a fat cat (Mr Wu), some kicking Irish coffee and an urn containing the ashes of its founder.

LAFITTE'S BLACKSMITH SHOP BAR

Map p234 (☑504-593-9761; www.lafittesblacksmithshop.com; 941 Bourbon St; ⊙10:30am-3am Sun-Thu, to 4am Fri & Sat) This gutted brick cottage claims to be the country's oldest operating bar – it certainly is the oldest in the South, and one of the most atmospheric in the Quarter. Rumors suggest it was once the workshop of pirate Jean Lafitte and his brother Pierre. Whether true or not (historical records suggest not), the house dates to the 18th century.

PAT O'BRIEN'S BAR

Map p234 (☑504-525-4823; www.patobriens.com; 718 St Peter St; ⊙noon-2am Mon-Thu, 10am-4am Fri-Sun) Yes, it's a campy tourist trap, but Pat O'Brien's has genuine atmosphere and history, and where else can you see copper-clad steampunk-esque dueling pianos playing different versions of '80s Billy Joel hits? The courtyard, lit by flaming fountains, is genuinely lovely, but folks mainly pack in for their Hurricanes, a blend of rum, juice and grenadine.

NAPOLEON HOUSE BAR

Map p234 (☑504-524-9752; www.napoleonhouse.com; 500 Chartres St; ⊙11am-10pm Sun-Thu, to 11pm Fri & Sat) By all appearances, the Napoleon House's stuccoed walls haven't received so much as a dab of paint since the place opened in 1805. The diffused glow pouring through open doors and windows in the afternoon draws out the room's gorgeous patina. The bar serves a good range of stiff mixed drinks, cold beer, and a popular Pimm's Cup.

CHART ROOM BAR

Map p234 (☑504-522-1708; 300 Chartres St; ⊙11am-4am) The Chart Room is simply a great bar. There's a historical patina on the walls, creaky furniture inside, outdoor seating for people-watching and a cast of characters plucked from Fellini's 8½ casting call. You may even meet Pocahontas. Or someone who believes he is her.

DEJA VU BAR

Map p234 (☑504-523-1931; http://dejavunola.com; 400 Dauphine St; ⊙24hr) Deja Vu is everything a neighborhood bar should be: mainly, it's there when you are, be that 7:30am or midnight. Open 24/7, Deja Vu has cheap

beers, decent cocktails, a friendly vibe, super-sweet bartenders, and even food. Nothing hoity-toity here, just a good local bar. Did we mention that it's open 24 hours?

LATITUDE 29 COCKTAIL BAR

Map p234 (☑504-609-3811; http://latitude-29nola.com; 321 N Peters St; ⊙3-11pm Sun-Thu, 1pm-midnight Fri & Sat) Jeff 'Beachbum' Berry is a tiki-bar scholar. If a drink has rum, is served in a faux-Polynesian cup or comes with an umbrella and some fruit, the man has written on it. These drinks from across the tropics are served in Latitude 29, Jeff's bar devoted to all things tiki. They're excellent and the bartenders are knowledgeable and friendly.

CAFÉ LAFITTE IN EXILE GAY

Map p234 (☑504-522-8397; www.lafittes.com; 901 Bourbon St; ⊙24hr) This spot, with its huge across-street projection and mood lighting, doesn't exactly feel historical, but it's the oldest dedicated gay bar in the USA. Tennessee Williams and Truman Capote both drank here. What's in a name? The owners once ran Lafitte's Blacksmith Shop; when they lost their lease in 1953, they moved here and opened Lafitte in Exile.

SPITFIRE COFFEE COFFEE

Map p234 (www.spitfirecoffee.com; 627 St Peter St; ⊙8am-8pm) This spot specializes in pour-over coffee and espresso drinks ($3.50 to $4.50). It serves some of the Quarter's strongest coffee, eschewing the usual amounts of milk. It's a take-out spot, so grab that coffee, wander over to nearby Jackson Sq, and fuel up for some caffeine-powered sightseeing. The Hellfire Mocha ($5.50) is a fiery concoction any chili addict should try.

TROPICAL ISLE BAR

Map p234 (☑504-529-4109; http://tropicalisle.com; 721 Bourbon St; ⊙noon-2am Sun-Thu, to 4am Fri & Sat) This touristy bar serves 'Hand Grenades'; drinking more than two is likely to buy you a ticket to Regret Town, characterized by dancing on the table, bead tossing, bead receiving... and the eventual gathering of the limp shreds of your dignity the next day. But why are you on Bourbon St, if not for that? Woo!

DOUBLE PLAY GAY & LESBIAN

Map p234 (☑504-523-4517; 439 Dauphine St; ⊙7:30pm-2am) Double Play is technically a bar but this friendly spot is also drag central. You'll likely see a lot of queens here, along with every other walk of life. Drag or no drag, the drinks are delightful.

OLD ABSINTHE HOUSE BAR

Map p234 (📞504-524-0113; www.ruebourbon.com/old-absinthe-house; 240 Bourbon St; ⏰9am-2am Sun-Thu, to 4am Fri & Sat) The Old Absinthe House, a casual spot where 1940s football helmets hang from the ceiling, is also one of the bars that served absinthe before the liquor was outlawed in 1914. Absinthe's legal again, and you can have it the traditional way: with water dripped over a sugar cube. When the sugar vanishes, the 'Green Fairy' is ready. Cheers!

PIRATE'S ALLEY CAFE BAR

Map p234 (📞504-524-9332; www.piratesalleycafe.com; 622 Pirate Alley; ⏰noon-midnight Sun-Thu, 10am-2am Fri & Sat) The narrow pedestrian alley in the shadow of St Louis Cathedral is a natural spot for a tiny bar, and this nook fits the bill perfectly. It has the atmosphere of a little Montparnasse hideaway, replete with several water drips for a tipple of the 'Green Fairy'. You can grab a quick drink here before departing on a tour.

OZ GAY & LESBIAN

Map p234 (📞504-593-9491; www.ozneworleans.com; 800 Bourbon St; ⏰24hr) Your traditional, commonplace, shirtless, drag-diva, loud-music, lots-of-dancing-boys bar, where there are bowls of condoms set out for the customers. Though it claims to be 'open when you are,' bartenders admit that it's most reliably open 24 hours from Thursday to Sunday. It's still a great party until 1am, 3am, or sunrise, depending.

COSIMO'S BAR

Map p234 (📞504-522-9715; 1201 Burgundy St; ⏰4pm-2am Mon & Tue, to 5am Wed-Thu, 2pm-5am Fri & Sat, 2pm-2am Sun) There aren't a ton of bars in the Quarter that we'd call neighborhood bars, but Cosimo's fits the bill, and does so superlatively well. Dark wood, big windows, gambling machines, a good jukebox, pool tables and bartenders with the right amount of tender and toughness; this is simply a very fine bar, and it deserves your patronage.

ERIN ROSE BAR

Map p234 (📞504-522-3573; 811 Conti St; ⏰10am-6am Sun-Thu, to 8am Fri & Sat) The Rose is only half a block from Bourbon St, but feels a world away. Few tourists make it

in here, but it's the go-to cheap spot for off-shift service folks, who hit it up for a beer, banter and a shot or five. Excellent po'boys ($10 to $14) are served in the back.

BOURBON PUB & PARADE GAY

Map p234 (📞504-529-2107; www.bourbonpub.com; 801 Bourbon St; ⏰10am-3am Sun-Thu, 24hr Fri & Sat) The Bourbon is the heart of New Orleans' gay nightlife. Many of the events that pepper the city's gay calendar either begin, end or are conducted here; during Southern Decadence (p24), in particular, this is the place to be. Ladies are welcome, but this is pretty much a bar for the boys.

⭐ ENTERTAINMENT

⭐FRITZEL'S EUROPEAN JAZZ PUB JAZZ

Map p234 (📞504-586-4800; www.fritzelsjazz.net; 733 Bourbon St; ⏰noon-midnight Sun-Thu, to 2am Fri & Sat) There's no cover charge at this awesome venue for live jazz, which is so small that you really can't have a bad seat. The seating is kind of rustic: benches and chairs so tightly packed that you'll be apologizing for disturbing people each time you go to the bathroom. But the music is great, everything New Orleans jazz should be.

⭐PRESERVATION HALL JAZZ

Map p234 (📞504-522-2841; www.preservation-hall.com; 726 St Peter St; cover Sun-Thu $15, Fri & Sat $20, reserved seats Sun-Thu $35-45, Fri & Sat $40-50; ⏰showtimes 8pm, 9pm & 10pm, also 5pm & 6pm Thu-Sun) Preservation Hall, housed in a former art gallery dating from 1803, is one of New Orleans' most storied live-music venues. The resident performers, the Preservation Hall Jazz Band, are ludicrously talented, and regularly tour the world. 'The Hall' dates from 1961, when Barbara Reid and Grayson 'Ken' Mills formed the Society for the Preservation of New Orleans Jazz.

There are some caveats to seeing a show here: first, the set is only about an hour long. Still, you're paying to see musical history as much as music, so we're OK with that. But hey, we also want to be able to see the band. The Hall is atmospheric, but it is also small and popular, and you need to show up early – at least an hour before – to snag a seat. Otherwise you'll be standing and, likely as not, your view will be blocked by people in front of you. Of course, you

CASKET GIRLS & WORKING GIRLS

During the early days of their work at the Ursuline Convent (p56), the nuns quickly observed that an unusually high proportion of the colony's women were working the world's oldest profession, leading to a shortage of possible wives for the men. They decided the solution was to call in marriageable teenage girls from France (generally recruited from orphanages or convents). The girls arrived in New Orleans, Biloxi and Mobile with their clothes packed in coffin-like trunks, and thus became known as the 'casket girls.' Educated by the nuns, the girls were brought up to make proper wives for the Frenchmen of New Orleans. Over the centuries, the casket-girl legacy became more sensational as some in New Orleans surmised the wood boxes may have contained French vampires.

Of course, prostitution never lost its luster in this steamy port. New Orleans' fabled bordellos are one of the earliest foundations upon which the city's reputation as a spot for sin and fun are built. It's immortalized in the famous song, 'The House of the Rising Sun,' which tells the tale of a ruined life in New Orleans; there's some ambiguity about whether the lyrics refer to a real brothel.

The most famous 'sporting' houses were elegant mansions, reputedly decorated with some of the finest art and furnishings of their era, and staffed with a multiracial cast of employees ranging from white to Creole to black. Around the turn of the 20th century, famously puritan city alderman (councillor) Sidney Story wrote an ordinance that moved the bordellos out of the city's posh residential neighborhoods and into the side of the French Quarter that borders the Tremé. Never ones to pass up good irony, New Orleanians dubbed their red-light district 'Storyville' in honor of Sidney.

Although there were no Lonely Planet books around at the time, visitors could explore Storyville with the help of the 'Blue Book,' a guide to the area's dubious attractions. Each book was imprinted with the line: 'Order of the Garter: *Honi Soit Qui Mal Y Pense*' (Shame to Him Who Evil Thinks). Jazz was largely popularized by visitors listening to music in Storyville's storied pleasure houses. One of the most famous houses, the Arlington, operated at 225 North Basin St (look for the onion-domed cupola, all that's left of the demolished bordello).

Storyville was shut down in 1917 by the federal government. At the time, Mayor Martin Behrman lamented that, while the authorities could make prostitution illegal, 'you can't make it unpopular'.

---

can reserve seats online, but you pay for the privilege. When it's warm enough to leave the window shutters open, those not fortunate enough to get inside can join the crowd on the sidewalk to listen to the sets.

Also note that no alcohol or snacks are served, and the bathroom is in next-door Pat O'Brien's bar.

FLEUR DE TEASE   DANCE
Map p234 (📞504-975-1245; http://fleurde tease.com) If you're in the mood for something a bit risqué, we'd recommend catching this burlesque show. These talented ladies, many of whom claim professional dance backgrounds, blend vintage vibe with a modern, in-your-face post-feminist sexuality that is pretty enticing for both men and women. They perform all over town, including at One Eyed Jacks every other Sunday.

ONE EYED JACKS   LIVE MUSIC
Map p234 (📞504-569-8361; www.oneeyedjacks. net; 615 Toulouse St; cover $10-25) If you've been thinking, 'I could use a night at a bar that feels like a 19th-century bordello managed by Johnny Rotten,' you're in luck. Jacks is a great venue; there's a sense that dangerous women in corsets, men with Mohawks and an army of bohemians with absinthe bottles could come charging out at any moment. The musical acts are consistently good.

HOUSE OF BLUES   LIVE MUSIC
Map p234 (📞504-310-4999; www.houseofblues. com/neworleans; 225 Decatur St; tickets $11-50) This national chain of blues venues has put a lot of admirable work into making their New Orleans outpost distinctive: there's tons of folk art and rustic, voodoo-themed murals and sculptures, and the effect is more powerful than kitschy.

PALM COURT JAZZ CAFÉ
LIVE MUSIC

Map p234 (☑504-525-0200; www.palmcourt-jazzcafe.com; 1204 Decatur St; cover around $5; ⊘7-11pm Wed-Sun) Fans of trad jazz who want to hang out with a mature crowd should head to this supper-club venue. Palm Court is a roomy spot that has a consistently good lineup of local legends; you really can't go wrong if you're a jazz fan. Shows start at 8pm.

LE PETIT THÉÂTRE
DU VIEUX CARRÉ
THEATER

Map p234 (☑504-522-2081; www.lepetittheatre.com; 616 St Peter St) Going strong since 1916, Le Petit Théâtre is one of the oldest theater groups in the country. In its Jackson Sq home, the troupe offers good repertory, with a proclivity for Southern dramas and special children's programming. Shows are sometimes followed by an informal burlesque performance, with the cast, audience and a resident ghost (so we hear) mingling over drinks.

BALCONY MUSIC CLUB
LIVE MUSIC

Map p234 (☑504-301-5912; www.balconymusicclub.com; 1331 Decatur St; ⊘5pm-2am Mon-Thu, 3pm-4am Fri-Sun) Balcony is all about the acts: if there's a dud band playing, you can walk on by without breaking your stride, but on good nights it's a convenient step in the French Quarter–Faubourg Marigny stumble o' fun along Decatur St.

🛍 SHOPPING

You can get almost anything, and we mean anything, in the French Quarter – most of it is even legal, too. From soaps to souvenirs, clothing to crafts, everything's for sale here and often it's on extravagant display.

★FIFI MAHONY'S
COSMETICS

Map p234 (☑504-525-4343; 934 Royal St; ⊘noon-6pm Sun-Wed, 11am-7pm Thu-Sat) New Orleans is the most costume-crazy city in the USA, and Fifi Mahony's is the place to go to don a wig. There's a stunning selection of hairpieces here that runs the gamut from the glittered to the beehived, presented in a veritable rainbow of colors. An on-site beauty salon and sassy staff round out the experience.

★MS RAU ANTIQUES
ANTIQUES

Map p234 (☑504-523-5660; www.rauantiques.com; 630 Royal St; ⊘9am-5:15pm Mon-Sat) With a huge 30,000-sq-ft showroom, and after a century of doing business, MS Rau ranks among New Orleans' most venerated dealers of antiques. It's all a bit serious – these are the sort of frosty antiques that require their own insurance policies – but it's a family business and the professional salespeople are warm and approachable.

★SECONDLINE ART
& ANTIQUES
ARTS & CRAFTS

Map p234 (☑504-875-1924; www.secondline-nola.com; 1209 Decatur; ⊘8am-8pm Sun-Wed, to 10pm Thu, to midnight Fri & Sat, market 5pm-1am Thu-Mon) Get unique crafts, art, antiques and souvenirs at this co-op, which includes an indoor gallery space and a courtyard night market outside. Meet the artists, chat with craftspeople and know that your purchase goes directly to the creators themselves. Everything from moose heads to jewelry to votive candles might be found. Come in and browse!

★LITTLE TOY SHOP
GIFTS & SOUVENIRS

Map p234 (☑504-523-1770; http://littletoyshops.com; 513 St Ann St; ⊘8:30am-8:30pm) Packed nearly floor to ceiling with toys and gifts for the younger set, this bustling shop has just about anything your kids, nieces, nephews or other such relatives might want. Choose between books, games, jokes, string dolls, voodoo and magic sets, stuffed animals and pet rocks.

BOUTIQUE DU VAMPYRE
GIFTS & SOUVENIRS

Map p234 (☑504-561-8267; www.feelthebite.com; 709 St Ann St; ⊘10am-9pm) This dungeon-esque store stocks all kinds of vampire-themed gifts. Come here for books, curses, spells, souvenirs and witty banter with the awesome clerks who oversee this curious crypt. Among the items is a deck of tarot cards with truly surreal, somewhat disturbing artwork. If your fangs have chipped, their on-call fangsmith can even shape you a new custom pair.

Now, don't quote us: keep this on the down low. But the store's lovely guardians may – if you look undead enough, come from Transylvania or can shape-shift into a bat on command – reveal the password to enter a secret vampire-themed speakeasy, Passions (p66), which is located above a popular bar nearby. Don't be crushed if they don't, as vampires are as fickle as it gets. And remember, you didn't hear this from us.

FAULKNER HOUSE BOOKS　BOOKS

Map p234 (☑504-524-2940; www.faulkner-housebooks.com; 624 Pirate Alley; ⊙10am-5pm) The erudite owner of this former residence of author William Faulkner sells rare first editions and new titles in an airy, elegant and charming independent bookshop. And, yes, there are a number of Faulkner titles on sale as well.

FRENCH QUARTER
POSTAL EMPORIUM　GIFTS & SOUVENIRS

Map p234 (☑504-525-6651; www.frenchquarterpostal.net; 1000 Bourbon St; ⊙9am-6pm Mon-Fri, 10am-3pm Sat) The wide variety of gifts here ranges from raunchy Bourbon St tropes (gag gifts, wince-worthy quips on T-shirts and mugs) to the genuinely beautiful, such as art, crafts and other souvenirs.

LUCULLUS　ANTIQUES

Map p234 (☑504-528-9620; http://lucullusantiques.com; 610 Chartres St; ⊙9am-5pm Mon-Sat) Peeking in the window, you'll see a battery of ancient copper pots that appear to have generations of dents tinkered out of their bottoms. Owner Patrick Dunne is an advocate of using, not merely collecting, antiques. Follow his advice and add more ritual and elegance to your life with an antique café au lait bowl or an absinthe spoon.

★HOVÉ PARFUMEUR　COSMETICS

Map p234 (☑504-525-7827; www.hoveparfumeur.com; 434 Chartres St; ⊙10am-6pm Mon-Sat, from 11am Sun) Grassy vetiver, bittersweet orange blossoms, spicy ginger – New Orleans' exotic flora has graciously lent its scents to Hové's house-made perfumes for almost a century. In its 90th year, female-owned and -operated for more than four generations, it's an inspiring spot that will leave your head swirling with images of the Vieux Carré's magnificent past.

CHIWAWA GAGA　FASHION & ACCESSORIES

Map p234 (☑504-581-4242; www.chiwawagaga.com; 511 Dumaine St; ⊙noon-6pm) What's not to love about a pet shop specifically dedicated to costumes? Not just dogs – they've proudly dressed snakes, pigs, iguanas, rabbits and even Tony the llama! The folks who run this store are dedicated to sourcing, and often creating by hand, some fantastically elaborate getups for your little (or big!) best friend.

QUEORK　FASHION & ACCESSORIES

Map p234 (☑504-481-2585; www.queork.com; 838 Chartres St; ⊙10am-6pm) 🗡 Besides boasting a punny name, Queork has a cool, sustainable gimmick: all of the bags, belts and accessories sold here are made from cork. The products both look and feel cool; the fascinating texture belies some pretty fashionable goods.

ESOTERICA OCCULT
GOODS　GIFTS & SOUVENIRS

Map p234 (☑504-581-7711; www.onewitch.com; 541 Dumaine St; ⊙noon-6pm) There are many *(many)* hokey magic/voodoo/spell shops in the French Quarter, but Esoterica is one of our favorites. There's a sense of sincerity regarding the occult here; these folks genuinely want to help you with spells and karmic realignment. Pop in for some mystical consultation.

LIBRAIRIE BOOKS　BOOKS

Map p234 (☑504-525-4837; 823 Chartres St; ⊙10am-5pm) A jam-packed little shop of delights for the avid bookworm and collector. The emphasis here is on very old (and sometimes dusty) volumes. You might dig up an ancient copy of Herbert Asbury's *The French Quarter*, or other tales of old New Orleans. And there are scholarly texts and ample material of more general interest as well.

TRASHY DIVA　CLOTHING

Map p234 (☑504-522-8861; www.trashydiva.com; 712 Royal St; ⊙11am-7pm) If all these drag shows have you feeling like your undergarments (or your life!) need a bit of spicing up, head to this vintage-inspired lingerie store – impossible to miss on its corner of Royal St, where a half-dozen scantily-dressed mannequins advertise the wares.

DIRTY COAST　CLOTHING

Map p234 (☑504-324-6730; www.dirtycoast.com; 713 Royal St; ⊙11am-7pm) Dirty Coast offers a wide range of T-shirts and other gifts that bring environmental, social, or other local issues to light. Don't expect to find 'I'm more wasted than a liberal arts degree!' on anything here. Expect socially aware, often scathing or tongue-in-cheek commentary on current issues and societal shortcomings.

REV ZOMBIE'S HOUSE
OF VOODOO　GIFTS & SOUVENIRS

Map p234 (☑504-486-6366; www.voodooneworleans.com; 723 St Peter St; ⊙10am-11:30pm Sun-Thu, to 1:30am Fri & Sat) Step inside and you'll see this is one religious store that's not bent on snuffing out the party. An altar at the entry includes a serious request that you not take photos, but then comes a truly splendiferous display of plaster-of-Paris statuettes imported from the Santería realms of Brazil. All are fun and charming; many are simply beautiful.

TABASCO® COUNTRY STORE
FOOD

Map p234 (☑504-539-7900; www.nolacajun-store.com; 537 St Ann St; ☺10am-8pm) Bet you thought Tabasco was either red or green and always hot, right? Guess again: here you'll find Tabasco ketchup, mayonnaise, cook-books, plenty of souvenirs and a fairly in-credible range of hot (and not-so-hot) sauces. Need a 500-count pack of mini-Tabasco bot-tles? This is the place. Also sells all manner of Cajun and New Orleans–themed kitsch.

JAMES H COHEN & SONS
ANTIQUES

Map p234 (☑504-522-3305; www.cohentiques.com; 437 Royal St; ☺9:30am-5:15pm Mon-Sat) From the sidewalk, you might be inclined to pass this one by: it's full of guns, including flintlocks, colts, and Winchester '73s. Beyond weaponry, however, the place is like a museum, stuffed with relics and historical curiosities, from jewelry and coins to swords and maps.

OD AOMO
CLOTHING

Map p234 (☑504-460-5730; www.odaomo.com; 839 Chartres St; ☺10am-6pm Mon-Sat, to 5pm Sun) 🍃 Dr Sophia Aomo Omoro has worn many hats in her life: runway model, surgeon, phi-lanthropist and now proprietor of a high-end fashion boutique. All of the clothes under her label are made in her native Kenya, where she is dedicated to providing increased em-ployment. Her style sits at a hip intersection of ethnic patterns and contemporary chic.

JAVA HOUSE IMPORTS
GIFTS & SOUVENIRS

Map p234 (☑504-581-1288; 523 Dumaine St; ☺10am-5pm) Java House Imports does in-deed have cool imports and statues from Java, as well as Balinese masks, Indone-sian-style Buddhas, lacquer-work from Lombok, and all the other items to prove what a savvy traveler you are.

LEAH'S PRALINES
FOOD

Map p234 (☑504-523-5662; www.leahspralines.com; 714 St Louis St; ☺10am-6pm) This old candy shop specializes in that special Cre-ole confection, the praline. If you've already tried pralines elsewhere and decided that you don't care for them, we suggest you try some at Leah's before making up your mind completely. Did someone say Bacon Pecan Brittle, for instance? Or Sweet Potato? Scrumptious.

MASKARADE
GIFTS & SOUVENIRS

Map p234 (☑504-568-1018; www.themaskstore.com; 630 St Ann St; ☺10am-5pm) Do not con-fuse this with a joke shop or a spot for those Groucho Marx nose 'n' glasses. Decades old, this place deals in high-quality masks by lo-cal and international artisans. The selection includes everything from classic *commedia dell'arte* masks from Venice to masks worn by the Cirque du Soleil. Think hang-on-the-wall art, not wear-for-Mardi-Gras.

FLEUR DE PARIS
FASHION & ACCESSORIES

Map p234 (☑504-525-1899; www.fleurdeparis.net; 523 Royal St; ☺10am-6pm) Fleur de Paris proves that millinery stores not only exist, but can thrive – this is the largest one in the USA. Their custom hats are bouquets of plumage, felt, lace and, here and there, a snatch of black netting. The evening gowns are devastating showstoppers.

MOSS ANTIQUES
ANTIQUES

Map p234 (☑504-522-3981; www.mossantiques.com; 411 Royal St; ☺9am-5pm Mon-Sat, by appoint-ment Sun) Watch your head when you enter this gallery of low-hanging chandeliers. Moss is a Royal St institution in the local antiques trade – only the finest quality antiques and objets d'art are sold here. You'll find the per-fect thing for your Garden District mansion.

BECKHAM'S BOOKSHOP
BOOKS

Map p234 (☑504-522-9875; 228 Decatur St; ☺10am-5pm) This large, well-organized store has been selling books for nearly 40 years. With two floors of used books, as well as used classical LPs, it's definitely worth a browse.

HUMIDITY SKATE SHOP
SPORTS & OUTDOORS

Map p234 (☑504-529-6822; www.humiditynola.com; 515 Dumaine St; ☺11am-7pm Mon-Sat, noon-6pm Sun) Graffiti chic, Vans shoes, Palace, Deluxe, Scumco decks and Spitfire wheels – if any of that makes sense to you, make your way up to Dumaine St.

COLLECTIBLE ANTIQUES
ANTIQUES

Map p234 (☑504-566-0399; 1232 Decatur St; ☺noon-6pm) You never know what you'll find between the piles of old furniture stacked along the walls of this large, garage-like em-porium of tantalizing junk. Perhaps you col-lect old photographic portraits from long-de-funct studios? Or maybe you're after an Art Deco martini shaker, a dented trumpet, a

Pee-wee Herman doll, a heavy army-surplus coat or some silverware? It's all here.

LE GARAGE ANTIQUES

Map p234 (☑504-522-6639; 1234 Decatur St; ⊗noon-6pm) This place lives up to its name: it's literally a garage, loaded with interesting stuff to paw through. There are odd items of clothing, hats, army surplus, curtains, yellowed pool balls, tattered Mardi Gras costumes from yesteryear, knitted beer-can caps, furniture and oodles of *objets d'art* to ogle or buy. Treasures galore: dive in.

ARCADIAN BOOKS & ART PRINTS BOOKS

Map p234 (☑504-523-4138; 714 Orleans Ave; ⊗9:30am-5:30pm Mon-Sat, 11:30am-4pm Sun) Arcadian is a small, crowded shop that's filled with Southern literature and history, as well as many volumes written in French. Owner Russell Desmond speaks French fluently and is a wonderful, if cynical, ambassador for New Orleans.

SPORTS & ACTIVITIES

NEW ORLEANS CULINARY HISTORY TOURS WALKING

Map p234 (☑877-278-8240; http://noculinarytours.com; 823 Decatur St; per person $55-84) It's hard to beat a tour that is delicious and intellectually stimulating. That's what Kelly Hamilton, a history instructor at Xavier University, offers with these tours that plumb both the past and local pantries.

MAGIC TOURS TOURS

Map p234 (☑504-588-9693; www.magictoursnola.com; 441 Royal St; adult $25, student & senior $20; ⊗8am-8pm) Led by local teachers, historians, preservationists and journalists, these tours explore the French Quarter daily at 4pm, among their other options. Magic Tours admirably gets under the skin of the city.

TOURS BY JUDY CULTURAL

Map p234 (☑504-416-7777, 504-416-6666; www.toursbyjudy.com; per person from $15) Judy Bajoie, a local scholar and historian, leads well-crafted tours of the city she loves. Tours depart from outside St Louis Cathedral, Jackson Sq; contact Judy for more information.

FRIENDS OF THE CABILDO WALKING

Map p234 (☑504-523-3939; www.friendsofthecabildo.org; 523 St Ann St; adult/student $20/15; ⊗10am & 1:30pm Mon-Sun) These walking tours are led by knowledgeable (and often funny) docents, who will give you a great primer on the history of the French Quarter, the stories behind some of the most famous streets and details of the area's many architectural styles. Tours depart from the 1850 House Museum store.

NEW ORLEANS SCHOOL OF COOKING COOKING

Map p234 (☑504-525-2665; www.nosoc.com; 524 St Louis St; courses per person $28-33) A food demonstration – not a hands-on class. Menus rotate daily, but rest assured you'll be watching creations such as gumbo, jambalaya, and pralines at the end of class, all the while learning about the history of the city as told by the charismatic chefs.

AMERICAN BICYCLE RENTAL CO CYCLING

Map p234 (☑504-324-8257; www.amebrc.com; 318 N Rampart St; per 4hr/8hr/24hr $25/30/40; ⊗9am-5pm) Rents out cruiser-style bikes for adults and kids.

ROYAL CARRIAGE TOURS TOURS

Map p234 (☑504-943-8820; www.neworleanscarriages.com; at Decatur St & Jackson Sq; private tour up to 4 people per 30min/1hr $100/200, shared carriage per 30min/1hr $20/40; ⊗8:30am-midnight) The conductors of these mule-drawn carriage tours know their stuff, revealing the locations of celebrity homes and sites of historic minutiae that constantly impress. Royal Carriages has a good animal-welfare track record; it's licensed by the city and doesn't conduct tours if the weather is more than 95°F (35°C).

AMERICAN PHOTO SAFARI TOURS

Map p234 (☑504-298-8876; www.americanphotosafari.com; per person $69) A cleverly focused tour: the photo-safari docents don't just show you the sights, they give you lessons in how to take pictures of them as well. Call ahead to make a reservation; the tour meeting point is Jackson Sq, by St Louis Cathedral.

HAUNTED HISTORY TOURS HISTORY

Map p234 (☑504-861-2727; www.hauntedhistorytours.com; 723 St Peter St; adult/child $25/14, student & senior $18; ⊗6pm & 8pm year-round, 3pm 26 Dec-31 Jul & 1 Oct-30 Nov) Sure, these tours are a little cheesy, but they're fun too, and you'll learn a bit about the shady side of city history.

Mardi Gras & Jazz Fest

Band of zombies? Check. Revelers riding giant neon shoes? Check. New Orleans' flights of fancy and indulgence are realized like at no other time during these two events...

Festival Season in New Orleans

No two events encapsulate New Orleans like Mardi Gras and Jazz Fest. These festivals are more than celebrations: they contain within them every thread of the colorful, complicated New Orleans tapestry.

'Stop exaggerating,' you may say, to which we reply: 'There's no need to exaggerate.' These festivals are incredible. Imagine a bunch of grown men and women riding giant neon shoes and plaster dinosaurs through the street; or Bruce Springsteen, Al Green, Dr John, Tom Petty, Cee-lo, Feist and the Carolina Chocolate Drops playing in the same venue in one weekend; or that you slip through the looking-glass into MOM's Ball and see a band of zombies playing for naked folks in body paint and a cast of costumes that appear to be lifted from Jim Henson's most lurid fantasies.

During Mardi Gras and Jazz Fest, all this happens. The city's flights of fancy and indulgence are realized like at no other time. And everything that makes New Orleans...well...New Orleans becomes a lot more...*New Orleansy*. Let's take the food. The best eats in the city turn up as booth fare in Jazz Fest. Restaurants throw open their doors during Mardi Gras to folks dressed as

goblins and fairies. This all speaks to the creativity of the city, expressed in a multitude of ways, from music to visual arts, crafts and theater (as exemplified by Mardi Gras floats and costumes). These festivals reveal the soul of a city that is obsessed with beauty, while both redefining the concept and appreciating it in every way possible.

Finally, these festivals speak to the history of the city. Jazz Fest is such a celebration because New Orleans is the most important musical city in America, and artists from around the world come here to pay tribute to that fact. Mardi Gras has an older, more mysterious history, one that dates at least as far back as the early Catholic Church, and perhaps further into antiquity.

Between late January, when Carnival Season begins, and late April/early May, when Jazz Fest happens, it's pretty much back-to-back celebrations in New Orleans, or as folks down here like to call it: 'festival season.' There are lulls here and there, but by the time mid-March rolls around it feels like there's a small festival bridging these two big events every weekend.

So are we saying there's basically a half-year of festivals in New Orleans?

....

1. Tarriona 'Tank' Ball of Tank and the Bangas performing at Jazz Fest **2.** A Mardi Gras sign on Magazine Street

Of course not. The party *never* stops in New Orleans. It just picks up between Mardi Grass and Jazz Fest.

Anatomy of a Celebration

The parade season is a 12-day period beginning two Fridays before Fat Tuesday. Early parades are charming, neighborly processions that whet your appetite for the later parades, which increase in size and grandeur until the spectacles of the 'superkrewes' emerge during the final weekend.

A Sensory Carnival

A popular preseason night procession, usually held three Saturdays before Fat Tuesday, is Krewe du Vieux. By parading before the official parade season and marching on foot, Krewe du Vieux is permitted to pass through the French Quarter. The themes of this notoriously bawdy and satirical krewe clearly aim to offend puritanical types.

Watch for Le Krewe d'Etat, whose name is a clever, satirical pun: d'Etat is ruled by a dictator rather than a king. Another favorite is Muses, an all-women's krewe that parades down St Charles Ave with thousands of members and some imaginative, innovative floats; their throws (the goodies that the krewes throw to the crowd) include coveted hand-decorated shoes.

Mardi Gras weekend is lit up by the entrance of the superkrewes, who arrive with their monstrous floats and endless processions of celebrities, as flashy as a Vegas revue. On Saturday night the megakrewe Endymion stages its spectacular parade and Extravaganza, as it calls its ball in the Superdome. On Sunday night the Bacchus superkrewe wows an enraptured crowd along St Charles Ave with its celebrity monarch and a gorgeous fleet of crowd-pleasing floats.

On Mardi Gras morning, Zulu rolls along Jackson Ave, where folks set up barbecues on the sidewalk and krewe members distribute their prized

1. Mardi Gras revelers take part in the Society of St Anne parade 2. A Mardi Gras Indian (p157)

hand-painted coconuts. The 'King of Carnival,' Rex, waits further Uptown; it's a much more restrained affair, with the monarch himself looking like he's been plucked from a deck of cards.

Costume Contests

Mardi Gras is a citywide costume party, and many locals take a dim view of visitors who crash the party without one. For truly fantastic outfits, march with the Society of St Ann on Mardi Gras morning. This collection of artists and misfits prides itself on its DIY outfits, which seem to have marched out of a collision between a David Bowie video and a '60s acid trip. The creativity and pageantry on display really needs to be seen to be believed. Other parades that feature great homemade costumes include the Box of Wine parade, the Chewbacchus parade and the Red Beans & Rice procession.

Walking Krewe Review

Some of the best parades of Carnival Season are put on by DIY bohemian walking krewes, groups of friends who create a grassroots show. Casual observers are always welcome to participate. Just bring a costume!

Barkus Dress up your furry friends for this all-pet parade (www.barkus.org).

Box of Wine Crazily costumed revelers march up St Charles Ave ahead of the Bacchus (god of wine) parade, distributing free wine from boxes along the way.

OUR FAVORITE BIG PARADES

Krewe de Vieux Old-school walking parade with sharply satirical floats.

Muses All-female krewe with creative floats.

Zulu Traditionally African American krewe that throws coconuts to the crowd.

Rex Old-line royalty of Mardi Gras.

Thoth Family-friendly Uptown day parade.

Intergalactic Krewe of Chewbacchus
Dress up as your favorite sci-fi character at this wonderful parade for geeks, nerds and other people we might hang out with on weekends (http://chewbacchus.org).
Red Beans & Rice On Lundi Gras (the day before Mardi Gras), folks dress up in costumes made from dry beans or as Louisiana food items.
Society of St Anne Traditionally made up of artists and bohemians, St Anne marches on Mardi Gras morning from the Bywater to the Mississippi and features the best costumes of Carnival Season.

New Orleans Jazz & Heritage Festival

Jazz Fest sums up everything that would be lost if the world were to lose New Orleans. Much more than Mardi Gras, with its secret balls and sparkly trinkets, Jazz Fest reflects the generosity of New Orleans, its unstoppable urge to share its most precious resource – its culture – with the rest of the world. Of course, the Fest is first and foremost about music, but it isn't just about jazz. It's jazz *and* heritage, which means any music that jazz came from, and any music that jazz inspired. The multitude of stages and tents feature everything that pours in and out of jazz – blues, gospel, Afro-Caribbean, folk, country, zydeco (p209), Cajun, funky brass, and on and on.

Roots of Roots Music

Jazz Fest began in 1970, when the idea of staging a big music festival in

New Orleans couldn't have been more natural. The first festival, held in Louis Armstrong Park, featured a remarkable lineup of legendary artists, including Duke Ellington, Mahalia Jackson, Clifton Chenier, Fats Domino and the Meters. Mardi Gras Indians performed, and every now and then a Second-Line parade (p158) swept through the audience. The ingredients were already in place for a major cultural event with a genuine regional significance. Outside talent, such as Ellington, complemented the local talent and beefed up the event's exposure.

Only 350 people attended that first Jazz Fest. Most likely, the low numbers were due to poor promotion outside New Orleans. Out-of-towners arrived in much greater numbers for the '71 Fest, and with them came a far stronger local response. To accommodate another anticipated jump in attendance, the Fest was moved to the far larger Fair Grounds Race Course a year later, and Jazz Fest really hasn't looked back since. By the late 1970s, the festival had grown from one weekend to two, with many legendary moments already solidifying the event's cultural importance.

Mesmerizing performances by the likes of James Booker, the Neville Brothers and Professor Longhair have been recorded for posterity. The musical lineup soon expanded to include big-time national acts, such as Lenny Kravitz, Bruce Springsteen and Bon Jovi, as well as international acts from South America, the Caribbean and Africa.

Experiencing Jazz Fest

Some people choose to do Jazz Fest over and over again, year after year, so obviously there's something addictive about the experience. It doesn't hurt that there are umpteen ways to approach this gargantuan feast of music, food and culture, which takes place over the last weekend of April and the first weekend of May.

Seeing the Stage

The first thing to decide is: one weekend of Jazz Fest or two? And if one's enough, then which one?

1. A marching band performs during Mardi Gras **2.** Rex, the 'King of Carnival' (p77)

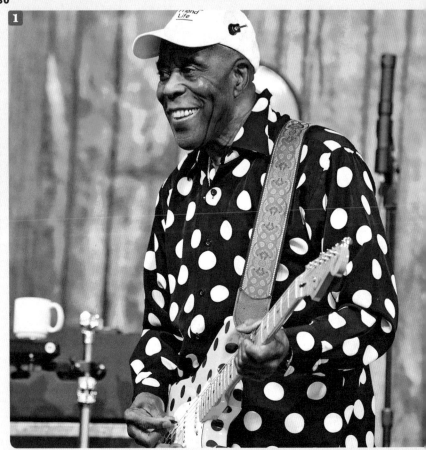

No one will laugh if you choose one weekend. The drawback is you may have to pick your dates before the Fest schedule is announced. The schedule isn't announced until early February at the earliest. Still, there's statistical logic to making blindfolded decisions this way, as both weekends are always equally packed with big-name show-stoppers and unheard-of talents. Sometimes you'll miss out on a personal favorite if you're not attending every day of the Fest, but in the end something along the way will make up for the loss.

For those who make their Jazz Fest plans late – that's to say, after February – there's the advantage of knowing the schedule. Free-spenders are still likely to find a pricey suite of rooms in the French Quarter at this point, but thrifty types might be frustrated with finding accommodations. If you decide to do both weekends, you'll have four days for bopping around town, or maybe driving out to Cajun Country for Festival International de Louisiane (www.festivalinternational.com) in Lafayette. 'Festival' is the largest free francophone music festival in North America, and is held during the last weekend of April.

It's worth noting that the area of Esplande Ave just outside of the Fair Grounds becomes as festive as Jazz Fest itself. Folks crowd around spots like Liuzza's and a general street party takes over the streets parallel to the Fair Grounds for about two weeks. In the days in between actual Jazz Fest weekends, many fest performers put on shows at venues around town – sometimes unexpectedly, and for free!

At the Fair Grounds

It takes a well-bred racehorse about two minutes to circumnavigate the Fair Grounds track, but the average human will require up to 10 minutes to get from one stage to the next. The only way to get from stage to stage is to walk or half-jog through dense crowds and all kinds of tempting food stalls and vendors. Be on the lookout for the Louisiana Folklife Village, which has plenty of demonstrations of Louisiana folk crafts. Jazz Fest consists of over a dozen performance tents:

Gospel Tent A cherished chapel of earth-shaking live gospel music.

Jazz Tent The lineup here leans more toward the contemporary side of the jazz genre.

Jazz & Heritage Stage Smaller stage where brass bands and the Mardi Gras Indians perform.

Economy Hall Tent Stomp your feet to New Orleans trad jazz with the likes of the Preservation Hall Jazz Band and the Tremé Brass Band.

Lagniappe Stage Varied entertainment. The stage's isolation from the rest of the Fair Grounds makes it ideal for intimate performances.

Blues Tent Blues, R&B, funk and, occasionally, some rock.

Fais-Do-Do Stage Cajun and zydeco music is the emphasis at this always-hopping stage.

Congo Square This stage has become the venue for world acts from Africa and Latin America.

Acura Stage Main stage where the biggest names appear.

Gentilly Stage Secondary main stage.

Kids Tent Children's music and family-friendly activities.

Allison Miner Music Heritage Stage Mainly hosts lectures and panel discussions with Jazz Fest artists.

Food Demonstration Stages Local live cooking lessons at these two stages.

Food, Glorious Food

In addition to the obvious musical draw, Jazz Fest is justifiably famous for its food stalls, many of which have cult followings. Some of the more popular Fest foods include fried soft-shell crab, Crawfish Monica (cream crawfish sauce over fusilli pasta), crawfish bread, *cochon de lait* (roast suckling pig), po'boys, spinach and artichoke casserole, Cuban sandwiches and Jamaican chicken. Of course, you'll also find jambalaya, red beans and fried catfish.

1. Buddy Guy performing at Jazz Fest **2.** Jambalaya

Faubourg Marigny & Bywater

Neighborhood Top Five

1 Frenchmen Street (p84) Wandering around at, say, 7pm when the music starts, having dinner, listening to music, dancing a bit, seeing who's playing on the corner of Chartres, scarfing down some late-night tacos, then listening to more music.

2 Crescent Park (p84) Spotting container ships

from the banks as they meander up the Mississippi.

3 Marigny Opera House (p91) Catching dance, puppetry and all manner of shows at this unique performance venue, which occupies the grounds of a former church.

4 St Claude Avenue (p91) Listening to music, from punk to bluegrass to hip-hop, on this street filled with eclectic performance venues.

5 The Barmuda Triangle (p89) Embarking on a pub crawl for the ages around the neighborhood bars of Bywater.

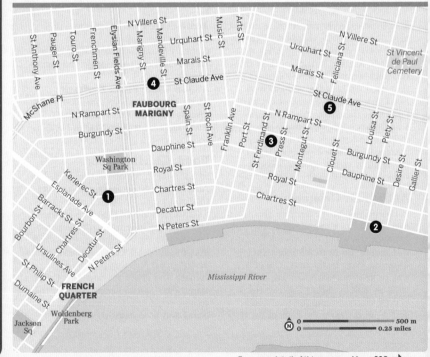

For more detail of this area see Map p238 ➡

Explore Faubourg Marigny & Bywater

Faubourg Marigny sits adjacent to the French Quarter, beginning just after Esplanade Ave. Marigny is divided by Elysian Fields Ave. Further downriver (east) are the Press St railroad tracks, marking the beginning of Bywater, which extends to the Industrial Canal.

Wander around Marigny by walking up Decatur St and onto Frenchmen St. Then head east along Royal St, taking in the architecture and sampling the local fare at some of the cafes and restaurants along the way. When night falls, head back to Frenchmen St to either party, listen to music, or both.

From the French Quarter, you can either bike or walk out to Bywater. You can explore compact Bywater easily on foot or with two wheels, eating, drinking and shopping wherever the spirit moves you. In the evening, head out to catch music or theater along St Claude Ave, or see if there's anything interesting showing at one of the local theaters.

Marigny is bounded by Rampart St to the west, the railroad tracks at Press St to the east and Esplanade Ave to the south. Bywater extends from Press to Poland St. St Claude Ave is, for our purposes, the northern border of both neighborhoods, but as there are more and more places of interest opening north of St Claude, we include some of those spots as well. The southern boundary of Bywater is easy to spot: it's the Mississippi River.

Local Life

Theater It takes plenty of forms here, from the brick-and-mortar playhouses such as Marigny Opera House (p91) to the street theater of local artists putting on impromptu performances.

Bars Even if you're not big on drinking, rubbing shoulders with locals at spots like BJ's (p89) gets you under the skin of the city.

Markets From the Healing Center (p84) to Palace Market (p84), these are the places to peruse and discover local goods.

Getting There & Away

Bus Bus 5, which you can catch on Canal and Decatur Sts, runs up Decatur and onto Poydras and Dauphine into the heart of Marigny and Bywater.

Car Free street parking is quite plentiful in Bywater, and only a little less common in Marigny. There are no time restrictions, except on Esplanade Ave.

Bike It's a pleasant, easy bike ride out here. If you're heading to Bywater, you can ride through Crescent Park, but the access point on St Peters St is by elevator, while the exit point is all the way down on Bartholomew St.

Lonely Planet's Top Tip

By far the easiest way of exploring these two neighborhoods is by bicycle. On two wheels you're never more than 20 minutes from the edge of the French Quarter and the borders of Bywater. Be warned that streets are pretty potholed; Chartres is reliable past Press St, but is heavily trafficked.

 Best Places to Eat

➡ Bacchanal (p88)

➡ Red's Chinese (p86)

➡ Cake Café & Bakery (p86)

For reviews, see p86➡

☆ Best Entertainment

➡ Spotted Cat (p90)

➡ Marigny Opera House (p91)

➡ d.b.a. (p91)

For reviews, see p90➡

🛏 Best Places to Sleep

➡ Bywater Bed & Breakfast (p180)

➡ Lookout Inn of New Orleans (p180)

➡ Dauphine House (p180)

For reviews, see p180➡

 Best ~ Nightlife

➡ BJ's (p89)

➡ Buffa's (p89)

➡ Mimi's in the Marigny (p89)

➡ R Bar (p90)

For reviews, see p88➡

◉ SIGHTS

There's a lot of pleasure to be had just wandering around streets like Royal St, Dauphine St and Rampart St, and admiring local houses. You can also find art bazaars, streets full of music, riverside parks and the odd cemetery scattered amid the pastel homes and crumbling streets.

CRESCENT PARK
PARK

Map p238 (☑504-636-6400; www.crescentparknola.org; Piety, Chartres & Mazant Sts; ◷6am-7:30pm; P ♿ 🐾) ✏ This waterfront park is our favorite spot in the city for taking in the Mississippi. Enter over the enormous arch at Piety and Chartres Sts, or at the steps at Marigny and N Peters Sts, and watch the fog blanket the nearby skyline. A promenade meanders past an angular metal-and-concrete conceptual 'wharf' (placed next to the burned remains of the former commercial wharf). A dog park is located near the Mazant St entrance.

FRENCHMEN STREET
STREET

Map p238 (from Esplanade Ave to Royal St) The 'locals' Bourbon St' is how Frenchmen St is usually described to those who want to know where New Orleanians listen to music. The predictable result? Frenchmen St is now packed with out-of-towners each weekend. Still, it's a ton of fun, especially on weekdays when the crowds thin out but music still plays. Bars and clubs are arrayed back to back for several city blocks in one of the best concentrations of live-music venues in the country.

PALACE MARKET
MARKET

Map p238 (☑504-249-9003; www.palacemarketnola.com; 619 Frenchmen St; ◷6pm-1am) Independent artists and artisans line this alleyway market, which has built a reputation as one of the better spots in town to find a unique gift to take home as your New Orleans souvenir. The selections include T-shirts with clever New Orleans puns, hand-crafted jewelry, trinkets and a nice selection of prints and original artwork.

HEALING CENTER
MARKET

Map p238 (☑504-940-1130; www.neworleanshealingcenter.org; 2372 St Claude Ave; ◷varies by store; P) The bright-orange Healing Center is a sort of warehouse of all things organic, spiritual, New Age and conscious-raising. Inside, you'll find yoga studios, performance spaces, a sustainable food co-op, and a central entrance hall that houses large voodoo shrines that are utilized by local adherents of the religion.

ART GARDEN
MARKET

Map p238 (☑504-912-6668; 613 Frenchmen St; ◷6pm-midnight Thu-Mon) Art Garden is an arts-bazaar space filled with painters working on their projects while you shop. It's a good spot to find unique or limited-edition work from local artists, and is a nice respite from the bustle of Frenchmen St. It's located next to another arts market, the Palace Market.

PRESS STREET GARDENS
GARDENS

Map p238 (www.pressstreetgardens.com; 7 Press St, btwn Dauphine & Burgundy Sts; ◷sunrise-sunset) ✏ The New Orleans Center for Creative Arts runs this plot of land as part of its culinary education program. You'll find wandering chickens, placid goats and rows of organic vegetables used for educating the next generation of New Orleans chefs. Frequent events and markets are held on the grounds of the gardens.

Volunteers are welcome at the gardens from 9am-noon on Tuesdays.

CLOUET GARDENS
PARK

Map p238 (707 Clouet St; ◷sunrise-sunset; ♿ 🐾) ✏ This formerly empty lot has been transformed by its Bywater neighbors into a neat little park filled with murals and generally appealing weirdness. Performances, concerts and neighborhood get-togethers are frequently held here.

ST VINCENT
DE PAUL CEMETERY
CEMETERY

Map p238 (1401 Louisa St; ◷8am-3:30pm) As New Orleans cemeteries go, this one feels completely off the tourist radar. And yet, it's as atmospheric and gloomy as any other 'city of the dead.' Be on the lookout for inscriptions written in French and a slew of immigrant names encompassing émigrés from across Europe. Take a taxi or drive out here.

NINTH WARD VICTORY ARCH
MONUMENT

(Map p238 Burgundy St, btwn Pauline & Alvar Sts) Walk down Burgundy street in Bywater and, seemingly out of nowhere, an Arc de Triomphe–style monument stands next to a high school football field. Oddly imposing and showing signs of neglect, this is the Ninth Ward Victory Arch, dedicated to the

THE LOWER 9TH WARD

Following almost complete inundation from rising floodwaters, the Lower 9th Ward received the most media attention following Hurricane Katrina, even though neighborhoods such as Lakewood and Gentilly were similarly affected. Parts of the Lower 9th remain pretty devastated, still more wilderness than ruins. From Bywater, drive a few minutes across the Industrial Canal on Claiborne or St Claude St and make your second left on Deslonde; you'll see a mix of empty lots and the architectural oddity of LEED Green Building–certified homes built by Brad Pitt's Make It Right Foundation (www.makeitrightnola.org).

The popular narrative of the Lower 9th is that it was devastated after Katrina, and this is true – but what is left is less urban wasteland, and more reclaimed nature. Those who wanted to move back to the neighborhood are already here, and that number was never enough to repopulate the entire area. In between the homes that are now occupied, one can find miles of empty lots and jungle-esque overgrowth. In many ways, the neighborhood is doing better than similarly hit areas – celebrity and media attention has at least brought money and volunteers. For all the talk of 'bringing the Lower 9th back,' what's here now is likely to be what will be here for the foreseeable future.

Ronald Lewis, a 9th Ward native and former streetcar worker and union rep, showcases the heritage of his home neighborhood in his actual home, which has been converted into the **House of Dance & Feathers** (☏504-957-2678; http://houseofdance-andfeathers.org; 1317 Tupelo St✆). This museum-turned-community-center brims with exhibits on Mardi Gras Indians, and Social Aid and Pleasure Clubs (African American civic organizations), and is emblematic of a unique American neighborhood. To get here you'll need a car; call Ronald beforehand, as the museum is open by appointment only. Admission is free, but donations are gratefully accepted.

Sankofa is a community organization that participates in several initiatives aimed at improving life here and across the city. It runs a twice-a-week **Fresh Market** (☏504-872-9214; http://sankofanola.org/fresh-stop-market; 5029 St Claude Ave; ⏰9am-1pm Sat & 2-5pm Wed) ✆ and is at work expanding a **wetland and nature trail** (☏504-872-9214; 6400 Florida Ave; ⏰sunrise-sunset; Ⓟ) ✆FREE in the neighborhood.

Rather than simply driving through the neighborhood or visiting via a tour bus, make an appointment with **Confederacy of Cruisers** (p94) for its Ninth Ward Rebirth Bike Tours. It works closely with Lower 9th Ward residents to provide a tour that acts as a dialogue between visitors and locals. Stops include local businesses and the House of Dance & Feathers.

local veterans of WWI. The names on the monument are segregated by race.

Because of this segregation, Take 'Em Down, the group that led a campaign against the city's Confederate memorials, listed this monument as offensive in 2017. Others argue that an explanatory plaque or signage would allow the monument to still honor the soldiers it lists while providing historical context to the public.

MARKEY PARK   PARK

Map p238 (700 Piety St; ⏰sunrise-sunset; 👶🐕) ✆ This small green space has a playground. It's a popular spot for Bywater families, and a good place to let younger kids run off some energy, especially given its proximity to Pizza Delicious (p86) (always good for hungry kids).

PLESSY V FERGUSON PLAQUE   HISTORIC SITE

Map p238 (cnr Press & Royal Sts) FREE This plaque marks the site where Homer Plessy, in a carefully staged act of civil disobedience, tried to board a whites-only train car. That action led to the 1896 *Plessy v Ferguson* trial, which legalized segregation under the 'separate but equal' rationale. The plaque was unveiled by Keith Plessy and Phoebe Ferguson, descendants of the opposing parties in the original trial, now fast friends.

WASHINGTON SQUARE PARK   PARK

Map p238 (cnr Frenchmen & Royal Sts; ⏰sunrise-sunset; 🐕) Also known as 'Marigny Green,' this park is a popular spot for locals to play with their dogs, toss Frisbees and, based on the frequent smell, smoke things that aren't cigarettes. There's a touching HIV/AIDS memorial on the northern side of the park.

Be aware the park can be a congregation point for the homeless and those suffering from addiction and mental-health issues.

VOODOO SPIRITUAL TEMPLE   MUSEUM
Map p238 (☑504-943-9795; www.voodoospiritualtemple.org; 1428 N Rampart St; donations accepted; ☺by appointment) Mexican crucifix? Check. Tibetan mandala? Ditto. Balinese Garuda? Why not? Miriam William's voodoo temple is a mash-up of global religions, New Age mysticism, and, of course, voodoo. The temple is big on the tour-group circuit and it can be entertaining to watch Miriam give her lectures on life, the universe and everything else. Some think her enlightening, others find her rambling. She doesn't keep set hours, so you should call ahead and bank on visiting before 5pm (she tends to close up around then).

EATING

The food cachet of Marigny and Bywater is increasing by the month, and there's a general bohemian vibe and plethora of good eats in this part of town.

★PIZZA DELICIOUS   ITALIAN $
Map p238 (☑504-676-8482; www.pizzadelicious.com; 617 Piety St; pizza by slice from $2.25, whole pie from $15; ☺11am-11pm Tue-Sun; 🚸♿🐾) The thin-crust pies here are done New York–style and taste great. The preparation is simple, but the ingredients are fresh and consistently top-notch. An easy, family-friendly ambience makes for a lovely spot for a casual dinner, and it serves good beer too if you're in the mood. Vegan pizzas are available. The outdoor area is pet-friendly.

★RED'S CHINESE   CHINESE $
Map p238 (☑504-304-6030; www.redschinese.com; 3048 St Claude Ave; mains $5-18; ☺noon-11pm; 🐾) Red's has upped the Chinese cuisine game in New Orleans in a big way. The chefs aren't afraid to add lashings of Louisiana flavor, yet this isn't what we'd call 'fusion' cuisine. The food is grounded deeply in spicy Szechuan flavors, which pairs well with the occasional dash of cayenne.

★CAKE CAFÉ & BAKERY   BREAKFAST $
Map p238 (☑504-943-0010; www.nolacakes.com; 2440 Chartres St; mains $6.25-13; ☺7am-3pm Wed-Mon) On weekend mornings the line quite literally extends out the door

here. Biscuits and gravy (topped with andouille – smoked pork sausage), fried oysters and grits (seasonally available), and all the omelets are standouts. Lunch is great, too, as are the cakes (goat cheese and apple king cake!) whipped up in the back.

BYWATER BAKERY   BAKERY $
Map p238 (☑504-336-3336; www.bywaterbakery.com; 3624 Dauphine St; mains $6-9; ☺7am-5pm; 🚸) This bakery is doing things right. It serves breakfasts – say, shrimp and grits or biscuits and gravy – in a cup (it works!), fantastic quiches, open-faced sandwiches, and slices of some of the most drop-dead delicious cakes you've ever tried. The king cake is so addictive it should be banned. Just kidding.

KEBAB   MIDDLE EASTERN $
Map p238 (☑504-383-4328; www.kebabnola.com; 2315 St Claude Ave; mains $6.50-9.50; ☺11am-11pm Sun, Mon, Wed, & Thu, to midnight Fri & Sat, closed Tue; 🚸) Americans are learning what Europeans and Middle Easterners have long known: when you're drunk (and, to be fair, even when sober), shaved meat or falafel served on flatbread with lots of delicious sauces and vegetables is *amazing*. Kebab has come to preach this gospel in New Orleans, and does so deliciously.

POKE-CHAN   ASIAN $
Map p238 (☑504-571-5446; www.poke-chan.com; 2809 St Claude Ave; mains $11-17; ☺11am-10pm; 🚸) Poke-chan adds a welcome bit of fresh Asian-inspired flavor to St Claude Ave. The menu features traditional Hawaiian *poke* – raw seafood salad – as well as bowls inspired by pan-Asian cuisine, with varied ingredients such as Korean pork belly, Thai chicken, seaweed and more.

SNEAKY PICKLE   VEGAN $
Map p238 (☑504-218-5651; www.yousneakypickle.com; 4017 St Claude Ave; mains $5-9.25; ☺11am-9pm; 🌿) 🍃 This city has been sorely in need of a vegan-friendly spot that can hold its own against the city's famously meat-heavy cuisine. Enter Sneaky Pickle, a little spot on St Claude that dishes out tempeh Reubens on sourdough, beet flatbreads and a ton of unexpected, tasty specials, including one changing meat dish.

RAMPART FOOD STORE   SANDWICHES $
Map p238 (☑504-944-7777; 1700 N Rampart St; po'boys $7-11; ☺8am-8pm Mon-Sat) This convenience store is run by Vietnamese

immigrants who know how to make some of the best, most overstuffed shrimp po'boys in New Orleans. Pass on everything else, and be prepared for long lines.

JOINT
BARBECUE $

Map p238 (☑504-949-3232; www.alwayssmokin.com; 701 Mazant St; mains $7.50-18; ☺11:30am-10pm Mon-Sat) The Joint's smoked meat has the olfactory effect of the Sirens' sweet song, pulling you, the proverbial traveling sailor, off course and into a savory meat-induced blissful death (classical Greek analogies ending *now*). Enjoy some ribs, pulled pork or brisket with some sweet tea in the backyard garden and learn to love life if you haven't already.

ST ROCH MARKET
MARKET $

Map p238 (☑504-609-3813; www.strochmarket.com; 2381 St Claude Ave; prices vary by vendor; ☺7am-10pm Sun-Thu, to 11pm Fri & Sat; ☑🎵) The St Roch Market was once the seafood and produce market for a working-class neighborhood. But after it was nearly destroyed by Hurricane Katrina, it was renovated into a shiny food court. The airy interior space now hosts 13 restaurants serving a broad range of food, including crepes, burritos, Haitian cuisine and coffee.

QUEENIE'S
SOUTHERN US $

Map p238 (☑504-558-4085; 3200 St Claude Ave; mains $7-13; ☺10am-10pm Mon-Sat, to 9pm Sun) In a neighborhood full of flashy new restaurants, Queenie's is appealingly old-school, even though it opened in 2017. This is a counter-style spot with frozen daiquiris for a hot day and delicious hand pies. The kitchen also slings a good po'boy, as well as good-value soul-food hot plates, from shrimp and grits to chicken and waffles.

HORN'S
SOUTHERN US $

Map p238 (☑504-459-4676; www.hornsnola.com; 1940 Dauphine St; mains $6-17; ☺7am-3pm Mon-Wed, to 9pm Thu-Sun; ☑) This colorful little spot has plenty of New Orleans character – and characters. This is a good spot to recover from a hangover; inked-up waitstaff cart out excellent breakfasts, from latkes (potato pancakes) topped with crawfish, eggs and spinach to cornbread waffles and pulled pork. Lunch and dinners lean more towards hot plates, po'boys and sandwiches.

SHANK CHARCUTERIE
SOUTHERN US $

Map p238 (☑504-218-5281; www.shankcharcuterie.com; 2352 St Claude Ave; mains $9-16;

☺11am-7pm Tue-Thu, to 8pm Fri & Sat, to 5pm Sun) Operated by a dedicated team of butchers, Shank is unapologetically accommodating to carnivores. For breakfast, you can try an unctuous headcheese (a kind of terrine) platter; for lunch and dinner, try a pimento cheese burger or simple, delicious grilled pork chops. The meats behind the glass case are perfect for an evening of grilling.

JUNCTION
AMERICAN $

Map p238 (☑504-272-0205; www.junctionnola.com; 3021 St Claude Ave; mains $9-13; ☺11am-2am) Junction takes a tight-focused approach to cuisine: it does cheeseburgers, and does them well. Variations include an Iowa burger with corn relish, blue cheese and bacon. The cheeseburgers come with hand-cut fries, and there are fine salads and wings on the menu, too. An enormous beer menu also tempts. Junction is a 21-and-over establishment.

KUKHNYA
EASTERN EUROPEAN $

Map p238 (☑504-265-8855; 2227 St Claude Ave; mains $5.50-10; ☺4pm-midnight; ☑) This restaurant in the Siberia (p91) live-music bar serves, appropriately enough, Eastern European and Russian grub. The blinis (crepes) run the gamut from savory (ham and cheese) to sweet (apple), nicely complemented by hearty beef stroganoff and delicious mushroom and cabbage rolls. The burger and the Reuben are both standouts.

WHO DAT COFFEE CAFE & CAFE NERO
CAFE $

Map p238 (☑504-872-0360; 2401 Burgundy St; coffees & pastries $3-5, mains $7-15; ☺Who Dat 7am-10pm, Cafe Nero 8am-3pm Mon-Wed, to 10pm Thu-Sun; 🎵☑) This comfortable coffee shop has good pastries, better sandwiches, lovely coffee and cupcakes, many baked with a bit of booze. The on-site restaurant, Cafe Nero, is a hidden treasure. The breakfast menu in particular is excellent; the Not Yo Mama's corn cakes, drowning in a cheesy egg sauce, are ridiculously tasty.

LOST LOVE
VIETNAMESE $

Map p238 (☑504-949-2009; 2529 Dauphine St; mains $5.25-12; ☺6pm-midnight) This divey neighborhood bar also has a Vietnamese kitchen in the back serving great pho, *banh mi* (Vietnamese po'boys) and spring rolls. Just be aware the atmosphere isn't standard Vietnamese American dive (Formica, old Republic flag, karaoke); this place is more of an inked-up hideaway.

SATSUMA
CAFE $

Map p238 (☑504-304-5962; www.satsumacafe.com; 3218 Dauphine St; mains $5.50-10.50; ☉7am-5pm; ☑☑) With its chalkboard menu of organic soups and sandwiches, ginger limeade and graphic- and-pop art-decorated walls, Satsuma is hip and fun. Kids' books and indulgent staff make this an ideal spot for your children.

DAT DOG
AMERICAN $

Map p238 (☑504-309-3362; www.datdognola.com; 601 Frenchmen St; mains $5-8; ☉11am-midnight Sun-Thu, to 3am Fri & Sat) The Frenchmen St outpost of this popular local franchise serves sausages ranging from 'duck dogs' to alligator sausage to hot Cajun sausage layered with toppings such as remoulade or crawfish. For what it's worth, regular, excellent sausages and down-to-earth toppings are available as well. There's a great balcony here for viewing the Frenchmen St scene below.

BAO & NOODLE
CHINESE $

Map p238 (☑504-272-0004; www.baoandnoodle.com; 2700 Chartres St; mains $5-14; ☉11:30am-2pm & 5-10pm Tue-Sat; ☑) You'll find casual yet refined Chinese in this Creole shack, which boasts a dining room and a menu that is small and delicious. Elegant steamed *bao* (dumplings) are served alongside savory bowls of spicy pork noodles, while lamb shoulder is braised in soy sauce and cumin.

13 MONAGHAN
DINER $

Map p238 (☑504-942-1345; www.13monaghan.com; 517 Frenchmen St; mains $6-11; ☉11am-4am; ☑) As it's usually called, '13' is a diner with a twist: much of its delicious greasy-spoon fare is actually vegetarian. A Philly cheesesteak, for example, comes with portobello mushrooms or tofu instead of beef. There's also a meat version, plus great pizza and other diner classics.

GENE'S
SANDWICHES $

Map p238 (☑504-943-3861; 1040 Elysian Fields Ave; po'boys $8; ☉24hr) It's hard to miss Gene's: with its pink-and-yellow exterior, it's one of the most vividly painted buildings on Elysian Fields Ave. The hot sausage po'boy with cheese, and the fact it is served 24/7 with a free drink, is the reason you come here.

★BACCHANAL
AMERICAN $$

Map p238 (☑504-948-9111; www.bacchanalwine.com; 600 Poland Ave; mains $8-21, cheese from $6; ☉11am-midnight Sun-Thu, to 1am Fri & Sat) From the outside, Bacchanal looks like a leaning Bywater shack; inside are racks of wine and stinky-but-sexy cheese. Musicians play in the garden, while cooks dispense delicious meals on paper plates from the kitchen in the back; on any given day you may try chorizo-stuffed dates or seared diver scallops that will blow your gastronomic mind.

ELIZABETH'S
CAJUN, CREOLE $$

Map p238 (☑504-944-9272; www.elizabethsrestaurantnola.com; 601 Gallier St; mains $11-26; ☉8am-2:30pm & 6-10pm Mon-Sat, 8am-2:30pm Sun) Elizabeth's is deceptively down-at-heel, but the food's as good as the best New Orleans chefs can offer. It's all friendliness, smiling sass, weird artistic edges and over-indulgence on the food front. Brunch and breakfast are top draws – the praline bacon is no doubt sinful, mixing greasy salt and honeyed sweet sugar, but consider us happily banished from the Garden.

ADOLFO'S
ITALIAN $$

Map p238 (☑504-948-3800; 611 Frenchmen St; mains $9-24; ☉5:30-10:30pm) If you take a date to this intimate Italian cubby squeezed on top of a jazz club (the Apple Barrel (p92)) and don't feel sparks, maybe it wasn't meant to be, because Adolfo's is romantic as can be. The food isn't bad either, all stick-to-your-ribs Italian–American fare with some requisite New Orleans zing.

BYWATER AMERICAN BISTRO
AMERICAN $$$

Map p238 (http://bywateramericanbistro.com; 2900 Chartres St, Bywater; ☉5-10pm Wed-Sat) This modern American restaurant in a former rice mill uses local ingredients and impeccable technique to compose inventive, flavorsome dishes. Many, like the warmly spiced rabbit curry, draw inspiration from owner Nina Compton's native Caribbean, but the menu is a melting pot of influences. Try the bresaola-style tuna toast or pickled shrimp (a variation on ceviche).

🍷 DRINKING & NIGHTLIFE

The bars on this side of town are legendary, encompassing wine shops, cozy neighborhood watering holes and some of the city's most popular gay bars (including a gay bathhouse). All of this simply means that when it comes

THE BARMUDA TRIANGLE

There are a lot of good neighborhood bars in New Orleans, but Bywater has a particular concentration of excellent dives where locals rub elbows and drink in convivial excess. If by chance you choose to sail the seas of old 9th Ward imbibery, beware of what the locals like to call the Barmuda Triangle! Many a drunken sailor has vanished in this boozy sector of space time, only to re-emerge the following day, nursing vague happy memories and a splitting headache. If you dare to embark on this alcohol-fueled adventure, chart a course for...

Vaughan's (p92) The most central port of call for a Barmuda expedition.

BJ's Always good for a cheap High Life and a shot.

Bar Redux (p90) It has outdoor seating, and a breath of fresh air may keep you afloat.

J&J's Avast! Dangerously cheap and strong drinks here.

Bud Rip's If ye have made it through the four bars listed above, take a small hike to the center of Bywater and enjoy one of its oldest bars.

to having a good time, you're kind of spoiled for choice in this part of town.

★ BUFFA'S · BAR

Map p238 (☑504-949-0038; www.buffasrestaurant.com; 1001 Esplanade Ave; ☺24hr) Buffa's wears a lot of hats. First and foremost, it's a neighborhood bar with a backroom stage that hosts the occasional band, quiz night, open-mic night and TV/movie screening. Second, it's a 24-hour spot that serves one of the best cheeseburgers in town.

★ MIMI'S IN THE MARIGNY · BAR

Map p238 (☑504-872-9868; www.mimismarigny.com; 2601 Royal St; ☺3pm-late Mon-Fri, 11am-late Sat & Sun) The name of this bar could justifiably change to 'Mimi's *is* the Marigny' – it's impossible to imagine the neighborhood without this institution. It's an attractively disheveled place, with comfy furniture, pool tables, an upstairs dance hall decorated like a Creole mansion gone punk, and dim brown lighting like a fantasy in sepia. The bar closes when the bartenders want it to.

BUD RIP'S · BAR

Map p238 (☑504-945-5762; 900 Piety St; ☺1pm-late) One of the oldest bars in Bywater, Bud Rip's clientele is at the junction of the old Bywater working class crowd and the new hipster kids who are moving in around them. Drinks are strong and cheap, and DJs spin on weekends.

J&J'S · BAR

Map p238 (☑504-942-8877; www.jjssportslounge.com; 800 France St; ☺9am-4am) A neighborhood dive extraordinaire, J&J's has incredibly cheap (and strong) drinks and a clientele of charmingly crazy locals. Despite the posted hours, this place will often stay open for 24 hours if customers are sticking around.

SOLO ESPRESSO · CAFE

Map p238 (☑504-408-1377; www.soloespressobar.com; 1301 Poland Ave; ☺7am-3pm Mon-Sat, 9am-1pm Sun) This little shack serves very fine, strong, small-batch coffee, and its espresso drinks are seriously delicious.

BJ'S · BAR

Map p238 (www.facebook.com/bjs.bywater; 4301 Burgundy St) This Bywater dive attracts a neighborhood crowd seeking cheap beers, chilled-out banter and frequent events, from blues-rock gigs to sci-fi readings by local authors. How great is this place? Robert Plant felt the need to put on an impromptu set here when he visited town. Cash only.

LOST LOVE · BAR

Map p238 (☑504-949-2009; 2529 Dauphine St; ☺2pm-2am Mon-Fri, from 11am Sat & Sun) Dark and sexy, Lost Love is that vampy Marigny goth or moody artist your momma told you to stay away from, mixed with a bit of blue-collar dive-bar sensibility. The drinks are cheap, the pours are strong, there are regular trivia nights, movies and TV shows are projected onto a big screen, and there's an excellent Vietnamese kitchen in the back.

COUNTRY CLUB · BAR

Map p238 (☑504-945-0742; www.thecountryclub-neworleans.com; 634 Louisa St; ☺10am-1am daily) From the front, it's a well-decorated Bywater house. Walk inside and there's a restaurant, sauna, leafy patio with bar, heated outdoor pool, 25ft projector screen and a hot tub. There's a $10 towel rental fee if you want to hang out in the pool area, which is a popular carousing spot for the gay and lesbian community (all sexualities welcome).

JOHN
BAR

Map p238 (☑504-942-7159; 2040 Burgundy St; ☺24hr) The clever name comes courtesy of the toilet bowl seats and tables arrayed around an otherwise pretty open interior space. The *extremely* strong drinks, served in mason jars, come courtesy of friendly bartenders. An excellent dive spot to start a Frenchmen St bar crawl.

R BAR
BAR

Map p238 (☑504-948-7499; www.royalstreetinn. com; 1431 Royal St; ☺3pm-3am Sun-Thu, to 5am Fri & Sat) This grotty spot seamlessly blends punk-rock sensibility with the occasional confused French Quarter tourist. Like many older New Orleans businesses, R Bar's appeal lies in its rough edges: a beer and a shot cost a few bucks, the pool tables constantly crack, the jukebox is great and everyone seems to stop by on Mardi Gras day.

PARLEAUX BEER LAB
MICROBREWERY

Map p238 (☑504-702-8433; www.parleauxbeer-lab.com; 634 Lesseps St; ☺Mon, Thu & Fri 3-10pm, from 11am Sat, from 10am Sun) A diverse menu of beers, ranging from the hoppy to the fruity, is sold at this 'nanobrewery,' which also has a lush little courtyard where parents bring their kids on many a warm Bywater evening. Food trucks are frequently present, and some of the best restaurants in the neighborhood are a hop, skip and jump away.

BAR REDUX
BAR

Map p238 (☑504-592-7083; www.facebook. com/BarRedux; 801 Poland Ave; ☺4pm-2am Sun-Thu, to 3am Fri & Sat) A friendly little bar with an outdoor courtyard that's full of offbeat local art, the sound of the nearby train tracks and lots of live performances, ranging from cabaret to theater and from comedy to music. There's a kitchen on-site slinging decent bar food and a warm, idiosyncratic vibe that's very Bywater.

FAUBOURG WINES
WINE BAR

Map p238 (☑504-342-2217; www.faubourgwines. com; 2805 St Claude Ave; ☺noon-9pm Sun-Thu, to 10pm Fri & Sat) Faubourg (as many call it) is

primarily a wine shop but also offers tons of wine classes, and an in-house bar provides a spot for some nice sipping with the locals. The owners make a point of providing affordable bottles, including a rack of under $10 vintages.

BIG DADDY'S BAR
BAR

Map p238 (☑504-948-6288; 2513 Royal St; ☺24hr) If it's too crowded at popular Mimi's (p89) across the street, or if you're tired of the *thumpa-thumpa-bass* queer scene on Bourbon, head to this friendly 'gayborhood' bar, where all sexualities are welcome for friendly banter and cheap drinks.

ORANGE COUCH
CAFE

Map p238 (☑504-267-7327; 2339 Royal St; ☺7am-9pm, to 8pm Jun-Aug; 🛜) An icebox-cool cafe, all Scandi-style furniture, polished stone flooring, local artwork and photography on the walls, graffiti-lined restrooms and, yes, an orange leather couch in the midst of it all. The sort of place where a tattooed attorney takes out a laptop and a tort law manual and works for hours.

MARKEY'S
BAR

Map p238 (☑504-943-0785; 640 Louisa St; ☺2pm-2am Mon-Thu, from 11am Fri-Sun) Markey's stands out for two reasons: its barn-red exterior and the fact that it is a straight-up good neighborhood hangout. There's shuffleboard, cheap beer, sports on the TV and an excellent jukebox. Closing hours are flexible.

☆ ENTERTAINMENT

★ ALLWAYS LOUNGE
THEATER, LIVE MUSIC

Map p238 (☑504-218-5778; www.theallway-slounge.net; 2240 St Claude Ave; cover $5-10; ☺6pm-2am Sun-Thu, to 4am Fri & Sat) In a city full of funky music venues, AllWays stands out as one of the funkiest. On any given night of the week you may see experimental guitar, local theater, thrash-y rock, live comedy, burlesque or a '60s-inspired shagadelic dance party. Also, the drinks are super cheap. A cover fee applies only during shows.

★ SPOTTED CAT
LIVE MUSIC

Map p238 (www.spottedcatmusicclub.com; 623 Frenchmen St; cover $5-10; ☺2pm-2am Mon-Fri, noon-2am Sat & Sun) The Cat might just be your sexy dream of a New Orleans jazz club, a thumping sweatbox where drinks are served in plastic cups, impromptu dances break out at the drop of a feathered hat and the music is always exceptional. Fair warning, though, it can get crowded.

★HI HO LOUNGE LIVE MUSIC
Map p238 (☑504-945-4446; www.hiholounge.net; 2239 St Claude Ave; ⊙5pm-1am Sun-Thu, to 3am Fri & Sat) Hip-hop, punk, brass bands, dance parties, live storytelling events and Mardi Gras Indians regularly pop up at Hi Ho, one of the most eclectic venues in an eclectic city. It can get pretty packed, but this remains one of the best mid-sized venues in town for a live act. May stay open later on weekends.

MARIGNY OPERA HOUSE PERFORMING ARTS
Map p238 (☑504-948-9998; www.marignyoperahouse.org; 725 St Ferdinand St) This former church has been remodeled into a performing arts space that's infused with the sort of romantic dilapidation that very much fits the New Orleans aesthetic. The Opera House gained national prominence when Solange Knowles (Beyonce's sister) got married here; on other days, the venue hosts theater and music performances and showcases its own dance company.

KAJUN'S PUB KARAOKE
Map p238 (☑504-947-3735; www.kajunpub.com; 2256 St Claude Ave; ⊙24hr) FREE Kajun's is guaranteed for a good cast of characters. This bar is technically a live-music venue too...if you count karaoke as live music. In any case, the karaoke is awesome (sometimes awesomely bad, sometimes surprisingly good) and the beer flows 24/7. Many people pass a night here, stumble into the morning light and wonder what they've done with their lives.

CAFE NEGRIL LIVE MUSIC
Map p238 (☑504-383-5131; 606 Frenchmen St; cover $5; ⊙6pm-2am Sun-Thu, from 4pm Fri & Sat) When you spin the Frenchmen St musical wheel, Negril is the stop for reggae, blues, Latin and world music. So if you're craving that sort of groove, and the dancing that goes with it (this is definitely one of the 'dancier' clubs on Frenchmen), roll on in.

D.B.A. LIVE MUSIC
Map p238 (☑504-942-3731; www.dbaneworleans.com; 618 Frenchmen St; cover $10-15; ⊙4pm-5am; 🛜) Swank d.b.a. consistently schedules some of the best live-music events in town. Listening to John Boutté's sweet tenor is one of the best beginnings to a night in New Orleans. Brass bands, rock shows, blues – everything plays here. Plus, there's an amazing beer selection.

SIBERIA LIVE MUSIC
Map p238 (☑504-265-8855; www.siberianola.com; 2227 St Claude Ave; cover $5-10; ⊙4pm-late) There's always an interesting crowd in Siberia, which hosts everything from punk rock to singer-songwriter nights and from heavy metal to bounce shows. The on-site Eastern European–themed restaurant, Kukhnya (p87), satisfies any cravings you may have for blinis and burgers.

SNUG HARBOR JAZZ
Map p238 (☑504-949-0696; www.snugjazz.com; 626 Frenchmen St; cover $10-20; ⊙shows at 8 & 10pm) There may be bigger venues but Snug

LOCAL KNOWLEDGE
THE ST CLAUDE SHUFFLE

One of the best live-music strips in New Orleans can be found along St Claude Ave, at the stretch between Touro and Mandeville St. Just don't expect jazz; the clubs here play hip-hop, rock, punk, EDM (electronic dance music) and all manner of genre-bending fun. If you want a night out with locals and good music, head up here to check out **Hi Ho Lounge** or any of these other great venues:

AllWays Lounge Cheeky burlesque, brass-band shows, swing-dance parties and R&B dance nights are all in the potential cards when you come by this popular performance hall.

Siberia This sweaty venue is a regular spot for loud punk, singer songwriters, bounce and hip-hop, and just about any other music genre under the sun.

Kajun's Pub The talent of the karaoke cast at Kajun's ranges from operatic renditions of glam metal to drunken slurring of '90s R&B. But everyone has a good time, helped in part by extremely strong drinks coming from the bar.

Harbor is still one of the best jazz clubs in the city. That's partly because it usually hosts doubleheaders, giving you a good dose of variety, and partly because the talent is kept to an admirable mix of reliable legends and hot up-and-comers; in the course of one night you'll likely witness both.

SATURN BAR
LIVE MUSIC

Map p238 (☑504-949-7532; 3067 St Claude Ave; cover $5; ☺7pm-late) In the solar system of New Orleans bars, Saturn is planet odd. Originally it was an eclectic neighborhood bar where regulars appreciated the outsider art, leopard-skin furniture and a general, genuinely unique aesthetic. Today the old punks and new scenesters are united by neon-lighting fixtures, flashy gambling machines and great live music. There is no cover charge on most nights.

VAUGHAN'S
LIVE MUSIC

Map p238 (☑504-947-5562; 800 Lesseps St; cover $5-15; ☺noon-late) On most nights of the week this is a Bywater dive, but on Thursdays regular live music brings the house down. As small, intimate venues go, this can't be beat. It also hosts frequent drag shows and neighborhood parties.

BLUE NILE
LIVE MUSIC

Map p238 (☑504-948-2583; www.bluenilelive.com; 532 Frenchmen St; cover $10-20; ☺8pm-late Mon-Wed, 7pm-4am Thu-Sat, 5:30pm-1am Sun) Hip-hop, reggae, jazz, soul and funk are the live-music staples downstairs section of the Nile. Things get pretty sweaty and sensual in the upstairs balcony room, with its dedicated dance floor, as the night goes on.

CAFÉ ISTANBUL
ARTS CENTER

Map p238 (☑504-975-0286; www.cafeistanbul-nola.com; 2372 St Claude Ave) This small live-performance venue hosts an eclectic mash-up of shows, ranging from live storytelling to bounce DJ nights and from slam poetry to amateur theater.

THREE MUSES
JAZZ

Map p238 (☑504-252-4801; 536 Frenchmen St; ☺5-11pm Sun-Thu, to midnight Fri & Sat) This excellent restaurant hosts jazz performances every night. It's perfect for when you need to combine good food with music loud enough to enjoy, but soft enough to keep your ears from hurting. The kitchen closes at 10pm on weekdays and 11pm on weekends.

DRAGON'S DEN
LIVE MUSIC

Map p238 (☑504-940-5546; www.dragonsden-nola.com; 435 Esplanade Ave; cover $5-10; ☺7pm-late) When it comes to rock, dance hall, Latin, punk, EDM (electronic dance music) and hip-hop, the Den consistently hosts some of the best acts in New Orleans. Burlesque shows pop off on Saturdays. Closing time is flexible; the bar stays open to around 4am on weekends, earlier during the week.

APPLE BARREL
LIVE MUSIC

Map p238 (☑504-949-9399; 609 Frenchmen St; ☺3pm-4am Mon-Thu, from 1pm Fri-Sun) The Barrel is roughly the size of its namesake: you can fit perhaps a dozen customers in here without going elbow to elbow. It fits in musicians, too, who play very fine jazz, blues and folk.

MAISON
LIVE MUSIC

Map p238 (☑504-371-5543; www.maisonfrench-men.com; 508 Frenchmen St; cover $5-10; ☺4pm-2am Mon-Thu, 1pm-4am Fri & Sat, 10am-2am Sun) With three stages, a kitchen and a decent bar, Maison is one of the more varied performance spaces on Frenchmen St. On any given night you may be hearing Latin rumba in one hour, indie rock in another and brass to round out the evening.

CHECKPOINT CHARLIE
LIVE MUSIC

Map p238 (☑504-281-4847; 501 Esplanade Ave; cover $5-10; ☺24hr) Charlie's is so grungy it could start a band in early '90s Seattle. Acts you've likely never heard of (plus some you might know) play a mix of rock, metal and punk, most of it very good.

PHOENIX BAR
GAY

Map p238 (☑504-945-9264; www.phoenixbar-nola.com; 941 Elysian Fields Ave; ☺11am-midnight Mon-Fri, noon-2am Sat & Sun) This is where the leather-and-denim community meets to rub each other's stubble. Much more of a locals' scene than similar spots in the Quarter.

NEW MOVEMENT THEATER
THEATER

Map p238 (www.facebook.com/TNMnola; 2706 St Claude Ave) New Movement hits well above the average number of laughs for improv theater. The company has a cast of regular local players and a stable schedule of classes that train new talent in the art of off-the-cuff comedy.

ART GARAGE
PERFORMING ARTS

Map p238 (☑504-717-0750; www.facebook.com/theartgarageonstclaude; 2231 St Claude Ave)

This spot – truly, a former auto garage – frequently hosts events, readings and concerts, as well as gallery nights that kick off on the third Saturday of each month. The art and general vibe of the place is punk-hipster, and the spot is accessible via the Rampart St Streetcar. Check its Facebook page for a schedule of what's happening.

MUDLARK THEATER
THEATER

Map p238 (www.facebook.com/mudlarkpublictheater; 1200 Port St) This funky theater shows all kinds of independent and fringe theater shows, but it's best known for its in-house puppet company, which performs with and creates its own giant, creepily beautiful puppets. The Mudlark players perform around town; check their Facebook page for upcoming shows.

 # SHOPPING

LOUISIANA MUSIC FACTORY
MUSIC

Map p238 (504-586-1094; www.louisianamusicfactory.com; 421 Frenchmen St; 10am-7pm) Here's your first stop if you're looking for music. The selection of new and used CDs delves deep into the musical culture of New Orleans and Louisiana, with recordings from the 1900s to the present. The listening stations are a great way to familiarize yourself with local artists. There's also a nice selection of cool T-shirts, along with books, DVDs and posters.

BYWATER BARGAIN CENTER
ANTIQUES

Map p238 (504-948-0007; 3200 Dauphine St; 11am-5pm) This emporium is a treasure trove of, well, treasures, if you follow the old adage that one person's junk is another's... well, you know. There are found objects, old door frames, handmade crafts, plaster alligators playing zydeco and a whole lot more. Most impressive is a collection of Mexican folk art, including Oaxacan sculptures and Dia del Muerte paraphernalia.

EUCLID RECORDS
MUSIC

Map p238 (504-947-4348; www.euclidnola.com; 3301 Chartres St; 11am-7pm) New Orleans is the kind of town that deserves really cool record shops, and Euclid is happy to oblige. It's got all the ingredients: racks of rare vinyl, old concert posters, knowledgeable staff and a board listing live-music performances you should see while in town.

STELLA!
....

Tennessee Williams fans, listen up. The home at the center of *A Streetcar Named Desire* is at 632 Elysian Fields Ave. Currently the building houses the shop **I.J. Reilly's** and the bicycle rental outfit A Bicycle Named Desire (p215). If you're tempted to stand outside in a tank top and yell at the top of your lungs, you may wish to save the 'Stella!' screams for the **Tennessee Williams Literary Festival** (www.tennesseewilliams.net) in late March.

If you've ever wondered where the title for the iconic play comes from – yes, it does allude to the 'desire' that rips apart the lives of the main characters; but it's also a literal reference to the old Desire streetcar line that once ran up Elysian Fields Ave.

I.J. REILLY'S
ARTS & CRAFTS

Map p238 (504-304-7928; www.facebook.com/I.J.Reillys; 632 Elysian Fields Ave; 10am-5pm Thu-Mon, 9am-4pm Wed) How deeply New Orleans is this store? It's named for Ignatious Reilly, protagonist of *A Confederacy of Dunces,* and located in the Kowalski house from *A Streetcar Named Desire.* Inside, the shop sells all manner of New Orleans gifts, from photography books to printed screens and local artwork.

PIETY STREET MARKET
MARKET

Map p238 (612 Piety St; 10am-4pm 2nd Sat of month) The monthly arts market held here gathers some of the most creative individuals in Bywater and Marigny. There's usually street food on sale and activities for the kids. Check the Facebook page for updates on market times.

FAUBOURG MARIGNY BOOK STORE
BOOKS

Map p238 (FAB; 504-947-3700; www.fabonfrenchmen.com; 600 Frenchmen St; noon-10pm) The South's oldest gay bookstore is a ramshackle, intellectual spot, and a good place to pick up local 'zines and catch up on the New Orleans scene, gay or otherwise.

DR BOB'S STUDIO
ART

Map p238 (504-945-2225; www.drbobart.net; 3027 Chartres St; 10am-5pm Mon-Sat, to 4pm Sun) Self-taught outdoor artist Dr Bob is a fixture in Bywater, and you're sure to recognize his signature work – the 'Be Nice or

Leave' signs that appear in restaurants and bars around town. Garbage-can lids, bottle caps, trashed musical instruments and more are all turned into art.

NEW ORLEANS ART SUPPLY ART

Map p238 (☎504-949-1525; www.nolabarkmarket.com; 3041 N Rampart St; ☺9am-7pm Mon-Fri, to 5pm Sat, 10am-5pm Sun; ⊛) If you like to sketch while traveling, here's a good place to go for a fresh supply of pencils, paint and pads. The selection is very high quality. There's an attached pet shop (the Bark Market!), too, if you're traveling with furry friends.

5 PRESS GALLERY ART

Map p238 (☎504-249-5624; www.5pressgallery.com; 5 Press St, btwn Chartres & Royal Sts; ☺10am-3pm Thu-Sun) The New Orleans Center for Creative Arts is a fine regional arts-magnet school, and this gallery exhibits work by faculty, alumni students and visiting artists. It also hosts receptions from 6pm to 9pm on the second Saturday of each month.

RUBBER LIBRARY
& FLOWER BODEGA BOOKS

Map p238 (☎504-945-4662; www.rubberlibrary.net; 3240 Dauphine St; ☺11am-6pm Tue-Sat) This two-story shop is what the name suggests: there's a florist on the ground floor, and a used bookstore on the top floor with a kid-friendly reading nook and a radical political bent. If you're in need of a gift for your sweetie and he or she likes wisteria and Emma Goldman, you're in the perfect spot.

ISLAND OF SALVATION BOTANICA MARKET

Map p238 (☎504-948-9961; www.islandofsalvationbotanica.com; 2372 St Claude Ave; ☺10am-5pm Mon-Thu & Sat, to 8pm Fri, 11am-5pm Sun) Run by genial owners who sell voodoo spells, cards, spell components and the like for serious practitioners of the faith.

NEW ORLEANS ART CENTER ART

Map p238 (☎504-383-4765; www.theneworleansartcenter.com; 3330 St Claude Ave; ☺noon-6pm) The largest gallery in Bywater features a constantly shifting tableau of exhibitions, ranging from photography to sculpture to mixed media to paintings. There's a major social scene here from 6pm to 9pm on the second Saturday of each month.

LA46 VINTAGE

Map p238 (☎504-220-5177; 2232 St Claude Ave; ☺11am-7pm Mon-Sat) There are legions of thrift stores in this part of town, but LA46

is carefully curated, and the antiques, hi-fis, clothes, garden gear, furniture, decor, etc run the range from the beautifully strange to the strangely beautiful.

ARTISANS' WELL ART

Map p238 (☎504-376-5006; 2372 St Claude Ave; ☺12:30-6pm Tue-Fri, to 4:30pm Sat) This lovely little shop, operated by a Panamanian historian, specializes in indigenous arts and crafts from Mexico and Central America.

ELECTRIC LADYLAND BODY ART

Map p238 (☎504-947-8286; www.electricladylandtattoo.com; 610 Frenchmen St; ☺noon-midnight Mon-Sat, to 10pm Sun) New Orleans is an old port filled with bars and a tattoo is just about the coolest souvenir you can get. This is a clean, brightly lit spot with talented ink artists on staff.

🏃 SPORTS & ACTIVITIES

CONFEDERACY OF CRUISERS CYCLING

Map p238 (☎504-400-5468; www.confederacyofcruisers.com; 634 Elysian Fields Ave; tours $49-89) This company sets you up on cruiser bikes that come with fat tires and padded seats for Nola's flat, potholed roads. The 'Creole New Orleans' tour takes in the best architecture of Marigny, Bywater, Esplanade Ave and the Tremé. Confederacy also does a 'History of Drinking' tour (for those 21 and over) and a tasty culinary tour.

WILD LOTUS YOGA YOGA

Map p238 (☎504-899-0047; www.wildlotusyoga.com; 2372 St Claude Ave; class/1 week $33/50; ☺9am-8pm Mon-Thu, to 6:15pm Fri & Sun, to 5pm Sat) Wild Lotus is a beloved local yoga institution. Its classes, from mellow flow to hot vinyasa, are open to visitors to town. Check the website for a complete class schedule.

NEW ORLEANS
BOULDER LOUNGE CLIMBING

Map p238 (☎504-962-7609; www.climbnobl.com/st-claude; 2360 St Claude Ave; day pass adult/child $16/10; ☺noon-10pm Mon-Sat, to 7pm Sat & Sun; ⊛) In a city and state that aren't exactly known for their elevation and altitude, the New Orleans Boulder Lounge is there to feed your climbing fix. You'll be climbing without rope and harness; the walls range from 12–14ft and there are padded foam floors to land on. Shoe rental is $4.

CBD & Warehouse District

Neighborhood Top Five

❶ **Ogden Museum of Southern Art** (p98) Appreciating the moody landscapes and then strolling around the galleries that line Julia St.

❷ **Contemporary Arts Center** (p99) Engaging with the next generation of art and expression or taking in a new temporary exhibition

at the city's most modern museum.

❸ **Aquarium of the Americas** (p99) Watching tropical fish swim amidst Mayan ruins, otters play, penguins dive and an albino alligator, all while the kids lose their minds.

❹ **National WWII Museum** (p97) Learning about the

conflict that shaped the world at this interactive, educational theme park.

❺ **Insectarium** (p99) Strolling through a Japanese garden full of flitting butterflies, snacking on fried bugs and learning all about local cockroaches and termites.

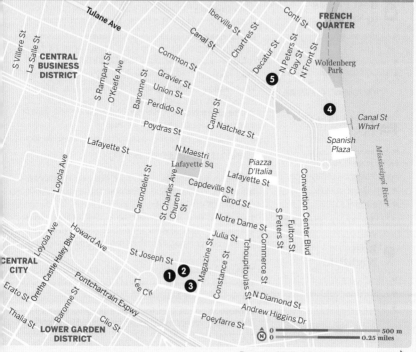

For more detail of this area see Map p242 ➡

Lonely Planet's Top Tip

Canal St separates the French Quarter from the CBD. If you want to be near but not in the Bourbon St craziness, book a hotel room in the CBD.

🍸 Best Hotel Bars

➡ Alto (p105)
➡ Piscobar (p105)
➡ Sazerac Bar (p105)

For reviews, see p104 ➡

🍴 Best Places to Eat

➡ Carmo (p101)
➡ Peche Seafood Grill (p102)
➡ Restaurant August (p104)

For reviews, see p101 ➡

🔒 Best Places to Shop

➡ Ogden Museum Store (p108)
➡ Ariodante (p108)
➡ Stonefree (p108)

For reviews, see p108 ➡

🛏 Best Places to Sleep

➡ Roosevelt New Orleans (p183)
➡ Le Pavillon (p182)
➡ The Catahoula (p183)
➡ Ace Hotel (p183)

For reviews, see p181 ➡

🍸 Best Nightlife

➡ Handsome Willy's (p105)
➡ CellarDoor (p105)
➡ Circle Bar (p107)

For reviews, see p104 ➡

CBD & WAREHOUSE DISTRICT

Explore the CBD & Warehouse District

The Central Business District (CBD) and Warehouse District stretch from I-10 and the Superdome to the river, and are bordered by Canal St and the elevated I-90. Poydras St divides the two neighborhoods, with the Warehouse District sitting 'above' (south) of Poydras.

Along Canal St, you'll find an odd mix of cheap and tatty gift stores and down-at-heel business chains. On the other side of the spectrum, there are theaters like the Joy and Saenger, two Audubon museums and the posh Shops at Canal Place (p109), plus several upscale hotels.

If you're heading south, once you pass Poydras St you're in the Warehouse District. You can walk down pedestrian Fulton St to soak in some of the old warehouse-style architecture. Julia St is the home of many of the city's most expensive art galleries. Around Camp St and St Joseph St, you'll find a cluster of important museums.

The eastern edge of the Warehouse District is taken up by the enormous New Orleans Convention Center, as well as the Outlet Collection at Riverwalk (p109). The northwest edge includes the Superdome, Claiborne Ave and I-10.

Local Life

Walk this way It's an easy walk from downtown offices and hotels to Warehouse District restaurants.

Lunch deals The city's nicest restaurants often serve affordable lunches. Enjoy top chefs' creations at Herbsaint (p103), Drago's (p103) and Emeril's (p104).

Free festivals Enjoy live music with families during **Wednesday at the Square** (http://ylcnola.org; Lafayette Sq; ⊙Mar-May) or stroll with the pretty people during **White Linen Night** (Center for Contemporary Arts, Julia St art galleries; ⊙First Sat evening in Aug).

Getting There & Away

Car From the airport, most hotels are easily accessible off the elevated I-90. Cars coming in from the east should exit off the I-10.

Taxi or shuttle A cab from Louis Armstrong Airport to the CBD costs $36 for up to two people (for more, it's $15 per person). Shuttles cost $24 per person one way.

Train/bus The Amtrak and Greyhound stations, also known as the Union Passenger Terminal, border Loyola Ave near the Superdome.

Streetcar The St Charles and Canal Streetcars run along their respectively named streets. The Riverfront Streetcar runs from the Quarter to the Outlet Collection at Riverwalk. The Rampart Streetcar connects the Union Passenger Terminal to Elysian Fields Ave.

TOP SIGHT
NATIONAL WWII MUSEUM

The National WWII Museum drops you into the action. Wall-sized photographs capture the confusion of D-Day. Riveting oral histories tell remarkable stories of survival. A stroll through the snowy woods of Ardennes feels eerily cold. Exhibits like these make this grand facility engaging; artifacts, battles and war strategies are humanized through personal recollections and heat-of-the-action displays.

The museum continues to open in several stages across three pavilions. The Campaigns of Courage Pavilion spotlights the European and Pacific theaters. Inside, the Road to Berlin galleries cover European battlefronts. A reconstructed Quonset hut – with a bombed-out roof – brings the air war powerfully close. The Road to Tokyo galleries highlight the Pacific theater, with visitors treading a route that begins in the days after Pearl Harbor and ends with the unconditional Japanese surrender. *Beyond All Boundaries* takes a 4D look at America's involvement in the war on a 120ft-wide screen. Get ready for rumbling seats and a dusting of snowflakes! *Final Mission* is a similar experience that places visitors in the USS submarine *Tang*.

DON'T MISS

➡ Road to Berlin
➡ *Beyond All Boundaries*
➡ Road to Tokyo

PRACTICALITIES

➡ Map p242
➡ ☎504-528-1944
➡ www.nationalww2museum.org
➡ 945 Magazine St
➡ adult/senior/child $27/23.50/17.50, plus 1/2 films $5/10
➡ ⊙9am-5pm

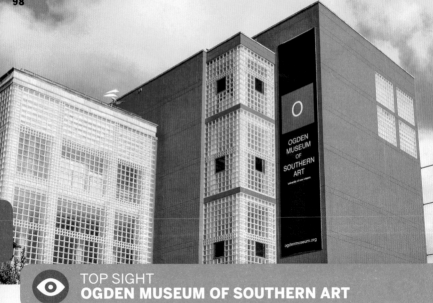

TOP SIGHT
OGDEN MUSEUM OF SOUTHERN ART

Although the Ogden Museum sits just a few steps away from the pedestal that once enshrined Robert E Lee, this vibrant collection of Southern art is not stuck in the past. It's one of the most engaging museums in New Orleans, managing to be beautiful, educational and unpretentious all at once.

The collection got its start more than 30 years ago when Roger Ogden and his father began purchasing art as gifts for Roger's mother. Ogden soon became a passionate collector and by the 1990s the New Orleans entrepreneur had assembled one of the finest collections of Southern art anywhere. Today his namesake museum and its galleries hold pieces that range from impressionist landscapes and outsider folk art to contemporary installation work. The Ogden is affiliated with the Smithsonian Institute in Washington, DC, giving it access to that bottomless collection.

The glass-and-stone Stephen Goldring Hall, with its soaring atrium, provides an inspiring welcome to the grounds. The building, which opened in 2003, is home to the museum's 20th- and 21st-century exhibitions as well as the Museum Store and its **Center for Southern Craft & Design**. 'Floating' stairs connect the different floors.

DON'T MISS

➡ Southern Landscapes
➡ Self-Taught, Outsider and Visionary Art
➡ Museum Store
➡ Ogden After Hours (after-hours performances on Thursdays)

PRACTICALITIES

➡ Map p242
➡ ☎504-539-9650
➡ www.ogdenmuseum.org
➡ 925 Camp St
➡ adult/child 5-17yr $13.50/6.75
➡ ⏱10am-5pm Fri-Wed, to 8pm Thu

👁 SIGHTS

Hotels and skyscrapers fill the CBD, a no-nonsense grid of bland buildings anchored by the hulking Superdome. A few historic buildings add character, particularly in the area surrounding Lafayette Sq, the heart of the former Faubourg St Mary. The old warehouses that line most of the streets in the Warehouse District have proved perfectly suitable for the Arts District that now thrives here. The museums and galleries are joined by some of the city's finest restaurants.

OGDEN MUSEUM OF
SOUTHERN ART   MUSEUM
See p98.

INSECTARIUM   ZOO
Map p242 (📞504-581-4629; https://audubon-natureinstitute.org/insectarium; 423 Canal St, US Custom House; adult/child/senior $23/18/20; ⏰10am-4:30pm Tue-Sun; 🚼) We'll be honest: if you're not a fan of bugs and creepy-crawlies, you may be happier elsewhere, because at this lively museum, you'll do more than stare at insects: you'll listen to them, touch them and, if you dare, even taste them. It's a multisensory adventure that's especially fun for kids. Our favorite exhibit? The Japanese-inspired Butterfly Garden, a tranquil slice of Zen pathways where clouds of butterflies hover over pools of koi fish.

Adventurous visitors can munch on 'chocolate-chirp cookies' (topped with crickets) or mango chutney with waxworms in the Bug Appetit room. The Louisiana Swamp Gallery and Insects of New Orleans display highlight regional creepy-crawlies. The latter exhibit examines yellow fever, a mosquito-borne virus that killed more than 40,000 people in the city between 1805 and 1905. Other fascinating exhibits include the mesmerizing leaf-cutter ants, toiling daily for their queen and for your viewing enjoyment.

The museum is located inside the carriageway of the city's historic US Custom House. Construction of the building began in 1848, but it took 33 years and nine architects to complete it. Confederate soldiers were imprisoned on the site when Union forces occupied New Orleans during the Civil War. Today, because it is a federal building, visitors' bags will be searched.

NATIONAL WWII MUSEUM   MUSEUM
See p97.

AQUARIUM OF THE AMERICAS   AQUARIUM
Map p242 (📞504-581-4629; www.audubon-institute.org; 1 Canal St; adult/senior/child $30/25/22; ⏰10am-5pm Tue-Sun; 🚼) The immense Aquarium of the Americas is loosely regional, with exhibits delving beneath the surface of the Mississippi River, Gulf of Mexico, Caribbean Sea and far-off Amazon rain forest. The impressive Great Maya Reef lures visitors into a 30ft-long clear tunnel running through a 'submerged' Mayan city, now home to exotic fish. Upstairs, the penguin colony, the sea-horse gallery, a bird jungle and a tank for otters are perennially popular. In the Mississippi River Gallery, look for the white alligator.

On the way out, you'll pass by the the 400,000 gallon Gulf of Mexico tank – home to sharks swimming placidly around a replica of oil-rig pilings. To that end, it may not surprise you that this exhibit was paid for by several major oil companies. 'Reef Rescue,' ($6) a virtual-reality undersea-exploration activity, is the latest addition to the aquarium's slate of activities.

The adjacent IMAX theater screens educational and commercial movies throughout the day. There are a few pay parking lots around; we prefer the garage at the nearby Shops at Canal Place (p109) – the Aquarium will validate your parking ticket, which provides a decent discount.

LOUISIANA CHILDREN'S
MUSEUM   MUSEUM
Map p242 (📞504-523-1357; www.lcm.org; 420 Julia St; $10; ⏰9:30am-4:30pm Tue-Sat, noon-4:30pm Sun; 🚼) This educational museum is like a high-tech kindergarten where the wee ones can play in interactive bliss till nap time. Lots of corporate sponsorship equals lots of hands-on exhibits. The Little Port of New Orleans gallery spotlights the five types of ships found in the local port. Kids can play in a galley kitchen or they can load cargo. Elsewhere, kids can check out optical illusions, shop in a pretend grocery store or frolic in a paper-and-cardboard story forest.

Children under 16 must be accompanied by an adult. The museum is slated to move to a new location in City Park in mid-2019.

CONTEMPORARY
ARTS CENTER   ARTS CENTER
Map p242 (CAC; 📞504-528-3805; www.cacno.org; 900 Camp St; adult/student/child $10/$8/free; ⏰11am-5pm Wed-Mon) From the outside, the CAC is pretty unassuming. But once inside, with the grand modernist entrance,

ℹ AUDUBON EXPERIENCE

Families and travelers who *really* like animals may want to visit all three of the facilities managed by the Audubon Institute: the aquarium (p99) and insectarium (p99) (in the CBD), and the zoo (p127) (in Audubon Park in Uptown). If that's the case, buy the **Audubon Experience package** (www.auduboninstitute.org) and see all three within 30 days, as well as an IMAX movie, at a reduced overall price of adult/concession $45/35.

an airy, spacious vault with soaring ceilings and conceptual metal and wooden accents, it's impressive. The best reason to visit? A good crop of rotating exhibitions by local as well as international artists, plus a packed events calendar that includes plays, skits, dance and concerts.

Admission for school children (K–12) is free.

ARTHUR ROGER GALLERY   GALLERY

Map p242 (☑504-522-1999; www.arthurroger-gallery.com; 432 Julia St; ⊙10am-5pm Tue-Sat) One of the most prominent galleries on Julia St, Arthur Roger represents several dozen artists from around the South. This spot hosts frequent gallery nights, exhibition openings and a slate of other events where wine is poured and art is discussed.

LEMIEUX GALLERIES   GALLERY

Map p242 (☑504-522-5988; www.lemieuxgalleries.com; 332 Julia St; ⊙10am-5:30pm Mon-Sat) Gulf Coast art is the emphasis in nationally recognized LeMieux Galleries, a good place to get a handle on the breadth of the regional arts scene.

CONFEDERATE
MEMORIAL HALL MUSEUM   MUSEUM

Map p242 (Louisiana's Civil War Museum; ☑504-523-4522; www.confederatemuseum.com; 929 Camp St; adult/child $10/5; ⊙10am-4pm Tue-Sat) Tattered gray uniforms, rebel swords and faded diaries – this collection of Civil War memorabilia pays homage to the Confederacy and locals who fought for that cause. The museum used to be a center of Confederate apologia. Today it's been largely politically corrected – note the different names it is known by – but it remains a collection of things, as opposed to a contemporary,

interpretation-driven educational museum. With that said, many of the personal effects are fascinating.

SCRAP HOUSE   MONUMENT

Map p242 (Convention Center Blvd, near John Churchill Chase St) **FREE** Built entirely out of found and recycled material, this eye-catching sculpture by artist Sally Heller honors the victims of Hurricane Katrina. A ruined shack that resembles Dorothy's house blown off-track, the sculpture sits in a tree constructed from pieces of oil drums. Inside, a light shines for those seeking to return home. It's a powerful piece of work in an appropriate setting – across from the Convention Center, where so many refugees were displaced in the aftermath of the storm.

GALLIER HALL   HISTORIC BUILDING

Map p242 (☑504-658-3627; www.nola.gov/gallier-hall; 545 St Charles Ave) Architect James Gallier Sr designed this Greek-Revival structure, dedicated in 1853. It served as New Orleans' city hall until the 1950s and far outclasses the city's current one (a few blocks away). Today the building is only open for private functions and is a focal point for Mardi Gras parades, many of which promenade past the grandstand erected here on St Charles Ave. The **LUNA Fête** (www.artsneworleans.org/event/luna-fete/; Lafayette Sq & nearby blocks; ⊙early Dec) light festival is partially projected onto the sides of Gallier Hall.

Both Confederate president Jefferson Davis and local R&B legend Ernie K-Doe have lain in state here – only in New Orleans.

NEW ORLEANS
COTTON EXCHANGE   HISTORIC BUILDING

Map p242 (231 Carondelet St) For much of its history, the economy of New Orleans was built on cotton and slavery. The former industry was largely brokered out of this building, where the city's Cotton Exchange was founded in 1871. In its heyday, thousands of cotton contracts were traded at this site, but, in time, Dallas replaced New Orleans as the nation's most important cotton-trading center. The building here, dating from the 1920s, is the third Cotton Exchange to occupy this site.

Today, the building hosts a bank, offices and parts of a hotel.

LEE CIRCLE   MONUMENT

Map p242 This traffic circle was called Place du Tivoli until it was renamed to honor Confederate General Robert E Lee after the

Civil War. In 2017, after many political battles and protests, the statue of Lee finally came down from its column. For now, the statue is yet to be replaced and the circle is yet to be renamed.

PRESERVATION
RESOURCE CENTER HISTORIC BUILDING
Map p242 (☎504-581-7032; www.prcno.org; 923 Tchoupitoulas St; ◷9am-5pm Mon-Fri) **FREE** If you're interested in the architecture of New Orleans or a self-guided walking tour, then start here. The welcoming Preservation Resource Center, located inside the 1853 Leeds-Davis building, offers free pamphlets with walking-tour maps for virtually every part of town. The helpful staff shares information about everything from cycling routes to renovating a historic home. Check the website for details about the Shotgun House tour in March and the popular Holiday Home tour in December. The neighborhood brochures are also available online.

GEORGE SCHMIDT GALLERY GALLERY
Map p242 (☎504-592-0206; www.george-schmidt.com; 626 Julia St; ◷12:30-4:30pm Tue-Sat) New Orleans artist George Schmidt describes himself as a 'historical' painter. Indeed, his canvases evoke the city's past, awash in a warm, romantic light. His Mardi Gras paintings are worth a look.

SOREN CHRISTENSEN GALLERY GALLERY
Map p242 (☎504-569-9501; www.sorengallery.com; 400 Julia St; ◷10am-5:30pm Tue-Fri, 11am-5pm Sat) This impressive space showcases the work of nationally renowned painters and sculptors. The gallery is known for its nontraditional sensibility and its strong collection of regional, contemporary art.

✖ EATING

New Orleans' downtown isn't great for cheap eats (with a few exceptions), but as far as fine dining goes, you've hit the mother lode. Many of the city's big-name chefs – Donald Link, Emeril Lagasse etc – have posh outposts downtown. That said, even the high-end restaurants here have affordable lunchtime menus, if you want to sample fine food on the cheap.

★CARMO VEGETARIAN $
Map p242 (☎504-875-4132; www.cafecarmo.com; 527 Julia St; lunch $9-12, dinner $9-15; ◷11am-3pm Mon, to 10pm Tue & Wed, to 11pm Thu-Sat; ✐) Carmo isn't just an alternative to the fatty, carnivorous New Orleans menu – it's an excellent restaurant by any measuring stick. Both the aesthetic and the food speak to deep tropical influences, from Southeast Asia to South America. Dishes range from pescatarian to full vegan; try Peruvian style sashimi or Burmese tea leaf salad and walk away happy.

★DRIP AFFOGATO ICE CREAM $
Map p242 (☎504-313-1611; www.dripaffogatobar.com; 703 Carondelet St; affogato $8.25; ◷10am-10pm; ◑) Drip serves all kinds of gelato and espresso, but it truly shines when it combines the two into an affogato – espresso or coffee poured onto ice cream. The result is culinary dynamite.

ST JAMES CHEESE COMPANY DELI $
Map p242 (☎504-304-1485; https://stjamescheese.com; 641 Tchoupitoulas St; mains $7-14; ◷11am-6pm Mon-Wed, to 8pm Thu & Fri, 9am-8pm Sat) When it comes to grabbing a sandwich downtown, we're always torn between this spot and Cochon Butcher. St James does possess an advantage on the actual cheese front – this is partly a cheese shop – and you'd be remiss not to try their simple, perfect ham and brie on a baguette.

COCHON BUTCHER SANDWICHES $
Map p242 (☎504-588-7675; www.cochonbutcher.com; 930 Tchoupitoulas St; mains $10-14; ◷10am-10pm Mon-Thu, to 11pm Fri & Sat, to 4pm Sun) Tucked behind the slightly more formal Cochon, this sandwich and meat shop calls itself a 'swine bar and deli.' We call it one of our favorite sandwich shops in the city, if not the South. From the convivial lunch crowds to the savory sandwiches to the fun-loving cocktails, this welcoming place encapsulates the best of New Orleans.

PHO TAU BAY VIETNAMESE $
Map p242 (☎504-368-9846; www.photaubayrestaurant.com; 1565 Tulane Ave; mains $6.50-13; ◷10am-7pm Mon-Fri; ✐) If you ever have a health emergency around lunchtime, head here – this beloved New Orleans Vietnamese hangout is packed with medical staffers in scrubs on an almost daily basis. They come for delicious mains from *banh mi* (Vietnamese sandwiches) to *bun cha* (char grilled pork and vermicelli) to, of course, pho.

COMPANY BURGER BURGERS $
Map p242 (☎504-309-9422; www.thecompanyburger.com; Girod & S Rampart Sts; mains $8-12; ◷11am-10pm) This outpost of the beloved

LOCAL KNOWLEDGE

CBD LANDMARKS

Scattered throughout the CBD are historic buildings that once controlled industries that participated in some of the darkest chapters of American history. Keep an eye out for them when wandering through the neighborhood. Note that both the Cotton Exchange and United Fruit Company have long closed or moved out of the below addresses.

New Orleans Cotton Exchange (p100) Although slavery was abolished by the time the New Orleans Cotton Exchange opened in 1871, it helped shape a regional geography that was the basis of the future cotton industry: a network of almost feudal plantations worked by generations of sharecroppers.

United Fruit Company Map p242 (321 St Charles Ave) The tropical fruit that frames the entrance to this building implies a sunny history, but United Fruit Company was notorious for supporting some of the worst dictators of 20th century Latin America. Indeed, the term 'Banana Republic' – a powder keg country dependent on the export of a resource – was invented to describe the nations manipulated by United Fruit.

Freret St burger joint of the same name (p130) does burgers and tater tots, and it does them exceedingly well. They've got 'Not Burgers' too – hot dogs, grilled cheese sandwiches, fried chicken sandwiches etc – but, jeez, those burgers hit the spot when you've got a craving.

RUBY SLIPPER – DOWNTOWN   BREAKFAST **$**
Map p242 (www.therubyslippercafe.net; 200 Magazine St; mains $8-14; ⏰7am-2pm Mon-Fri, to 3pm Sat & Sun) This rapidly growing local chain specializes in down-home Southern breakfasts prepared with decadent oomph. How does fried chicken on a biscuit with poached eggs and tasso (spicy cured pork) cream sauce sound? Soon after the doors open, this lively joint is full up with solos, families, college-age kids, renegade convention-goers and folks revving up before the party that is New Orleans.

MOTHER'S   DELI **$**
Map p242 (☎504-523-9656; www.mothersrestaurant.net; 401 Poydras St; breakfast $3-12, mains lunch & dinner $11-27; ⏰7am-10pm) At lunchtime, expect to see a line out the door. Mother's is a longtime crowd-pleaser that has drawn locals and tourists for years. The quality isn't what it was, but the history and come-as-you-are hospitality make the difference. Mother's invented the 'debris' po'boy (roast beef marinated in its own juices) and serves the justifiably famous 'Ferdi Special' – a po'boy loaded up with ham, roast beef and debris.

★**PECHE SEAFOOD GRILL**   SEAFOOD **$$**
Map p242 (☎504-522-1744; www.pecherestaurant.com; 800 Magazine St; small plates $9-14, mains $14-27; ⏰11am-10pm Sun-Thu, to 11pm Fri & Sat) Coastal seafood dishes are prepared simply here, but unexpected flourishes – whether from salt, spices or magic – sear the deliciousness onto your taste buds. The vibe is convivial, with a happy crowd savoring among the exposed-brick walls and wooden beams. A large whole fish, made for sharing, is a signature preparation, but we recommend starting with something from the raw bar.

★**SEAWORTHY**   SEAFOOD **$$**
Map p242 (☎504-930-3071; www.seaworthynola.com; 630 Carondelet St; mains $17-30; ⏰brunch 11am-3pm Sat & Sun, dinner 5-11pm daily, bar menu 11pm-1am daily) 🌿 Many new restaurants in New Orleans have not lived up to the city's intimidating culinary legacy. Seaworthy is not such a place. They serve, simply, seafood – gorgeously fresh, brilliantly executed seafood, from yellowfin and sea bass to redfish in chili butter to one of the finest raw oyster selections in the city.

COCHON   CAJUN **$$**
Map p242 (☎504-588-2123; www.cochonrestaurant.com; 930 Tchoupitoulas St; small plates $8-14, mains $19-32; ⏰11am-10pm Mon-Thu, to 11pm Fri & Sat) The phrase 'everything but the squeal' springs to mind at Cochon, regularly named one of New Orleans' best restaurants. Donald Link pays homage to his Cajun culinary roots and the menu revels in

most parts of the pig, including pork cheeks with sweet potato gratin and fried boudin (spicy sausage).

HERBSAINT
LOUISIANAN **$$**

Map p242 (☏504-524-4114; www.herbsaint.com; 701 St Charles Ave; mains $16-34; ☉11:30am-10pm Mon-Fri, from 5:30pm Sat) Herbsaint's duck and andouille (smoked sausage) gumbo might be the best restaurant gumbo in town. The rest of the food ain't too bad either – it's very much modern bistro fare with dibs and dabs of Louisiana influence, courtesy of owner Donald Link. On our last visit, we enjoyed divine cornmeal fried oysters and crispy goat served alongside curried cauliflower.

LUKE
BISTRO **$$**

Map p242 (☏504-378-2840; www.lukeneworleans.com; 333 St Charles Ave; mains $16-35; ☉7am-11pm) This spin on a European bistro has an elegantly simple tiled interior and a menu that will make you reconsider the limits of Louisiana-French fusion; the primary muse is the smoky, rich cuisine of Alsace, the French–German border. Yellowfin tuna is rubbed with tasso, while an entrecôte ribeye comes doused in a sinfully rich bearnaise.

BALISE
SOUTHERN US **$$**

Map p242 (☏504-459-4449; www.balisenola.com; 640 Carondelet St; mains $16-34; ☉lunch & brunch 11:30am-2pm Fri, to 2:30pm Sat & Sun, dinner 4:30-10pm Sun-Thu, to 11pm Fri & Sat) Peeling plaster and brick accents ensconce a warm, wooden interior where decadent, yet classically inspired, Southern cuisine rules the roost – try the fried-chicken sandwich, a strip steak with roasted bone marrow or fries smothered in pork-cheek gravy and cheese.

DOMENICA
ITALIAN **$$**

Map p242 (☏504-648-6020; www.domenicarestaurant.com; 123 Baronne St; mains $15-34; ☉11am-11pm; ☏) With its wooden refectory tables, white lights and soaring ceiling, Domenica feels like a village trattoria gone posh. The 'rustic' pizza pies at this lively, often-recommended spot are loaded with nontraditional but enticing toppings – clams, prosciutto, smoked pork – and are big enough that solo diners might just have a slice or two left over.

PUBLIC SERVICE
AMERICAN **$$**

Map p242 (☏504-962-6527; www.publicservicenola.com; 311 Baronne St; lunch $7-14, dinner

$10-30; ☉6:30am-10pm, to 11pm Fri & Sat) There's a whole eclectic mash-up of farm-to-table treats served in this airy, grand dining hall, which is attached to the NOPSI Hotel (p183). Mix up your small plates (steak and cheese fries, black bean hummus) with flat breads (white anchovy and manchego) and some fine burgers and pasta.

CAFÉ ADELAIDE
CREOLE **$$**

Map p242 (☏504-595-3305; www.cafeadelaide.com; 300 Poydras St; mains lunch $16-27, dinner $24-33; ☉6:30am-10:30am & 11:30am-2pm Mon-Thu, to 2:30pm Fri, 7am-1:30pm Sat & Sun, dinner 5:30-9pm Sun-Thu, to 10pm Fri & Sat) This jazzy restaurant is a Brennan family tribute to their endearingly eccentric aunt Adelaide. We love the pop-art portraits of her that hang above the dining room. The motto here is the namesake's own: 'Eat, drink and carry on,' a philosophy realized by haute Creole cuisine – garlic and chili shrimp, Cajun-roasted drum fish, and pork shoulder cooked in milk.

DRAGO'S SEAFOOD RESTAURANT
SEAFOOD **$$**

Map p242 (☏504-584-3911; www.dragosrestaurant.com; 2 Poydras St; mains lunch $14-22, dinner $18-46; ☉11am-10pm) Charbroiled oysters at Drago's? Heaven on the half shell. This sprawling restaurant is loaded with tourists, but oyster creations are the real deal thanks to Drago Cvitanovich, a Croatian immigrant who brought a heady knowledge of shellfish from the Dalmatian Coast to the Gulf. Oysters drip with butter, garlic, parmesan and their own juices after kissing an open fire.

WILLA JEAN
SOUTHERN US **$$**

Map p242 (☏504-509-7334; www.willajean.com; 611 O'Keefe Ave; mains $13-19; ☉7am-9pm) Willa Jean sells itself as a contemporary Southern bakery/breakfast and lunch counter – you'll find braised short ribs and poached eggs in a decadent breakfast bowl and New Orleans-style barbecue-shrimp toasts in the afternoon. Everything tastes pretty good, but the slick, loungey atmosphere and inflated prices aren't the New Orleans norm.

MAYPOP
ASIAN **$$**

Map p242 (☏504-518-6345; http://maypoprestaurant.com; 611 O'Keefe Ave; mains $15-32; ☉11am-10pm) This New Orleans spin on haute Asian fusion is popular with business-lunch types, foodies on the prowl for the next big thing and well-heeled tourists.

A changing menu mixes up the American South and Southeast Asia via dishes like fried 'hot chicken' in vindaloo curry and softshell crab *almandine* (cooked with almonds) spiced up with coconut.

AMERICAN SECTOR
AMERICAN **$$**

Map p242 (☑504-528-1940; www.american-sector.com; 945 Magazine St; lunch $10-14, dinner $14-28; ☺11am-7pm Sun-Thu, to 8pm Fri & Sat) This ode to the Greatest Generation looks like a 1940s doo-wop diner: white-capped waitstaff beside the tables and black-and-white photos on the wall. Look for burgers and sandwiches at lunch, and mains with a Southern spin at dinner, including Mississippi rabbit, pork chops with boudin dirty rice, and shrimp and grits.

JOHNNY SANCHEZ
MEXICAN **$$**

Map p242 (☑504-304-6615; www.johnny-sanchezrestaurant.com; 930 Poydras St; lunch $8-22, dinner $8-28; ☺11am-10pm Sun-Thu, to 11pm Fri & Sat) Day of the Dead meets vintage New Orleans at this stylish 'taqueria'. The rallying line is traditional Mexican dishes with innovative flavors, sourced from local fishers and farms. Highlights include crispy brussels sprouts, lamb enchiladas, and tacos with savory fillings ranging from *carne asada* (spicy steak) to pork belly, goat and shrimp.

★COMPÈRE LAPIN
CARIBBEAN **$$**

Map p242 (☑504-599-2119; http://comperelapin.com; 535 Tchoupitoulas St; lunch $14-28, dinner $26-31; ☺dinner 5:30-10pm daily, lunch 11:30am-2:30pm Mon-Fri, brunch 10:30am-2pm Sat & Sun; ☑) Chef Nina Compton became a household name via the TV show *Top Chef,* but her New Orleans restaurant is anything but a celebrity flash in the pan. This is wonderful cuisine that sits at the intersection of the Caribbean and Louisiana Creole taste universes, serving curry goat and sweet potato gnocchi and jerk drum fish.

★RESTAURANT AUGUST
CREOLE **$$$**

Map p242 (☑504-299-9777; www.restaurantaugust.com; 301 Tchoupitoulas St; lunch $23-38, dinner $34-48, 5-course tasting menu $98, with wine pairings $163; ☺5-10pm daily, 11am-2pm Fri; ☑) For a little romance, reserve a table at Restaurant August. This converted 19th-century tobacco warehouse, with its flickering candles and warm, soft shades, earns a nod for most aristocratic dining room in New Orleans, but somehow manages to be both intimate and lively. Delicious meals take you to another level of gastronomic perception.

The five-course, two-hour tasting menu makes local foodies weep; there's a specially tailored version for vegetarians as well ($77). There's also a prix-fixe lunch ($28) with various options. Solo diners do just fine at the easygoing but professional bar.

LA BOCA
STEAK **$$$**

Map p242 (☑504-525-8205; www.labocasteaks.com; 870 Tchoupitoulas St; mains $38-60; ☺5:30-10pm Mon-Wed, to midnight Thu-Sat) The steakhouse scene in New Orleans has been steadily improving over the last decade, and La Boca has given the city no small push in the polls. Meticulously sourced beef is cooked and cut Argentine style, from hanger steaks to sweetbreads to sirloin flap.

EMERIL'S
CREOLE **$$$**

Map p242 (☑504-528-9393; www.emerils.com; 800 Tchoupitoulas St; mains lunch $12-25, dinner $29-45; ☺11:30am-2pm Mon-Fri, 6-10pm daily) The noise level can be deafening, but Emeril's remains one of New Orleans' finest dining establishments. The kitchen's strengths are best appreciated by ordering the daily specials. The full-on Emeril experience includes partaking of the cheese board with a selection from the restaurant's eclectic wine list. The bar is a favorite with visiting celebrities and is a fun see-and-be-seen local spot.

BON TON CAFÉ
CAJUN **$$$**

Map p242 (☑504-524-3386; www.thebontoncafe.com; 401 Magazine St; mains $18.50-48; ☺11am-2pm & 5-9pm Mon-Fri) Whoa, where did all these people come from? Bon Ton looks low-key and stuffy beneath its Magazine St awnings, but come lunchtime you'd think half of downtown is here. This classy but sassy joint, an old-style Cajun restaurant that's been open for half a century, maintains an old-school menu of redfish, rice, steak and lots of butter.

⊖ DRINKING & NIGHTLIFE

Downtown may look like a nightlife wasteland, but there's some great live music peppered about the office blocks.

More pertinently, New Orleans, while home to many great dives, can lack in the hip lounge stakes; the CBD works to remedy this situation.

ALTO
ROOFTOP BAR

Map p242 (📞504-900-1180; www.acehotel.com/neworleans/alto; 600 Carondelet St; ⊙10am-9pm) If you want a good view of the city, or a good view of a bunch of millennials enjoying a good view of the city, head to the Ace Hotel's rooftop bar. There's lush greenery, cold mixed drinks, hot breezes and a general sexy-times vibe – as well as a small menu of bar bites.

HANDSOME WILLY'S
BAR

Map p242 (📞504-525-0377; 218 S Robertson St; ⊙11am-11pm Mon-Wed, to 1am Thu, to 2am Fri, 4pm-2am Sat, to midnight Sun) Willy's is one of the oddest bars in New Orleans, a neighborhood-style dive in a patch of empty parking lots that lacks a neighborhood. It's consistently fun – there's a nice outdoor area and DJs frequently spin excellent hip-hop and dance tracks.

CELLARDOOR
COCKTAIL BAR

Map p242 (📞504-265-8392; www.cellardoornola.com; 916 Lafayette St; ⊙4-11pm Mon-Thu, 4pm-1am Fri, 5pm-1am Sat) Although the CellarDoor is technically a gastropub, we tend to skip the New Southern food menu and lean into the excellent, extensive cocktail list and historic-chic ambiance. Once a brothel, this lovely space now doubles (or triples?) as a bar and miniature art gallery.

CAFÉ AT ROULER
CAFE

Map p242 (📞504-603-2781; www.rouler.cc/service/the-cafe-at-rouler; 601 Baronne St; ⊙7am-9pm; 🐾) This cafe serves as an excellent CBD meet-up corner and is popular with the local cycling community – unsurprising, as it's connected to a **bicycle shop and rental outfit** (504-327-7655; www.spinlister.com/profile/rouler; per hr $5-20, day $35-100; ⊙7am-7pm Sun-Thu, to 9pm Fri & Sat). Wi-fi is fast and the coffee is strong, so this is a good spot for getting work done (or procrastinating and ignoring said work).

PISCOBAR
COCKTAIL BAR

Map p242 (📞504-603-2442; www.catahoulahotel.com/piscobar/; 914 Union St; ⊙1-10pm Sun-Thu, to midnight Fri & Sat) One of the more haute and hip options in downtown New Orleans, the downstairs bar at the Catahoula (p183) specializes in pisco-based cocktails, in case it wasn't obvious (Pisco, for the uninitiated, is a brandy from Peruvian and Chilean wine regions). You'd think this would make for a one-trick-pony bar, but the cocktails here are diverse and delicious.

SWIZZLE STICK BAR
BAR

Map p242 (📞504-595-3305; www.cafeadelaide.com; 300 Poydras St; ⊙11:30am-11pm Mon-Thu, to midnight Fri, 10am-midnight Sat, to 11pm Sun) This swell bar is the tipsy companion to Café Adelaide, and its good-time vibe seems poised to spill into the lobby of the adjoining Loews Hotel. A dash of adult fun massaged with heavy levels of quirkiness, it's a snazzy spot for an after-work drink or pre- or post-convention tipple.

BARCADIA
BAR

Map p242 (📞504-335-1740; www.barcadianeworleans.com; 601 Tchoupitoulas St; ⊙11am-2am Mon-Sat, to midnight Sun) This sprawling, high-energy bar celebrates the games of your youth in a big and flashy way. There's life-size Jenga, towering Connect Four, air hockey, pop-a-shot and loads of '80s arcade games. Nope, it's not relaxing and it can be a bit broy, but it's also a potentially fun way to mingle.

RUSTY NAIL
BAR

Map p242 (📞504-525-5515; www.rustynailnola.com; 1100 Constance St; ⊙4pm-1am Mon-Thu, 2pm-3am Fri, 11am-3am Sat, noon-1am Sun) The Rusty Nail is a dive bar for newbies. Yeah, it lurks in a dark spot under the I-90 overpass, but it's also flanked by loft complexes that look downright trendy. The twinkling white lights are kinda cute. Come on in, have a beer or a scotch (there's a long list) and kick back.

WINE INSTITUTE OF NEW ORLEANS (WINO)
WINE BAR

Map p242 (📞504-324-8000; www.winoschool.com; 610 Tchoupitoulas St; ⊙2-10pm Sun-Wed, to midnight Thu-Sat) Topping our list of New Orleans acronyms, WINO is the place to spend an evening wine tasting or learning more about a certain varietal or wine region. But we're going to assume you're simply keen to try some wines. Pop by to sample well over 100 different types of vino on tap, plus a fair amount of pâté and cheese.

SAZERAC BAR
BAR

Map p242 (📞504-648-1200; http://theroosevelt neworleans.com; 130 Roosevelt Way;

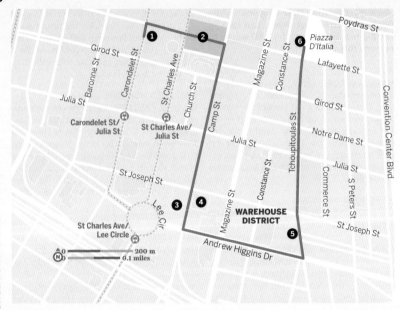

Local Life
The Past is the Present is the Future

In the Warehouse District, more so than any other New Orleans neighborhood, the city's well-worn historical identity rubs shoulders with a 21st-century sense of contemporary cool. On this little tour you'll take in elements of New Orleans ranging from its deep past to its envisioned new horizons.

Start at the ❶ **Ace Hotel & Seaworthy**. The drop-dead gorgeous Ace Hotel (p183) chain can sometimes feel painfully hip and grounded in global hipster aesthetic. Yet the on-site restaurant, Seaworthy (p102), goes to great pains to specifically draw from the bounty of local waters. We respect that, and the oyster bar, which you should partake of. Oysters = good walking fuel.

As millennial fresh as the Ace may be, walk just a few blocks east (or, in local parlance, towards the river) and you're in ❷ **Lafayette Sq**, second-oldest park in the city, named for a Revolutionary War hero and studded with statues of said hero's contemporaries.

Within the ❸ **Ogden Museum of Southern Art** (p98), you'll find both old-school and modern interpretations of the American South: its landscapes, its peoples, its hopes and its visions.

Across the street from the Ogden is the ❹ **Contemporary Arts Center** (CAC; p99), where the cutting edge of contemporary art is exhibited. In contrast to the solid, brick 19th- and early 20th-century architecture of the nearby warehouses, the flash CAC practically screams its modernity to the city.

At the ❺ **Preservation Resource Center** (p101), dedicated to preserving the city's historical character, you can learn all about the deep histories of each of New Orleans' neighborhoods.

Finish this walk at ❻ **Compère Lapin** (p104), a restaurant that fuses the food and folkways of both the Caribbean and Creole Louisiana with a distinctly 21st-century approach to food presentation and sourcing. Bonus: the cocktails are delish.

11am-midnight daily) Walking through Hotel Roosevelt's chandeliered lobby and into the polished glow of the Sazerac Bar, you feel as if you've stepped back into a well-heeled era of hushed wheeling and dealing and high-society drinking. With its art deco murals, subdued lighting and plush couches, the Sazerac Bar is an OK – but over-priced – alternative to the rowdy French Quarter bars nearby.

LUCY'S RETIRED SURFERS BAR
BAR

Map p242 (504-523-8995; www.lucysretired-surfers.com; 701 Tchoupitoulas St; 11am-midnight Mon-Wed, to 2am Thu & Fri, 10am-2am Sat, 10am-midnight Sun) There's always somebody sipping a drink at one of the sidewalk tables at Lucy's, a beach-bum kinda spot oddly plopped in the middle of downtown. It draws the 20- and 30-something crowd, but it's also decent for an after-work drink. Closing time is flexible based on how busy it is.

POLO CLUB LOUNGE
BAR

Map p242 (504-523-6000; 300 Gravier St; 11:30am-midnight Sun-Thu, to 1am Fri & Sat) Need to prep for the fox hunt? Try this bar in the Windsor Court. The overstuffed chairs, tweedy bookshelves, nightly jazz and soft clink of hushed merry-making are meant to evoke aristocratic old England. A wine cobbler or port, anyone?

LOA
LOUNGE

Map p242 (504-553-9550; www.ihhotel.com/loa; 221 Camp St; 5pm-2am) Off the lobby of the fashionable International House hotel, Loa is a stylish, candlelit place to sip a well-crafted cocktail. If you practice voodoo, or you're after a full-coverage religious plan, you can leave an offering at the voodoo altar on your way out. Loa, if you're wondering, are voodoo spirits.

FULTON ALLEY
SPORTS BAR

Map p242 (504-208-5569; www.fultonalley.com; 600 Fulton St; bowling lane rental $30; 4-11pm Mon-Thu, 11am-1am Fri & Sat, 11am-11pm Sun) This is the downtown spot for bowling, bocce (a boules-style game), shuffleboard, foosball and similar activities – basically, a good spot to take friends who want fun sans alcohol. That said, there is a full bar on the premises. It's a bit cheesy and plastic, but it does the trick if you're in the mood for the above sort of games.

ENTERTAINMENT

The venues on S Peters St are within walking distance of several good restaurants, hotels and bars. To make a night of it, grab dinner before a show then see what's happening later on.

CIRCLE BAR
LIVE MUSIC

Map p242 (504-588-2616; www.circlebarneworleans.com; 1032 St Charles Ave; 4pm-2am) Picture a grand Victorian mansion, all disheveled and punk, and you've caught the essence of this strangely inviting place to drink. Live acts of varying quality – folk, rock and indie – occupy the central space, where a little fireplace and lots of grime speak to the coziness of one of New Orleans' great dives.

HOWLIN' WOLF
LIVE MUSIC

Map p242 (504-529-5844; www.thehowlinwolf.com; 907 S Peters St; cover from $5; hours vary) One of New Orleans' better venues for live blues, alt-rock, jazz, comedy and roots music, the Howlin' Wolf draws a lively crowd. The attached 'Den' features smaller acts in a much more intimate venue.

ORPHEUM THEATER
PERFORMING ARTS

Map p242 (504-274-4870; https://orpheumnola.com; 129 Roosevelt Way) Built back in 1918, this Beaux Arts beauty is a grand-dame theater that has undergone many incarnations – vaudeville stage, movie house etc – and is now the home of the Louisiana Philharmonic Orchestra. It also hosts a ton of gigs and performances – it's a popular spot for visiting artists, who love the restored glory of this venue.

LOUISIANA PHILHARMONIC ORCHESTRA
CLASSICAL MUSIC

Map p242 (504-523-6530; www.lpomusic.com; 129 Roosevelt Way, Orpheum Theater) The Louisiana Philharmonic Orchestra is the only musician-owned and -managed professional symphony. It is based out of the Orpheum Theater. The season generally runs from September to May, and tickets range from $20 to $140 for premium box seats.

JOY THEATER
LIVE PERFORMANCE

Map p242 (504-528-9569; www.thejoytheater.com; 1200 Canal St; cover $10-30) This intimate little art deco–style theater is a joy (ha ha) and hosts acts ranging from comedy to

CBD & WAREHOUSE DISTRICT ENTERTAINMENT

brass band shows to EDM (electronic dance music) minifestivals.

REPUBLIC NEW ORLEANS
LIVE MUSIC

Map p242 (☑504-528-8282; www.republicnola. com; 828 S Peters St; cover $10-50; ☺hours vary) Republic showcases some pretty awesome live acts, but on any given night the crowd could range from a bunch of music-obsessed fanatics to some aggro meatheads coming in from the 'burbs. With that said, the curation of acts has gotten better and better over the years and the sight lines to the small stage are awesome.

MERCEDES-BENZ SUPERDOME
STADIUM

Map p242 (☑504-587-3822, 504-587-3663; www.mbsuperdome.com; Sugar Bowl Dr) The Superdome hovers like a giant bronze hubcap between the elevated I-10 freeway and downtown's skyscrapers. The immense indoor stadium, which seats more than 73,200, has hosted NCAA Final Four basketball games, presidential conventions, the Rolling Stones (largest indoor concert in history), Pope John Paul II and seven Super Bowls.

CINEBARRE CANAL PLACE 9
CINEMA

Map p242 (☑888-943-4567; 333 Canal Place, Shops at Canal Place; tickets $12) The screens at this multiplex are small, but if you're without a car in the Quarter or CBD, this is the closest available movie theater. Shows the usual Hollywood fare and the occasional oddball indie screening.

FOUNTAIN LOUNGE
LIVE MUSIC

Map p242 (☑504-648-5486; www.theroosevelt neworleans.com; 130 Roosevelt Way; ☺4-10pm Tue-Thu & Sun, to midnight Fri & Sat) Ever so chic, the Fountain Lounge inside the Roosevelt Hotel is an upscale place to listen to live music, from modern jazz to cool lounge classics. Check online for times.

ENTERGY GIANT
SCREEN THEATER
THEATER

Map p242 (☑504-565-3033; https://audubon natureinstitute.org/theater; 1 Canal St; ☺show-times vary, closed Mon; 🚻) This 5½ story IMAX theater sits beside the Audubon Aquarium of the Americas. It shows frequent nature movies and kid-friendly Hollywood blockbusters. Tickets are included with aquarium admission, but these cannot be used at various special screenings.

HARRAH'S CASINO
CASINO

Map p242 (☑800-427-7247; www.caesars.com/ harrahs-new-orleans; 8 Canal St; ☺24hr) You'd think all manner of vice would be welcome in the Big Easy, but Harrah's, near the foot of Canal St, doesn't get much local love. It's a big casino – 115,000 sq ft for gaming – that's part of a national chain and it pretty much feels exactly like that.

🛍 SHOPPING

This part of town is chiefly concerned with business and art. It's not good for window shopping, but if you know what you're looking for, you may find yourself zeroing in on that perfect little specialty shop.

★OGDEN MUSEUM STORE
ART

Map p242 (☑504-539-9606; http://ogdenmu-seum.org; 925 Camp St; ☺10am-5pm Fri-Wed, to 8pm Thu) The Ogden boasts a very fine museum store, stuffed with prints, crafts and books that explore the theme of regional art. Start with graphite pencils, move on to locally penned coffee table books on New Orleans art and music, then finish with a handcrafted sycamore bowl.

STONEFREE
CLOTHING

Map p242 (☑504-304-5485; http://shopstone-free.com; 611 O'Keefe Ave; ☺10am-8pm Mon-Sat, to 6pm Sun) This hip little boutique feels plucked out of Magazine St – or Brooklyn for that matter. Fun spangly dresses and styles that comfortably juke between vintage and modern are all present and accounted for.

KEIFE AND CO
FOOD & DRINKS

Map p242 (☑504-523-7272; www.keifeandco. com; 801 Howard Ave; ☺10am-8pm Tue-Sat) This chic gastronomic boutique is packed with fancy charcuterie, teas, caviar, condiments, wines, spirits and all the other ingredients of a fairly expensive, if extremely enjoyable picnic.

ARIODANTE
ARTS & CRAFTS

Map p242 (☑504-524-3233; www.ariodantegal-lery.com; 535 Julia St; ☺9:30am-4pm Mon-Sat, to 1:30pm Sun) This small but well-stocked gallery sells jewelry, glass works, ceramics and fine art by local and regional artists. It's a fun place to browse.

MEYER

THE HATTER
FASHION & ACCESSORIES

Map p242 (☑504-525-1048; www.meyerthe hatter.com; 120 St Charles Ave; ☺10am-5:45pm Mon-Sat) This cluttered shop a half-block from Canal St has a truly astounding inventory of world-class hats. Biltmore, Dobbs and Stetson are just a few of the milliners represented. Fur felts dominate in fall and winter, and flimsy straw hats take over in spring and summer. The selection of lids for the ladies isn't as deep.

OUTLET COLLECTION

AT RIVERWALK
MALL

Map p242 (☑504-522-1555; www.riverwalk neworleans.com; 500 Port of New Orleans Pl; ☺10am-9pm Mon-Sat, to 7pm Sun) Got your walking shoes? This outlet mall is half a mile long, stretching from Poydras to Julia St along the river. Retailers include Coach, Crocs, Forever 21, the Guess Factory Store and Neiman Marcus Last Call Studio.

SHOPS AT CANAL PLACE
MALL

Map p242 (☑504-5229200; www.canalplacestyle. com; 333 Canal St; ☺10am-7pm Mon-Fri, to 8pm Sat, noon-7pm Sun) No, you didn't come to New Orleans to shop at Ann Taylor, Brooks Brothers, J Crew or Saks Fifth Avenue, but if someone spills a hurricane over your last white shirt or you forgot to pack your heels, this glossy mall will be a blessing.

The attached parking garage is a good alternative to finding street parking in the Quarter or CBD.

SPORTS & ACTIVITIES

ESCAPE MY ROOM

NEW ORLEANS
LIVE CHALLENGE

Map p242 (☑504-475-7580; https://escape myroom.com; 633 Constance St; tickets $30) If you're not familiar with the Escape My Room concept, it goes like this: you and a team (of two to eight) are locked in a room. You scavenger hunt for clues to escape said room within a time limit. This local twist on the escape room genre is gorgeous, utilizing old art and history to deliver classic mystery scenarios.

St Charles Avenue Streetcar

The clang and swoosh of the St Charles Avenue Streetcar is as essential to Uptown and the Garden District as live oaks and mansions. New Orleanians are justifiably proud of their moving monument, which began life as the nation's second horse-drawn streetcar line, the New Orleans & Carrollton Railroad, in 1835.

Laying the Line

In 1893 the line was among the first streetcar systems in the country to be electrified. Now it is one of the few streetcars in the USA to have survived the automobile era. Millions of passengers utilize the streetcar every day despite the fact the city's bus service tends to be faster. In many ways, the streetcar is the quintessential vehicle for New Orleans public transportation: slow, pretty and, if not entirely efficient, extremely atmospheric.

Another streetcar line plies Canal St and you should ride it but, if we're honest, the route isn't as pretty as the St Charles line. There are plans to build a new line from Canal St, up Rampart St to Elysian Fields Ave.

Along the Avenue

It's only slightly hyperbolic to claim St Charles Ave is the most beautiful street in the USA. Once you enter the Garden District, the entire street is shaded under a tunnel of big, old live oak trees that look like they could have wiped the floor with an orc army in a Tolkien novel.

1. The St Charles Avenue Streetcar **2.** St Charles Avenue during Carnival season **3.** A historic home on St Charles Avenue

Gorgeous houses, barely concealed behind the trees, house the most aristocratic elite of the city. Those same elite often ride in the floats that proceed along St Charles during Carnival season; look up to the tree branches and you'll see many are laden with shiny beads tossed from Mardi Gras floats. Within the Neutral Ground, or median space that houses the streetcar tracks, you'll often see joggers and families passing through the verdant corridor. By far the best way of experiencing this cityscape is via the slow, antique rumble of the streetcar; free from driving, your eyes are free to gaze on all the beauty.

A STREETCAR NAMED DESIRE

Tennessee Williams' play *A Streetcar Named Desire* is the most famous stage (and, arguably, film) depiction of New Orleans. The story follows Blanche Dubois as she moves in with her sister, Stella, and brother-in-law, Stanley Kowalski. In the ensuing drama, everyone gets along and no one suffers crippling emotional trauma. Just kidding! Of course, it's the reverse.

The name of the play derives from both the flawed desire of the characters and the actual streetcar that ran to Desire St. That streetcar has been replaced by the No 80 Desire–Louisa bus line, which, sadly, lacks Marlon Brando screaming in a tank top.

Garden, Lower Garden & Central City

Neighborhood Top Five

❶ Lafayette Cemetery No 1 (p114) Learning about the past at this cemetery, where above-ground crypts hold tragic tales draped with vines and spreading tree roots.

❷ Southern Food & Beverage Museum (p115) Studying BBQ, hot sauce

and absinthe in this temple to Southern gastronomy.

❸ McKenna Museum of African American Art (p116) Wandering past paintings of local musicians, political icons and Mardi Gras festivities.

❹ Magazine Street (p123) Popping into the fashion and clothing boutiques as

well as the art galleries, music shops and day spas that line the city's largest shopping street.

❺ Bar Crawls (p120) Wandering and imbibing at spots such as Bulldog along Magazine St and St Charles Ave, which are both perfect for a nightlife expedition.

For more detail of this area see Map p246 ➡

Explore Garden, Lower Garden & Central City

The Garden District, Lower Garden District and Central City are three distinct neighborhoods, each offering a different experience. Two days is enough to explore all three.

The Garden District exudes Old Southern excess with its historic mansions, lush greenery, chichi bistros and upscale boutiques. Your first morning, soak up the mixture of fecund tropical beauty and white-columned old-money elegance on a walking tour, where stately homes and colorful gardens shimmer beside sidewalks bursting with roots. The Garden District is a rectangular grid bounded by St Charles Ave, Jackson Ave, Magazine St and Louisiana Ave. Magazine St and St Charles Ave are the main commercial thoroughfares; Prytania St is the most scenic (and the quickest).

Between the CBD and the Garden District, the Lower Garden District is somewhat like the Garden District but not quite as posh. Here the houses are pleasant, not palatial. There's a studenty vibe, and plenty of bars and restaurants for those with university-stunted wallets and university-sized appetites for fun. The Lower Garden District is upriver (in this case, south) from the CBD. Magazine St is the main thoroughfare.

Central City, which lies between the CBD and Lower Garden District, is very much in transition. While there are large stretches of urban blight here, there is also a wonderful concentration of community activist organizations rebuilding what was once one of the city's most important African American neighborhoods. It is also home to the Southern Food & Beverage Museum (p115), found on the area's main thoroughfare, Oretha Castle Haley Blvd.

Local Life

Breakfast joints At Surrey's Juice Bar (p116), everything's seriously good, from the boudin (spicy sausage) to the shrimp and grits. The vibe is rock and roll at Slim Goodie's (p119), but the crowd is all ages.

Commander's Palace Every New Orleanian has a story about celebrating a big occasion at this Creole restaurant (p119). And they know 'dressing up' adds to the fun.

Neighborhood bars Some call 'em dive bars, others call 'em home. These scruffy joints typically offer TV, pool tables, dartboards and cheap beer.

Getting There & Away

Bus Bus 11 runs along Magazine St from Canal St to Audubon Park.

Streetcar The St Charles Avenue Streetcar travels through the CBD, the Garden District and Uptown.

Lonely Planet's Top Tip

Avoid parking hassles on Magazine St by using public transportation. From the French Quarter and CBD, hop on the St Charles Avenue Streetcar at Canal St in the morning, then catch bus 11 on Magazine St to return to your hotel in the afternoon.

✕ Best Places to Eat

➡ Surrey's Juice Bar (p116)
➡ Stein's Deli (p116)
➡ Coquette (p119)
➡ Commander's Palace (p119)

For reviews, see p116 ➡

🔒 Best Places to Shop

➡ GoGo Jewelry (p123)
➡ Aidan Gill for Men (p123)
➡ Funky Monkey (p123)
➡ Tchoup Industries (p122)

For reviews, see p122 ➡

🛏 Best Places to Sleep

➡ Creole Gardens (p184)
➡ Henry Howard Hotel (p185)
➡ Garden District B&B (p184)

For reviews, see p184 ➡

🍷 Best Nightlife

➡ Bulldog (p120)
➡ Avenue Pub (p120)
➡ Barrel Proof (p120)

For reviews, see p120 ➡

GARDEN, LOWER GARDEN & CENTRAL CITY

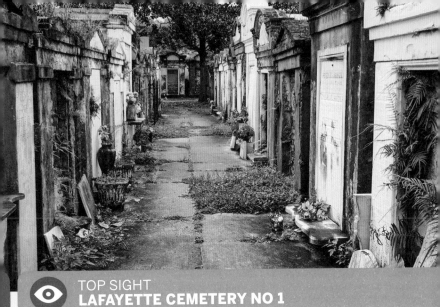

TOP SIGHT
LAFAYETTE CEMETERY NO 1

A thick wall surrounds a battalion of gray crypts at this moody place, a tiny bastion of history, tragedy and Southern Gothic charm in the heart of the Garden District.

Established in 1833 by the former City of Lafayette, the cemetery is divided by two intersecting footpaths that form a cross. Look out for the structures built by fraternal organizations such as the Jefferson Fire Company No 22, which took care of its members and their families in large shared crypts. Some of the wealthier family tombs were built of marble, with elaborate detail rivaling the finest architecture in the district, but most tombs were constructed simply of inexpensive plastered brick. You'll notice many German and Irish names on the above-ground graves, testifying that immigrants were devastated by 19th-century yellow-fever epidemics.

In July 1995, author Anne Rice staged her own funeral here. She hired a horse-drawn hearse and a brass band to play dirges, and wore an antique wedding dress as she laid down in a coffin. The event coincided with the release of one of Rice's novels.

On your visit, you might find that the spell cast by the cemetery is broken the moment a black-and-white-clad waiter strides past its grated gates, hurrying to his shift at the neighboring Commander's Palace restaurant. He's a vivid reminder that time marches on and that, yes, perhaps you are ready for lunch and a 25¢ martini. This is New Orleans after all.

DON'T MISS
➡ Social society crypts
➡ Save Our Cemeteries tour

PRACTICALITIES
➡ Map p246
➡ ☎504-658-3781
➡ Washington Ave, at Prytania St
➡ admission free
➡ ⊘7am-3pm

⊙ SIGHTS

There's joy to be had just wandering around the Garden and Lower Garden Districts. In the former neighborhood, you'll find grand homes and palatial villas. The Lower Garden District also has its share of attractive architecture – look out for the area's signature double-story townhouses. In both areas, sights are concentrated near Magazine St and St Charles Ave. Central City was once a magnet for African American businesses and social clubs. This neighborhood underwent degradation following desegregation, but its main thoroughfare, Oretha Castle Haley Blvd, is undergoing a steady renaissance.

LAFAYETTE CEMETERY NO 1   CEMETERY
See p114.

BLAINE KERN'S
MARDI GRAS WORLD   MUSEUM
(☑504-475-2057; www.mardigrasworld.com; 1380 Port of New Orleans Pl; adult/senior/child 2-11yr $22/17/14; ☺tours 9am-5:30pm, last tour 4pm; P ♿) We dare say Mardi Gras World is one of the happiest places in New Orleans by day – but at night it must turn into a terrifying fun-house. It's all those *faces:* the dragons, clowns, kings and fairies, leering and dead-eyed. That said, we love touring Mardi Gras World – the studio-warehouse of Blaine Kern (Mr Mardi Gras) and family, who have been making jaw-dropping parade floats since 1947. Tours last about 90 minutes, and are given by a crew of knowledgeable, personable docents.

There are never less than 2000 props in the inventory, and the company builds about 50 or 60 new ones each year. Kern learned the trade from his father and passed it down to his sons.

If you're staying at a nearby hotel, you may be able to catch the company's free shuttle. Otherwise, parking costs $10 in the lot beside the entrance.

SOUTHERN FOOD
& BEVERAGE MUSEUM   MUSEUM
Map p246 (☑504-569-0405; www.natfab.org/southern-food-and-beverage; 1504 Oretha Castle Haley Blvd; adult/child under 12yr $10.50/free; ☺11am-5:30pm Wed-Mon) You don't have to be a gourmet or mixologist to enjoy this made-from-scratch museum, which celebrates Southern cooking and cocktails with

exhibits – some fascinating, others less so – sourced from every state south of the Mason-Dixon line. The well-stocked **Museum of the American Cocktail** displays old elixir bottles, cocktail-making tools, tiki glasses and old pictures of impressively mustachioed bartenders. Check the website for details about cooking classes in the demo kitchen.

ASHÉ CULTURAL
ARTS CENTER   ARTS CENTER
Map p246 (☑504-603-6394; www.ashecac.org; 1712 Oretha Castle Haley Blvd; ☺10am-6pm Mon-Sat) An important anchor for the local African American community, Ashé (from a Yoruba word that could loosely be translated as 'Amen') regularly showcases performances, art and photography exhibitions, movie screenings and lectures with an African, African American or Caribbean focus, and beyond. Check the online calendar for upcoming events.

The on-site Diaspora Boutique (p123), which stocks clothing, earrings and crafts, is also worth a look.

IRISH CHANNEL   AREA
Map p246 The name Irish Channel is a bit of a misnomer. Although this historic neighborhood, which borders the Garden Districts, was settled by poor Irish immigrants fleeing the 1840s potato famine, many German and African American residents coexisted here in a multicultural gumbo. This is a rapidly gentrifying cluster of shotgun houses, and in general it's pleasant for ambling, although you should exercise caution at night.

The area runs between Magazine St to the north, the Mississippi River to the south, Toledano St to the west and, depending on who you ask, First or Jackson St to the east. Come St Patrick's Day, a big block party takes over Constance St in front of Parasol's (p116).

COLISEUM SQUARE   PARK
Map p246 (1708 Coliseum St; ☺24hr) Much of the Lower Garden District was designed as a settlement zone for those Americans who began arriving in New Orleans after the Louisiana Purchase. Coliseum Square was envisaged as a sort of triangular village green for these residents and, to be fair, the space still serves as a center of gravity and recreational area for locals looking for fresh air. The park does attract the occasional shady hanger-on come nightfall.

MCKENNA MUSEUM
OF AFRICAN AMERICAN ART   MUSEUM

Map p246 (☎504-323-5074; www.themckenna-museum.com; 2003 Carondelet St; adult/student $5/3; ⊙by appointment) Although the displayed work at this beautiful two-story institution comes from all over the African diaspora, most of it was created by local New Orleans artists. Images of Mardi Gras and the New Orleans music scene are highlights. The artwork is part of a collection amassed over some 30 years by Dr Dwight McKenna, a local physician, politician and the first black coroner in the city's history. Visiting is by appointment only – call well ahead.

ST VINCENT'S
INFANT ASYLUM   HISTORIC BUILDING

Map p246 (☎504-666-8300; www.frenchquarterphantoms.com; 1507 Magazine St; tour $50; ⊙tours 7pm & 10pm Wed-Sun) This large red-brick orphanage was built in 1864 with assistance from federal troops occupying the city. It helped relieve the overcrowded orphanages filled with youngsters of all races who had lost their parents to epidemics and the Civil War. The orphanage is a guesthouse these days (not recommended), and can be visited on a two-hour tour with the tour company French Quarter Phantoms.

EATING

Foodies can pick and choose from Vietnamese soup shops, old-line Creole cafes, great sandwich shops and some truly excellent breakfast joints. With a high student population, there's a decidedly young, hip and economical bent to the food on offer in the Lower Garden. There's not as much variety in the Garden District – just some of the most storied restaurants in the country. Central City's renaissance is evident in the form of new restaurants – ranging from old-school cheap spots to fancier new food-court-style options – arrayed along Oretha Castle Haley Blvd.

★SURREY'S JUICE BAR   AMERICAN $

Map p246 (☎504-524-3828; www.surreysnola.com; 1418 Magazine St; mains $6.50-13; ⊙8am-3pm; ☑) Surrey's makes a simple bacon-and-egg sandwich taste – and look – like the most delicious breakfast you've ever been served. And you know what? It proba-

bly *is* the best. Boudin biscuits; eggs scrambled with salmon; biscuits swimming in salty sausage gravy; and a shrimp, grits and bacon dish that should be illegal. And the juice, as you might guess, is blessedly fresh.

Surrey's has an Uptown branch with the same menu and hours at 4807 Magazine St.

★STEIN'S DELI   DELI $

Map p246 (☎504-527-0771; www.steinsdeli.net; 2207 Magazine St; sandwiches $7-13; ⊙7am-7pm Tue-Fri, 9am-5pm Sat & Sun) You may get a no-nonsense 'what?' when you step up to the counter, but it's just part of the schtick at this scruffy deli. For quality sandwiches, cheese and cold cuts, this is as good as the city gets. Owner Dan Stein is fanatical about keeping his deli stocked with great Italian and Jewish meats and cheeses, and fine boutique beers.

DRYADES PUBLIC MARKET   MARKET $

Map p246 (☎504-644-4841; http://dryadespublicmarket.com; 1307 Oretha Castle Haley Blvd; hot plates $8-13; ⊙8am-8pm Mon-Thu, to 9pm Fri & Sat, to 6pm Sun; ☑) This enormous market is stocked with fresh groceries representing a good range of local vendors, and there are several hot-food bars – the menu varies, but it's invariably good (and good value). On some days we've had great oysters and fried chicken here, on others, excellent teriyaki. Grab some groceries for a picnic too.

POKE LOA   HAWAIIAN $

Map p246 (☎504-309-9993; www.eatpokeloa.com; 3341 Magazine St; mains $11.50-15; ⊙11am-9pm; ☑) A welcome and popular addition to the New Orleans dining firmament, Poke Loa brings Hawaiian-style *poke* bowls (raw fish mixed with vegetables, spices, sauces and other bits of goodness) to Magazine St. There are over 15 toppings and tons of protein and green options to round out your bowl, but the end result is invariably tasty.

PARASOL'S   SANDWICHES $

Map p246 (☎504-302-1533; 2533 Constance St; po'boys $7-16; ⊙11am-9pm) Parasol's isn't just in the Irish Channel neighborhood; it sort of *is* the Irish Channel, serving as community center, nexus of gossip and watering hole. It's first and foremost a bar, but you can order some of the best po'boy sandwiches in town from the seating area in the back. That big ol' roast beef is a messy, juice-filled conduit of deliciousness.

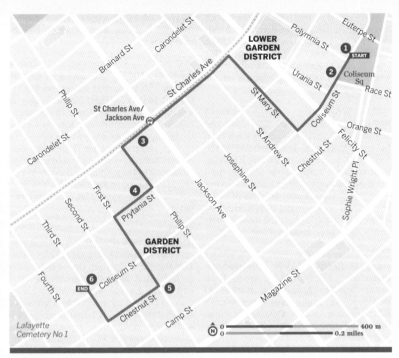

Neighborhood Walk
Garden District Stroll

START GOODRICH-STANLEY HOUSE
END WALTER GRINNAN ROBINSON HOUSE
LENGTH 1 MILE; 2½ HOURS

At 1729 Coliseum St, the historic double-gallery ❶ **Goodrich-Stanley House** was built in 1837 by jeweler William M Goodrich. Goodrich sold the house to the British-born merchant Henry Home Stanley, whose adopted son, Henry Morton Stanley, went on to win fame for finding the missing Scottish missionary, Dr David Livingstone.

At 1749 Coliseum St, behind a handsome wrought-iron fence, ❷ **Grace King House** was named for the Louisiana historian and author who lived here from 1905 to 1932. It was built in 1847 by banker Frederick Rodewald, and features Greek Ionic columns on the lower floor as well as Corinthian columns above. Like the Goodrich-Stanley House, it's not open to the public.

The ❸ **House of Broel**, built in the 1850s, is a bit madcap. The entire two-story building was elevated in 1884 to allow for the construction of a new first floor; the owner wanted to throw elaborate parties for his three daughters. Today the house showcases gowns and an astounding collection of highly detailed dollhouses.

At 2343 Prytania St, the ❹ **McGehee School for Girls**, formerly the Bradish Johnson House, looks like a stately opera house that was dropped into the heart of the Garden District. The 1872 building was designed by James Freret in the Second Empire style, an architectural school not known for its subtlety.

If the home at 1239 First St looks like it could house an aristocratic vampire or a cabal of witches, you've either got a great imagination or have read Anne Rice. This home, known as the ❺ **Brevard-Rice House**, used to be the author's residence. The 1857 Greek Revival masterpiece has two stories of columns and wrought-iron balconies.

The columned double-decker ❻ **Walter Grinnan Robinson House** sticks out on a relatively modest block of Third St like an exceptionally ornate sore thumb. It was built in 1859 and designed by the famed Irish New Orleans architect Henry Howard.

There's a mad cast of characters both behind and at the bar, but don't feel threatened; all in all this is one of the friendliest neighborhood spots in New Orleans. This place is also St Paddy's Day headquarters, when a huge block party happens on the street.

MAIS AREPAS
COLOMBIAN $

Map p246 (☑504-523-6247; 1200 Carondelet St; mains $8-20; ⊙11:30am-2:30pm & 6-9:45pm Tue-Sat, 6-9:15pm Sun) If the cuisine of the Southern US isn't far enough south for you, head to South America via Mais Arepas. Their specialty is, unsurprisingly, arepas (corn cakes) topped with all sorts of goodies: chicken, avocado and lime juice; fried oysters and salsa; and grilled steak, onions and black beans – to name a few examples.

SEED
HEALTH FOOD $

Map p246 (☑504-302-2599; www.seedyour-health.com; 1330 Prytania St; mains $7-14; ⊙11am-10pm Mon-Fri, from 10am Sat & Sun; 🍴) Vegetarians and vegans can now nosh with abandon in New Orleans, just like their more carnivorous friends. This spare and boxy addition to the Lower Garden District calls its menu 'garden-based' and whips up delicious salads and sandwiches plus a few heartier mains, such as vegetarian spaghetti and pad Thai. Blended juices and cocktails, all made with fresh juice, add to the fun.

CAFÉ RECONCILE
DINER $

Map p246 (☑504-568-1157; http://reconcile-neworleans.org; 1631 Oretha Castle Haley Blvd; mains $6-15; ⊙11am-2:30pm Mon-Fri) 🍴 Café Reconcile fights the good fight by recruiting and training at-risk youth to work as kitchen and floor staff. The food is simple and, frankly, really good. It's very much of the humble New Orleans school of home cookery: red beans and rice, fried chicken, shrimp Creole and the like, with the spotlight on daily specials.

SUCRÉ
SWEETS $

Map p246 (☑504-520-8311; www.shopsucre. com; 3025 Magazine St; confectionary $2-9; ⊙9am-10pm Sun-Thu, to 11pm Fri & Sat) Willy Wonka's chocolate factory has put away its top-hat and purple suede coat and gone decidedly upscale. Artisanal chocolates, chocolate bars, toffee, marshmallows, gelato and other confections beckon from behind the glass counter. One macaroon will

set you back $2 – but you can gain comfort from the fact that Sucré is widely considered the best chocolate in town.

DISTRICT
PASTRIES $

Map p246 (☑504-570-6945; www.donutsandsliders.com; 2209 Magazine St; donuts & pastries $3-6, sliders $4-11; ⊙7am-9pm) District makes us feel naughty – and we like it. In the morning, truly decadent donuts lure customers to the counter – we enjoyed the piled-high cookies and cream. After 11am, fancy sliders step onto the scene; fortunately they are also small, so the guilt is not overwhelming. Note that the 'brew' here is coffee, not beer.

If the fried-oyster slider is available, get it.

SLICE
PIZZA $

Map p246 (☑504-525-7437; www.slicepizzeria. com; 1513 St Charles Ave; pizzas $13-23; ⊙11am-11pm Mon-Sat, to 10pm Sun) One of those places you'll find yourself returning to again and again if you're staying in the Lower Garden District for more than a few days. Highlights? Nice staff, happy-hour specials and damn good pizza. Toppings for the thin-crust pies can be as artisanal or run-of-the-mill as you like. Slices start at at $3.

TRACEY'S
SANDWICHES $

Map p246 (☑504-897-5413; www.traceysnola. com; 2604 Magazine St; mains $9-15; ⊙11am-10pm Sun-Thu, to midnight Fri & Sat, bar 11am-late) This neighborhood bar, known for its roast-beef po'boys, is where you go to watch the Saints play on a lazy Sunday afternoon – the joint's got 20 TVs. Order your pub grub at the window, grab a buzzer, then settle in until you're buzzed (in both senses of the word).

The crowd sitting outside can look kind of scruffy, but c'mon in – it's a welcoming place. The trendy exposed-brick wall will give urban hipsters a modicum of comfort, and parasols hang from the ceiling.

BIG FISHERMAN SEAFOOD
SEAFOOD $

Map p246 (☑504-897-9907; 3301 Magazine St; crawfish from $4; ⊙11am-6pm Mon-Fri, from 10am Sat, 10am-5pm Sun) If you're here in the spring during crawfish season, you may develop a taste for the little mudbugs. But you haven't had the full-on crawfish experience unless you've been invited to a crawfish boil in someone's backyard. This busy little shop will pack some up for you so you can carry 'em back to your own bungalow or someone else's.

Prices fluctuate, so call ahead – depending on the time of year and the harvest, a pound of cooked crawfish goes for around $4 to $6.

JUAN'S FLYING BURRITO
MEXICAN $

Map p246 (☎504-569-0000; www.juansflyingburrito.com; 2018 Magazine St; mains $7-15; ⊙11am-10pm Sun-Thu, to 11pm Fri & Sat) The answer to that perennial question, 'What happens when you cross a bunch of skinny-jeans-clad hipsters with a tortilla?', is (ta da) Juan's. The food is about as authentically Mexican as Ontario, but that doesn't mean it's not good; the hefty burritos pack a satisfying punch. The margaritas are tasty and the quesadilla comes with ground beef, bacon and blue cheese – yes, please.

SLIM GOODIE'S DINER
DINER $

Map p246 (☎504-891-3447; 3322 Magazine St; mains $5.50-16; ⊙6am-3pm) The grease is as prevalent as the '70s rock in this laid-back place, where hipsters in dirty tennis shoes serve hipsters in wool caps. Burgers, shakes, American breakfasts and other short-order standards anchor the menu. It's good, if not exactly awe-inspiring. And we jest about the hipsters – they're just the most eye-catching folks in the all-ages, all-fashion crowd.

★COQUETTE
FRENCH $$

Map p246 (☎504-265-0421; www.coquettenola.com; 2800 Magazine St; brunch mains $13-23, dinner mains $20-30; ⊙5:30-10pm Mon-Fri, 10:30am-2pm & 5:30-10pm Sat & Sun) Coquette mixes wine-bar ambience with friendly service and a bit of white linen; the result is a candlelit place where you don't feel bad getting tipsy. Explore beyond the respectable wine menu, though – there's some great Louisiana-sourced food here, often with an innovative global spin. Choices may include charred broccoli and kohlrabi, or speckled trout with shrimp and sausage dressing.

The small plates are eclectic and highly recommended. Menus change daily. At the low-key but inviting bar, you might just find yourself seated beside a recognizable TV actor, dining and relaxing after a day on set.

CENTRAL CITY BBQ
BARBECUE $$

Map p246 (☎504-558-4276; http://centralcitybbq.com; 1201 S Rampart St; mains $11-20; ⊙11am-9pm) 'Who does the best barbecue in town' is a subject of low-intensity foodie debate in New Orleans, but Central City BBQ is a respectable answer. The spot is the love-child of two local chefs with a passion for barbecue and wood smoke. The interior is airy and modern by New Orleans standards, and the food is on point.

While you may find burnt ends (meat cut from the 'point' of the brisket that soaks up a ton of flavor) at other barbecue spots, Central City has a particular passion for these holy grails of the carnivore firmament.

CASA BORREGA
MEXICAN $$

Map p246 (☎504-427-0654; http://casaborrega.com; 1719 Oretha Castle Haley Blvd; lunch mains $7-12, dinner mains $11-24; ⊙11am-9:30pm Tue-Thu, to 10:30pm Fri & Sat, to 3pm Sun) Borrega is a good Mexican restaurant, yes. It's also a concert venue and a gallery for Latin American art that ranges from striking contemporary to colorful folk. Beyond all of this, Casa Borrega has become a major center of community gravity for the Latino New Orleans community. Also, the shrimp in butter-garlic-tequila sauce is *fantastic*.

SAKE CAFÉ UPTOWN
JAPANESE $$

Map p246 (☎504-894-0033; www.sakecafeonmagazine.com; 2830 Magazine St; sushi $3.75-18, mains $12-16.25; ⊙11:30am-10:30pm Mon-Thu, to 11:30pm Fri & Sat, 12:30pm-10:30pm Sun) Believe it or not, fish in this town doesn't have to come fried, swimming in a thick sauce or stuffed with bacon, crawfish or crabmeat. Sake Uptown (the original is in Metairie) serves decent sushi that's popular with the young types who populate the Lower Garden District and surrounds.

★COMMANDER'S PALACE
CREOLE $$$

Map p246 (☎504-899-8221; www.commanderspalace.com; 1403 Washington Ave; dinner mains $32-43; ⊙11:30am-1pm & 6:30-10:30pm Mon-Fri, from 11am Sat, from 10am Sun) Commander's Palace is a dapper host, a seer-suckered bon vivant who wows with white-linen dining rooms, decadent dishes and attentive Southern hospitality. The nouveau Creole menu shifts, and can run from crispy oysters with brie-cauliflower fondue to pecan-crusted gulf fish. The dress code adds to the charm: no shorts or T-shirts, and jackets preferred at dinner. It's a *very* nice place – and lots of fun.

Owner Ella Brennan takes pride in her ability to promote her chefs to stardom; Paul Prudhomme and Emeril Lagasse are among her alumni. And note that some of that stiff-upper-lip formality is put on; the lunch special, after all, is the 25¢ martini. Reservations are required.

DRINKING & NIGHTLIFE

Bars in this part of New Orleans tend to attract a youngish student and post-student crowd. Magazine St is, in its way, as much fun as Bourbon and Frenchmen Sts in the French Quarter and Faubourg Marigny neighborhoods. It's wild without being ridiculous or idiotic and, while it lacks Frenchmen's live-music scene, it makes up for that with a better variety of bars.

AVENUE PUB   PUB
Map p246 (☑504-586-9243; www.theavenuepub.com; 1732 St Charles Ave; ⊙24hr) From the street, this scruffy pub looks like a nothing-special neighborhood dive. But with more than 40 beers on tap and another 135-odd in bottles, plus staff with serious dedication to the taste of their drafts, this two-story beer bar is earning national accolades. The upstairs patio is a fine place to watch the world go by.

BULLDOG   BAR
Map p246 (☑504-891-1516; http://bulldog.draftfreak.com; 3236 Magazine St; ⊙11:30am-2am) With 40 or so brews on tap and more than 100 by the bottle or can – from Louisiana and Mexico to Italy and points beyond – the Bulldog works hard to keep beer enthusiasts happy. The best place to sink a pint is the courtyard, which gets packed with the young and beautiful almost every evening when the weather is warm.

VERRET'S LOUNGE   BAR
Map p246 (☑504-895-9640; 1738 Washington Ave; ⊙3pm-3am Sun-Thu, to 4am Fri & Sat) This is the kind of old-school dive where you'd expect to find a bunch of retirees propping up the bar. Instead, the clientele is a younger (not student young) crowd, enjoying cheap, strong drinks and the strung up Christmas lights.

BARREL PROOF   BAR
Map p246 (☑504-299-1888; www.barrelproofnola.com; 1201 Magazine St; ⊙4pm-1am Sun-Thu, to 2am Fri & Sat) Do you like whiskey? We

sincerely hope so, because there are almost 300 to pick from here, including smoky, smooth and sublime. The crowd is young professional and dressed to impress, but the ties loosen up as the brown liquor flows. Plenty of other spirits and beers on tap as well.

URBAN SOUTH   MICROBREWERY
Map p246 (☑504-267-4852; http://urbansouthbrewery.com; 1645 Tchoupitoulas St; ⊙4-9pm Mon-Wed, from noon Thu & Fri, from 11am Sat & Sun; ⊕) In an industrial dystopia of warehouses and concrete jungle, you'll find a big, booming beer hall packed with happy folks and, yes, laughing kids. Urban South keeps a couple of things on tap, as it were – over a dozen award-winning beers, and a children's play area with daycare, donated toys and an old arcade game.

They offer free brewery tours at 5pm and 7pm on Friday, 3pm, 5pm and 7pm on Saturday, and 2pm and 4pm on Sunday.

COURTYARD BREWERY   MICROBREWERY
Map p246 (www.courtyardbrewing.com; 1020 Erato St; ⊙4:30-9:30pm Mon-Wed, 11am-10:30pm Thu-Sat, 11am-9:30pm Sun; ⊕) Beyond their home-brewed products, Courtyard also carries a few dozen beers from around the world, and hosts a regular, rotating slate of food trucks. Pets and kids are welcome and have a great time running around, although not as much as their parents and owners.

NOLA BREWING   BREWERY
(☑504-301-1117; www.nolabrewing.com; 3001 Tchoupitoulas St; ⊙taproom 11am-11pm, tours 2-3pm Fri, 2-4pm Sat & Sun) This cavernous brewery welcomes guests throughout the weekend for a free brewery tour that kicks off with sloshy cups of craft brew and a food truck or two out front. The rest of the week? Stop by the taproom, which has plenty of beers on tap and a roof deck.

As for the brewery tour, it's a high-energy gathering of youngish folks and beer enthusiasts who want to get gently buzzed and hang out in a festival-like setting – and maybe learn about beer. Beloved originals include the NOLA Blonde and the Hopitoulas.

HIVOLT COFFEE   CAFE
Map p246 (☑504-324-8818; http://hivoltcoffee.com; 1829 Sophie Wright Pl; ⊙7am-5pm; ⊛) A clean, airy interior and excellent shots of espresso – plus a great counter of baked

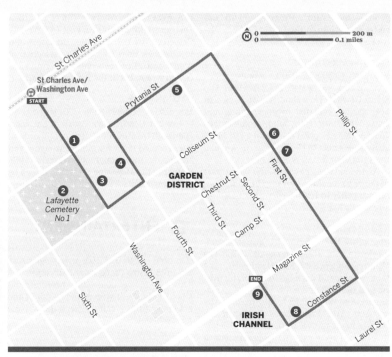

Neighborhood Walk
Green, Green New Orleans

START THE RINK
FINISH TRACEY'S
LENGTH 1 MILE; TWO TO THREE HOURS

Soak up the 'green' of New Orleans, from the historic, magnolia-shaded streets of the Garden District to the Emerald Isle heritage of the Irish Channel.

From the CBD, take the St Charles Avenue Streetcar to Washington Ave. Walk one block south to **1 The Rink**, an 1880s skating rink turned 21st-century mini-mall. **2 Lafayette Cemetery No 1** (p114), one of the city's oldest cemeteries, stands across Prytania St, as does the dapper **3 Commander's Palace** (p119), the elegant crown jewel of the Brennan restaurant empire. Around the corner at 1448 Fourth St is **4 Colonel Robert Short's House**, designed by architect Henry Howard. Once the home of a Confederate officer, it's an exemplary double-gallery home with fine cast-iron details.

Continue to the **5 Women's Guild of the New Orleans Opera Association** at 2504 Prytania, a Greek Revival home designed by William Freret in the late 1850s.

Turn right onto First St where you'll find **6 Joseph Carroll House** at No 1315, a beautiful center-hall house with double galleries laced with cast iron. At the back there's a similarly impressive carriage house.

The grand home at 1239 First St is the former residence of author Anne Rice. The spinner of vampire tales lived in the 1857 home, known as the **7 Brevard-Rice House**, for many years, and regularly invited fans to tour inside. Which, by the way, is beautiful but disappointingly free of bats, organ music and Tom Cruise mooning about in a frilly jacket. It's no longer open to the public.

As you move upriver from First St, homes quickly become shotgun shacks. This is the Irish Channel, home to working-class Irish, German and African American communities. Head down First St, turn right into Constance and wander along until you come to **8 Parasol's** (p116) on the corner of Third St and **9 Tracey's** (p118) on the corner of Third and Magazine Sts. These are two quintessential New Orleans neighborhood bars with dueling roast-beef po'boy sandwiches. Dig in.

goods – makes for an excellent wi-fi and coffee emporium in the Lower Garden District.

SAINT BAR & LOUNGE
BAR

Map p246 (☎504-523-0500; www.thesaintneworleans.com; 961 St Mary St; ☉7pm-late) The Saint? Of what? How about a great backyard beer garden enclosed in duck blinds and filled with tattooed young professionals, Tulane students, good shots and a fair bit of attitude. It's not the cleanest bar (nickname: the Taint), but it sure is a fun one.

As the bartender told us, the worst part of the city's smoking ban may be that, 'People are going to realize what this place really smells like.'

RENDEZVOUS
BAR

Map p246 (☎504-891-1777; www.therendezvoustavern.com; 3101 Magazine St; ☉3pm-late Mon-Fri, from 1pm Sat & Sun) Dartboard, pool table, a long and dark bar, old-looking mirrors on the wall and a few video poker machines. And Billy Squier's *The Stroke* on the speakers. Yup, Rendezvous meets all the requirements for a legitimate New Orleans dive bar. This locals' hangout attracts a mixed bag of college students and yuppies, plus a few outliers to keep it real.

HALF MOON
BAR

Map p246 (☎504-522-0599; www.halfmoongrillnola.com; 1125 St Mary St; ☉5pm-2am) On an interesting corner, just half a block from Magazine St, the Half Moon beckons with a cool neighborhood vibe. This dive bar is good for a beer, short-order meal or an evening shooting stick. Look for the sweet neon sign. Hours can be fungible, but they try to keep the kitchen open as long as the bar is open.

IGOR'S LOUNGE
BAR

Map p246 (☎504-568-9786; 2133 St Charles Ave; ☉24hr) Play pool, tap your foot to the rock on the speakers *and* do your laundry? Yep, and you know it's time to leave this dive if the sinuous bar counter starts looking straight. Igor's constant rotation of characters makes it a good place to drop into, or make it your terminus if staying nearby.

STILL PERKIN'
CAFE

Map p246 (☎504-899-0335; 2727 Prytania St; ☉7am-6pm Mon-Fri, 8am-6pm Sat, to 5pm Sun; ☎) Perched on the corner of Prytania St and Washington Ave, this bright coffee shop

is a great place to start or finish a Garden District walking tour or a visit to Lafayette Cemetery No 1. In addition to lattes and iced coffees, there's a decadent selection of scones and other treats plus a few sandwiches and wraps. It's in the Rink mini-mall.

BALCONY BAR
BAR

Map p246 (☎504-894-8888; 3201 Magazine St; ☉4pm-2am Mon-Thu, noon-3am Fri & Sat, noon-2pm Sun) This student-centric neighborhood bar is a good place for pizza, carousing and sitting on the eponymous balcony while watching the Magazine St parade march by on balmy nights. The kitchen is open late.

 ENTERTAINMENT

ZEITGEIST
CINEMA

Map p246 (☎504-352-1150; www.zeitgeistnola.org; 1618 Oretha Castle Haley Blvd; tickets $8) This old movie house has been around since the 1920s. It screens independent and art-house films – call or check the website for a schedule.

 SHOPPING

Magazine St is by far New Orleans' best shopping strip, and as a center for commercial activity it begins in the Lower Garden District, near its intersection with Felicity St. From here, you can follow Magazine west all the way to Audubon Park and shop or window browse in antiques stores and boutiques almost the entire way.

★TRASHY DIVA
CLOTHING

Map p246 (☎504-299-8777; www.trashydiva.com; 2048 Magazine St; ☉noon-6pm Mon-Fri, from 11am Sat, 1-5pm Sun) It isn't really as scandalous as the name suggests, except by Victorian standards. Diva's specialty is sassy 1940s- and '50s-style cinched, hourglass dresses and Belle Époque undergarments – lots of corsets, lace and such. The shop also features Kabuki–inspired dresses with embroidered dragons, and retro tops, skirts and shawls reflecting styles plucked from just about every era.

TCHOUP INDUSTRIES
SPORTS & OUTDOORS

Map p246 (☎504-872-0726; www.tchoupindustries.com; 1115 St Mary St; ☉11am-6pm

Mon & Tue, Thu-Sat, noon-5pm Sun) A nice bag may turn heads, but it'll drop jaws when your friends notice the canvas siding, vintage metal clasps, or exterior made from a repurposed rice bag. These are all locally sourced materials that go into these immensely popular bags 'for city and swamp', which are often produced from found or sustainable materials.

DISKO OBSCURA
MUSIC

Map p246 (www.diskoobscura.com; 1113 Saint Mary St; ⊙noon-6pm Fri-Mon) You'd think it was hard enough to be a record shop in this day and age, but along comes Disko Obscura, a record shop specializing in underground disco, techno, post-punk and synth-based LPs. That's *niche,* but Obscura is also a small recording studio and has a dedicated international clientele.

SIMON OF NEW ORLEANS
ARTS & CRAFTS

Map p246 (☑504-524-8201; 1028 Jackson Ave, Antiques on Jackson; ⊙10am-5pm Mon-Sat) Local artist Simon Hardeveld has made a name for himself by painting groovy signs that hang like artwork in restaurants all over New Orleans. You'll probably recognize the distinctive stars, dots and sparkles that fill the spaces between letters on colorfully painted signs such as 'Who Died & Made You Elvis?'

The gallery is part of Antiques on Jackson, an antiques shop that Hardeveld owns with his wife Maria.

AIDAN GILL FOR MEN
FASHION & ACCESSORIES

Map p246 (☑504-587-9090; www.aidangillformen.com; 2026 Magazine St; ⊙10am-6pm Mon-Wed & Fri, to 7pm Thu, 9am-6pm Sat, noon-6pm Sun) Shave and a haircut: 40 bits. Or $40. Apiece. But who's counting at this suave barbershop, where smartly dressed Prohibition–era mobsters would surely have felt comfortable? It's all about looking neat and stylish, in a well-heeled, masculine sort of way. High-end shaving gear and smart men's gifts are sold in front, and the barber shop is in back.

GOGO JEWELRY
JEWELRY

Map p246 (☑504-529-8868; www.ilovegogo jewelry.com; 2036 Magazine St; ⊙11am-5pm Mon-Sat, from noon Sun) If you're looking for stylish, one-of-a-kind jewelry – rings, necklaces and cuffs – with a bit of sass, GoGo is a good place to start.

FUNKY MONKEY
VINTAGE

Map p246 (☑504-899-5587; www.funkymonkeynola.com; 3127 Magazine St; ⊙11am-6pm Sun-Wed, to 7pm Thu-Sat) You'll find wigs in every color at Funky Monkey, which sells vintage attire for club-hopping men and women. This fun-house of frippery is also a good spot for Mardi Gras costumes. It's tiny, though, and can get jam-packed with customers. In addition to wigs, look for jeans, jewelry, tops, sunglasses, hats and boots.

Annoyingly, it has turned into one of those vintage shops where the secondhand stuff is as expensive as new clothes from a big brand name, but the clothes are admittedly very hip-to-trip. The welcoming staff is a bonus.

THOMAS MANN GALLERY I/O
JEWELRY

Map p246 (☑800-875-2113; www.thomasmann.com; 1810 Magazine St; ⊙11am-5pm Mon-Sat) A giant crawfish, a robot made of wood, jewelry, baskets and candle holders: if you need a funky but finely designed gift, pop in here. The 'I/O' in the name stands for 'insight-full objects'. Local craftsman Thomas Mann specializes in jewelry and sculpture, and his gallery is a smorgasbord of glass and metal.

RHINO
ARTS & CRAFTS

Map p246 (Right Here In New Orleans; ☑504-523-7945; http://rhinocrafts.com; 2028 Magazine St; ⊙10am-5pm Mon-Sat, from noon Sun) This cool gallery is run by a nonprofit that gathers some of the city's most talented artists and craftspeople. The artists participate in arts education programs aimed at the public, conduct a ton of workshops, and display quirky work in all kinds of major media. A great spot for a local souvenir.

DIASPORA BOUTIQUE
JEWELRY

Map p246 (☑504-569-9070; www.facebook.com/ashediasporaboutique; 1712 Oretha Castle Haley Blvd; ⊙9am-5:30pm Mon-Sat) Sells clothing, jewelry and crafts from across the African diaspora. Some of the prints are stunning, and the shop also has books by small print publishers.

ANTON HAARDT GALLERY
ART

Map p246 (☑504-891-9080; www.antonhaardtgallery.com; 2858 Magazine St; ⊙noon-4pm Tue-Sat) The bold, expressive work of outsider and folk art (produced by those with no formal arts education) is an aesthetic that seems to particularly fit funky,

GARDEN, LOWER GARDEN & CENTRAL CITY SHOPPING

idiosyncratic New Orleans. With work sourced from across the American South, this gallery represents an excellent repository of outsider artistic vision.

GARDEN DISTRICT
BOOKSHOP   BOOKS

Map p246 (☑504-895-2266; www.gardendistrict-bookshop.com; 2727 Prytania St; ☉10am-6pm Mon-Sat, to 5pm Sun) Want a book about New Orleans history or a coffee-table tome about Mardi Gras? Then stop by this well-stocked indie bookstore inside the Rink mini-mall. The store also sells travel guides, bestsellers, cookbooks, postcards and a select collection of 1st-edition works. Check the online calendar for book signings with local authors, who drop in every now and then.

FLEURTY GIRL   CLOTHING

Map p246 (☑504-301-2557; www.fleurtygirl.net; 3117 Magazine St; ☉11am-6pm Mon-Thu, 10am-7pm Fri & Sat, 11am-5pm Sun) Fleurty Girl celebrates New Orleans and the city's unofficial symbol – the fleur-de-lis – with a feminine, cheeky style. T-shirts sporting local and topical messages, often involving football, are its raison d'être.

MAGAZINE ANTIQUE MALL   ANTIQUES

Map p246 (☑504-896-9994; 3017 Magazine St; ☉10am-5pm Mon-Sat, from 11:30am Sun) Scary baby dolls, hats, chandeliers, old soda-brand memorabilia: inside this overstuffed emporium, rummagers are likely to score items of interest in the dozen or so stalls, where independent dealers peddle

an intriguing and varied range of antique bric-a-brac. Bargain hunters aren't likely to have much luck, though – some of this stuff is way overpriced.

SPORTS & ACTIVITIES

SAVE OUR CEMETERIES   HISTORY

Map p246 (☑504-525-3377; www.saveourcemeteries.org; adult/child under 12yr $15/free; ☉tours 10:30am & 1pm) This nonprofit leads tours of Lafayette Cemetery No 1 (p114) daily, and the entire proceeds are used for cemetery restoration and documentation. Reservations are recommended because spots are limited, but tours need three people or more to depart. Tours meet at the Washington Ave entrance.

BELLADONNA DAY SPA   SPA

Map p246 (☑504-891-4393; www.belladonna-dayspa.com; 2900 Magazine St; deep tissue massage 25/80 min $55/130; ☉9am-6pm Mon & Tue, Fri & Sat, to 8pm Wed & Thu, noon-5pm Sun) After a few hard days of getting stuffed with rich Creole food and sloshed on pints of NOLA Blonde, it's time to treat yourself to a little cleansing experience at the Belladonna Day Spa. When you're done spoiling yourself, take home fragrant lotions and colorful cleansers for some homegrown renewal.

A full detox (aromatic bath, seaweed wrap and deep-tissue massage) runs $225.

Uptown & Riverbend

Neighborhood Top Five

❶ Audubon Zoo (p127) Strolling beneath live oaks in Audubon Park then ogling alligators, foxes and swamp monsters.

❷ St Charles Avenue Streetcar (p129) Riding the world's oldest running streetcar while taking in the mansions and grandeur of this beautiful part of New Orleans.

❸ Potsalot (p137) Grabbing a ceramic souvenir while chatting with the friendly owners of this Magazine St pottery hub.

❹ Tulane University (p129) Learning about art, jazz and African American history on this scenic campus.

❺ Jacques-Imo's Café (p132) Savoring a blue-cheese-smothered steak and a slice of alligator-sausage cheesecake.

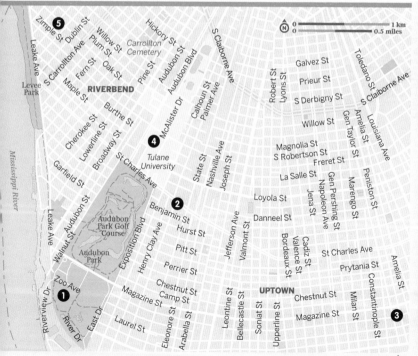

For more detail of this area see Map p248 ➡

Lonely Planet's Top Tip

Magazine St stretches from downtown to Audubon Park, covering 4 miles in the Garden District and Uptown. To get a handle on its shops, galleries and restaurants before your trip, order the guide published by the Magazine St Merchants Association (www.magazinestreet. com). You can also pick it up at many member stores. Visit the website for a listing of upcoming events.

Best Nightlife

➡ Cure (p134)

➡ Monkey Hill Bar (p135)

➡ Columns Hotel (p135)

➡ Bouligny Tavern (p134)

For reviews, see p134 ➡

Best Places to Eat

➡ Jacques-Imo's Café (p132)

➡ Gautreau's (p134)

➡ DTB (p133)

➡ Wayfare (p129)

For reviews, see p129 ➡

Best Places to Shop

➡ Potsalot (p137)

➡ Hazelnut (p137)

➡ Peaches Records & Tapes (p137)

For reviews, see p136 ➡

Best Places to Sleep

➡ Park View Historic Hotel (p185)

➡ Columns Hotel (p185)

➡ Alder Hotel (p185)

For reviews, see p185 ➡

Explore Uptown & Riverbend

If you've only got one day, check out the Audubon Zoo in the morning. Magazine St runs past the zoo, so after your visit with the elephants and giraffes, spend the rest of the day exploring the shops and art galleries that line this busy thoroughfare. Enjoy dinner on Freret St, located above St Charles Ave, then catch a band or grab drinks at a local joint such as Tipitina's.

If you've got another day, ride the St Charles Avenue Streetcar to Tulane University for a bit of wandering. Continue into Riverbend to check out the shops and restaurants off S Carrollton Ave, particularly along Maple St and Oak St. For dinner, relax with a perfectly crafted cocktail and some Cajun comfort food at DTB.

Maps of New Orleans rarely agree on the area's extents, but we'll say Uptown includes everything west of Louisiana Ave, between Magnolia St and the river, including the universities and Audubon Park. St Charles Ave, Magazine and Tchoupitoulas Sts are the main routes that more or less follow the contours of the river. The Riverbend is the area above the campuses and Audubon Park. Where St Charles Ave meets S Carrollton Ave is the nexus of the Riverbend area.

Local Life

Exercising Lush Audubon Park (p128), with its 100-year-old live oaks and paved jogging trail, is beloved by runners, walkers and cyclists.

Shopping Magazine St lures the masses with indie shops, galleries and, yes, a branch of **Whole Foods** (☑504-899-9119; www.wholefoodsmarket.com; 5600 Magazine St; ⊙8am-9pm), while boutiques and thrift stores alike draw students to Riverbend.

Dive bars Spending a blurry evening at grungy but lovable dives, from Ms Mae's (p135) to Snake & Jakes (p135), is part of what it means to be a New Orleanian.

Getting There & Away

Bus Bus 11 ($1.25) runs along Magazine St from Canal St to Audubon Park. Pick it up at the corner of Canal and Magazine Sts in front of the Sheraton Hotel.

Streetcar The St Charles Avenue Streetcar ($1.25) travels through the CBD, the Garden District and into Uptown/Riverbend.

Car Metered parking ($2 per hour) is required along much of Magazine St between 8am and 7pm Monday through Saturday. Look for free parking on side streets.

TOP SIGHT
AUDUBON ZOO

The zoo is inside Audubon Park, a lovely riverside spot with 1.8 miles of multi-use paved trail unfurling beneath a shady canopy of live oaks. It's a large zoo with numerous different sections, including African, Asian and South American landscapes and fauna, and many of the popular animals from elephants to giraffes that kids love to see.

The zoo's sections have names such as the **Louisiana Swamp**: a Cajun wonderland of bald cypresses and Spanish moss, natural wonders of southern Louisiana bayou country. Bobcats, lynx, alligators, bears and otters are on view here, and you may see a red fox chilling on a log in the swamp scrub.

There's also the **Reptile Encounter**, displaying some of the largest snakes in the world – from the king cobra, which grows to more than 18ft in length, to the green anaconda that reaches 38ft. Other memorable sections include the Mayan-style **Jaguar Jungle** and the **South American Pampas** with its raised walkway.

Behind the zoo is the Fly (p129), Audubon Park's waterfront section where people toss Frisbees and chill out, just beyond the levee.

DON'T MISS

➡ Louisiana Swamp
➡ White alligators
➡ Jaguar Jungle
➡ Reptile Encounter

PRACTICALITIES

➡ Map p248
➡ ☎504-861-2537
➡ www.auduboninstitute.org
➡ 6500 Magazine St
➡ adult/child 2-12yr/senior $23/18/20
➡ ⏰10am-5pm Mon-Fri, to 6pm Sat & Sun Sep-Mar, 10am-4pm Tue-Fri, to 5pm Sat & Sun Apr-Aug
➡ P ♿

⊙ SIGHTS

This quiet and scenic part of the city has several iconic sights and many small nooks and crannies that offer fun discoveries. You can get your bearings while on the St Charles Avenue Streetcar, as much a sight itself as for the views it provides. Audubon Zoo and the surrounding park are a lovely place to relax, and those with walking shoes can visit the river as part of the visit as well. Though far more sedate than the French Quarter, the stately university campuses of Tulane and Loyola are worth a gander, as are their museums.

★ NEWCOMB ART MUSEUM   MUSEUM
Map p248 (☑504-865-5328; http://newcombartmuseum.tulane.edu; Woldenberg Art Center, Tulane University; ⊙10am-5pm Tue-Fri, 11am-4pm Sat) FREE Part of Tulane University and flanked by beautiful Tiffany stained-glass triptychs, the Newcomb Art Museum is a great spot to soak up some art, with works from colonial portraiture to engravings by John James Audubon. Just outside is a pretty green, where students sunbathe, toss Frisbees and generally recede into the happiest rhythms of American higher ed.

AUDUBON ZOO   ZOO
See p127.

AUDUBON PARK   PARK
Map p248 (⊙5am-10pm) This lovely spot, riverside of St Charles Ave, is home to Audubon Zoo. A 1.8-mile multi-use paved trail loops around the central golf course, unfurling beneath a shady canopy of live oaks.

ALEX BEARD STUDIO   GALLERY
Map p248 (☑504-309-0394; www.alexbeardstudio.com; 3926 Magazine St; ⊙10am-6pm Mon & Wed-Sat) The lovely paintings of Alex Beard are somewhere between a fairy-tale and dreams given pigment form. From puzzles to children's books to fine art, his adventures in 'abstract realism' will pull you in for a closer look.

SOUTHEASTERN ARCHITECTURAL ARCHIVE   MUSEUM
Map p248 (6801 Freret St, 3rd fl, Jones Hall, Tulane University, Tulane University; ⊙9am-noon & 1-5pm Mon-Fri) Stop by for changing exhibits that highlight different aspects of architecture in the Gulf South, which stretches from Louisiana east to the Florida Keys.

LEVEE PATH   PARK
Map p248 Part of the Mississippi River Trail, this unique public greenway runs atop the levee space that follows the curves of the Mississippi River all the way from the Fly behind Audubon Park to Jefferson Parish and beyond. It's a nice spot for walking, jogging or biking, but views onto the river are occasionally so-so.

TOURO SYNAGOGUE   SYNAGOGUE
Map p248 (☑504-895-4843; www.tourosynagogue.com; 4238 St Charles Ave; ⊙services 6pm Fri, 10:30am Sat, tours by appointment) Despite the fact that Jews were officially banned from New Orleans under the Code Noir (Black Code), which was in effect from 1724 until the Louisiana Purchase in 1803, they have been calling the Crescent City home since the 18th century. Founded in 1828, Touro is the city's oldest synagogue (and the oldest in the country outside the original 13 colonies) and bears a slight resemblance to a red-brick Byzantine temple, with squat buttresses and bubbly domes.

LOYOLA UNIVERSITY   UNIVERSITY
Map p248 A private university with more than 4700 students, opened as a Jesuit college in 1904. It's one of America's more scenic campuses, with live oaks, beautiful buildings and open quads – worthy of a stroll on a sunny day.

MILTON H LATTER MEMORIAL LIBRARY   NOTABLE BUILDING
(☑504-596-2625; www.nolalibrary.org; 5120 St Charles Ave; ⊙10am-8pm Mon-Thu, to 5pm Fri & Sat, 1-5pm Sun) Poised elegantly above shady stands of palms, the Latter Memorial Library was once a private mansion. The Isaac family – who owned the building from 1907 to 1912 and installed Flemish-style carved woodwork, Dutch murals and French frescoed ceilings – passed the property to aviator Harry Williams and his silent-film-star wife, Marguerite Clark (1912–39). The next owner was local horse racer Robert S Eddy, followed by Mr and Mrs Harry Latter, who gave the building to the city in 1948.

HOGAN JAZZ ARCHIVE   ARCHIVES
Map p248 (☑504-865-5688; http://jazz.tulane.edu; 6801 Freret St, 3rd fl, Jones Hall, Tulane University, Tulane University; ⊙8:30am-5:30pm Mon-Fri) Jazz heads, and really anyone interested in New Orleans music, should pop into the Hogan Jazz Archive. Although most of its

great wealth of material is not on exhibit, the librarian will retrieve items from the stacks for you. The collection includes stacks of 78rpm recordings, such as early sides by the Original Dixieland Jazz Band in 1917.

AMISTAD RESEARCH CENTER ARCHIVES

Map p248 (☑504-862-3222; www.amistadre-searchcenter.org; 6823 St Charles Ave, Tilton Memorial Hall, Tulane University, Tulane University; ⊙8:30am-4:30pm Mon-Fri, 9am-1pm Sat) FREE Part of Tulane University, the Amistad Research Center is one of the nation's largest repositories of African American history. The Amistad is not a museum, but it does display items from its collection in rotating exhibits that offer insights on ethnic heritage that you're not likely to get from any other source. These exhibits are on the 2nd floor. Advance notice is required to visit the impressive Aaron Douglas Collection, which features the work of this well-known African American painter.

FLY PARK

Map p248 (Riverview Dr; ⊙dawn-dusk) The Fly is a popular spot for river viewing, picnics, Frisbee tossing, or just plain lazing about. Joggers trot by, families push strollers or release their toddlers, and on a sunny day (that's not sweltering) it's hard to beat coming here to let the 'Easy' soak in.

TULANE UNIVERSITY UNIVERSITY

Map p248 (☑504-865-5000; www.tulane.edu; 6823 St Charles Ave) The campus of Tulane, a premier Southern university, is an attractive tableau of live oaks, red-brick buildings and green quads spread across 110 acres above Audubon Park. This is one of the prettiest colleges in the country, and it's a pleasant place to stop and stretch your legs if you're riding the St Charles Avenue Streetcar across town.

✖ EATING

Uptown and Riverbend are arguably the hottest food corridors in the city. There's no shortage of options, including shotgun-shack diners, po'boy-slinging bars and cute garden cottages hiding some of the best Creole fine dining in town. Freret St, which has undergone a remarkable renaissance since Hurricane Katrina, is the latest foodie hub, where new eateries put a

ST CHARLES AVENUE STREETCAR

A buck twenty-five gets you on the **St Charles Avenue Streetcar** (☑504-248-3900, TTY 504-827-7832; www.norta.com; per ride $1.25, all-day pass $3; ⊙24hr; ♿ 🚋) which plies the world's oldest continuously operating street railway system. It travels through the CBD, the Garden District and into Uptown/Riverbend. The transit authority offers an all-day $3 option that gives you unlimited rides for a full 24 hours.

gourmet spin on old favorites such as pizza, hamburgers and hot dogs.

★BA CHI CANTEEN VIETNAMESE $

Map p248 (☑504-373-5628; www.facebook.com/bachicanteenla; 7900 Maple St; mains $4-12; ⊙11am-2:30pm Mon-Fri, to 3:30pm Sat, 5:30-9pm Mon-Wed, to 10pm Thu-Sat) Do not be skeptical of the 'bacos' ($3), as odd as they sound. These pillowy bundles of deliciousness – a *banh bao* crossed with a taco – successfully merge the subtle seasonings of Vietnamese fillings with the foldable convenience of a taco-shaped, steamed flour bun. Pho and *banh mi* – dubbed po'boys here – round out the menu.

★WAYFARE PUB FOOD $

Map p248 (☑504-309-0069; www.wayfare-nola.com; 4510 Freret St; mains $12-15; ⊙11am-10pm Mon-Thu & Sat, to 11pm Fri, to 9pm Sun) This former takeout joint has gone all-in and now hovers in that delicious middle ground between pub (with inventive craft cocktails such as the Porkbelly Old Fashioned, garnished with a piece of bacon!) and restaurant (with a scrumptious eggplant-banh-mi sandwich that you wish you could take home to meet your parents). Either way, it's all about *yum*.

NOMIYA JAPANESE $

Map p248 (www.nomiyaramen.com; 4226 Magazine St; ramen $13.50; ⊙11:30am-9:30pm Tue-Sun) *Irasshaimase!* That's what they yell whenever you enter a business in Japan, and it's what the servers say here as well. New Orleans has been in dire need of a good ramen place, and Nomiya has come to the rescue. Admire the comic-book and

FRERET STREET

Freret Street's rapidly expanding eating options make it one of the city's most popular dining destinations. The eight-block strip, which stretches from Jefferson Ave to Napoleon Ave, had been in a state of serious decline for decades. Named for 19th-century mayor and cotton baron William Freret, the street was a prosperous business corridor in the 1920s and 1930s. The neighborhood lost families to white flight from the 1950s into the 1970s, and the fatal shooting of a popular business owner in front of his store in the mid-1980s hastened the slide. Mother Nature seemed to deal the final blow in 2005, when the levee broke and several feet of water doused the neighborhood.

A few community stalwarts started the Freret Street Farmers Market (p138) in 2007, but the revitalization really began after Neal Bodenheimer and Matthew Kohnke transformed a 100-year-old former firehouse into craft cocktail bar **Cure** (p134). City council member Stacy Head, who represents the district, helped the neighborhood win a more development-friendly zoning designation, and new eateries began trickling onto the strip. That trickle has become a storm; by 2011 there were 11 new restaurants on Freret St and today there are 16. The 2014 PBS documentary *Getting Back to Abnormal* examines the Freret district's 2010 city council race, spotlighting Head, her opponent, race relations and post-Katrina politics.

This new dining and drinking destination presents a bedeviling dilemma for gourmands who are only in town for a short time – how do you decide where to go? Fortunately it's hard to go wrong. You'll find topping-slathered hot dogs and sausages at **Dat Dog**, gourmet deep-dish pies at Midway Pizza (p133), natural burgers at the **Company Burger** ((☑504-267-0320; http://thecompanyburger.com; 4600 Freret St; mains $7.50-10; ☺11am-10pm), and comfort food from the bayou and the delta at **High Hat Cafe**. For craft beer and cocktails try the new Wayfare (p129). Visit www.thenewfreret.com for a list of the 20 or so eateries and bars in the neighborhood. Bon appétit!

graffiti murals, then order your soup and add whatever extras you please.

PHO CAM LY
VIETNAMESE $
Map p248 (☑504-644-4228; www.phocamly.com; 3814 Magazine St; mains $7-13; ☺11am-8:30pm Mon-Sat, to 7:30pm Sun) After much exhaustive research, this is our go-to bowl of pho in New Orleans (short of driving to New Orleans East). The Pho Cam Ly broth is rich and exciting and textured and makes you go all kinds of 'mmm'. There are plenty of excellent vermicelli bowls and rice dishes if you're not in a soup mood.

HIGH HAT CAFE
CAFE $
Map p248 (☑504-754-1336; www.highhatcafe.com; 4500 Freret St; mains $11-20; ☺11am-9pm Sun-Thu, to 10pm Fri & Sat) At this bustling neighborhood spot, simple bayou and delta dishes – fried catfish, BBQ shrimp and slow-roasted pork – are served with a hint of style. Look for pimento cheese grits as a side.

CREOLE CREAMERY
ICE CREAM $
Map p248 (☑504-894-8680; www.creolecreamery.com; 4924 Prytania St; scoops $3; ☺noon-

10pm Sun-Thu, to 11pm Fri & Sat) Every single flavor here sounds – and is – uniquely delicious: Steen's Molasses Oatmeal Cookie; I Scream Fudge!; Pine Forest; Lavender Honey; Pear and Ginger Sorbet. And the list goes on. The good news is you can't go wrong. Flavors rotate, but there's always vanilla and chocolate, and you'll get in their Hall of Fame for eating eight scoops with eight toppings.

DAT DOG
AMERICAN $
Map p248 (☑504-899-6883; www.datdog.com; 5030 Freret St; hot dogs $8; ☺11am-10pm Mon-Sat, to 9pm Sun; 🖵) Every part of your tasty dog, from the steamed link (sausage) to the toasted sourdough bun to the flavor-packed toppings, is produced with exuberance here. Sausage choices include duck, alligator and crawfish. If you like your dawgs spicy, try the Louisiana hot sausage from nearby Harahan. And grab about 10 napkins for every topping. Even better, there's a 5pm-to-7pm happy hour!

BEARCAT CAFE
CAFE $
Map p248 (☑504-309-9011; www.bearcatcafe.com; 2521 Jena St; mains $7-16; ☺7am-4pm

Tue-Sun; 🖼) 🍴 It's hard to find fault with a place that offers 'Good Cat' (healthy) and 'Bad Cat' (not for the dieters) options on its menu, but even better are the sustainably sourced coffees, house-made syrups and abundant vegan and gluten-free options. The stainless-steel and wood cafe almost seems like it might have been an Apple store in a previous life.

ST JAMES CHEESE CO
DELI $

Map p248 (🖼504-899-4737; www.stjamescheese.com; 5004 Prytania St; mains $9-16; ⊙11am-6pm Mon-Wed, to 8pm Thu-Sat, to 4pm Sun) Founded by an Englishman obsessed with all the right things (namely, meat and fermented milk products), St James is the city's best cheese shop, with a veritable atlas of cheese. From the grilled Gruyère to the French ham with brie, the sandwiches all sound enticing; we like the mozzarella with basil pesto and salami.

CASAMENTO'S
SEAFOOD $

Map p248 (🖼504-895-9761; www.casamentosrestaurant.com; 4330 Magazine St; mains $5-24; ⊙11am-2pm & 5:30-9pm Thu-Sat, 5-9pm Sun) One word: oysters. That's why you come here. Walk through the 1949 soda-shopesque interior, cross the tiled floors to a marble-top counter, trade a joke with the person shucking shells and get some raw boys with a beer. The thick gumbo with Creole tomatoes and the oyster loaf (a sandwich of breaded and fried oysters) are suitably incredible. Cash only.

GUY'S
SANDWICHES $

Map p248 (🖼504-891-5025; 5259 Magazine St; po'boys $8-15; ⊙11am-4pm Mon-Sat) It's very simple: Guy's is basically a one-man operation that does some of the best po'boys in town. Sandwiches are made fresh and to order, with a level of attention you don't get anywhere else in the city. Even when the line is out the door – and it often is – each po'boy is painstakingly crafted.

CAMELLIA GRILL
DINER $

Map p248 (🖼504-309-2679; 626 S Carrollton Ave; mains $5-12; ⊙8am-midnight Sun-Thu, to 2am Fri & Sat) Go ahead, accept the straw. You'll see what we mean after grabbing your seat. And the food? We love the burger-chili-Reuben diner fare, and the fact that they all call each other – and you – 'baby'. Plus, they dress in white shirts and black bow ties. What's not to like?

SATSUMA MAPLE
HEALTH FOOD $

Map p248 (🖼504-309-5557; www.satsumacafe.com; 7901 Maple St; mains $6-11; ⊙7am-5pm; 🖼) A stylish, bright-faced crowd lines up from the counter to the door at this popular health-food cafe, beloved for its light and gourmet breakfasts. Choices include house-made granola, tofu scramble ($9.50), and the 'green' breakfast sandwich ($7.50) with egg, arugula, tomato and avocado mash. Look for salads and sandwiches at lunch. Fresh organic juices are on offer, too.

REFUEL
CAFE $

Map p248 (🖼504-872-0187; www.refuelcafe.com; 8124 Hampson St; mains $9-15; ⊙7am-noon Mon, to 2pm Tue-Fri, 8:30am-2pm Sat & Sun) Hip Refuel packs 'em in tight on Sunday mornings, but still manages to look cute and breezy. It adds some chic to the local coffee scene, but it's hardly pretentious; service is some of the friendliest in town. Fresh food such as Baja omelets with avocado are served alongside Southern mainstays such as creamy cheese grits with andouille (smoked sausage).

BREADS ON OAK
BAKERY $

Map p248 (https://breadsonoak.com; 8640 Oak St; breads $3-7; ⊙7am-3pm Wed-Sun; 🖼) This clean and quirky coffee and bread shop has smiling staff and vegan options for those who need them. It also features a nice area where you can sit and use your laptop while watching the staff make the breads.

HANSEN'S SNO-BLIZ
DESSERTS $

Map p248 (🖼504-891-9788; www.facebook.com/snobliz; 4801 Tchoupitoulas St; snowballs $4-8; ⊙1-7pm Tue-Sun Mar-Oct) The humble snowball (shaved ice with flavored syrup) is New Orleans' favorite dessert. Citywide consensus is that Hansen's, in business since 1939, does the best ball in town. Founder Ernest Hansen actually patented the shaved-ice machine. Now his granddaughter, Ashley, runs the family business, doling out shaved ice under everything from root-beer syrup to uber-popular Bananas Foster.

BOURÉE
FOOD TRUCK $

Map p248 (🖼504-510-4040; http://bourreenola.com; 1510 S Carrollton Ave; mains $10-15; ⊙11am-10pm Sun-Thu, to 11pm Fri & Sat) Looking not unlike a large, rectangular eggplant, this bright purple food truck at Boucherie (p132) serves up frozen daiquiris and tasty wings, pork, brisket and ribs, in a setting that's as casual as can be. Pick up a plate, grab your drink, and eat outside at the plastic tables and chairs.

MAHONY'S PO-BOY SHOP
SANDWICHES $

Map p248 (☑504-899-2374; www.mahonyspoboys.com; 3454 Magazine St; po'boys $9-23; ☺11am-9pm Mon-Fri, from 9am Sat & Sun) A convenient po'boy place with a fun atmosphere, Mahony's is a welcome if sometimes expensive choice. Digs are a converted Magazine St house with a tiny front porch. The Peacemaker with fried oysters, bacon and cheddar is a crowd-pleaser, as is the grilled shrimp and fried green tomatoes, although at $14.95, it's a hefty price for a po' tourist.

DOMILISE'S PO-BOYS
CREOLE $

Map p248 (5240 Annunciation St; po'boys $6-18; ☺10am-6:30pm Mon-Sat) Domilise's is everything that makes New Orleans great: a white shack by the river serving Dixie beer, staffed by long-timers and prepping some of the city's best po'boys. Locals tell us to opt for the half-and-half (oysters and shrimp) with gravy and cheese, but we think the oyster, dressed but otherwise on its own, is the height of the po'boy-maker's craft.

PIZZA DOMENICA
PIZZA $

Map p248 (☑504-301-4978; www.pizzadomenica.com; 4933 Magazine St; pizzas $12-20; ☺noon-9pm Sun-Thu, to 10pm Fri & Sat) Fans of wood-fired pizza can burn off calories with the short walk between the St Charles Avenue Streetcar and the renowned Pizza Domenica, which opened in 2014 on Magazine St.

TEE-EVA'S OLD-FASHIONED PIES & PRALINES
CREOLE $

Map p248 (☑504-899-8350; www.tee-evapralines.com; 5201 Magazine St; pralines $3-6, pint of gumbo/jambalaya $5; ☺11am-6pm Mon-Sat, noon-5pm Sun) It's impossible to nibble a praline from Tee-Eva's over the course of a day. Trust us, after one bite, you're a goner for the whole thing – right then. Tee-Eva once sang backup to the late, great local legend Ernie K-Doe; now she whips up snowballs ($2) and pralines ($3), some fine hot lunches and great Louisiana sweet and savory pies.

★BOUCHERIE
SOUTHERN US $$

Map p248 (☑504-862-5514; www.boucherie-nola.com; 1506 S Carrollton Ave; mains lunch $12-23, dinner $18-30; ☺11am-3pm Tue-Sat, 5:30-9:30pm Mon-Sat, 10:30am-2:30pm Sun) The thick, glistening cuts of bacon on the BLT can only be the work of the devil – or chef Nathanial Zimet, whose house-cured meats and succulent Southern dishes are lauded citywide. Savor boudin (Cajun sausage) balls with garlic aioli ($9), blackened shrimp in bacon vinaigrette, and smoked Wagyu-style brisket. The Krispy Kreme bread pudding with rum syrup ($7) is a wonder.

★JACQUES-IMO'S CAFÉ
LOUISIANAN $$

Map p248 (☑504-861-0886; http://jacquesimos.com; 8324 Oak St; mains $20-34; ☺5-10pm Mon-Thu, to 11pm Fri & Sat) Ask locals for restaurant recommendations in New Orleans, and almost everybody mentions Jacques-Imo's. We understand why: cornbread muffins swimming in butter, steak smothered in blue-cheese sauce, and the insane yet wickedly brilliant shrimp and alligator-sausage cheesecake. That's the attitude at Jack Leonardi's exceedingly popular restaurant: die, happily, with butter and heavy sauces sweating out of your pores.

★AVO
SICILIAN $$

Map p248 (☑504-509-6550; http://restaurantavo.com; 5908 Magazine St; mains $17-32; ☺4-10pm Mon-Thu, from 5pm Fri & Sat) Avo is a new kid on the Magazine St block, serving pastas cooked to perfection – as one would expect, with the owner-chef hailing from Sicily. It's clean, cozy, and convenient – a perfect stop if you're strolling along shopping and need a bite. They also offer impressive takes on classic cocktails and a 4pm-to-6pm happy hour (cocktails $6, wine half price).

COWBELL
BURGERS $$

Map p248 (www.cowbell-nola.com; 8801 Oak St; mains $12-32; ☺11:30am-9pm Tue-Thu, to 10pm Fri & Sat) Cowbell has a scruffy charm – scuffed wooden floors, Elvis on the ceiling, a bottle-cap mosaic on one of its bars – that makes you want to stay awhile. The juicy grass-fed beef burgers are a must for most, but non-beef options include grilled Gulf fish tacos and lime-grilled organic chicken. We hear the mac 'n' cheese is divine.

DELACHAISE
INTERNATIONAL $$

Map p248 (☑504-895-0858; www.thedelachaise.com; 3442 St Charles Ave; small plates $8-28, cheese plates $13-28; ☺5pm-2am Mon-Thu, from noon Fri-Sun) If you're looking for a place to relax, sip wine and watch the world go by, Delachaise is a great choice. It's just steps from the St Charles Avenue Streetcar line. The small plates are wonderful in their

UPTOWN ON THE CHEAP

Uptown can be daunting for the budget traveler, what with so much snazzy shopping and fine dining where the per-person tab is likely to include at least two (and probably three) digits – especially if there's been a beverage or two consumed.

The area doesn't have to be expensive though. First of all, check out happy hours, especially on Freret St: Wayfare (p129) offers 50% off all its cocktails and select appetizers on weekdays from 3pm to 6pm. Check around and you may find that fancy dinner you want is within your budget after all, provided you can eat a little earlier in the day.

Other places just do cheap (and do it well!) all day long. Here are some spots where you'll get great meals at prices that stay nicely inside the budget range:

Ba Chi Canteen (p129) Try their 'bacos' for about $3 each.

Bearcat Cafe (p130) Wide range of cheap breakfasts and lunches.

Bourée (p131) Purple food truck with tasty chicken.

Dat Dog (p130) Who dat? Dat dog. Cheap and tasty hot dogs with unique fillings.

Domilise's Po'boys that are still within reach of poor boys (and girls).

Midway Pizza Tasty pies that, split between two to three people, will satisfy without breaking anyone's bank.

indulgent way, especially the over-the-top grilled cheese sandwich with house-made apple butter. And everyone lovingly recalls the *pommes frites* – fried in goose fat.

DANTE'S KITCHEN LOUISIANAN $$
(☑504-861-3121; www.danteskitchen.com; 736 Dante St; mains $23-27, brunch $10-14; ☺6-10pm Wed-Mon, 10:30am-2pm Sat & Sun) It's hard not to feel like you've stepped into the pages of the J Crew catalog during Sunday brunch at Dante's, a country cottage on the Mississippi levee. Tulane kids, grandmas and grandpas, girlfriends who brunch and a few well-behaved babies – it feels as if half of New Orleans is here. The menu melds French, American and Louisiana traditions.

LA PETITE GROCERY FRENCH $$
(☑504-891-3377; www.lapetitegrocery.com; 4238 Magazine St; mains $16-30; ☺11:30am-2:30pm Tue-Sat, 10:30am-2:30pm Sun, 5:30-9:30pm Sun-Thu, 5:30-10:30pm Fri & Sat) Petite is one of the many cozy and popular bistros squeezed into the crowded Uptown dining scene. We like the lunches, which consist of some very fine sandwiches and salads. The dinners are good but not great for the price, and include bistro mainstays such as Gulf shrimp ($25) and grits.

Chef Justin Devillier is a three-time James Beard nominee for Best Chef: South. Look for another Devillier venture, Balise (p103) in the CBD.

MIDWAY PIZZA PIZZA $$
Map p248 (☑504-322-2815; www.midwaypizzanola.com; 4725 Freret St; pizzas $15-21; ☺11:30am-11pm Sun-Wed, to midnight Thu-Sat) The King Creole pizza at this deep-dish pizza joint is topped with Creole *fredo* sauce and and Gulf shrimp marinated in garlic. Their tasty pies, split between two to three people, will satisfy without breaking anyone's bank.

★CLANCY'S CREOLE $$$
Map p248 (☑504-895-1111; www.clancysneworleans.com; 6100 Annunciation St; mains lunch $17-20, dinner $28-40; ☺11:30am-1:30pm Thu & Fri, 5:30-10pm Mon-Sat) This white-tablecloth neighborhood restaurant embraces style, the good life and Creole cuisine with a chattering joie de vivre and top-notch service. The city's professional set comes here to gossip and savor the specialties: fried oysters and brie ($15), veal with crabmeat and béarnaise ($28), and lobster and mushroom risotto ($30). Reservations recommended.

★DTB CAJUN $$$
Map p248 (Down The Bayou; ☑504-518-6889; http://dtbnola.com; 8201 Oak St; mains $25-35; ☺10:30am-2:30pm Fri-Sun, 5-10pm Sun-Thu, 5-11pm Fri & Sat) DTB is the new place on Oak everyone's talking about. Get melt-in-your-mouth meats, crisp salads, and creative takes on Cajun comfort food (roasted cauliflower, for instance, or stuffed banana beignets) in an airy spot finished with

scrubbed steel, wood and marble – with Spanish moss hanging from the lamps. The cocktails, unique recipes crafted with care, are fun, inventive and refreshing.

Happy hour at the bar runs from 3pm to 5pm Monday to Friday.

★GAUTREAU'S   AMERICAN $$$

Map p248 (☑504-899-7397; www.gautreaus-restaurant.com; 1728 Soniat St; mains $30-45; ☺6-10pm Mon-Sat) There's no sign outside Gautreau's, just the number 1728 discreetly marking a nondescript house. Cross the threshold to find a refined but welcoming dining room, where savvy diners, many of them New Orleanian food aficionados, enjoy fresh, modern American fare.

PATOIS   FRENCH $$$

Map p248 (☑504-895-9441; www.patoisnola.com; 6078 Laurel St; mains brunch $15-20, lunch $13-22, dinner $22-34; ☺5:30-10pm Wed & Thu, to 10:30pm Fri & Sat, 11:30am-2pm Fri, 10:30am-2pm Sun) The interior of Patois feels like the cozy house of very good friends – who happen to be very good cooks. Head chef Aaron Burgau went through his paces in New Orleans' top restaurants, including Commander's Palace (p119), before opening Patois. The setting has an unaffectedly rustic and romantic vibe, while the menu is French haute with New Orleans accents (or patois).

LILETTE   FRENCH $$$

Map p248 (☑504-895-1636; www.liletteres-taurant.com; 3637 Magazine St; mains lunch $12-26, dinner $26-39; ☺11:30am-2pm Tue-Sat, 5:30-9:30pm Mon-Thu, 5:30-10:30pm Fri & Sat) Where has all the romance gone? Perhaps to this white-linen bistro that sparkles with a traditional but lively European vibe. Chef John Harris adds innovative spins to familiar dishes. The white-truffle parmigiana toast with wild mushrooms is a nice start, and the solid lineup of mains that change seasonally, such as hanger steak or poultry, leaves nothing to be desired.

Lunch here is a pleasant way to pass an afternoon on Magazine St. Harris owns the equally stylish Bouligny Tavern next door.

🍷 DRINKING & NIGHTLIFE

There's not much difference between this drinking scene and the fun going on in the Lower Garden District; Magazine St maintains a generally young, hip, neighborhood vibe throughout. Bars in Riverbend attract more of a student crowd.

★CURE   BAR

Map p248 (☑504-302-2357; www.curenola.com; 4905 Freret St; ☺5pm-midnight Mon-Thu, 3pm-2am Fri & Sat, 3pm-midnight Sun) This stylish purveyor of cocktails and spirits flickers like an ultramodern apothecary shop, a place where mysterious elixirs are expertly mixed to soothe whatever ails you. A smooth and polished space of modern banquettes, anatomic art and a Zen-garden outdoor area, Cure is where you come for a well-mixed drink, period. It's drinks for adults in a stylish setting.

The premise here is that a good cocktail is the height of a bartender's craft. Classics such as the Sidecar and the Rob Roy are given an innovative spin with spices, citrus additions and, occasionally, chocolate. On Friday and Saturday evenings, men will be asked to remove their baseball caps – a tactic intended to filter out rowdy undergrads.

LE BON TEMPS ROULÉ   BAR

Map p248 (☑504-897-3448; 4801 Magazine St; ☺11am-3am) A neighborhood bar – a very good one at that – with a mostly college and post-college crowd attracted by two pool tables and a commendable beer selection. Late at night, high-caliber blues, zydeco or jazz rocks the joint's little back room. The Soul Rebels play Thursday nights to huge acclaim. It sometimes opens 24 hours.

BOULIGNY TAVERN   BAR

Map p248 (☑504-891-1810; www.boulignytavern.com; 3641 Magazine St; ☺4pm-midnight Mon-Thu, to 2am Fri & Sat) Sexy lighting, Mad Men decor, inventive cocktails and an extensive wine list – it all comes together in a lively, flattering tableau. A fashionable addition to the Magazine St bar scene, Bouligny draws after-work crowds and those prepping their palate for a meal at chef John Harris' companion restaurant, Lilette (p134), next door.

The small plates are divine, particularly the bruschetta and the gouda beignets. You don't like blue? Try one of their gin cocktails – we're guessing you'll change your mind. This low-key hideaway is in a house fronted by a live oak, and it's easy to miss. Look for the alluringly lit alleyway patio.

UPTOWN & RIVERBEND DRINKING & NIGHTLIFE

MONKEY HILL BAR BAR

Map p248 (📞504-899-4800; 6100 Magazine St; ◷3pm-2am Mon-Thu, to 3am Fri, 1pm-3am Sat, noon-2am Sun) Toward the quiet end of Magazine St, Monkey Hill looks and feels like a neighborhood bar, but it's also one of the best happy-hour spots (3pm to 7pm weeknights) in this part of town and hosts some good live music on a monthly basis. The craft cocktails here are excellent, and if it's not busy the bartenders will stop and chat.

ST JOE'S BAR

Map p248 (📞504-899-3744; www.stjoesbar.com; 5535 Magazine St; ◷3pm-2am Sun-Thu, noon-3am Fri & Sat) New Orleanians have voted St Joe's the best in town several times. Patrons come to this dark-but-inviting place for the Japanese lantern decor, the well-used pool table, and the near-sacred jukebox. Mainly a 20s and 30s crowd, they are friendly and chatty, as are the staff.

The layout is also a draw – the narrow front leads past a series of faux Catholic shrines to a spacious backyard that feels like a cross between an Indonesian island and a Thai temple. And the jukebox? Well stocked with jazz, rock and blues.

RUE DE LA COURSE CAFE

Map p248 (📞504-861-4343; www.ruedelacourse. com; 1140 S Carrollton Ave; ◷6:30am-11pm Mon-Fri, 7am-11pm Sat & Sun; 🛜) The setting alone – a cavernous former bank building on the corner of Carrollton Ave and Oak St – is reason enough to step inside for a look-see. With the pastries, hot and cold javas, and local syrups, you'll surely be tempted to settle in and soak up the atmosphere, or just listen to the classical music playing and stare at the gargoyles.

Sandwiches go for $10, coffee for $5.

COOTER BROWN'S TAVERN & OYSTER BAR BAR

Map p248 (📞504-866-9104; www.cooterbrowns. com; 509 S Carrollton Ave; ◷11am-2am; 🛜) Cooter's scores points with locals because it served as a community gathering place in the aftermath of Katrina. College kids, local characters and Uptown swells drop in for brews and freshly shucked oysters, and to shoot pool or watch sports on TV. It also takes beer seriously, with 84 taps. The Back Bar spotlights craft brews.

Pause to appreciate the tavern's 'Celebrity Hall of Foam and Beersoleum' – a gallery of more than 100 plaster bas-relief statuettes of mostly 1970s celebs from Liberace to Chairman Mao, each holding a bottle of beer. This curious, still-growing exhibit is the work of the uniquely talented Scott Conary.

COLUMNS HOTEL BAR

Map p248 (📞504-899-9308; www.thecolumns. com; 3811 St Charles Ave; ◷3pm-midnight Mon-Thu, 11am-2am Fri & Sat, to midnight Sun) With its antebellum trappings – a raised front porch, white Doric columns, a flanking live oak – the Columns Hotel (p185) harks back to a simpler era. Here we're going to party like it's 1859. But, truthfully, it's not as aristocratic as all that; it's more a place where college students and just-graduates drink beneath the grandeur of the Old South.

This hotel bar is a great place to sit back with a cool glass of gin while fanning yourself and watching the St Charles Avenue Streetcar crank past.

OAK WINE BAR WINE BAR

Map p248 (📞504-302-1485; www.oaknola.com; 8118 Oak St; ◷5-11pm Tue-Thu, to midnight Fri & Sat) With a setting both swanky and spare, Oak's vibe is hard to place, but if you'd like a glass of wine or a specialty cocktail in a nondivey setting, this is a nice choice. You can catch live jazz and acoustic folk here on Friday and Saturday nights at 9pm. They offers 30 wines by the glass.

SNAKE & JAKES BAR

(Map p248 📞504-861-2802; www.snakeandjakes.com; 7612 Oak St; ◷7pm-5am) Looking like a bayou bait shack tarted up for Christmas, Snake & Jakes is an institution. Some say the place messes with the space-time continuum – enter at 3am and a mere five minutes later you're stumbling outside as the sun rises. If this happens to you, pat yourself on the back: you're now a fully fledged honorary New Orleanian.

If you end up here any time before 3am, it's probably too early. When you're out with your buddies and someone says, 'Let's go to Snakes,' that's a sure sign the night is either going to get much better or immeasurably worse.

MS MAE'S BAR

Map p248 (📞504-218-8035; 4336 Magazine St; ◷24hr) Ms Mae sold the bar in 2010, but this legendary place keeps on. Despite its gritty reputation, this dive bar is a popular

UPTOWN & RIVERBEND DRINKING & NIGHTLIFE

spot for pool, arcade games (think 1970s!), and local beers served ice-cold on draft.

F&M'S PATIO BAR
BAR

Map p248 (☑504-895-6784; www.fandmpatio-bar.com; 4841 Tchoupitoulas St; ☺7pm-4am Sun-Wed, 9pm-5am Thu-Sat) If you're old enough to be paying off your student loans, you may want to give F&M a pass on weekends, when every college student in Louisiana tests the structural integrity of the bar's pool tables by dancing on them. Otherwise this is a reasonably chill spot, with a grill and a semi-outdoor area for a cold beer.

ENTERTAINMENT

Many bars in Uptown and Riverbend offer live music – several venues do it particularly well and are worth a special trip.

★ TIPITINA'S
LIVE MUSIC

Map p248 (☑504-895-8477; www.tipitinas.com; 501 Napoleon Ave; cover $5-20; ☺8pm-2am) 'Tips', as locals call it, is one of New Orleans' great musical icons. The legendary Uptown nightclub, which takes its name from Professor Longhair's 1953 hit single, is the site of some of the city's most memorable shows, particularly when big names such as Dr John come home to roost. Outstanding music from local talent packs 'em in year-round.

This is one of the few non–French Quarter nightspots regularly drawing tourists. The joint really jumps in the weeks prior to Mardi Gras and during Jazz Fest.

★ MAPLE LEAF BAR
LIVE MUSIC

Map p248 (☑504-866-9359; www.mapleleafbar.com; 8316 Oak St; cover $10-20; ☺3pm-2am) The premier night-time destination in the Riverbend area, the legendary Maple Leaf's dimly lit, pressed-tin caverns are the kind of environs you'd expect from a New Orleans juke joint. Work up a sweat on the small dance-floor or relax at the bar in the next room. The Grammy Award–winning Rebirth Brass Band plays Tuesdays, starting between 10pm and 11pm.

Scenes from the film *Angel Heart* (1987), in which the late, great blues man Brownie McGhee starred, were shot here, as well as more recent classics such as *Ray* (2004), about the life of music legend Ray Charles.

There's also a nice back patio on which to cool your heels.

PRYTANIA THEATRE
CINEMA

Map p248 (☑504-891-2787; www.theprytania.com; 5339 Prytania St; tickets adult $11.75, child under 12yr & senior $9.75, matinee $6) This old movie house has been around since 1914, and screens independent art films, classics and mainstream releases. One of the finest spots to catch a flick in the city.

LUPIN THEATRE
THEATER

Map p248 (☑504-865-5105; 16 Newcomb Blvd, Dixon Annex) New Orleans has a strong theatrical bent; numerous local theater companies and a few large venues for touring productions frequently stage shows. Student plays are often performed at Tulane University's Lupin Theatre.

GASA GASA
LIVE MUSIC

Map p248 (☑504-338-3567; www.gasagasa.com; 4920 Freret St; ☺bar 2pm-midnight Tue-Sun, shows Mon) We're unsure what is most interesting at this performance and drinking space inside an art gallery: the art, the music or the patrons. Come for an eclectic array of live music, including jazz, folk and indie.

Big Freedia was on the lineup for Gasa Gasa's first anniversary.

ROCK 'N' BOWL
LIVE MUSIC

(☑504-861-1700; www.rockandbowl.com; 3000 S Carrollton Ave; cover $10; ☺11:30am-midnight Mon-Thu, to 2am Fri & Sat, 4:30-11pm Sun) The Rock 'N' Bowl is a strange combination of bowling alley, deli and huge live-music and dance venue, where patrons get down to New Orleans roots music while trying to avoid that 7-10 split. The best place in the city to experience zydeco is the weekly Thursday-night dance party held here.

The bowling is expensive (starting at $24 an hour) and crowded – go for the music and dancing.

SHOPPING

Magazine St is the city's best shopping strip. You can take a good multi-mile window-shopping hike stretching from Audubon Park to Louisiana Ave. The area around Maple St in Riverbend is another hopping carnival of consumption. Fashionable shops and restaurants front a small square on

Dublin St near S Carrollton Ave, where it meets St Charles Ave. On the river (north) side of S Carrollton, Oak St is reasonably compact for strolling and offers a few interesting businesses, along with restaurants and the stellar Maple Leaf Bar.

★PEACHES RECORDS & TAPES   MUSIC
Map p248 (☑504-282-3322; www.peaches-recordsneworleans.com; 4318 Magazine St; ☺10am-7pm) Peaches has been around since 1975, doing the holy work of promoting, cataloging and marketing the best in local New Orleans music. Once in the French Quarter and now on Magazine St, it's a must-see for anyone who wants to take home a piece of the city's musical heritage.

★YVONNE LA FLEUR   CLOTHING
Map p248 (☑504-866-9666; www.yvonnelafleur. com; 8131 Hampson St; ☺10am-6pm Mon-Wed, Fri & Sat, to 8pm Thu) They don't make them like this anymore – neither the clothes, millinery, lingerie nor Yvonne herself, a businesswoman who has outfitted generations of local ladies for weddings, debuts and race days. She makes her own floral perfumes and gorgeous hats, overflowing with silk flowers, that seem to belong to another era. Gentility, grace, style – thy name is Yvonne La Fleur.

Among newer popular items are her line of Magic Pants, and her cards with suggested gifts based on price. Need a stocking stuffer for under $10? She's got suggestions. Need a graduation gift that's around $75? That's here too. All of it's beautifully designed, but you come here to be sublimely taken care of by Yvonne herself. If all retail experiences were like this, online shopping wouldn't have the boa-constrictor grip it does today.

★POTSALOT   ARTS & CRAFTS
Map p248 (☑504-899-1705; www.potsalot.com; 3818 Magazine St; ☺10am-5pm Tue-Sat) Owners Alex and Cindy Williams, who have made and sold pottery from their Magazine St shop since 1993, call their exquisite creations functional art. Their unique, personally tested pieces, made for use in the kitchen, bathroom and den, include bowls, platters, lamps, vases and, yep, lotsa pots.

Their eye-catching sinks – with scallops, dimples and rolled lips – are particularly cool. If you're lucky, they may even give you some clay to squeeze out your stress with

as you ponder a purchase. They sometimes open on Monday.

FRENCH LIBRARY   BOOKS
Map p248 (☑504-267-3707; www.thefrenchlibrary. com; 3811 Magazine St; ☺9am-6pm Tue-Sat, noon-5pm Sun) This place is so *cute* – or should that be *mignon*? Or *joli*? We haven't taken French in a few years, but we could brush up here – the largest French children's bookstore in the country. There are all kinds of lovingly bound titles, and the owners throw parties and private events for *les enfants* as well.

PELICAN COAST CLOTHING CO   CLOTHING
Map p248 (☑504-309-2314; www.pelicancoast-clothing.com; 5509 Magazine St; ☺10am-6pm Mon-Sat, noon-5pm Sun) Dapper dudes and Tulane students get their preppy on at this small and friendly shop. It's packed tight with colorful ties and sports shirts, plus some cool travel bags.

COLE PRATT GALLERY   ART
Map p248 (☑504-891-6789; www.coleprattgal-lery.com; 3800 Magazine St; ☺10am-5pm Tue-Sat) This fine-art gallery showcases the work of 42 contemporary Gulf Coast and Southern artists. The works here include Susan Downing-White's Gulf Coast landscapes and David Armentor's haunting black-and-white photos of sugar farms and mills, as well as many others.

BERTA'S & MINA'S ANTIQUITIES   ART
Map p248 (☑504-895-6201; 4138 Magazine St; ☺10am-7pm) This painting-cluttered gallery specializes in regional folk art, especially the works of the late Nilo Lanzas, whose daughter operates the shop. Lanzas began painting at 63 and produced an impressive body of work, most of it outsider art with a religious bent. Museums and serious collectors have snatched up many of Lanzas' paintings. You'll find dozens of pieces, all eye-catching.

His daughter, Mina, also paints – her works show alongside her father's and a few other artists from the city and its surrounds. The gallery is one of the oldest on Magazine St.

HAZELNUT   HOMEWARES
Map p248 (☑504-891-2424; www.hazelnutne-worleans.com; 5525 Magazine St; ☺10am-6pm Mon-Sat) Actor Bryan Batt of *Mad Men* fame (he played art director Salvatore Romano) co-owns this elegant, pleasantly eclectic

gift and homewares shop. In addition to classically cool New Orleans–print toile, the shop sells gilded glassware, postmodern ceramics and other interior-decor must-haves for the stylishly modern.

If you accidentally knock over a display of poinsettas after the Christmas holidays, and it starts falling...the gracious, unflappable Batt might just swoop in and save it. Not that we'd, er, know anything about that.

PIED NU FASHION & ACCESSORIES

Map p248 (☑504-899-4118; www.piednunola.com; 5521 Magazine St; ☺10am-5pm Mon-Sat) If you need a hand-poured candle that lasts 60 hours, try one of the sweet-smelling Diptyques on sale here. As you soak up that vanilla-scented goodness, browse elephant-printed cotton T-shirt dresses, cinched poet-dresses and low-joe sneakers. Set it all off with tiny leaf earrings – you'll make yourself almost as endearing as this precious luxury shop.

DIRTY COAST CLOTHING

Map p248 (☑504-324-3745; www.dirtycoast.com; 5631 Magazine St; ☺10am-6pm) You're not a cool new New Orleanian if you haven't picked up one of the clever T-shirts or bumper stickers (eg 'make wetlands, not war'), all related to local issues, inside jokes and neighborhood happenings, in this ridiculously cool store. There's a French Quarter location (p71) as well.

FRERET STREET MARKET MARKET

(www.freretmarket.org; cnr Freret St & Napoleon Ave; ☺11am-4pm 1st Sat of month Sep-May) This combined farmers, flea and art market offers a great mix of local culture.

UPTOWN COSTUME & DANCEWEAR CLOTHING

Map p248 (☑504-895-7969; 4326 Magazine St; ☺11am-6pm Mon-Thu, to 7pm Fri, 10am-6pm Sat) A one-stop emergency shop for anyone caught completely unprepared for Mardi Gras, Halloween or any other occasion that calls for a disguise. It's an emporium of goofy get-ups, packed with boas, masks, Elvis capes, ballerina tutus and a truly astounding selection of cheap wigs. Fun stuff for the entire family, guaranteed to keep you from blending into the woodwork.

CRESCENT CITY COMICS COMICS

Map p248 (☑504-891-3796; www.crescentcitycomics.com; 4916 Freret St; ☺1-7pm Wed-Sat, noon-6pm Sun) The helpful, on-the-ball staff members are what make Crescent City Comics shine. The store is compact but well stocked, with sections dedicated to everything from local comics to underground graphic reads. Neil Gaiman books and sci-fi action figures are also in the stacks. Check it out.

FEET FIRST SHOES

Map p248 (☑504-899-6800; www.feetfirststores.com; 4122 Magazine St; ☺10am-6pm Mon-Sat, to 5pm Sun) Feet First has been selling shoes to New Orleans' fashionistas for more than 30 years. Pop into this bright store for sandals, boots and heels as well as jewelry, frocks and T-shirts.

BLOOMIN' DEALS VINTAGE

Map p248 (☑504-891-1278; www.jlno.org; 4645 Freret St; ☺10am-6pm Tue-Sat, noon-5pm Sun) This Junior League–run thrift store isn't exactly Bloomingdale's, but some of the donations may have originated there. The women's collection is extensive – lots of jeans – and you might just pick up a unique ball gown from Mardi Gras season that was only worn once. Lots of used books for sale, too (from 25¢).

C COLLECTION FASHION & ACCESSORIES

Map p248 (☑504-861-5002; www.ccollectionnola.com; 8141 Maple St; ☺10am-5:30pm Mon-Sat) This boutique, preening fashionably inside a converted house, does its best to keep the female population of Tulane University (and the women of Riverbend region in general) looking smart, with its range of short shorts, flowy skirts, cute dresses and silky shirts plus fashionable sunglasses, scarves, jeans and shoes. New outfits are posted at www.instagram.com/ccollection.

Mid-City, Bayou St John & City Park

Neighborhood Top Five

1 **City Park** (p141) Spending a lazy afternoon at this park, checking out art, outdoor sculptures, gardens and a toy train, then blissing out under an oak tree as the world spins by.

2 **Bayou St John** (p143) Lazing the day away by this man-made waterway that runs through the heart of the city, or heading out here with a kayak and a paddle.

3 **Sydney & Walda Besthoff Sculpture Garden** (p143) Wandering around the statuary and green landscaping.

4 **Esplanade Avenue** (p143) Marveling at one of the most gorgeous streets in the city, packed end to end with beautiful homes and mansions.

5 **New Orleans Museum of Art** (p143) Soaking up the arts at this elegant institution, filled with both regional and global art.

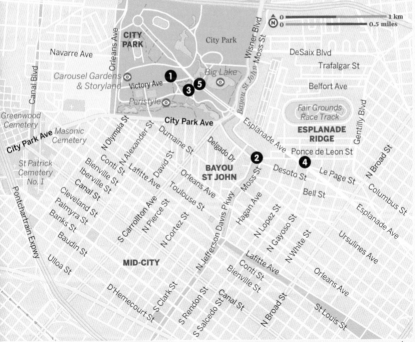

For more detail of this area see Map p252 ➡

Lonely Planet's Top Tip

Mid-City and its surrounding neighborhoods are best explored by car or at least bicycle. Sights are spread out in small clusters of activity across the cityscape. Walking around parts of Mid-City at night, especially near Orleans Ave and Tulane Ave, is not recommended. On the flip side, the cityscapes around Esplanade Ave, City Park Ave and Carrollton Ave between Canal St and Esplanade are some of the prettiest blocks in town.

Best Places to Eat

➡ Marjie's Grill (p146)
➡ Liuzza's By The Track (p145)
➡ 1000 Figs (p146)
➡ Parkway Tavern (p145)

For reviews, see p145 ➡

Best Nightlife

➡ Twelve Mile Limit (p148)
➡ Pal's (p148)
➡ Second Line Brewing (p148)
➡ Treo (p148)
➡ Chickie Wah Wah (p149)

For reviews, see p148 ➡

Explore Mid-City, Bayou St John & City Park

A bike ride may be the most pleasant way to explore the 'green' sections of these neighborhoods. If you cycle independently, just roll up attractive Esplanade Ave and take it all the way to City Park, stopping at St Louis Cemetery No 3 along the way. Explore the park and the New Orleans Museum of Art, and afterwards stop in for dinner at Café Degas or 1000 Figs. In the evening, enjoy a drink at Pal's or Twelve Mile Limit.

The next day, have lunch at Marjie's, then drive around Bayou St John, enjoy the serenity and consider dinner at Parkway Tavern.

Starting from the southwest, near Banks St, Mid-City is a mix of commercial lots and residential blocks. Northeast is Bayou St John, ringed with historic houses, and the great green stretches of City Park. In the southeast, Esplanade Ave runs to the French Quarter, passing through the Tremé on the way.

Local Life

Food These leafy neighborhoods are chock full of unassuming restaurants serving fantastic comfort food. The low-key friendliness of these joints just adds to the allure.

Green spaces City Park is the obvious contender for top green space in New Orleans, but there's also Bayou St John, Esplanade Ave and plenty of tree-lined streets.

Nightlife As with the food scene, there's a ton of unexpected nightlife gems in this corner of town, from convivial bars to great music venues.

Getting There & Away

Streetcar The City Park spur of Canal St hits Carrollton St, then heads up that road all the way to City Park.

Bus The 91 runs up Esplanade Ave, turns into Mid-City and drops by City Park. The 27 follows Louisiana Ave and also hits the park. The 94 bus runs along Broad, cutting through both Mid-City and the Tremé.

Car Free street parking is plentiful throughout these neighborhoods.

Bike You can pedal up here via Esplanade Ave, which has a bicycle lane, or the Lafitte Greenway.

TOP SIGHT
CITY PARK

In many ways City Park is a near perfect expression of a local 'park,' in the sense that it is an only slightly tamed expression of the forest and Louisiana wetlands (Bayou Metairie runs through the grounds) that are the natural backdrop of the city. Golf courses mar this narrative, but there's still enough wild to get lost in.

A Touch of History

City Park occupies the site of the former Allard Plantation; much of the infrastructure and improvements, including pathways, bridges and art deco flair, were built by the Works Progress Administration (WPA) during the Great Depression. The arboreal life is magnificent and includes strands of mature live oaks – thousands of them, some as old as 600 years – along with bald cypresses, Southern magnolias and other species. During Hurricane Katrina, nearby canals flooded and inundated more than 90% of the park in up to 8ft of salt water. Though the ground has recovered, many priceless trees were lost. One tree that wasn't was the **Singing Oak** (or Singing Tree), which stands festooned with chimes, some up to 14ft in length. Standing under the tree during the slightest breeze is pretty magical.

DON'T MISS

➡ Sydney & Walda Besthoff Sculpture Garden
➡ Botanical Gardens
➡ New Orleans Museum of Art

PRACTICALITIES

➡ Map p252
➡ ☎504-482-4888
➡ www.neworleans citypark.com
➡ Esplanade Ave & City Park Ave
➡ P ♿ 🐾

Botanical Gardens & Peristyle

The Botanical Gardens (p144) have been the site of many a New Orleans wedding, and in their green depths you'll find examples of flora from both around the world and across the backyard of Louisiana.

Overlooking Bayou Metairie like a Greek temple is the Peristyle (pictured above; p143), a classical pavilion featuring Ionic columns, built in 1907. Four concrete lions stand watch, while weddings, dances, recitals and curious tourists meander through.

CELEBRATION IN THE OAKS

This City Park celebration (www.neworleanscitypark.com/celebration-in-the-oaks; adult/child under 3 $9/free; ☉6-10pm Mon-Thu, 6-11pm Fri, 5-11pm Sat, 5-10pm Sun late Nov & Dec; c) is New Orleans' take on Christmas in America, with 2 miles of oak trees providing the lit-up superstructure. You can view it in its entirety from your car or in a horse-drawn carriage.

City Park is larger than Central Park and it has alligators, so really, what are you waiting for? If alligators aren't your thing, it is also home to long lines of live oaks and weeping willows; a botanical garden that contains New Orleans in miniature; ice cream; Greek columns; a sculpture garden that surrounds the New Orleans Museum of Art; and a singing tree, festooned with wind chimes and romance.

Couturie Forest

The wildest section of the park is this scad of hardwood forest, where live oaks shade leafy underbrush and mushrooms peek out of the moist soil. Park your car in the lot off the Harrison Ave traffic circle and you'll see a road that extends back into the forest; take any branching trail and get pleasantly lost.

New Orleans Museum of Art

Looking like a vague cross between Lenin's tomb and a Greek temple, the New Orleans Museum of Art (p143) is one of the finest art museums in the South. There's strong representation from regional and American artists, but the work of masters, such as Edgar Degas, who have passed through the city is also prominent.

Popp Fountain

The Popp Fountain is wonderful, and another impressive example from the WPA. Promenades planted with perennials and 26 Corinthian columns surround the centerpiece of water erupting from a bronze base of cavorting dolphins.

Sydney & Walda Besthoff Sculpture Garden

Three of George Rodrigue's 'Blue Dogs' – in red, yellow and blue – await your arrival in the pleasant Sydney & Walda Besthoff Sculpture Garden, which sits beside the New Orleans Museum of Art. The garden opened in 2003 with pieces from the world-renowned Besthoff collection and today holds more than 60 pieces, dotted across 5 acres. Most are contemporary works by artists such as Antoine Bourdelle, Henry Moore and Louise Bourgeois.

Theme Parks

Anyone who doesn't like the charmingly dated Carousel Gardens must surely have a heart of stone. The lovingly restored antique carousel is housed in a 1906 structure with a stained-glass cupola. You can board the tiny City Park Railroad here as well, plus a little Ferris wheel, bumper cars and a tilt-a-whirl.

Storyland (p144) doesn't have rides, just fun statues of fairy-tale heroes and villains. If the characters seem strangely similar to Mardi Gras floats, it's because they were created by master float-builder Blaine Kern. During the Christmas season it's lit up like a Christmas tree and all very magical.

⊙ SIGHTS

Two of the main sights in this area are in the name of the neighborhood: Bayou St John and City Park. Both are lovely spots for just wandering around and soaking up greenery; City Park has the added advantage of being enormous and full of its own 'sub' sights. There's a lot to be said for just wandering up and down Esplanade Ave and Ursuline Ave, both of which are undeniably attractive. Beyond that, this area is one of the more residential, less touristy parts of the city.

CITY PARK   PARK
See p141.

★SYDNEY & WALDA
BESTHOFF SCULPTURE GARDEN   GARDENS
Map p252 (www.noma.org/sculpture-garden; 1 Collins Diboll Circle; ⊙10am-6pm Apr-Sep, to 5pm Oct-Mar) FREE The sculpture garden that sits just outside the New Orleans Museum of Art is a wooded quilt of streams, pathways, lovers' benches and, of course, sculpture, mainly of the modern and contemporary sort. During spring and summer, theatrical productions are often put on here, but it's a lovely spot for a stroll any time of year.

BAYOU ST JOHN   RIVER
Map p252 (Moss St & Wisner Ave; 🚲🎣) Back in the day, this was a true bayou – an overgrown morass of Spanish moss and prowling alligators. Native Americans, fur trappers and smugglers would use the waterway as a natural road that led over the dark wetlands to the shores of Lake Pontchartrain. Today, the bayou has been partially dredged and beautified into a narrow green space that makes for a breezy, altogether pleasant green ribbon that snakes across the center of the city.

Don't swim here – the bottom is shallow, has sharp rubble underfoot and there are still alligators here!

ESPLANADE AVENUE   STREET
Map p252 (btwn Rampart St & City Park) Esplanade is one of the most beautiful streets in New Orleans, yet barely recognized by visitors as such. Because of the abundance of historical homes, Esplanade, which follows the 'high ground' of Esplanade Ridge, is known as the Creole St Charles Ave. Both streets are shaded by rows and rows of leafy live oaks, but whereas St Charles is full of large, plantation-style American villas, Esplanade is framed by columned, French Creole–style mansions.

NEW ORLEANS MUSEUM OF ART   MUSEUM
Map p252 (NOMA; ☎504-658-4100; www.noma.org; 1 Collins Diboll Circle; adult/child 7-17yr $12/6; ⊙10am-6pm Tue-Thu, to 9pm Fri, 10am-5pm Sat, 11am-5pm Sun) Inside City Park, this elegant museum was opened in 1911 and is well worth a visit for its special exhibitions, gorgeous marble atrium and top-floor galleries of African, Asian, Native American and Oceanic art. Its sculpture garden contains a cutting-edge collection in lush, meticulously planned grounds. Other specialties include Southern painters and an ever-expanding collection of modern and contemporary art.

PITOT HOUSE   HISTORIC BUILDING
Map p252 (☎504-482-0312; www.pitothouse.org; 1440 Moss St; adult/child under 12yr & senior $10/7; ⊙10am-3pm Wed-Sat) The Pitot House, perched prettily beside Bayou St John, is an excellent example of classical French New Orleans architecture. Constructed circa 1799, it's the only Creole Colonial house along the bayou that is open to the public. The shaded verandah served as a living area whenever the weather got too hot. The house is named for resident James Pitot, who served as first mayor of incorporated New Orleans and lived here from 1810 to 1819. Visitation is by guided tour.

PERISTYLE   ARCHITECTURE
Map p252 (http://neworleanscitypark.com/rentals-and-catering/venues/peristyle; City Park; sunrise-sunset) FREE This eye-catching pavilion in City Park, built in 1907, is marked by Ionic columns and flanked by four lions. It looks like it was summoned via some time machine from ancient Greece, but today it's a great spot to sit with a sweetie and watch the sun set. The structure was originally built for private events and many weddings happen here.

CAROUSEL GARDENS
AMUSEMENT PARK   AMUSEMENT PARK
Map p252 (☎504-483-9402; www.neworleanscitypark.com/in-the-park/carousel-gardens; 7 Victory Ave, City Park; adult/child 36in & under $4/free, each ride $4; ⊙11am-6pm Sat & Sun Mar-May & Aug-Oct, 11am-5pm Tue-Fri, to 6pm Sat & Sun Jun & Jul) This little amusement park is

anchored by a 1906 carousel that's a gem of vintage carny-ride happiness. Other thrills include a Ferris wheel, bumper cars and a tilt-a-whirl. If you want to stay for awhile, buy an $18 pass for unlimited rides. The park is closed outside of the above seasonal hours, although it is open on evenings during Celebration in the Oaks (a festival of lights in late November and December).

METAIRIE CEMETERY CEMETERY

Map p252 (☑504-486-6331; 5100 Pontchartrain Blvd; ☉7:30am-5:30pm) Established in 1872 on a former racetrack (the grounds, you'll notice, still follow the oval layout), this is the most American of New Orleans' cities of the dead. Highlights include the Brunswig mausoleum, a pyramid guarded by a sphinx statue; the Moriarty monument, reputedly the 'tallest privately owned monument' in the country; and the Estelle Theleman Hyams monument, its stained-glass fixture casting a somber blue light over a slumped, despondent angel. A car helps for exploring the 150-acre grounds.

ST LOUIS CEMETERY NO 3 CEMETERY

Map p252 (☑504-596-3050; 3421 Esplanade Ave; ☉9am-3pm Mon-Sat, to noon Sun) FREE This long but compact cemetery was established in 1854 at the site of the old Bayou Cemetery and is worth strolling through for a few minutes (longer if you're a cemetery enthusiast). Of particular note is the striking monument James Gallier Jr designed for his mother and father who were lost at sea. It's a few steps to the right just after you enter from Esplanade Ave. The cemetery's wrought-iron entrance gate is a beauty.

BOTANICAL GARDENS GARDENS

Map p252 (☑504-483-9488; www.neworleanscitypark.com/botanical-garden; City Park; adult/child/under 3 $8/4/free; ☉10am-5pm; ℗) Located within City Park, both local and international flora is exhibited here. You'll also find stirring examples of WPA workmanship and art deco design in the form of pavilions and function halls such as the Pavilion of Two Sisters and Lath House. In the northwest corner, the Train Garden replicates the city in 1:22 scale miniature size, cut through with 1300ft of rail.

FAIR GROUNDS RACE COURSE LANDMARK

Map p252 (☑504-944-5515; www.fairgroundsracecourse.com; 1751 Gentilly Blvd) Laid out in 1852, this is the third-oldest racetrack in the nation. During the Civil War, you could catch bear fights here. Today, besides horse races, the Fair Grounds is the site of the annual Louisiana Derby (in March) and the Jazz Fest. Buried in the infield are derby winners from a past era. The racing season runs from late November through March and includes, along with the horses, ostrich, dachshund and guys-in-T-rex races,

STORYLAND AMUSEMENT PARK

Map p252 (http://neworleanscitypark.com/in-the-park/storyland; 5 Victory Ave, City Park; adult/child 36in & under $4/free; ☉10am-5pm; ⊞) There are no rides at Storyland, located next to Carousel Gardens, but the fairy-tale statuary provides plenty of fuel for young imaginations. Children can play with – and climb upon – the Jabberwocky from *Alice in Wonderland* or enter the mouth of the whale from *Pinocchio*.

ALCEE FORTIER PARK PARK

Map p252 (3100 Esplanade Ave; ☉24hr; ⊞☺) FREE This pretty park, strung up with lights and lanterns and decked out with funky furniture, sits across the road from one of the most attractive stretches of Esplanade Ave, an area replete with restaurants, shops and a general breezy ambience. Movies are sometimes screened here on evenings, especially for kids.

A good spot for a picnic, but you should know there are occasionally homeless people around as well.

OUR LADY OF THE ROSARY RECTORY HISTORIC BUILDING

Map p252 (☑504-488-2659; 1342 Moss St; ☉Mass 7am Mon-Fri, 4pm Sat, 9am, 11am & 6pm Sun) Built around 1834 as the home of Evariste Blanc, Our Lady of the Rosary Rectory exhibits a combination of styles characteristic of the region. The high-hipped roof and wraparound gallery seem reminiscent of West Indies houses but were actually the preferred styles of French Canadians who originally settled Bayou St John. However, it's the house's neoclassical details that make it obvious that this building is from a later period.

During Jazz Fest, Mass is held at 7:30am and 9am on Sundays.

SANCTUARY HISTORIC BUILDING

Map p252 (924 Moss St) This historic house was built by Evariste Blanc from 1816 to 1822 on land originally granted in 1720

NEW ORLEANS: BORN ON THE BAYOU

Today, Bayou St John is a pleasant backdrop for a stroll or a short paddle in a kayak. But take a closer look. This sometimes smelly creek is the reason this city exists. It was originally used by Native Americans as a wet highway to the relatively high ground of Esplanade Ridge before French explorers realized the waterway was the shortest route between the Mississippi River – and by extent the Gulf of Mexico – and Lake Pontchartrain. It was essentially for this reason that New Orleans was built in its commanding position at the mouth of the Mississippi. Eventually a canal built by Governor Carondelet extended the bayou to the edge of the French Quarter, and the bayou acted as the city's chief commercial harbor. Life in the area thrived; beautiful houses lined the bayou (many remain here today) and voodoo queen Marie Laveau and followers supposedly conducted rituals on the waterfront.

The era of steamboats made direct navigation up and down the Mississippi easier, and the bayou began to be eclipsed. Navigation ended with the filling of the canal in 1927, but the bayou remained an important geographic point of reference. Since 2005 it has also become a bone of contention between local residents and the Army Corps of Engineers. The Corps insists St John is a potential source of floodwater and have proposed sealing it off from Pontchartrain. Some residents say opening sector gates on the bayou's pump houses could facilitate the natural flow of water, which would freshen up the bayou (which can grow darkly stagnant), improve water quality and reintroduce important flora and fauna to the bayou bank.

The issue is still being fought. In the meantime, come out here to stroll along the bayou (stagnant or not, it is scenic and supremely serene, especially at sunset), enjoy a po'boy from the **Parkway Tavern**, catch one of the many concerts played on the median that runs through the bayou and gape at the gorgeous residences. You are able to visit Pitot House (p143), a restored mansion with a lovely set of gardens in the back.

to French Canadians. The once-swampy property was later transferred to Don Andrés Almonaster y Roxas, the real-estate speculator who commissioned St Louis Cathedral on Jackson Sq in the French Quarter. It's a private residence today.

EATING

There are loads of neighborhood restaurants out this way that serve excellent New Orleans cuisine (and increasingly, food from further afield). Local restaurants charge local prices; you can eat a lot cheaper here than in the Quarter or CBD.

★ LIUZZA'S BY THE TRACK   DINER $

Map p252 (☎504-218-7888; www.liuzzasnola.com; 1518 N Lopez St; mains $7-16; ⊙11am-7pm Mon-Sat) Mmmm, that gumbo. This quintessential Mid-City neighborhood joint does some of the best in town. The barbecue shrimp po'boy is to die for and the deep-fried garlic oysters are legendary. The atmosphere is unforgettable: we've seen a former city judge and a stripper dining together here, which is as 'Only in New Orleans' an experience as you can get.

Liuzza's is nearly impossible to squeeze into during Jazz Fest, which is held at the nearby Fair Grounds Race Course.

★ PARKWAY TAVERN   SANDWICHES $

Map p252 (☎504-482-3047; www.parkwaypoorboys.com; 538 Hagan Ave; po'boys $8-14; ⊙11am-10pm Wed-Mon; P🞄) Who makes the best po'boy in New Orleans? Honestly, who can say? But tell a local you think the top sandwich comes from Parkway and you will get, at the least, a nod of respect. The roast beef in particular – a craft some would say is dying among the great po'boy makers – is messy as hell and twice as good.

Take one down to nearby Bayou St John, and munch that sandwich in the shade. Louisiana bliss. The homemade bread pudding with rum sauce is also divine – and secretly our top choice at Parkway.

NAMESE   VIETNAMESE $

Map p252 (☎504-483-8899; www.namese.net; 4077 Tulane Ave; mains $7-18; ⊙11am-10pm

Mon-Sat; P ✗ ⚲) We get a little leery when folks try to modernize a cuisine that's already great, but Namese executes this concept with care and precision. Folks pack in for shrimp and pork-belly papaya salad, cornish hen with Dijon ginger and even a vegan bowl of pho. There's a kids' menu for the little ones.

ANGELO BROCATO   ICE CREAM $

Map p252 (✆504-486-0079; www.angelobroca-toicecream.com; 214 N Carrollton Ave; scoop of gelato $3.25, pastries under $4; ⊙10am-10pm Tue-Thu, to 10:30pm Fri & Sat, to 9pm Sun) When an ice-cream parlor passes the 100-year mark, you gotta step back and say, 'Clearly, they're doing something right.' Opened in 1905 by Signor Brocato himself, a Sicilian immigrant who scraped together his savings from working on a sugar plantation, this is the oldest ice-cream shop in New Orleans. Inside, silky gelatos, perfect cannoli and crispy biscotti wow the tastebuds.

BISCUITS & BUNS ON BANKS   BREAKFAST $

Map p252 (✆504-273-4600; www.biscuitsand-bunsonbanks.com; 4337 Banks St; mains $9-12; ✗ ⚲) Need some carbs in your life? Have them with a side of delicious at Biscuits & Buns. The fluffy breads come slathered with gravy and topped with fried chicken or apples, walnuts and grilled goat cheese. Kids come here a lot, and while there isn't a dedicated children's menu, little ones are well looked after.

IDEAL MARKET   SUPERMARKET $

Map p252 (✆504-822-8861; http://laidealmar-ket.com; 250 S Broad St; hot plates $5-10; ⊙6am-9pm; P) The Ideal Market chain is the largest grocery purveyor serving the Louisiana Latino community. Ideal is filled with imported items that may be hard to find elsewhere and has a hot-plate bar where you can easily feed yourself, and likely a friend, for under $10. Rotating specials include slow-cooked pork, yellow rice, plantains, stewed chicken and other goodies.

NONNA MIA CAFÉ & PIZZERIA   ITALIAN $

Map p252 (✆504-948-1717; www.nonnamia.net; 3125 Esplanade Ave; pizza $12-20, mains $10-16; ⊙11am-9pm Sun-Thu, to 10pm Fri & Sat; ✗) Getting tired of heavy, rich Creole cuisine? How about a fresh slice of pizza and some ice tea in Nonna Mia's outdoor courtyard? The caramelized onions, goat cheese and artichoke hearts are proof pizza doesn't need pepperoni to be perfect.

CANSECO'S   SUPERMARKET $

Map p252 (✆504-322-2594; www.cansecos.com; 3135 Esplanade Ave; hot plates $7-10; ⊙7am-10pm) If you're self-catering or just need some picnic food before Jazz Fest, head to this little grocery store – their hot plates (fried chicken, pasta and other comfort-food fare) are delicious and cheap.

MORNING CALL   BREAKFAST $

Map p252 (http://neworleanscitypark.com/in-the-park/morning-call; Dreyfous Ave, City Park; mains $2-10; ⊙24hr) Just a few steps from the Besthoff Sculpture Garden, Morning Call serves coffee, gumbo and very good beignets (arguably better than another famous beignet spot that begins with a 'C' and ends with 'afé du Monde') around the clock. Cash only.

RUBY SLIPPER   BREAKFAST $

Map p252 (✆504-525-9355; www.therubyslip-percafe.net; 315 S Broad St; mains $9-20; ⊙7am-2pm Mon-Fri, to 3pm Sat & Sun; ✗) The Slipper has become a small local chain and serves basic American breakfast food prepared with a touch of gourmet flair: the hollandaise has a kick, the French toast is stuffed, yummy and gooey, and a poached egg tops the crispy chicken biscuit. That said, it's not as great as its popularity may imply.

★MARJIE'S GRILL   ASIAN $$

Map p252 (✆504-603-2234; www.marjiesgrill.com; 320 S Broad St; mains $8-26; ⊙11am-2:30pm & 5:30-10pm Mon-Fri, 4-10pm Sat) In one word: brilliant. Marjie's is run by chefs who were inspired by Southeast Asian street food, but rather than coming home and doing pale imitations of the real thing, they've turned an old house on Broad St into a corner in Hanoi, Luang Prabang or Chiang Mai. With that said, there's a hint of New Orleans at work.

Coal-roasted fish has a flaky, wonderfully charred skin, while cornmeal-battered chicken goes down a treat with sambal and cane syrup. The simple pork steak is a godsend: sliced, wonderfully cooked and served with a small mountain of fresh herbs.

★1000 FIGS   MIDDLE EASTERN $$

Map p252 (✆504-301-0848; www.1000figs.com; 3141 Ponce de Leon St; small plates $5-16; ⊙11am-9pm Tue-Sat; ✗) Although the menu isn't exclusively vegetarian, 1000 Figs serves our favorite vegetarian fare in town. The falafel, hummus, baba ghanouj and lentil soup are just *good* – freshly prepared and expertly executed. The dining space is well lit and seating makes you feel as if you're eating in a best friend's stylish dining room.

A full sampler platter of more or less everything on the menu is $32.

TOUPS' MEATERY
LOUISIANAN **$$**

Map p252 (☑504-252-4999; www.toupsmeatery.com; 845 N Carrollton Ave; lunch $14-22, small plates $11-17, mains $22-34; ⏰11am-2:30pm Tue-Sat, 5-10pm Tue-Thu, 5-11pm Fri & Sat) Cheese plates. Charcuterie boards. These are standard appetizers at restaurants across the land. But they are nothing compared to the chest-pounding glory that is the Toup's Meatery Board, a Viking-worthy platter of MEAT. Housemade and cured, this carnivore's feast will harden your arteries in a single glance. But oh, that butter-soft marrow on the bone.

At this Mid-City hot spot, which looks like a hunting lodge dressed up nice, meat includes beef, pork, goat, quail, lamb, chicken and seafood, with boudin (Cajun sausage) balls, cracklin' and hog's head cheese available as sides. New Orleans beers are on tap and Pimms cups are available by the pitcher.

CAFÉ DEGAS
FRENCH **$$**

Map p252 (☑504-945-5635; www.cafedegas.com; 3127 Esplanade Ave; lunch $8-18, dinner $14-31; ⏰11am-3pm Wed-Fri, from 10:30am Sat & Sun, 5:30-10pm Wed-Sat, to 9.30pm Sun) A pecan tree thrusts through the floor and ceiling of the enclosed deck that serves as Café Degas' congenial dining room. A rustic, romantic little spot, Degas warms the heart with first-rate French fare. Meals that sound familiar on the menu – *steak frites au poivre,* parmesan-crusted veal medallions – are arranged with extraordinary beauty on the plate.

Brunch is gorgeous; the crab crepe with hollandaise is decadent.

BEVI SEAFOOD CO.
SEAFOOD **$$**

Map p252 (☑504-488-7503; http://beviseafoodco.com; 236 Carrollton Ave; mains $8-20; ⏰11am-8pm Tue-Sat, to 4pm Sun & Mon) Inside, Bevi's has less atmosphere than the moon, but if you don't mind the bare walls and cafeteria seating, there's excellent local seafood to be had, from boiled crawfish to head-on barbecue shrimp to a po'boy with fried oysters, melted Gouda cheese and bacon (!).

BROWN BUTTER
SOUTHERN US **$$**

Map p252 (☑504-609-3871; www.brownbutterrestaurant.com; 231 N Carrollton Ave; mains $12-19; ⏰11am-3pm Tue-Fri, 5:30-10pm Tue-Sat,

10:30am-3pm Sat, 10am-3pm Sun; ⓟ) Contemporary Southern food has been a culinary trend in New Orleans for decades, but Brown Butter executes the genre with midrange prices and menu items that are high-end quality. For lunch, grab an oyster sandwich or a boudin *banh mi;* come dinner, oak-smoked brisket and chili-lathered chicken make an appearance.

LOLA'S
SPANISH **$$**

Map p252 (☑504-488-6946; www.lolasneworleans.com; 3312 Esplanade Ave; mains $13-34; ⏰5:30-9:30pm Sun-Thu, to 10pm Fri & Sat) Enjoy wine and conversation with crowds of Mid-City locals who swear by Lola's paellas and *fideuàs* (an angel-hair pasta variation on the former). Inside, it's all elbows and the buzz of conversation and good grub. This isn't haute Barcelona cuisine; it's the Spanish peasant fare Hemingway wrote chapters about: rabbit, meats, fresh seafood, olive oil and lots of delicious garlic.

KATIE'S
CREOLE **$$**

Map p252 (☑504-488-6582; www.katiesinmidcity.com; 3701 Iberville St; mains $11-24; ⏰11am-9pm Mon-Thu, to 10pm Fri & Sat, 9am-3pm Sun; ⓐ) Katie's is how New Orleans does a family restaurant. Everything is taken over the top to new levels of decadent enjoyment; onion rings swim in remoulade sauce, fries are tossed with garlic butter and blue cheese, and the oysters Slessinger, doused in cheese, shrimp and bacon...oh wow. Portions are enormous.

NEYOW'S
CREOLE **$$**

Map p252 (☑504-827-5474; www.neyows.com; 3332 Bienville St; mains $8.75-19; ⏰11am-9pm Mon-Thu, to 11pm Fri & Sat) Neyow's is a New Orleans standby, the sort of spot that churns out relatable, reliable blue-chip dishes like breaded pork chops, smothered chicken, and grilled catfish stuffed with lump crab meat. It's enormously popular, so be prepared to wait for a table (no reservations).

MOPHO
VIETNAMESE **$$**

Map p252 (☑504-482-6845; www.mophonola.com; 514 City Park Ave; lunch $7-18, dinner $8-23; ⏰11am-10pm Sun-Thu, to 11pm Fri & Sat; ⓟ☑) At this innovative kitchen, traditional Vietnamese dishes often come with a Louisiana kick, from Gulf shrimp spring rolls to *banh mi*–style po'boys. We give props for the stylish digs, attentive service and the great name. The pho? Solid, not swoon-inducing.

We're bigger fans of the super rich, slow-roasted lamb curry.

MANDINA'S
ITALIAN $$

Map p252 (☑504-482-9179; www.mandinas-restaurant.com; 3800 Canal St; mains $12-23; ☺11am-9:30pm Mon-Thu, to 10pm Fri & Sat, noon-9pm Sun) In the Italian American New Orleans community, funerals were followed by a visit to Mandina's for turtle soup. The menu may be conservative, but when you've been around for more than 100 years you stick to what you know. In this case that's Sicilian Louisiana food: trout almandine, red beans and veal cutlets, and bell peppers stuffed with macaroni and meat.

The dining room is as historic as any building in the city and just as crucial to its culture.

CRESCENT CITY STEAKS
STEAK $$$

Map p252 (☑504-821-3271; http://crescentcitysteaks.com; 1001 N Broad St; steaks $26-31; ☺11:30am-9:30pm Tue-Thu, to 10pm Fri, 4-10pm Sat, noon-9pm Sun) Is this the best steak in the city? No. But the venue is older than old school; there are little private booths where you can have mafia-style dinners without having to look at the common folk. Plus the steak, which comes out sizzling in butter with potatoes Lyonnaise (sliced and fried with shallots), is still pretty great.

🍷 DRINKING & NIGHTLIFE

There are some decent bars out this way, but they tend to be neighborhood places that out-of-towners may not consider worth the hike. But there are a few key exceptions. In general the scene here is lively, local and happy to share a beer and a story with a stranger.

★ TWELVE MILE LIMIT
BAR

Map p252 (☑504-488-8114; www.facebook.com/twelve.mile.limit; 500 S Telemachus St; ☺5pm-2am Mon-Thu, 11am-2am Fri, 10am-2am Sat, 10am-midnight Sun) Twelve Mile is simply a great bar. It's staffed by people who have the skill, both behind the bar and in the kitchen, to work in four-star spots, but who chose to set up shop in a neighborhood, for a neighborhood. The mixed drinks are excellent, the match of any mixologist's cocktail in Manhattan, and the vibe is super accepting.

★ PAL'S
BAR

Map p252 (☑504-488-7257; www.palslounge.com; 949 N Rendon St; ☺3pm-late) This great neighborhood bar is a little more convivial for the older generation, although it's definitely an all-ages crowd. The men's bathroom, wallpapered with vintage pinups, is like a walk through *Playboy's* history, while the backroom air hockey is always enjoyable. Open until at least 3am Sunday through Thursday and at least 4am on Friday and Saturday.

You might not expect great cocktails at this little dive, but mixed drinks like the gingerita could hold their own in any fancy Manhattan or London mixology joint.

STATION
CAFE

Map p252 (☑504-309-4548; www.thestation.coffee; 4400 Bienville St; ☺6:30am-8pm Mon-Fri, 7:30am-5pm Sat & Sun) There are plenty of cafes in Mid-City, but Station is a significant caffeinated cut above the rest. The coffee is simply thoughtfully curated and brewed well; there's no need for crazy espresso concoctions here. Try the Vietnamese *cafe sua da* (iced coffee with condensed milk) – it's a treat on a hot day.

TREO
COCKTAIL BAR

Map p252 (☑504-304-4878; www.treonola.com; 3835 Tulane Ave; ☺4pm-midnight) My Whole Life Is Thunder. Shochu Wanna Party. The Rubio. Treo knows how to name a cocktail – and, more importantly, how to mix one. Tipplers have a choice of seasonal drinks and Louisiana-style small plates. For a touch of culture, check out the art gallery upstairs. And that cool art piece on the ceiling? A wooden map of New Orleans.

SECOND LINE BREWING
BREWERY

Map p252 (☑504-248-8979; www.secondline-brewing.com; 433 N Bernadotte St; ☺4-10pm Wed-Fri, noon-10pm Sat, to 8pm Sun; 🐾) Located at the end of some old railroad tracks, Second Line has turned a light industrial warehouse into a kicking brewery with a courtyard and kid-friendly play accoutrements. The frequent presence of food trucks makes this outdoor suds spot a popular place with families and those seeking beer and bites al fresco.

FINN MCCOOL'S
BAR

Map p252 (☑504-486-9080; www.finnmccools.com; 3701 Banks St; ☺11am-2am Mon-Thu, to 3am Fri-Sun) Want a surreal New Orleans experience? Arrive at 6am when premier league soccer or big international rugby games are playing. You'll see a mix of European sports enthusiasts, British expats and Hispanic locals packed into this bar. Finn's is an excellent spot for a beer any time (especially on St Paddy's Day), but we particularly love it for watching soccer.

Check the website or call for game days and hours.

MID-CITY YACHT CLUB   BAR

Map p252 (☎504-483-2517; www.midcityyachtclub.com; 440 S St Patrick St; ⊕11am-2am Mon-Thu, to 4am Fri, 10:30am-4am Sat & Sun) The Yacht Club is so much a part of the neighborhood that one of the owners took his boat out to save flooded Katrina victims (hence the name of the bar, which isn't near a lake or ocean). More than this, it is literally a part of the neighborhood: the bar is made from wood salvaged from storm debris.

The vibe is somewhere between a neighborhood watering hole and a sports bar. During big games (especially Saints football), folks pack in for game-day specials; at other times, you're rubbing elbows with and buying rounds for locals.

FAIR GRINDS   CAFE

Map p252 (☎504-913-9072; 3133 Ponce de Leon St; ⊕6:30am-9pm; 🐾) 🍴 Like many of the best indie coffee shops, Fair Grinds is comfy, hip and unpretentious. And, of course, it serves a good cup of joe. It also showcases local art and generally acts as the beating heart of Mid-City's bohemian scene; plus, it supports community development associations and hosts regular folk-music nights.

BAYOU BEER GARDEN   BAR

Map p252 (☎504-302-9357; www.bayoubeergarden.com; 326 N Jefferson Davis Pkwy; ⊕11am-2am) The Bayou has been sorely needed in New Orleans: a beer bar with an enormous outdoor deck that serves pub grub. Shows lots of sports and thus attracts an interesting mix of jocks and punky locals on game days.

BAYOU WINE GARDEN   WINE BAR

Map p252 (☎504-826-2925; http://bayouwinegarden.com; 315 N Rendon St; ⊕11am-2am Mon-Thu, to 3am Fri-Sun) Literally across the street from the back courtyard of Bayou Beer Garden, and managed by the same team, the wine garden is just that: a courtyard bar with dozens of wines available via either bottle or on tap. The interior of this spot is more brick and hardwood classy than the sporty beer garden.

SIDEBAR   BAR

Map p252 (☎504-324-3838; www.sidebarnola.com; 611 S White St; ⊕2pm-2am Mon-Sat, from 11am Sun) This is a classy little spot, the sort of bar that feels like a warm drinking den in your tasteful friend's home more than anything else. For all its looks, though, Sidebar is very casual – a spot to watch a game and that seems to draw in workers from the nearby courthouse and medical centers.

PEARL WINE CO   WINE BAR

Map p252 (☎504-483-6314; www.pearlwineco.com; 3700 Orleans Ave; ⊕4pm-midnight Wed-Sat) On the 1st floor of the American Can Building apartment complex, this wine shop and lounge is an inviting place to relax and sip wine after a morning exploring City Park or strolling Bayou St John. Hosts frequent free wine tastings.

☆ ENTERTAINMENT

CHICKIE WAH WAH   LIVE MUSIC

Map p252 (☎844-244-2543; www.chickiewahwah.com; 2828 Canal St; cover $5-10; ⊕5pm-midnight Mon-Fri, 7pm-midnight Sat & Sun) Despite the fact it lies in Mid-City on one of the most unremarkable stretches of Canal St, Chickie Wah Wah is a great music venue. Local legends, such as Sunpie Barnes and Alex McMurry, and plenty of international talent, all make their way across the small stage.

BANKS STREET BAR   LIVE MUSIC

Map p252 (☎504-486-0258; www.banksstreetbarandgrill.com; 4401 Banks St; ⊕11am-2am) While Banks Street Bar is a quintessential neighborhood dive, it's also renowned as a good place to catch local music seven nights a week. It's famous for its good rock shows, but it also hosts jazz, funk, brass and the rest, and doesn't charge a cover.

It gets loud in here, so don't plan on discussing representation and repression in the latter works of Terrence Malick between sets.

🛍 SHOPPING

Thanks to its historical infrastructure and architecture, New Orleans tends to lack the sprawling strip-mall development

you find in so many other American cities. But you'll find exceptions to this rule around N Carrollton Ave and Bienville St. There are also a few cool boutiques and smaller shops strung out along Carrollton Ave and Broad St.

★ TUBBY & COOS   BOOKS

Map p252 (📞504-598-5536; www.tubbyandcoos.com; 631 N Carrollton Ave; 10am-7pm Thu-Tue; 📶) Haven't found the droids you were looking for? Then stop by this self-proclaimed 'geeky' bookstore where books and movies loved by nerds take the spotlight. *Game of Thrones, Dr Who, Star Wars* – the gang is all here. They have a great kids section upstairs and rent out an enormous selection of board games.

★ F&F BOTANICA
SPIRITUAL SUPPLY   GIFTS & SOUVENIRS

Map p252 (📞504-482-9142; www.orleanscandleco.com; 801 N Broad Ave; 8am-5pm Mon, Tue & Thu-Sat) Hesitant to enter a 'voodoo store'? Don't worry, staff couldn't be more helpful at this jam-packed shop that's lined with colorful candles. Forget all the fake voodoo shops in the French Quarter, this is a genuine Puerto Rican botanica that sells issue-related candles (success, love, etc), *gris-gris* (spell bags or amulets) and spell components.

No tourist-oriented, Hollywood-style dolls here; real worshippers drop in to deal with real issues, which, according to the spell lists, seem to be mainly related to heartache, immigration and the law. We guarantee you'll walk away with one of their candles, which are used in voodoo and Santería (the latter is a Puerto Rican religion related to voodoo).

HOME MALONE   GIFTS & SOUVENIRS

Map p252 (📞504-324-8352; https://homemalonenola.com; 629 N Carrollton Ave; 10am-6pm Tue-Sat, noon-5pm Sun) You won't find Macaulay Culkin or improvised booby traps here, but this lovely shop is packed with bath bombs, New Orleans-ish home decor and local original art. A perfect shop for a South Louisiana souvenir.

MASSEY'S   SPORTS & OUTDOORS

Map p252 (📞504-648-0292; www.masseysoutfitters.com; 509 N Carrollton Ave; 10am-7pm Mon-Sat, 11am-6pm Sun) Massey's is a large, well-stocked local chain carrying an excellent selection of camping, hiking and general outdoors gear.

🏃 SPORTS & ACTIVITIES

KAYAKITIYAT   KAYAKING

(📞985-778-5034, 512-964-9499; http://kayakitiyat.com; tours per person $45-105) Kayakitiyat leads tours on the Bayou seven days a week. The best is the Pontchartrain Paddle ($65), a four-hour tour that traverses the length of the Bayou.

CITY PUTT   GOLF

Map p252 (📞504-483-9385; http://neworleanscitypark.com/in-the-park/city-putt; City Park; adult/child 4-12yr $8/6; 10am-10pm Sun & Tue-Thu, to midnight Fri & Sat) Home to two separate courses, the New Orleans Course and the Louisiana Course, this 36-hole putt-putt is the only minigolf attraction in the city. Open year-round.

NOLA GONDOLA   BOATING

Map p252 (📞504-450-4400; www.nolagondola.com; 8 Friedrichs Ave; per couple $90; tours 1-7pm Wed-Sun) Look into getting poled around with that special someone on a gondola in City Park with Nola Gondola. Your 50-minute ride comes with crackers, cheese and croony Italian music. The company will provide champagne or wine glasses, but bring your own bubbly or vino.

WHEEL FUN RENTALS   BOATING

Map p252 (📞504-300-1289; Big Lake Trail, City Park; boats per hr from $26; 10am-sunset Mon-Fri, from 9am Sat & Sun) Grab paddleboats for pottering around Big Lake, which anchors at the far southeast corner of City Park. It also rents bicycles and Surreys (pedal-powered carriages).

Tremé-Lafitte

Neighborhood Top Five

1 **Backstreet Cultural Museum** (p154) Learning about the city's deep well of unique African American institutions at this museum, dedicated to a street-level appreciation of local culture.

2 **Louis Armstrong Park** (p154) Catching live music or a parade in this culturally dynamic public space, which is a common starting point for protests and festivals.

3 **Lafitte Greenway** (p154) Biking or walking the length of Tremé to Mid-City along a well-groomed public green space.

4 **St Louis Cemetery No 1** (p153) Wandering amidst the tombs of the city's long-passed residents in one of the most famous cemeteries in the city.

5 **St Augustine Catholic Church** (p156) Watching the local gospel choir belt out their Sunday best at this storied African American church.

detail of this area see Map p254 ➡

Lonely Planet's Top Tip

Street parking is plentiful in Tremé-Lafitte, but this compact area can easily be explored by foot or bicycle. With that said, there's less for pedestrians to enjoy above Claiborne Ave, with some exceptions. A walk up Esplanade Avenue is a walk past some of the finest large home architecture in the city. While much of the area is safe, it's best to stick to well-lit areas and use taxis or ride-share services after dark.

✕ Best Places to Eat

➡ Willie Mae's Scotch House (p158)

➡ Buttermilk Drop (p156)

➡ Dooky Chase (p159)

➡ Pagoda Cafe (p157)

➡ Lil' Dizzy's (p157)

For reviews, see p156 ➡

🛏 Best Places to Sleep

➡ La Belle Esplanade (p186)

➡ Degas House (p186)

➡ Ashton's Bed & Breakfast (p186)

For reviews, see p186 ➡

🍷 Best Nightlife

➡ Sidney's Saloon (p159)

➡ Kermit's Treme Mother in Law Lounge (p159)

➡ Bullets (p159)

For reviews, see p159 ➡

Explore Tremé-Lafitte

For our purposes, Tremé-Lafitte is bound by Rampart St, the Lafitte Greenway, Broad St and St Bernard Ave. The historical core of the Tremé is the area between Rampart St, Claiborne Ave, St Bernard Ave and Basin St. Much of this real estate is taken up by Louis Armstrong Park (p154). This is where you'll find some of the most attractive streets in the neighborhood; the area where Gov Nicholls St intersects with Henriette DeLille St is particularly lovely. If you were a fan of the show *Treme,* the 1200 block of Tremé Street was a popular filming location. In general, the neighborhood becomes more rundown the closer you get to Basin St.

Between Claiborne Ave and Broad St, the neighborhood becomes almost purely residential. There are few outright tourist attractions here, but there are some very fine restaurants up this way. With that said, there are better areas of the city for walking.

Local Life

Street parades Second Lines – neighborhood parades – can be found across New Orleans, but they often originate in, or at least pass through, Tremé-Lafitte.

Free festivals We're not exaggerating: there is basically at least one free music event in Louis Armstrong Park every month.

Bayou Road rambler Bayou Rd between Esplanade Ave and Broad St is a bricked-over thoroughfare that makes for a wonderful, short stroll.

Getting There & Away

Bus The area is relatively well served by city bus lines – the 51, 52, 57 and 91 buses all pass through Tremé-Lafitte.

Streetcar The Rampart Streetcar line runs along the edge of the neighborhood.

Bike The Lafitte Greenway begins (or ends, depending on where you're coming from) here. Esplanade Ave has a bicycle lane.

Car Parking is rarely an issue out here.

TOP SIGHT
ST LOUIS CEMETERY NO 1

New Orleans was historically influenced by the massive mausoleum-building cultures of the Spanish and French, and large above-ground necropolises are a common sight across town. The most famous is St Louis Cemetery No 1, opened in 1789. Ongoing vandalism forced the Archdiocese of New Orleans to limit visitation to relatives and organized tours. Our favorite tour group is Save Our Cemeteries (p124).

Group Graves

The Italian Mutual Benevolent Society Tomb is responsible for the tallest monument in the cemetery. Like other immigrant groups in New Orleans, the Italians formed a benevolent association to pool funds and assist in covering burial costs. In 1969, a demented rape scene in the movie *Easy Rider* was filmed here.

Marie Laveau

The supposed crypt of voodoo queen Marie Laveau (p155), where people leave offerings, is a big drawcard. Historically, this crypt has been a source of much of the vandalism that has plagued St Louis No 1. That's ironic (and tragic), as debates over which Marie Laveau – mother or daughter, if either – was actually buried here show no signs of reaching a resolution.

Other Famous Graves

St Louis No 1 is filled with some of the city's most prominent historical figures. Civil-rights figure Homer Plessy rests in the cemetery, as do real-estate speculator Bernard de Marigny (namesake of Faubourg Marigny) and architect Henry Latrobe (designer of the central tower of St Louis Cathedral, among other structures).

DON'T MISS

➡ Marie Laveau tomb
➡ Italian Mutual Benevolent Society Tomb
➡ Grave of Homer Plessy

PRACTICALITIES

➡ Map 254
➡ 504-596-3050
➡ www.saveourcemeteries.org/st-louis-cemetery-no-1
➡ 425 Basin St
➡ guided tour adult/child $20/free
➡ tours 10am, 11:30am & 1pm Mon-Sat, 10am Sun

⊙ SIGHTS

Many of the sights within the Tremé are actually at its edges, including the Louis Armstrong Park and St Louis Cemetery No 1 (p153). Other sites can be found within the neighborhood itself, which is, for our purposes, bisected by Claiborne Ave. While the Tremé is fairly light on sights, there's a lot to be said for just strolling in the area around Gov Nicholls and Henriette DeLille Sts; this is simply a very attractive part of the city. The Lafitte neighborhood is an area of mainly residential housing and the eponymous Lafitte Greenway.

★ BACKSTREET
CULTURAL MUSEUM   MUSEUM
Map p254 (☎504-522-4806; www.backstreet-museum.org; 1116 Henriette Delille St; $10; ☺10am-4pm Tue-Sat) Mardi Gras Indian suits grab the spotlight with dazzling flair – and finely crafted detail – in this informative museum examining the distinctive elements of African American culture in New Orleans. The museum isn't terribly big (it's the former Blandin's Funeral Home), but if you have any interest in the suits and rituals of Mardi Gras Indians, as well as Second Line parades and Social Aid and Pleasure Clubs (the local African American community version of civic associations), you need to stop by.

The guided tours are usually great, but sometimes feel rushed, so be sure to ask lots of questions. Ask for information about upcoming Second Lines so you can check one out firsthand.

LAFITTE GREENWAY   PARK
Map p254 (N Alexander & St Louis to Basin & St Louis; ☺24hrs; 🚻 👶) 🚲FREE This 2.6-mile green corridor connects the Tremé to City Park via Bayou St John, traversing the length of the Tremé and Mid-City along the way. It's a bicycle- and pedestrian-friendly trail that follows the course of one of the city's oldest transportation paths – this was originally a canal and, later, a railroad.

Over the years, the railroad right-of-way became decrepit; it is hoped the thoughtfully landscaped Greenway will reverse the legacies of that blight. The trail includes a raised asphalt path, energy-efficient trail lighting and wheelchair-accessible curb ramps. Although the Greenway is well lit, exercise caution late at night.

LOUIS ARMSTRONG PARK   PARK
Map p254 (701 N Rampart St; ☺sunrise-sunset) The entrance to this massive park has got to be one of the greatest gateways in the US, a picturesque arch that ought rightfully to be the final set piece in a period drama about Jazz Age New Orleans. The original Congo Sq is here, as well as a **Louis Armstrong statue** and a **bust of Sidney Bechet**. The Mahalia Jackson Theater (p159) hosts opera and Broadway productions. The park often hosts live-music festivals throughout the year.

CLOSING THE CONGO SQUARE CIRCLE
Near the main entrance to **Louis Armstrong Park** is one of the most important spots, arguably, in the development of modern music: **Congo Square**. Once known as Place de Negres, this area used to be just outside the city's walls (Rampart St, as the name suggests, was the town limit). Under French Colonial law, slaves were allowed to gather here on Sundays. The period of rest became one of both celebration and preservation of West African rituals, which largely revolved around song and dance. Sunday became a day of letting off steam and channeling latent discontent, and it must have been, at the time, the largest celebration of traditional African culture in continental North America – slaves were forbidden from practicing traditional culture in the American colonies.

The practice was shut down when US settlers took over New Orleans, but it was alive long enough to imprint its musical stamp on the city's cultural substrate. By the late 19th century, brass bands were blending African rhythms with classical music. These bands played on a weekly basis in Congo Sq and their sound eventually evolved, especially near the bordellos of nearby Storyville, into jazz – itself a foundation for the variations of pop music (R&B, rock and roll, even hip-hop) the USA would give the world in the 20th century.

VOODOO QUEEN

Voodoo became wildly popular in New Orleans after it was introduced by black émigrés from St Domingue (now Haiti) at the beginning of the 19th century, but very little is known with certainty about the legendary 19th-century voodoo queen Marie Laveau, who gained fame and fortune by shrewdly exploiting voodoo's mystique. Though details of her life are shrouded in myth and misconception, what has been passed down from generation to generation makes for a fascinating story.

She was born in 1794, a French-speaking Catholic of mixed black and white ancestry. Invariably described as beautiful and charismatic, at age 25 she married a man named Paris. He died a few years later and Marie became known as the Widow Paris. She had 15 children with another man, Glapion, who is believed to have migrated from St Domingue and may have been Laveau's first connection to voodoo.

In the 1830s she established herself as the city's preeminent voodoo queen and her influence crossed racial lines. Mostly she reeled in stray husbands and helped people avenge wrongs done to them. According to legend, she earned her house on St Anne St as payment for ensuring a young man's acquittal in a rape or murder trial.

Marie apparently had some tricks up her sleeve. She is said to have worked as a hairdresser in the homes of upper-class white women, and it was not uncommon for these women to share local society gossip while having their hair done. In this way, Laveau gained a familiarity with the vagaries of the elite and she astutely perceived the value of such information. At the peak of her reign as voodoo queen, she employed an entire network of spies, most household servants in upper-class homes.

Reports on Laveau's activities suggest there was more to her practice than non-practitioners were permitted to witness – which makes these reports suspect. Part of the Laveau legend involves rituals she presided over in the countryside around New Orleans. According to sensational accounts, Laveau's followers danced naked around bonfires, drinking blood and slithering on the ground like snakes before engaging in all-out orgies.

A brothel by Lake Pontchartrain called Maison Blanche was reputedly operated by Marie Laveau, but it is uncertain if this was the same Marie Laveau – there were two people known by the name, the second being the daughter of the original Marie Laveau. The elder Laveau died in 1881 and is believed to be buried in St Louis Cemetery No 1 (p153). The younger lived into the early 20th century.

ST LOUIS CEMETERY NO 1   CEMETERY

See p153.

CONGO SQUARE   HISTORIC SITE

Map p254 (Louis Armstrong Park; ☉sunrise-sunset) FREE In Louis Armstrong Park, Congo Sq was a Sunday gathering spot for slaves under the French Code Noir. For one day of the week, the enslaved could sing the songs and practice the cultural traditions of the continent they were exiled from. This was the groundwork of a uniquely New Orleanian link to Africa and much of the city's most iconic food, music and culture has been built on that foundation.

Today Congo Sq is marked by a few stylized statues and sculptures of the city's musical heritage and heroes. The space is also a major jumping-off point for protest marches, rallies and Second Lines.

LE MUSÉE DE F.P.C.   MUSEUM

Map p254 (Free People of Color Museum; ☎504-323-5074; www.lemuseedefpc.com; 2336 Esplanade Ave; tour regular/private $15/25; ☉tours 1-4pm Tue-Fri) Inside a lovely 1859 Greek Revival mansion in the Upper Tremé, this museum showcases a 30-year collection of artifacts, documents, furniture and art. It tells the story of a forgotten subculture: the 'free people of color' before the Civil War, who played a unique but prominent role in the development of the city. Visitation is by guided tour, which should be arranged in advance.

Rooms spotlight different eras in the city's history, with a focus on physician and newspaper publisher Dr Louis Charles Roudanez, born in 1823. The small but fascinating collection includes original documentation of slaves who became free, either

CEMETERY VISITS

The Archdiocese of New Orleans decided in 2015 to limit visitation to St Louis Cemetery No 1 to relatives of those interred in the cemetery and to approved tour groups.

The decision stemmed from ongoing acts of vandalism on cemetery grounds. One of the most notable occurred in 2013 when vandals painted the tomb of voodoo queen Marie Laveau bright pink. Not only did the vandals desecrate the tomb, but they also used moisture-trapping latex paint. Moisture is a key source of damage to brick-and-mortar tombs. Restoring the tomb cost $10,000. There is also a long history of visitors scrawling three X's across Laveau's crypt as part of a wish-fulfillment ritual. Elsewhere in the cemetery, vandals have stolen elaborate pieces of fencing and raided tombs.

Another reason for the new rule? By requiring tour companies to obtain a license, there is more oversight over their quality and behavior. For tours by experienced and knowledgeable guides, consider Save Our Cemeteries (p124).

by *coartación* (buying their own freedom) or as a reward for particularly good service.

ST AUGUSTINE'S CHURCH   CHURCH
Map p254 (☑504-525-5934; www.staugchurch.org; 1210 Governor Nicholls St; ⊘Mass 10am Sun, 5pm Wed) Open since 1841, 'St Aug's' is the oldest African American Catholic church in the country, a place where Creoles, émigrés from St Domingue and free persons of color could worship shoulder to shoulder, even as separate pews were designated for slaves. Call ahead to see if it's possible to arrange a visit. Don't miss the Tomb of the Unknown Slave, fashioned to resemble a grim cross assembled from chain links.

MORTUARY CHAPEL   CHURCH
Map p254 (Our Lady of Guadalupe; ☑504-525-1551; www.judeshrine.com; 411 N Rampart St; donations accepted; ⊘Mass 7am & noon Mon-Fri, 7am & 4pm Sat, 7:30am, 9:30am, 11:30am & 1:30pm Sun) A fear of yellow-fever contagion led the city to forbid funerals for fever victims at St Louis Cathedral. Built in 1826 near St Louis Cemetery No 1, the Mortuary Chapel offered services for victims, its bell tolling constantly during epidemics. In 1931 it was renamed Our Lady of Guadeloupe. Inside the chapel is a statue of St Jude, patron saint of impossible cases.

NEW ORLEANS
AFRICAN AMERICAN MUSEUM   MUSEUM
Map p254 (☑504-566-1136; www.noaam.org; 1418 Governor Nicholls St; adult/student/child $7/5/3; ⊘11am-4pm Wed-Sat & by appointment) This small museum is in the midst of a $6-million renovation and is closed to visitors, although it still offers Tremé-based walking tours. Before closing, the museum displayed an eclectic mix of exhibits mainly dating from the slavery and Reconstruction eras. Its location alone makes the spot of interest: the Meilleur-Goldthwaite House, aka the Tremé Villa, is the site of the city's first brickyard and an exemplar of the Creole architectural style. In the back are restored shotgun houses and slave quarters.

 ## EATING

As befits one of the nation's most storied African American neighborhoods, you'll find some of the city's landmark, African American–owned restaurants in Tremé-Lafitte. Although the vibe is generally pretty casual, there are a few dressier spots.

BUTTERMILK DROP   BAKERY $
Map p254 (☑504-252-4538; www.buttermilk-drop.com; 1781 N Dorgenois St; baked goods $1-4; ⊘6am-4pm Mon-Sat, to 3pm Sun) You came to New Orleans and thought, 'I have to get beignets,' right? And sure, beignets are fine, but the best dessert in town is the buttermilk drop – a small donut hole filled with roughly a metric ton of butter, so rich and smooth and glazed and good it haunts our dreams.

Buy your drops at this ramshackle bakery, which has dusty floors and barely anything that qualifies as seating (get the food to go), and know you have experienced culinary bliss.

LIL' DIZZY'S
CREOLE **$**

Map p254 (📞504-569-8997; www.lildizzyscafe. com; 1500 Esplanade Ave; breakfast $7-14, lunch $11-16, buffet $16-18; ⊗7am-2pm Mon-Sat, 8am-2pm Sun) One of the city's great lunch spots, Dizzy's does mean soul food specials in a historic shack owned by the Baquet family, who have forever been part of the culinary backbone of New Orleans. The fried chicken is excellent and the bread pudding is divine.

PAGODA CAFE
CAFE **$**

Map p254 (📞504-644-4178; www.pagodacafe. net; 1430 N Dorgenois St; breakfast $3-9, pastries under $5, sandwiches $8-10; ⊗7:30am-3pm Tue-Fri, 8am-3pm Sat & Sun; 📶🅿) In a land of dimly lit dive bars and heavy Creole buffets, Pagoda Cafe is a sprightly diversion. This compact place serves healthy fare with a global spin. In the morning, try bacon-and-egg tacos, toast with Nutella and bananas, and house-made granola. For lunch to-go, grab a turnover or sausage pastry or settle in for a lemongrass tofu *banh mi*.

Also sells coffee and teas. All seating is outdoors.

CAJUN SEAFOOD
SEAFOOD **$**

Map p254 (📞504-948-6000; http://cajunsea-foodnola.com; 1479 N Claiborne Ave; takeout $5-19; ⊗10:30am-8:30pm Mon-Sat, from 11am Sun) The name says it all: this is a grocery store–takeout that's a good budget option for seafood and cooked hot plates, such as fried chicken, boudin, fish plates and the like. The boiled shrimp is always freakishly huge, as are the shrimp po'boys.

MEET THE BOYS ON THE BATTLEFRONT

The most significant African American tradition of Carnival began in 1885 when a Mardi Gras Indian gang, calling itself the Creole Wild West, paraded the city's backstreets on Mardi Gras. Their elaborately beaded and feathered suits and headdresses made a huge impression and many more black Indian gangs soon followed – the Wild Tchoupitoulas, Yellow Pocahontas and Golden Eagles, among many others. The new tradition, some say, signified respect for Native Americans who constantly fought US expansion in the New World. A canon of black Indian songs was passed down from generation to generation, with lyrics often fusing English, Creole French, Choctaw and African words until their meaning was obscure.

From the beginning, 'masking Indian' was a serious proposition. Tribes became organized fighting units headed by a big chief, with spy boys, flag boys and wild men carrying out carefully defined roles. Tremendous pride was evident in the costly and expertly sewn suits, and when two gangs crossed paths, an intense confrontation would ensue as members of each tribe sized each other up. Often violence would break out. As is the case with many of Mardi Gras' strongest traditions, this was no mere amusement.

Big chiefs became pillars of communities, and some became legends – among them Big Chief Jolly of the Wild Tchoupitoulas and Tootie Montana of the Yellow Pocahontas. Chief Jolly, an uncle of the Neville Brothers, made his mark by recording black Indian classics backed by the Meters. The Wild Magnolias, long led by Big Chief Bo Dollis (who died in 2015), is one of the most dynamic Indian groups and appears at clubs in New Orleans and at Jazz Fest.

Over the years, black Indian suits gained recognition as extravagant works of folk art and they are exhibited as such at the Backstreet Cultural Museum (p154), at the Presbytère (p53) and at Jazz Fest. Layers of meaningful mosaics are designed and created in patterns of neatly stitched sequins. Multilayered feathered headdresses – particularly those of the big chiefs – are more elaborate and flamboyant than the headgear worn by Las Vegas show performers. The making of a new suit can take the better part of a year.

Visitors not in town for Mardi Gras are likely to have other opportunities to see the Indians at Jazz Fest or occasionally performing in clubs such as Tipitina's. They also parade annually on St Joseph's Night (roughly midway through the Lenten season) and on Indian Sunday (also known as Super Sunday).

SECOND LINE!

Second Lines aren't the alternate queue at the bank window, if you're wondering. No, Second Line specifically refers to New Orleans neighborhood parades, especially those put on by the city's African American Social Aid and Pleasure (S&P) Clubs. The S&P members deck themselves out in flash suits, hats and shoes, and carry decorated umbrellas and fans. This snazzy crowd, accompanied by a hired band, marches through the city pumping music and 'steppin' – engaging in a kind of syncopated marching dance that looks like a soldier in formation overcome by an uncontrollable need to get fun-kay.

This is the First Line and marching behind it is the Second Line: the crowds that gather to celebrate the music. Hundreds, sometimes thousands of people – the majority African American – dance in the Second Line, stopping for drinks and food all along the parade route. Many folks bring along coolers full of beer and soda, plus rolling grills, too.

So what are these S&P clubs? There are theories they have their roots in West African secret societies, cultural institutions that are a big part of the societies slaves were plucked from. While this theory has an appealing veneer of anthropological allure, the roots of Second Lines may be more based on economics. In the 19th and 20th centuries, S&P clubs functioned as insurance agencies for African Americans, as well as brokers who would help arrange the traditional (and expensive) New Orleans jazz funeral procession. The act of the parade, which the S&P helped fund, may have been eventually appended to these brokerage responsibilities.

While that role has faded, the S&P clubs remain important civic institutions. There are a few dozen in the city and traditionally Second Lines roll every weekend, except for summers, usually in the Tremé or Central City. They're not the easiest thing to find, but keep abreast of 90.7 WWOZ's Takin' it To The Streets section (www.wwoz. org) or stop by the Backstreet Cultural Museum (p154) to ask – and be on the lookout for parades and music if you're driving around on a Sunday.

Also note that folks here will throw a Second Line for just about any reason. There were huge parades thrown to honor Fats Domino, Prince and David Bowie when those artists died, or to protest about Donald Trump and the city's Confederate monuments. Other Second Lines have celebrated marriages or anniversaries.

MANCHU　　　　　　　AMERICAN, CHINESE $

Map p254 (☑504-947-5507; www.manchuchicken.com; 1413 N Claiborne Ave; mains $5-12; ⊙10:30am-9pm Mon-Sat, 11:30am-7pm Sun) Also known as the 'purple shop' (when you see it, you'll know why), Manchu is a dingy little takeout that is most famous for its fried chicken wings. You can also pick up fried seafood, grilled pork chops and bowls of yakamein – a sort of black New Orleans version of *pho*, renowned for its hangover-curing powers.

This place is ostensibly Chinese – they sell fried rice and egg rolls – but the dishes that will draw you in are New Orleans soul food.

WILLIE MAE'S
SCOTCH HOUSE　　　　　SOUTHERN US $$

Map p254 (☑504-822-9503; www.williemaes nola.com; 2401 St Ann St; fried chicken $15; ⊙10am-5pm Mon-Sat) Willie Mae's has been dubbed the best fried chicken in the world by the James Beard Foundation, the Food Network and other media, and in this case, the hype isn't far off – this is superlative fried bird. The white beans are also amazing. The drawback is everyone knows about it, so expect long lines, sometimes around the block.

GABRIELLE　　　　　　　　　CAJUN $$

Map p254 (☑504-603-2344; 2441 Orleans Ave; mains $16-32; ⊙5:30-10pm Tue-Sat) This old school, high-end Cajun spot has been refurbished into a lovely little blue-and-yellow cottage doling out sumptuous, rich plates of braised rabbit, slow-roasted duck and other favorites. The wine list is deep and, all in all, this is a perfect spot for a date.

DOOKY CHASE
CREOLE $$

Map p254 (📞504-821-0600; www.dookychase-estaurant.com; 2301 Orleans Ave; buffet $20, mains $20-25; ⏲11am-3pm Tue-Thu, 11am-3pm & 5-9pm Fri) Ray Charles wrote 'Early in the Morning' about Dooky's; civil rights leaders used it as informal headquarters in the 1960s; and Barack Obama ate here after his inauguration. Leah Chase's labor of love is the backbone of the Tremé and her buffets are the stuff of legend, a carnival of gumbo and fried chicken served in a white-linen dining room.

These days the food can be a little hit and...well, not miss, but not as much of a hit as it has been in the past. The vegetarian gumbo z'herbes, served on Thursday during Lent, is the great New Orleans dish done green with mustards, beet tops, spinach, kale, collards and Leah knows what else; committed carnivores should give it a try.

DRINKING & NIGHTLIFE

This is a land of neighborhood bars and live-music gigs held in packed taverns. You won't find a ton of tourists out here and, while folks are friendly, there are some bars where you'll get a little scrutiny if you're not a regular.

SIDNEY'S SALOON
BAR

Map p254 (📞504-224-2672; www.sidneyssaloon.com; 1200 St Bernard Ave; ⏲3pm-3am) Friendly bartenders, strong drinks, pop-up restaurants slinging food on the nearby street and a raucous clientele make Sidney's a winning stop any night of the week. Hosts trivia nights on Tuesdays, comedy on Thursdays and dance parties on the weekend.

⭐ ENTERTAINMENT

BROAD THEATER
CINEMA

Map p254 (636 N Broad St; ⏲1pm-midnight Mon-Wed, from 11am Thu-Sun) The Broad is a great movie theater, showcasing both Hollywood blockbusters and indie/art-house titles in the middle of the city. It's extremely popular with locals, and during busy shows, the parking lot is almost always full to capacity, so you may want to seek out street parking.

The on-site bar certainly helps with your cinematic relaxation.

BULLETS
LIVE MUSIC

(📞504-948-4003; 2441 AP Tureaud Ave; cover $5; ⏲bar 7am-2am, shows 6pm & 9pm) Don't be put off by the name; Bullets is just a sports bar. Well, sort of – this is New Orleans, so it's a sports bar, but a sports bar where live music kicks off on a regular basis. The crowd is friendly, the beer is cold, the drinks are strong and the music is good – what more do you want?

KERMIT'S TREME MOTHER IN LAW LOUNGE
LOUNGE

Map p254 (📞504-975-3955; www.kermitstrememotherinlawlounge.com; 1500 N Claiborne Ave; ⏲10am-midnight) Owned by iconic trumpeter Kermit Ruffins, this wonderfully odd bar is a Tremé standby and a popular spot for drinks during Second Lines. Or any time of day, really. Look for the big, bright building with lots of murals. Kermit himself is often dishing out free food at night.

This was formerly K-Doe's Mother in Law Lounge, owned by the late, great Ernie K-Doe. Besides being famous for writing the song 'Mother-in-Law,' Ernie would frequently proclaim his 'Emperorship of the Universe.'

SAENGER THEATRE
THEATER

(📞504-525-1052; www.saengernola.com; 1111 Canal St) The Saenger's ornate 1927 facade was designed by noted New Orleans architect Emile Weil. It has been refurbished and renovated into one of the finest indoor venues in the city. Shows range from comedy slams to off-Broadway hits.

MAHALIA JACKSON THEATER
THEATER

Map p254 (📞504-287-0350; www.mahaliajacksontheater.com; 1419 Basin St) Named for New Orleans' own Queen of Gospel, the Mahalia Jackson is one of the city's major mainstage venues. It often features performances ranging from ballet to stand-up comedy to classical music.

CANDLELIGHT LOUNGE
LIVE MUSIC

Map p254 (📞504-525-4748; 925 N Robertson St; cover $10; ⏲11am-late) This classic Tremé dive is a hit-or-miss experience. Great bands play here – Corey Henry and the Treme Brass Band, to name a few –

and on some nights the music infuses the place and everything is magic. On other nights the bands clearly phone it in and the whole experience is overpriced.

We've had good nights here, and it's a popular spot on the Second Line routes, but fair warning, the Candlelight does not always shine.

 ## SHOPPING

There isn't much of a dedicated shopping scene in the Tremé besides the occasional arts market that gets attached to festivals held in Louis Armstrong Park (p154).

★ KITCHEN WITCH   BOOKS
Map p254 (☑504-528-8382; http://kwcook-books.com; 1452 N Broad St; ☺11am-5:30pm) At a time when stores are becoming more and more homogeneous, Kitchen Witch is doing its own thing, selling antique and vintage cookbooks to a loving clientele who are dedicated to this niche of the written word. Some of these cookbooks are true works of art; others are fascinating collector's items. All have a gastronomic story.

 ## SPORTS & ACTIVITIES

THE VOODOO BONE LADY   TOURS
Map p254 (☑504-267-2040; http://voodooboneladytours.com; adult/child $25/15) The eponymous Voodoo Bone Lady – or one of her staff – leads these spooky-by-design tours of local cemeteries, haunted sites and pirate hangouts. The tours are fun and engaging, if not exactly academic.

Day Trips from New Orleans

River Road Plantions p162

An introduction to the palatial homesteads and troubled history of the region.

Down the Bayou p163

Explore the deep swamps and wetlands of South Louisiana.

St Francisville p165

An arty, antique-y sort of town with some good outdoor hikes.

Lafayette & Breaux Bridge p167

The heart of Cajun country has great food and better music.

Cajun Prairie p170

Dance the night away at the spot where Cajuns and cowboys collide.

River Road Plantations

One of the main draws here is visiting plantation homes, which are a source of intense debate – while their architecture is undeniably beautiful, they were built, literally, on the backbreaking toil of chattel slave labor. That stain on local history used to be glossed over in favor of tours that espoused a romantic narrative of Southern aristocratic genteelness, but plantation museums seem to be taking steps to recognize the culpability their historic properties had in the brutal institution of slave holding. The best plantation museums are now just that – educational spaces that provide visitors with a well-rounded history lesson.

Explore

Elaborate plantation homes dot the east and west banks of the Mississippi River between New Orleans and Baton Rouge. First indigo, then cotton and sugarcane, brought great wealth to the plantation owners; today, many plantations are open to the public. Most tours focus on the lives of the owners, the restored architecture and the ornate gardens of antebellum Louisiana.

The Best...

➡ **Sight** Whitney Plantation (p162)
➡ **Place to Eat** Mosca's (p163)

Getting There & Away

River Rd, which heads west from New Orleans, is where many plantations can be found. The plantations are anywhere from 25 to 55 miles from downtown New Orleans.

Need to Know

➡ **Area Code** ☑985

⊙ SIGHTS

★WHITNEY PLANTATION   HISTORIC SITE
(☑225-265-3300; www.whitneyplantation.com; 5099 Hwy 18, Wallace; adult/student/child under 6yr $22/10/free; ⊙museum 9:30am-4:30pm Wed-Mon, tours hourly 10am-3pm; ℗) The Whitney is the first plantation in the state to focus on slavery, and in doing so they've flipped the script on plantation tours. Whereas before the story told was that of the 'big house', here the emphasis is given to the hundreds who died to keep the residents of the big house comfortable. There's a museum on-site that you can self-tour, but admission to the plantation is by 1½-hour guided tour only.

In addition, the property is speckled with memorials and monuments to the area's slave population.

LAURA PLANTATION   HISTORIC SITE
(☑225-265-7690; www.lauraplantation.com; 2247 Hwy 18, Vacherie; adult/child $20/6; ⊙10am-4pm; ℗) This ever-evolving and popular plantation tour teases out the distinctions between Creole, Anglo, free and enslaved African Americans via meticulous research and the written records of the Creole women who ran the place for generations. Laura is also fascinating because it was a *Creole* mansion, founded and maintained by a continental European–descended elite, as opposed to Anglo Americans; the cultural and architectural distinctions between this and other plantations is obvious and striking. Tours are offered in English or French.

DESTREHAN PLANTATION   HISTORIC SITE
(☑985-764-9315; www.destrehanplantation.org; 13034 River Rd, Destrehan; adult/child 7-17yr/under 7yr $20/7/free; ⊙9am-4pm; ℗) Destrehan, the oldest plantation home remaining in the lower Mississippi Valley, was originally established for indigo production. In 1787 Antoine Robert Robin DeLongy commissioned the original French Colonial–style mansion, which uses *bousillage* (mud- and straw-filled) walls supported by cypress timbers. The house features a distinctive African-style hipped roof, no doubt the inspiration of the plantation's builder, who was partially of African descent. Viewing the historical-documents room, which contains original Louisiana Purchase–era artifacts, is a highlight.

OAK ALLEY PLANTATION   HISTORIC SITE
(☑225-265-2151; www.oakalleyplantation.com; 3645 Hwy 18, Vacherie; adult/student/child $22/8/5; ⊙9am-5pm Mar-Oct, 9am-4:30pm Mon-Fri, to 5pm Sat & Sun Nov-Feb; ℗) The most impressive aspect of Oak Alley Plantation is its canopy of 28 majestic live oaks lining the entry to the grandiose Greek Revival–style

home. The tour covers a blacksmith shop, a slavery exhibit and several other points of interest, and there are guest cottages (from $250) and a restaurant on-site.

EATING

MOSCA'S   ITALIAN $$
(📞504-436-8950; www.moscasrestaurant.com; 4137 US 90 West, Avondale; mains $7-34; ⊙5:30-9:30pm Tue-Sat) There's old school, and then there's Mosca's. This Italian joint looks like it's about to collapse into the mud, but it soldiers on, serving to-die-for oysters Mosca (cooked in cheese and bread crumbs) and garlicky spaghetti *bordelaise* that is heaven-sent. Dimly lit and romantic in a dilapidat-ed way, Mosca's is an experience, although they'll have to roll you home after dinner.

The restaurant is truly in the middle of nowhere, and they've stubbornly remained there because this is just how certain New Orleans restaurants do things (and yes, this is effectively a New Orleans restaurant, even if it's located about 15 miles west of town).

WAYNE JACOB'S
SMOKEHOUSE & RESTAURANT   CAJUN $$
(📞985-652-9990; www.wjsmokehouse.com; 769 W 5th St, LaPlace; mains $16-22; ⊙store 9am-5pm Mon-Fri, to 2pm Sat & Sun, restaurant 11am-2pm Mon-Fri, 9am-2pm Sun; 🚻) This is the place to stop on your way upriver for smoky pork goodness. LaPlace, located about 30 miles west of New Orleans, is known for its fantastic sausages, and Wayne Jacob's smokes up some of the best. Po'boys, red beans and rice, and Cajun comfort food fill out the menu, and portions are generous.

Whatever you choose, make sure to in-clude an order of the smoky chicken and an-douille (smoked pork sausage) Gumbo. It's some of the best we had in Southern Loui-siana. An amazing array of sausages are for sale in the store in back.

Down the Bayou

The maze of bayous and swamps arching southwest of New Orleans – 'down the bay-ou,' as locals say – is where the first Cajuns settled. Their traditional lifestyle is still

in evidence in small part, though now it's mostly older folks who speak French and make a living from fishing the waterways.

Explore
The best way to experience bayou culture is to take a swamp tour and afterwards pull up a big plate of fresh-caught crawfish. Stop in Houma for a swamp tour or drive to Thi-bodaux, where you can learn about Cajun culture in the wetlands region and pull off the road for a look at well-preserved slave cabins, stark reminders of the South's past. The Rig Museum in Morgan City shows the modern face of Cajun culture, with an ex-tensive history of the petroleum industry that has been a financial windfall for the region.

The Best...
➡ **Sights** Barataria Preserve (p163)
➡ **Place to Eat** White Bowl (p164)
➡ **Activities** Lost Land Tours (p165)

Getting There & Away
Most of this region lays within a 60-mile drive south of New Orleans. I-90 runs east-west through most of the bayou region, while Hwy 45 runs by Barataria Preserve. **Greyhound** (www.greyhound.com; 103 E Bayou Rd) bus services from New Orleans to Mor-gan City, Houma and Thibodaux are avail-able.

Need to Know
➡ **Area Code** 📞985
➡ **Thibodaux Tourist Office** (📞985-446-1187; www.thibodauxchamber.com/visitor-center; 318 E Bayou Rd; ⊙9am-5pm Mon-Fri)

SIGHTS

★BARATARIA PRESERVE   PARK
(📞504-689-3690; www.nps.gov/jela; 6588 Bara-taria Blvd, Marrero; ⊙parking lot for trails 9am-5pm, visitor center 9am-4:30pm Wed-Sun; 🅿)
🎫**FREE** This section of the Jean Lafitte Na-tional Historical Park and Preserve, south of New Orleans near the town of Marrero (and Crown Point), provides the easiest ac-cess to the dense swamplands that ring New Orleans. The 8 miles of boardwalk trails are a stunning way to tread lightly through the fecund, thriving swamp, home

to alligators, nutrias (basically big, invasive river rats), tree frogs and hundreds of species of birds.

Start at the **National Park Service Visitor Center (NPS)**, 1 mile west of Hwy 45 off the Barataria Blvd exit, where you can pick up a map or join a guided wetland walk or canoe trip (call for more information). To rent canoes or kayaks for a tour or an independent paddle, go to **Bayou Barn** (☑504-689-2663; www.bayoubarn.com; 7145 Barataria Blvd; canoe/kayak hire per person $20/25; ☉10am-6pm Thu-Sun) about 3 miles from the park entrance.

WETLANDS ACADIAN CULTURAL CENTER   CULTURAL CENTER
(☑985-448-1375; www.nps.gov/jela; 314 St Mary St, Thibodaux; ☉9am-7pm Mon & Tue, to 5pm Wed-Fri; ☻) ✦FREE This excellent National Park Service site is a comprehensive introduction to Cajun culture. The on-site museum gives an overview of Acadian history, but the real draws are the extensive activities schedule and events calendar, which include walking tours, boat tours on the bayou, Cajun music nights (5pm to 6:15pm Monday) and Francophone conversation circles (5:30pm to 7pm Tuesday) – it's an experience just to be a fly on the wall for that last engagement.

Call ahead or check the website to plan your trip here.

RIG MUSEUM   MUSEUM
(International Petroleum Museum & Exposition; ☑985-384-3744; www.rigmuseum.com; 111 1st St, Morgan City; adult/senior/child $5/4/3.50; ☉tours 10am & 2pm Mon-Sat; ℗) If you want to get a firsthand look at what it really means when American politicians say 'drill baby drill,' take the 1½-hour guided tour here. This informative tour winds up, down and around Big Charlie, the first ever offshore drilling rig. It was completed in 1954, eight years after it was first proposed by creator AJ Laborde of Marksville, LA.

The tour stops inside dorms, the kitchen and the rec area, and goes outside to the actual drill site. Questions are encouraged, and you will learn a lot about life on a floating rig and how it all works. In fact, Big Charlie is still used as a training facility.

The tour may not go down well if you're a believer in environmentalism or gender inclusivity, but it may nevertheless be interesting. Wear walking shoes, as you'll climb at least 26 steep steps and do a fair bit of walking around the rig.

LAUREL VALLEY VILLAGE PLANTATION   HISTORIC SITE
(☑985-446-7456; 595 Hwy 308; admission by donation; ☉11am-5pm; ℗) Among the cane fields, about 2 miles east of town on Hwy 308, this is one of the best-preserved assemblages of sugar-plantation structures in Louisiana. Overall, some 60 buildings (c 1755 and later) survive here, including the old general store and a school house.

✖ EATING

WHITE BOWL   VIETNAMESE $
(☑985-262-4093; 235 Enterprise Dr, Houma; mains $5-11; ☉10am-8:30pm Mon-Sat; ☻) Delicious Vietnamese food served in a simple space makes for a nice splash of diversity in the local dining scene. Delicious bowls of pho, stir-fries and *bun* (vermicelli) platters round out a standard but solid menu.

RITA MAE'S KITCHEN   SOUTHERN US $
(☑985-384-3550; 711 Federal Ave, Morgan City; mains $5-18; ☉8am-9pm Mon-Sat, to 8pm Sun; ☻) Rita Mae's comes recommended up, down and around the bayou. This little cottage near the Hwy 90 overpass serves up comfort food like grandma used to make, but maybe just a little bit better. Come for omelets in the morning, or juicy burgers, po'boys, fried chicken, and red beans and rice later in the day.

LEJEUNE'S   BAKERY $
(☑337-276-5690; www.lejeunesbakery.com; 1510 Main St, Jeanerette; baked goods $3-5; ☉7am until the bread runs out) For a quick but satisfying snack between Morgan City and New Iberia, swing off Hwy 90 at Jeanerette and drive though the small downtown to LeJeune's. If the red light is on that means it still has French bread available for sale. Trust us when we say people from Louisiana will fight over this bread: it's that good.

The LeJeune family has been operating the bakery since 1884 and still uses the same recipes. It's located about 10 miles southeast of New Iberia.

FREMIN'S   CAJUN $$$
(☑985-449-0333; www.fremins.net; 402 W Third St, Thibodaux; mains $25-45; ☉11am-2pm Tue-Fri, 5-9pm Tue-Thu, 5-10pm Fri & Sat) Fremin's is

one of the great granddaddies of high-end, classic Cajun cuisine. The menu doesn't change much, and while there are some items that could use an update, overall this is a solid menu. Case in point: soft-shell crab served over pasta with a very good mushroom brandy sauce.

DRINKING

FOUNDRY ON
THE BAYOU LOUNGE   LOUNGE
(☑985-387-4070; www.foundryonthebayou. com; 715 W 1st St, Thibodaux; ⊙5-9pm Wed-Thu, to 10pm Fri & Sat; 🐾) We like the Foundry, a massive dining-drinking-entertainment venue, for its live-music shows and generous drink specials. You'll find the former in their concert hall, and the latter in the open-air lounge area upstairs.

MUDBUG BREWERY   MICROBREWERY
(☑985-492-1610; www.mudbugbrewery.com; 1878 LA 3185, Thibodaux; ⊙5-10pm Thu, to midnight Fri & Sat) 'Mudbug' is a nickname for crawfish, which are amazing, and thus a great title for this town's local craft brewery. Stop by the brewery's tasting room for café au lait stouts or a blackberry-blossom Belgian *witbier* (among many other varieties).

ACTIVITIES

★LOUISIANA LOST
LAND TOURS   ECOTOUR
(☑504-858-7575; http://lostlandstours.org; tours for 4 people from $95) 🛶 This wonderful outfit conducts three- to four-hour kayak paddles into the wetlands. Excursions focus on land loss and wildlife threats, and are led by expert guides who genuinely love this land (or lack thereof, as you'll learn). Staff include Pulitzer Prize–winning journalist and outdoorsman Bob Marshall.

BAYOU WOMAN ADVENTURES   ECOTOUR
(☑985-851-7578; www.bayouwoman.com; 1917 Bayou Dularge Rd, Theriot; cruise per adult/ child $50/30) 🛶 Captain Wendy leads eco-oriented wetland tours and cruises across a swampland lake near the coast. The cruise is great, and Wendy is awesome – she's an avid outdoorswoman, writer and

environmental educator. Bayou Woman also offers two-day bird-watching and photography tours, which include lodging ($500 per person).

ANNIE MILLER'S SON'S
SWAMP & MARSH TOURS   BOATING
(☑985-856-8501; www.annie-miller.com; 4038 Bayou Black Dr, Houma; adult/child $15/10; 👪) This tour company is run by the son of a local storytelling legend. He, like his mom before him, has been feeding chicken drumsticks to the alligators for so long that the swamp critters rise from the muck to take a bite when they hear the motor. Find it 8 miles west of Houma.

CAJUN MAN'S SWAMP
TOURS & ADVENTURES   CRUISE
(☑985-868-4625; www.cajunmanadventures.com; Marina Dr, off Hwy 182/Bayou Black Dr; adult/child $25/15; ⊙tours 10:30am & 1:30pm Mon-Sat) Swamp tours are great, but they're even better with a bit of Cajun music. Captain Billy entertains his passengers with an accordion while piloting them through a jaw-droppingly beautiful stretch of Bayou Black. Billy knows the area well, and bald eagle and alligator sightings are common. The tour office is at Bob's Bayou Black Marina.

St Francisville

Lush St Francisville is the quintessential Southern artsy small town, a blend of historical homes, bohemian shops and outdoor activities courtesy of the nearby Tunica Hills (you read that right – hills in Louisiana). During the antebellum years (pre–Civil War) this was home to plantation millionaires, and much of the architecture these aristocrats built is still intact, forming a historic core that has magnetized tourists for over a century.

····································

Explore
In town, stroll down historic Royal St to catch a glimpse of antebellum buildings turned homes. The visitors center has self-guided tour brochures. You can easily lose a morning in St Francisville just pottering around, popping into antiques shops and generally lazing the day away.

Other destinations in the area, like Tunica Falls, are small day trips in their own right.

The Best...
➡ **Sight** Mary Ann Brown Preserve
➡ **Place to Eat** Birdman Coffee & Books

Getting There & Away
St Francisville lies about 115 miles north of New Orleans on Hwy 61, which winds right through town.

Need to Know
➡ **Area Code** ✆225

SIGHTS

MARY ANN BROWN
PRESERVE   NATURE RESERVE
(✆225-338-1040; www.nature.org; 13515 Hwy 965; ⏱sunrise-sunset; P) 🅿 **FREE** Operated by the Nature Conservancy, the 110-acre Mary Ann Brown Preserve takes in some of the beech woodlands, dark wetlands and low, clay-soil hill country of the Tunica uplands. A 2-mile series of trails and boardwalks crosses the woods – the same trees that John James Audubon tramped around when he began work on *Birds of America*.

TUNICA FALLS   WATERFALL
(www.stfrancisville.us; 119 Ft Adams Pond Rd, Woodville, MS; P) 🅿 Tunica Falls, technically called Clark Creek Nature Area, is about 30 minutes' drive from St Francisville. The pleasant, hilly trails here wind past lovely waterfalls – the main draw for hikers. Crude maps can be found at the general store in Pond, MS (at Hwys 24 and 969), the town where the trailhead is located and in which you can park.

OAKLEY PLANTATION
& AUDUBON STATE
HISTORIC SITE   HISTORIC SITE
(✆225-635-3739; http://audubonstatehistoric-site.wordpress.com; 11788 Hwy 965; $5; ⏱9am-5pm Wed-Sun; P) 🅿 Outside of St Francisville, this is where naturalist John James Audubon spent his tenure, arriving in 1821 to tutor the owner's daughter. Though his assignment lasted only four months (and his room was pretty spartan), he and his assistant finished 32 paintings of birds

found in the plantation's surrounding forest. The small West Indies–influenced house (1806) includes several original Audubon prints.

ROSEDOWN PLANTATION
HISTORIC SITE   HISTORIC SITE
(✆225-635-3332; www.crt.state.la.us; 12501 Hwy 10; adult/student $12/6; ⏱9am-5pm; P) Get your cameras out for the corridor of live oaks fronting this attractive plantation home. Commissioned by Daniel and Martha Turnbull, the 1835 cypress-and-cedar house still contains many original mid-19th-century furnishings. Tours are a little old fashioned, focusing on the minutiae of aristocratic plantation life, but the building and grounds are impressive. Outside, the formal gardens have been meticulously restored based on Martha's garden diaries. Be warned: Rosedown is a major stop on the tour-bus circuit.

EATING

BIRDMAN COFFEE & BOOKS   CAFE $
(✆225-635-3665; 5695 Commerce St; mains $5-8; ⏱7am-5pm Tue-Fri, 8am-2pm Sat, 8am-noon Sun; 🛜) Birdman is *the* spot for strong coffee, acoustic live music several times a month, a delicious local breakfast (old-fashioned yellow grits, sweet-potato pancakes, salty bacon) and local art.

MAGNOLIA CAFÉ   CAFE $
(✆225-635-6528; www.themagnoliacafe.net; 5687 Commerce St; mains $8-16; ⏱10am-4pm Mon-Wed, to 9pm Thu & Sat, to 10pm Fri) The Magnolia Café was once a health-food store and VW-bus repair shop. Today it's the nucleus of what's happening in St Francisville – it's where people go to eat, socialize and, on Friday night, dance to live music. Try the cheesy shrimp po'boy.

AL AQABA   LEBANESE $
(✆225-635-4035; 5712 Commerce St; mains $8-19; ⏱10am-9pm Mon-Thu, to 10pm Fri & Sat, to 8:30pm Sun) Lebanese food – particularly good Lebanese food – wasn't what we were expecting out in rural Louisiana, but when that smell of kofta kabobs, falafel and chicken shawarma hit our noses, we weren't complaining. Finish the meal off with some baklava, or some belly dancing (on Friday night, from 6:30pm).

THE FRANCIS SOUTHERN TABLE & BAR

SOUTHERN US $$

(☎225-635-0033; www.thefrancissoutherntable. com; 6747 Hwy 61; mains $10-32; ☺11am-9pm Sun-Thu, to 10pm Fri & Sat) The Francis has quickly become a local center of gravity in St Francisville. Louisiana classics – crawfish and andouille pasta, country-fried ribeye in white gravy, and grilled redfish – are served on a big patio, next to a bar slinging craft cocktails. Live music often kicks off on Saturday.

Lafayette & Breaux Bridge

There's an eerie beauty to this place, a land of tall cypress pines and thick deciduous oak, emerging from endless miles of flatwater bayou, creek, slough and river. Alligators wink from the black water, while deer perk their tails in the bottom land basins, and in the distance, the fires of the oil refineries flicker into the night. Stop into a local town, tune the radio into some Cajun dance music, and order some fried seafood and boudin – this is the Cajun country of legend.

Lafayette and adjacent Breaux Bridge are the major towns and bases of exploration in the area. East and south of Lafayette, the Atchafalaya Basin is the preternatural heart of the Cajun wetlands. Stop into the Atchafalaya Welcome Center to learn about the dense jungle protecting these swamps, lakes and bayous.

Explore

Lafayette is an excellent base for exploring all of Cajun country, collectively known as Acadiana, which includes Eunice and the Cajun Prairie. If you'd prefer slightly more quiet surroundings, stay in Breaux Bridge. The dance halls here are fun, but they're separated by decently long driving distances, so be aware when you're inevitably offered a cold beer.

Getting There & Away

Lafayette is about 135 miles (2.5 hours) west of New Orleans by car. From I-10, take exit 103A – the Evangeline Thruway (Hwy

167) goes to the center of town. **Greyhound** (☎337-235-1541; www.greyhound.com; 100 Lee Ave) operates from a hub beside the central commercial district, making several runs daily to New Orleans (3½ hours) and Baton Rouge (one hour). The **Amtrak** (www.amtrak. com; 100 Lee Ave) Sunset Limited service, which runs between New Orleans and Los Angeles, stops in Lafayette.

The Best...
➡ **Sights** Lake Martin (p168)
➡ **Place to Eat** French Press (p168)
➡ **Entertainment** Blue Moon Saloon (p169)

Need to Know
➡ **Area Code** ☎337
➡ **Atchafalaya Welcome Center** (☎337-228-1094; www.crt.state.la.us/tourism/welcome-centers/atchafalaya; 1908 Atchafalaya River Hwy, I-10, Exit 121; ☺8:30am-5pm)
➡ **Lafayette Visitors Center** (☎337-232-3737; www.lafayettetravel.com; 1400 NW Evangeline Thruway; ☺8:30am-5pm Mon-Fri, from 9am Sat & Sun)

⊙ SIGHTS

⊙ Lafayette

VERMILIONVILLE   MUSEUM
(☎337-233-4077; www.bayouvermiliondistrict. org/vermilionville; 300 Fisher Rd; adult/student $10/6, boat tour $12/8; ☺10am-4pm Tue-Sun; ⓟ♿) This tranquil, recreated 19th-century Cajun village wends along the bayou near the airport. Friendly, enthusiastic costumed docents explain Cajun, Creole and Native American history, and local bands perform on Sunday (1pm to 4pm). Guided boat tours of Bayou Vermilion are also offered at 10:30am Tuesday to Saturday in spring and fall.

ACADIAN VILLAGE   MUSEUM
(☎337-981-2364; www.acadianvillage.org; 200 Greenleaf Dr; adult/student $9/7; ☺10am-4pm Mon-Sat Jan-Oct, 5:30-9pm Dec; ⓟ♿) At the understated, educational Acadian Village, you follow a brick path around a rippling bayou to restored houses, craftsman barns and a church. Old-timers sometimes still hang out here, regaling visitors

NEW IBERIA

Settled by the Spanish in 1779, New Iberia prospered on the sugarcane of surrounding plantations. Today the town's best-known product is Tabasco hot sauce, famous the world over, and its best-known native son is mystery writer James Lee Burke, whose page-turning detective novels about Dave Robicheaux take place in and around New Iberia.

This is one of the more attractive mid-sized towns in the state, with a preserved main street in the center and handsome historic homes framed by live oaks and Spanish moss in the surrounding lanes. Most folks visit as a day trip from Lafayette.

The big draw is a little ways outside of town: the **McIlhenny Tabasco Factory** (☑337-359-9562; www.tabasco.com/visit-avery-island; Avery Island Rd; museum & factory tour $5.50; ⊙tours 9am-4pm; **P**) **FREE**, headquarters (but not main production facility) of the famous hot sauce. You can take a tour of the factory, but the real attraction is the **Jungle Gardens** (☑337-369-6243; www.junglegardens.org; adult/child $8/5, incl Tabasco Factory tour $12.50/9.50; ⊙9am-5pm) ✿, a self-contained park where you can drive or walk through 250 acres of moss-covered live oaks and subtropical jungle flora. There's an amazing array of waterbirds (especially snowy egrets, which nest here in astounding numbers) as well as turtles and alligators. In New Iberia itself, many visitors drop into **Shadows on the Teche** (☑337-369-6446; www.shadowsontheteche.org; 317 E Main St; adult/senior/student $10.50/8.50/6.75; ⊙10am-4pm Mon-Sat; ♿), a huge, gothic Greek Revival Plantation.

New Iberia is most often visited as a day trip from Lafayette, located about 20 miles north. There's a **Greyhound** (☑800-231-2222; www.greyhound.com; 304 S Lewis St) stop at the Texaco station a mile east of the Shadows on the Teche plantation house.

with Cajun songs and stories from days gone by.

ACADIAN CULTURAL CENTER   MUSEUM
(☑337-232-0789; www.nps.gov/jela; 501 Fisher Rd; ⊙9am-4:30pm Tue-Fri, 8:30am-noon Sat; **P** ♿) ✿ This National Parks Service museum has extensive exhibits on Cajun culture and is a good entry point for those looking to peer deeper into Acadian folkways.

◉ Breaux Bridge

LAKE MARTIN   BIRD SANCTUARY
(Lake Martin Rd; ⊙24hr) **FREE** This lake – a mossy green dollop surrounded by many trees and cypress trunks – serves as a wonderful, easily accessible introduction to bayou landscapes. A few walking paths, as well as a boardwalk, take visitors over the mirror-reflection sheen of the swamp, while overhead thousands of great and cattle egrets and blue herons perch in haughty indifference.

It's about 5 miles south of Breaux Bridge.

◉ Cajun Wetlands

CYPREMORT POINT STATE PARK STATE PARK
(☑337-867-4510; www.crt.state.la.us; 306 Beach Lane, Cypremort Point; adult/senior & child under 3yr $3/free; ⊙7am-9pm Sun-Thu, to 10pm Fri & Sat; **P** ♿) You can't get more end of the road than Cypremont Point, a lonely, windswept promontory of land buffeted by wind, seagull calls and foam spray off of the Gulf of Mexico. There's a little man-made beach and some picnic tables, but the highlight is the long, slightly surreal drive here, through miles of breeze-bent marshland and still, piney woods.

✕ EATING

✕ Lafayette

★**FRENCH PRESS**   BREAKFAST $
(☑337-233-9449; www.facebook.com/french-presslaf; 214 E Vermillion; mains $9-15; ⊙7am-2pm Mon-Fri, from 9am Sat & Sun; 🛜) This

French Cajun hybrid is one of the best culinary things going in Lafayette. Breakfast is mind-blowing, with a sinful Cajun Benedict (boudin instead of ham), cheddar grits (that will kill you dead) and organic granola (to offset the grits). Lunch ain't half bad either; the fried shrimp melt, doused in Sriracha mayo, is gorgeously decadent.

DWYER'S   DINER **$**

(📞337-235-9364; 323 Jefferson St; mains $7-16; ⏱6am-2pm; 📶) This family-owned joint serves Cajun diner fare, finally bringing gumbo for lunch and pancakes for breakfast into one glorious culinary marriage. It's especially fun on Wednesday mornings, when a French-speaking table is set up and local Cajuns shoot the breeze in their old-school dialect. Rotating lunch mains include smothered pork chops, fried chicken and shrimp stew.

JOHNSON'S BOUCANIÈRE   CAJUN **$**

(📞337-269-8878; www.johnsonsboucaniere. com; 1111 St John St; mains $4.25-10; ⏱7am-3pm Tue-Fri, to 5:30pm Sat) This resurrected, 70-year-old smoker business turns out detour-worthy boudin and an unstoppable smoked-pork-brisket sandwich topped with smoked sausage.

SOCIAL SOUTHERN TABLE   SOUTHERN US **$$**

(📞337-456-3274; www.socialsouthern.com; 3901 Johnston St; mains $12-32; ⏱11am-10pm Tue-Sat, 10:30am-2pm Sun) The hip culinary crowd out in Acadiana pack into Social to feast on fried chicken 'n' biscuits, wild mushroom flatbreads, and local vegetables drenched in curry, among other delights. This isn't the first restaurant to elevate Southern staples, but they're doing so at a level beyond most of the competition.

✖ Breaux Bridge

POCHE'S CAJUN RESTAURANT   CAJUN **$**

(📞337-332-2108; www.poches.com; 3015 Main Hwy; mains $10-16; ⏱4am-7:30pm Mon-Sat, to 5:15pm Sun) You'll be sweating Cajun cuisine when they roll you out of Poche's, and we mean all that in a good way. Feast on a menu full of daily specials – smothered pork chops, crawfish *étouffée* (a kind of stewed crawfish over rice), tasso (Cajun smoked ham) and other dishes that are terrible for your heart and amazing for your mouth.

ACTIVITIES

CHAMPAGNE'S SWAMP TOURS   BOATING

(📞337-230-4068; www.champagnesswamp-tours.com; 1151 Rookery Rd, Lake Martin; 2hr tour adult/child $20/10, kayak rentals per hour $10; ⏱tours 9am, 10:30am, 11:30am, 1pm, 3pm & 5pm) Get in a boat, grab some oars and say hello to that gator cruising by in Lake Martin...just kidding! Er, sort of. You may well see a gator, although it isn't guaranteed on this tour. What is guaranteed is a good time on the water, and the chance to experience a unique Louisiana ecosystem at eye level.

They also offer kayak and canoe rentals.

CAJUN COUNTRY SWAMP TOURS   BOATING

(📞337-319-0010; www.cajuncountryswamp-tours.com; adult/child $20/10; ⏱by appointment) Butch Guchereau, born and raised in the Bayou Teche area, offers two-hour eco-minded tours on quiet crawfish skiffs.

☆ ENTERTAINMENT

☆ Lafayette

BLUE MOON SALOON   LIVE MUSIC

(📞337-234-2422; www.bluemoonpresents.com; 215 E Convent St; cover $5-15; ⏱8am-1pm & 5pm-2am) This intimate venue on the back porch of the accompanying **guesthouse** (dm $23, r $75-95; 🅿❄@🛜) is what Louisiana is all about: good music, good people and good beer. What's not to love? Music tends to go off Wednesday to Saturday.

ARTMOSPHERE   LIVE MUSIC

(📞337-233-3331; www.artmosphere.vpweb.com; 902 Johnston St; ⏱5pm-2am Mon-Thu, from 4pm Fri, from 11am Sat, 11am-midnight Sun) Graffiti, hookahs, hipsters and an edgy lineup of acts – it's more CBGBs than Cajun dance hall, but it's a lot of fun, and there's good Mexican food to boot.

RANDOL'S   LIVE MUSIC

(📞337-981-7080; www.randols.com; 2320 Kaliste Saloom Rd; ⏱5-10pm Sun-Thu, to 10:30pm Fri & Sat) Dishes such as crab cake au gratin are quite tasty, but it's nightly live Cajun tunes that are the why-go. Regulars are always scooting around the floor; sit on the bench around the dance floor (separated from the tables by an awkward partition) and you will be asked out onto the floor.

☆ Breaux Bridge

LA POUSSIERE   LIVE MUSIC
(☎337-332-1721; www.lapoussiere.com; 1301 Grand Point Hwy; ◷7-11pm Sat, 2-7pm Sun) Cajun club La Poussiere doesn't serve food, just drinks and dance. Live bands play Saturday and Sunday; the cover charge and show times depends on who's playing.

☆ Cajun Wetlands

ATCHAFALAYA CLUB   LIVE MUSIC
(☎337-228-7512; www.patsfishermanswharf. com; 1008 Henderson Levee Rd, Henderson; ◷8pm-late Fri & Sat, 6-10pm Sun) Shuffling its feet beside **Pat's Fisherman's Wharf** (mains $12-26; ◷11am-9:30pm Sun-Thu, to 10:30pm Fri & Sat) in Henderson, the Atchafalaya Club hosts a great variety of Cajun bands. The Foret Tradition regularly belts out mean swamp pop, and you might see the talented Louisana Red among others. If nothing else, the enormous swamp mural is pretty impressive.

Cajun Prairie

Dancing cowboys? Works for us. Cajun and African American settlers in the higher, drier terrain north of Lafayette developed a culture based around animal husbandry and farming, and the 10-gallon hat still rules. In many ways, this region is a blend of both South Louisiana and East Texas.

Physically, this truly is prairie: wide expanses of green flatlands, broken up by rice and crawfish ponds. This is the heartland of zydeco music; come evening, keep your ears peeled for the accordion, fiddle and distinctive 'zzzzzzzzip' sound of the frottoir, a corrugated metal vest that is played as its own percussion instrument.

Explore

Eunice and Opelousas are the major towns in the prairie, but you'll also find interesting diversions in Mamou and Ville Platte. If you're interested in learning some background about Cajun culture, note that there are four museums in Eunice, and all of them are closed on Mondays. For education and music exposure, aim for a Saturday visit.

Getting There & Away

Eunice is about 170 miles (a three-hour drive) west of New Orleans. While this is a doable day trip from the Crescent City, it's best to combine with a visit to Lafayette, which makes a good base for exploring the Cajun Prairie. There's a Greyhound stop in Opelousas that has buses to Lafayette ($12 to $14, twice daily) and New Orleans ($34 to $42, three daily). The heart of the Cajun Prairie can best be accessed via I-49 or LA-13.

The Best...

➡ **Sights** Prairie Acadian Cultural Center
➡ **Place to Eat** Billy's Boudin & Cracklins)
➡ **Entertainment** Savoy Music Center

Need to Know

➡ **Area Code** ☎337
➡ **Visitors Center** (☎337-457-2565; www. eunicechamber.com; 200 S CC Duson St, Eunice; ◷9am-3pm Mon-Fri)

◉ SIGHTS

CHICOT STATE PARK   STATE PARK
(☎337-363-2403; www.crt.louisiana.gov; 3469 Chicot Park Rd, Ville Platte; $3; ◷6am-9pm Sun-Thu, to 10pm Fri & Sat; 🅿 ♿) ♪ A wonderful place to access the natural beauty of Cajun country. The excellent arboretum is fun for kids and informative for adults, and deserves enormous accolades for its open, airy design. Miles of trails extend into the nearby forests, cypress swamps and wetlands. If you can, stay for early evening – the sunsets over the Spanish-moss-draped trees that fringe Lake Chicot are superb.

There are boat rentals ($20 per day), campsites ($25 to $28 per night), eight-person cabins ($150 to $175) and 14-person lodges ($175 to $225) available.

PRAIRIE ACADIAN CULTURAL CENTER   MUSEUM
(☎337-457-8499; www.nps.gov/jela; 250 Park Ave, Eunice; ◷9:30am-4:30pm Wed-Fri, to 6pm

Sat) 🍴**FREE** This NPS-run museum has exhibits on rural life and Cajun culture, and shows a variety of documentaries explaining the history of the area. It's the perfect place to begin your exploration of the Cajun Prairie. Music and food demonstrations start at 2:45pm on Saturday, or arrive a little earlier for a Cajun French–language lesson (1pm to 2pm).

OPELOUSAS MUSEUM
& INTERPRETIVE CENTER   MUSEUM
(☏337-948-2589; www.cityofopelousas.com; 315 N Main St, Opelousas; ◷8am-4:30pm Mon-Fri) **FREE** Squatting sleepily alongside Hwy 49, Opelousas' historic downtown is home to this grandma's attic of exhibits, artifacts and esoterica related to the town.

CAJUN MUSIC HALL
OF FAME & MUSEUM   MUSEUM
(☏337-457-6534;   www.cajunfrenchmusic.org; 240 S CC Duson St, Eunice; ◷9am-4:30pm Tue-Sat) **FREE** This small collection of instruments and cultural ephemera caters to the die-hard music buff. Try to engage whoever is working on some tales of Cajun living and music.

KBON   MUSEUM
(☏337-546-0007; www.kbon.com; 109 S 2nd St, Eunice; ◷9am-4pm Mon-Fri) Visitors are welcome all day at KBON, 101.1FM, home of Cajun music, zydeco, swamp pop and all the other sounds of Acadiana. Browse the capacious Wall of Fame, signed by visiting musicians.

✗ EATING

BILLY'S BOUDIN & CRACKLINS   CAJUN $
(☏337-942-9150;   http://billysboudin.com; 904 Short Vine St, Opelousas; boudin per lb $9; ◷7:30am-6pm Mon-Fri, 8am-5pm Sat, 8am-2pm Sun) Folks will literally drive for hours, sometimes crossing state lines, to grab some of Billy's goods. Most folks treat this as a take-out counter, but there's a seating area and some coolers where you can snag a cold drink. There's cracklin', which is amazing, and some other pork products as well.

RUBY'S RESTAURANT   CAFE $$
(☏337-550-7665; 123 S 2nd St, Eunice; mains $9-25; ◷6-10am Mon-Fri, 5-10pm Thu-Sat) This Eunice institution serves popular plate lunches in a 1950s diner setting. Weirdly it

also serves sushi (Thursday only) – and why not? The more local menu features dishes such as meat loaf, grilled salmon and fried chicken.

Interestingly, they have a larger restaurant across the street where the lunch and dinner items are served; the cafe is for breakfast only. The phone number goes to both places depending on which is open, so they're essentially the same spot – split into two locations.

CRAWFISH HOUSE & GRILL   CAJUN $$
(☏337-948-0049; 1214 S Union St, Opelousas; mains $13-31; ◷11am-2pm Sun-Fri, 5-9pm Tue-Sat) This may be the prairie, but you can still find good seafood out here, and the Crawfish House & Grill is a good example. Fried baskets and Cajun spins on local seafood abound; give the Cajun Girl po'boy (crab, crawfish and shrimp with peppers and sauce) a whirl. A pound of boiled crawfish will run around $6.25.

CAFÉ MOSAIC   CAFE $
(☏337-534-8336;   www.revecoffeeroasters. com/pages/cafe-mosaic; 202 S 2nd St, Eunice; mains $4-8; ◷7am-7pm Mon-Wed, to 9pm Thu & Fri, 8am-9pm Sat; 🛜) This smart coffeehouse has fluffy waffles, grilled sandwiches and a cheerful community vibe that's pretty hard not to appreciate. Live-music acts occasionally traipse across the coffeehouse stage.

☆ ENTERTAINMENT

★ SAVOY MUSIC CENTER   LIVE MUSIC
(☏337-457-9563;   www.savoymusiccenter.com; 4413 US-190, Eunice; ◷9am-5pm Tue-Fri, to noon Sat) The best time to visit Eunice is on a Saturday from 9am to noon when this accordion factory and shop hosts a Cajun-music jam session. Musician Marc Savoy and his guitarist wife, Ann, often join in.

FRED'S LOUNGE   LIVE MUSIC
(☏337-468-5411; 420 6th St, Mamou; ◷7:30am-2pm Sat) Deep in the heart of Cajun country, Mamou is a typical South Louisiana small town six days of the week, worth a peek and a short stop before rolling on to nearby Eunice. But on Saturday morning, Mamou's hometown hangout, little Fred's Lounge, becomes the apotheosis of a Cajun dance hall.

DAY TRIPS FROM NEW ORLEANS CAJUN PRAIRIE

OK, to be fair, Fred's is more of a dance shack than a hall. Whatever it is, this small bar gets more than a little crowded from 8:30am to 2pm-ish, when the staff hosts a Francophone-friendly music morning, with bands, beer and dancing. Back in the day, owner Tante Sue herself would take to the stage to dispense wisdom and songs in Cajun French, all while taking pulls from a bottle of brown liquor she kept in a pistol holster. She has since passed, but something of her amazing, anarchic energy has been imbued into the very bricks of this place.

LIBERTY THEATER   THEATER

(☏337-457-7389; http://eunice-la.com/liberty-theater; 200 Park Ave, Eunice; admission $5; ◷6-7:30pm) Saturday evening's 'Rendez-Vous des Cajuns' is a Cajun country roundup of music and a little bit of banter; it's performed live here and broadcast on local radio.

 # SHOPPING

FLOYD'S RECORD SHOP   MUSIC

(☏337-362-2184; www.floydsrecordshop.com; 434 E Main St, Ville Platte; ◷8am-4pm Mon-Sat) A good way to round out your musical tour of the prairie is to stop by this record shop in Ville Platte, 14 miles northeast of Mamou. In 1957 Floyd Solieau left his DJ job to start both the shop and Flat Tire Music. The shop, still in the family, is a cultural icon and an excellent resource for all things Cajun – CDs, instruments, books and souvenirs.

Throughout the years, under various label names, Floyd has waxed records for dozens of French-language Cajun and swamp pop legends.

Sleeping

Because the bedrock of the New Orleans economy is tourism, accommodations are generally of a high standard. Hotels are found in the French Quarter and CBD. These are large, multistory affairs kitted out with amenities; hotels in the French Quarter tend to have a more boutique, historical feel, while CBD properties are more modern.

More intimate (and quirky) guesthouses and B&Bs are the norm in the Garden District, Uptown, Faubourg Marigny and the Bywater. There is one hostel in Mid-City.

Hotels

New Orleans hotels come in all the standard shapes and sizes. Most commonly you'll find either large purpose-built properties or cozier lodgings in older buildings. Figuring out which is which by an establishment's name alone is impossible (an 'inn' here might have five rooms or 500), so read reviews carefully. The two areas where you'll find large hotels are the French Quarter and the CBD; in the latter in particular, you'll find more modern accommodation geared at the convention crowd. Boutique hotels tend to crop up in the CBD and art-gallery heavy Warehouse District.

B&Bs

For charm, you can't beat the Crescent City's hundreds of B&Bs, which are housed in everything from colorful Creole cottages to stately town houses and megamansions. B&Bs provide intimate surroundings, interesting architecture and, in many cases, a peaceful courtyard in which to escape the madding crowds. The complimentary morning meal at B&Bs is almost always a continental breakfast, although in a city with this many great breakfast spots, there's no need to settle for juice and toast.

Each of the city's residential neighborhoods is brimming with B&Bs and guesthouses; there's a particularly large glut in Faubourg Marigny and the Bywater.

Room Rates & Seasons

Lodgings in New Orleans generally charge by room, rather than per person. The city is peculiar in that it's busy during the shoulder seasons of spring and fall (February through May and September through November) and slow during the summer months (due to seriously oppressive heat from June through August).

Rates usually drop like a stone from June until August. Most hectic and high-priced times are Mardi Gras (February or March), Jazz Fest (late April to early May) and other holidays and festivals. At these times rates can triple or more, and you may find places requiring three-night (or more) minimum stays. We list prices for high spring and fall.

Parking

Parking can seriously add to your bottom line (an extra $20 to $45 per night) if staying in the Quarter or the CBD. Parking in other neighborhoods is usually free; street parking is rarely an issue in the Garden District, Uptown, Mid-City, the Marigny or Bywater. If you like your car accessible in a dedicated, on-site lot, look for the parking icon in our reviews.

NEED TO KNOW

Price Ranges

In our listings, the following indicate the price of an en-suite double room in high season.

$	less than $150
$$	$150 to $250
$$$	over $250

Reservations

➡ Conventions can fill the city any time.

➡ You'll almost always get a better rate by booking ahead.

➡ For Mardi Gras or Jazz Fest, reserve rooms six months to a year in advance.

Online Resources

New Orleans Online (www.neworleansonline.com/book) Official tourism website for the city.

Louisiana Bed & Breakfast Association (www.louisianabandb.com) Directory of local B&Bs and guesthouses.

New Orleans Hotels (www.bestneworleanshotels.com) Has some links to private home rentals and national chains.

Lonely Planet (http://www.lonelyplanet.com/usa/new-orleans/hotels) A comprehensive, curated list of properties.

Gay Stays

Note that all properties we list are LGBT-friendly. New Orleans is a tolerant town.

Air-conditioning

All accommodations listed have air con. You'd melt in summer without it.

Lonely Planet's Top Choices

Audubon Cottages (p177) Gorgeous, deceptively spacious cottages in the French Quarter.

Soniat House Hotel (p178) Quintessential French Quarter historic hotel.

Park View Historic Hotel (p185) Beautiful mansion at the edge of lovely Audubon Park.

Melrose Mansion (p180) A gorgeous villa on the edge of Faubourg Marigny.

Best B&B

Bywater Bed & Breakfast (p180) Eccentric house decked out with folk art.

La Belle Esplanade (p186) Oozing character and warm hospitality.

Ashton's Bed & Breakfast (p186) An elegant B&B dripping with historical accents.

Best by Budget: $

Bywater Bed & Breakfast (p180) Occupies the golden mean between funky and cozy.

India House Hostel (p186) Well-run hostel with a fun clientele.

City House Hostel (p176) You can't beat the location of this spotless hostel within the French Quarter.

Best by Budget: $$

La Belle Esplanade (p186) Gorgeous historical home managed by an original New Orleans character.

Cornstalk Hotel (p179) Famous for its gate, the Cornstalk is stately and well located.

Dauphine House (p180) An elegant B&B with good service in the Marigny.

Best by Budget: $$$

Audubon Cottages (p177) Gorgeous Creole suites in the French Quarter.

Ace Hotel (p183) A bastion of contemporary cool in the CBD.

Saint (p178) Sleek and stylish accommodations that are near heavenly, pun intended.

Best Contemporary Cool

Ace Hotel (p183) As modern as anything, but has thoughtful historical touches.

NOPSI Hotel (p183) Plenty of hip swag within the CBD.

Loft 523 (p181) Almost perfectly fits the contemporary boutique label.

Best for Families

Prytania Park (p184) Lower Garden District at your family's fingertips.

Olivier House (p177) A French Quarter standby that's good with kids.

Dauphine Orleans (p179) Boutique-hotel style with family-friendly amenities.

Embassy Suites Hotel (p182) A central location gives young ones lots of activity options.

Best Historic Stays

Hotel Monteleone (p179) Has hosted some of the nation's top literary luminaries.

Columns Hotel (p185) A stately facade and a lobby with decades of stories.

Lafitte Guest House (p178) Boasts a great location within the historical Quarter.

Degas House (p186) Named for the painter who stayed and worked here.

Where to Stay

NEIGHBORHOOD	FOR	AGAINST
French Quarter	Centrally located, so no need for a car. High competition means high standards of accommodations.	Touristy and loud, sometimes bordering on obnoxious. If driving, it is difficult to find parking and maneuver in the narrow streets.
Faubourg Marigny & Bywater	Cozy, independently owned guesthouses and B&Bs. Some have an authentic bohemian vibe going; all are gay-friendly. Low-key, but close to some great live music.	Small properties means inconsistent access to major modern amenities such as 24-hour room service. Less privacy than larger hotels.
CBD & Warehouse District	Best area for modern amenities. Many hotels here have excellent attached bars and restaurants. Many family-friendly spots.	The least quintessentially 'New Orleans' part of New Orleans. Many hotels are boring, convention-style places. Parking can be expensive. Potentially far from French Quarter and Uptown.
Garden, Lower Garden & Central City	Charming B&Bs set in wonderful historic homes, plus a few larger hotels on St Charles Ave. Walking distance to Magazine St shopping.	Not for folks who need funkier edges to their accommodations. Having a car really helps if you stay out here.
Uptown & Riverbend	Posh hotels and smaller (but just as opulent) guesthouses for those needing beauty and quiet. Within striking (sometimes walking) distance of the most exciting restaurants in the city.	Far from French Quarter and Marigny, so having a car is recommended.
Mid-City, Bayou St John & City Park	Smaller guesthouses with character in beautiful historic neighborhoods far from the French Quarter's bustle.	You need a car out here. Sights and activities are scattered around rather than centralized. No larger hotels and their reams of amenities.
Tremé-Lafitte	Main accommodations are small B&Bs with personalized service and a lot of character.	You won't have much in the way of luxury amenities, and you're not within walking distance of some major sights.

SLEEPING

🛏 French Quarter

CITY HOUSE HOSTEL
NEW ORLEANS
HOSTEL $

Map p234 (☏504-571-9854; www.cityhousehostels.com/new-orleans; 129 Burgundy St; dm $21-28, d $165; ⊜❋☎) This newcomer can be meat-locker chilly if the temperature dips suddenly, but if it's warm you can't beat the spic-and-span, friendly hostel that's right in the French Quarter. Nightly activities, a huge TV and game console, and the spotless kitchen and bathrooms seal the deal. There are even private toilet-and-shower rooms, with locks and hooks for your towel and toiletry bag.

The main downside is the inability to alter the heat settings easily, meaning that, if they haven't planned weeks in advance to turn on the heat for the season, it's going to be freezing cold for hours or days.

One final drawback is that the dorms have no windows, meaning you don't know if it's 8am or 3pm until you look at your clock. It's a minor complaint though, all things considered, when you can stay affordably in the French Quarter and save your pennies for Bourbon St.

HISTORIC FRENCH MARKET INN
HOTEL $

Map p234 (☏504-561-5621; www.frenchmarketinn.com; 509 Decatur St; r $90-$340; P❋☎) This hotel has pleasant rooms with crisp linens, but not much daylight (consider it a boon if you get in late). Hidden within the complex is a pleasant courtyard and small pool that's better for drinking by than swimming. You're also not far from aromatic coffee at iconic Café du Monde (p63).

Room rates are as all over the map as a reveler stumbling home from a night on Bourbon St, but can be very reasonable at certain times and with online booking.

BIENVILLE HOUSE
HOTEL
BOUTIQUE HOTEL $$

Map p234 (☏504-529-2345; www.bienvillehouse.com; 320 Decatur St; r/ste from $150/250; P⊜❋☎❉❋) The Bienville is the definition of a well-executed historic French Quarter hotel. The wrought-iron balconies that ring the tiled lobby give way to a lovely courtyard with swimming pool; interior period design matches the promise of the Federal-meets-French-Creole exterior. Rooms are pretty, and a good size for the Quarter, which tends to offer rooms on the small side.

HOTEL ROYAL
BOUTIQUE HOTEL $$

Map p234 (☏504-524-3900; www.hotelroyalneworleans.com; 1006 Royal St; r from $150; ⊜❋☎) Lace-like ironwork balconies, gas lanterns and decorative topiaries – everything an 1833 New Orleans home should be. Inside, renowned architect and designer Lee Ledbetter has infused each of the individually decorated guest quarters with subtle, softly contemporary touches. A modern, dark-wood four-poster bed contrasts nicely with the rough, white-plaster walls and plantation shutters in the king suite.

Rooms can drop to $99 at certain times of year.

CHATEAU HOTEL
HOTEL $$

Map p234 (☏504-524-9636; www.chateauhotel.com; 1001 Chartres St; r incl breakfast $242; P⊜❋☎❉) Nothing is cookie-cutter here; rooms range in size and have varying floral motifs. Though they're on the smallish side, we'd opt for the courtyard rooms, which are cool and open up to a pool. In the late spring and summer low season, rates can fall as low as $99 per night.

GENTRY QUARTERS
B&B $$

Map p234 (☏504-525-4433; www.gentryhouse.com; 1031 St Ann St; r from $185; ⊜❋☎) This charming old Creole house contains five homey rooms with kitchenettes. Modest but comfortable furnishings give the rooms a lived-in feel, while linens and towels are fresh and clean. Most rooms open onto a lush garden patio, where you might be visited by Caesar the Great Dane. Some rooms are large enough for families. There's a two-night minimum.

Guests get free pastries from Wednesday to Monday.

NINE-O-FIVE ROYAL HOTEL
HOTEL $$

Map p234 (☏504-523-0219; www.905royalhotel.com; 905 Royal St; r/ste $194/569; ⊜❋☎) On a particularly scenic block, the Nine-O-Five eschews the usual NOLA shtick and opts for the timeless comfort you'd expect to find if this house belonged to a dignified aunt. Front rooms with balconies are the choice for those who want to survey always-entertaining Royal St, but for seclusion, get a room off the cute courtyard out back.

INN ON ST PETER
HOTEL $$

Map p234 (☏504-524-9232; www.frenchquarterguesthouses.com; 1005 St Peter St; r from $187; ⊜❋☎) This inn is located in a 19th-century treasure built during the Spanish Colonial period. Wraparound iron balconies and a lovely facade conceal rooms with surprising character – a carved bed here, exposed brick there. The St Peter is a little beyond tourist central, which has advantages (quiet) and disadvantages (you might want to take a cab home).

HOTEL PROVINCIAL
HOTEL **$$**

Map p234 (☎504-581-4995; www.hotelprovin-cial.com; 1024 Chartres St; r/ste from $169/249; P☻❋☎☒) Behind its stately stucco facade, this hotel fills much of the block with a series of finely restored buildings and a large parking area. The best rooms have high ceilings and open onto the interior courtyards. Others can be cramped and dark. Decor ranges from commercial standard to ornately historic. The back courtyard is a revelation, as is its lovely pool.

Its bar, the Ice House, is a nice spot to unwind after you unwind elsewhere. Room prices include breakfast.

OLIVIER HOUSE
HOTEL **$$**

Map p234 (☎504-525-8456; www.olivierhouse. com; 828 Toulouse St; d $229; ❋☎☒) The main house was built in 1838 by Marie Anne Bienvenu Olivier, a wealthy planter's widow, and is an uncommon beauty with Greek Revival touches. Rooms range from the relatively economical to the elaborate, with balconies and kitchens; most have furnishings evoking the early 19th century. The main courtyard is lush with trees and flowers; another courtyard has a small pool.

LE RICHELIEU
HOTEL **$$**

Map p234 (☎504-529-2492; www.lerichelieuhotel. com; 1234 Chartres St; r from $205; P☻❋☎☒) Le Richelieu's red-brick walls once housed a macaroni factory, a furniture store and a barracks, but extensive reconstruction in the 1960s converted it to a good-value hotel. Spacious rooms are decorated with standard synthetic floral spreads and can be musty, but the price includes parking (a big plus); you're within an easy walk of Frenchmen St; and there's a pool.

Prices drop precipitously in the slow summer season.

HOTEL ST MARIE
HOTEL **$$**

Map p234 (☎504-561-8951; www.hotelstmarie. com; 827 Toulouse St; r from $189; P❋☎☒) The St Marie was built to look historic from the outside, but is up-to-date on the inside.

Its best feature is the inviting courtyard, which has a swimming pool and umbrella-covered tables amid lush plantings. The neocolonial guest rooms are comfortable and well appointed, and their spacious dimensions do the trick. Just around the corner is Bourbon St at its most extreme.

HOTEL VILLA CONVENTO
HOTEL **$$**

Map p234 (☎504-522-1793; www.villaconvento. com; 616 Ursulines Ave; r from $179; ☻❋☎) Classic New Orleans, the Villa occupies an 1833 town house in the residential part of the Lower Quarter, complete with a three-story red-brick facade and wrought-iron balconies. Out back in the annex (probably former servants' quarters) are more rooms, all with traditional decor, from comfy quilts to lacy canopies. Prices for budget doubles fall as low as $99 when demand dwindles.

Even if you can't stay here, it's worth taking a quick peek at 'Mr Bones and Buffet' in the lobby, so named because the iconic singer Jimmy Buffet once lived here.

BOURBON ORLEANS HOTEL
HOTEL **$$**

Map p234 (☎504-523-2222; www.bour-bonorleans.com; 717 Orleans St; r from $245; ☻❋☎☒) A polished-marble classic whose gray exteriors and white trim are almost as stately as the grand foyer. It combines several buildings, mostly dating from the early 1830s, and some street-side rooms access the classic wrought-iron balconies. (Bourbon St, needless to say, can get noisy.) Traditional rooms feature comfortable beds and ergonomic desks, but note that standard rooms are on the small side.

PRINCE CONTI HOTEL
HOTEL **$$**

Map p234 (☎800-366-2743; www.princeconti-hotel.com; 830 Conti St; r/ste from $209/231; ☻❋☎) The three floors of this 19th-century structure house a glut of guest rooms decorated with early-20th-century-style furnishings and a general sense of dignified understatement. The lobby and parlor areas might have been plucked from a Jane Austen novel, but otherwise the property is suffused with modern amenities such as a turn-down service and cable TV.

★AUDUBON COTTAGES
HOTEL **$$$**

Map p234 (☎504-561-5858; www.auduboncot-tages.com; 509 Dauphine St; cottages $350-1200; P☻❋☎☒) At the Audubon Cottages, you get to sleep in one of seven immaculately

SLEEPING FRENCH QUARTER

HAUNTED HOTELS

An eerily cold 14th-floor hallway leads to a vision of children playing; cafe doors open and shut on their own; despite the bar being locked, guests see a patron who isn't there... Andrea Thornton, Director of Sales & Marketing at the **Hotel Monteleone**, had heard dozens of first-hand accounts of supernatural sightings when she decided investigation was in order. In 2003 the hotel invited the International Society of Paranormal Research (ISPR) to come spend several days, during which they identified 12 disparate spirits on the property, one a former employee named 'Red.' And, indeed, hotel records showed that an engineer who went by the nickname Red worked at the hotel in the 1950s.

Hearing or seeing children is the most common of the mischievous-but-benign activities people experience in the historic hotel. Numerous guests have reported seeing a little boy in a striped suit (aged about three) in room 1462. Speculation is that it's Maurice, son of Josephine and Jacques Begere, looking for his parents. While Maurice was in the hotel being watched by a nanny, his father was thrown from a coach and died instantly; his mother passed a year later.

In a town with such a strife-torn history – slavery, war, fever, flood – hauntings (if they exist) are hardly a surprise. And the Monteleone is far from the only hotel in the Quarter to report sightings. Among others, ghostbusters might want to check out the following:

Bourbon Orleans Hotel (p177) Once an orphanage and an African American convent; children have been seen and heard playing on the 6th floor.

Dauphine Orleans Bottles appear rearranged at May Bailey's bar, site of a once-infamous brothel, and moans and sounds of beds moving at night have been reported.

Hotel Provincial (p177) Building 5 was constructed on the site of a Civil War hospital; guests report sometimes-gruesome visions of wounded soldiers and bloody sheets.

Lafitte Guest House 'Marie,' a little girl who died of yellow fever, is said to appear in the mirror in room 21, where her mother stayed.

Le Pavillon (p182) Apparitions materialize bedside in this 1907 hotel, where the ISPR identified at least four resident spirits.

---

restored historical buildings, ranging from two-bedroom suites with private courtyards and walk-in showers to a former storage shed once used as a studio by John James Audubon. You'll have your own saltwater pool, attentive staff and the satisfaction of having privacy and quiet within the Quarter.

★**SAINT**　　　　　　　　　　　HOTEL **$$$**
Map p234 (☏504-522-5400; www.the-sainthotelneworleans.com; 931 Canal St; r/ste $242/874; ➔❋@�🛜) The Saint has the whole Heaven thing going on: apples in a bowl at the reception desk; feathered wings on the chairs; and clean duo-chromatic color schemes (white walls, dark wood floors) offset with little azure accents – quite contemporary, yet alleviated by the historic property's elegance. It's a luxury stay with some genuine friendliness, well worth the splurge.

If you're feeling more sinner than saint, dine at Tempt, the hotel's restaurant, where pitchforks and darkness surely await.

★**SONIAT HOUSE**
HOTEL　　　　　　　BOUTIQUE HOTEL **$$$**
Map p234 (☏504-522-0570; www.soniathouse.com; 1133 Chartres St; r/ste from $400/600; ➔❋🛜) The two houses here epitomize Creole elegance at its unassuming best. You enter into a courtyard filled with ferns and a fountain; some rooms open onto the courtyard, while winding stairways lead to elegant upstairs quarters. Singular attention has been paid to the art and antiques throughout, with gas lamps adding more ambiance.

Note that rates often dip weekdays.

LAFITTE GUEST HOUSE　BOUTIQUE HOTEL **$$$**
Map p234 (☏504-581-2678; www.lafitteguesthouse.com; 1003 Bourbon St; r $389; ➔❋🛜) This elegant, three-story 1849 Creole town house is at the quieter end of Bourbon St.

The guest rooms are lavishly furnished in period style, although the antique washbasins and fireplaces seem an odd contrast with flat-screen TVs. Many rooms have private balconies. Lafitte's Blacksmith Shop (p67), one of the street's more welcoming (and some say haunted) taverns, is on the opposite corner.

Room rates include breakfast.

HOTEL MONTELEONE   HOTEL $$$

Map p234 (☑504-523-3341; www.hotelmonteleone.com; 214 Royal St; r $190-270, ste from $370; ✆❀🖥🖥🖥) Perhaps the city's most venerable hotel, the Monteleone is also the Quarter's largest. Not long after it was built, preservationists put a stop to building on this scale below Iberville St. Since its inception in 1866, the hotel has lodged literary luminaries including William Faulkner, Truman Capote and Rebecca Wells. Rooms exude an old-world appeal with French toile and chandeliers.

RITZ-CARLTON NEW ORLEANS   HOTEL $$$

Map p234 (☑504-524-1331; www.ritzcarlton.com; 921 Canal St; r from $399; ✆❀🖥🖥) Sip tea surrounded by neoclassical antiques and French fabrics; dip into a magnolia-scented bath; or retire to the library. An ample number of smiling staff waits to attend, whether you're ready for turn-down service or need a complimentary shoe shine. The solid wood floors, tall beds and brick fireplaces would fit in at an English manor house.

Trivia factoid: the spa here is the largest in Louisiana.

W FRENCH QUARTER   HOTEL $$$

Map p234 (☑504-581-1200; www.whotels.com; 316 Chartres St; r/ste from $176/572; 🅿✆❀@🖥🖥) Like all W hotels, this one wears its style on its trendy sleeve, but not all Ws have tarot cards. Where the French Quarter has colonial charm, this is all palatial grandeur, even if understated in places. Rooms vary, but all boast contemporary sleekness; the best open onto an inner patio, where you can ponder the pool's azure waters.

WESTIN NEW ORLEANS
AT CANAL PLACE   HOTEL $$$

Map p234 (☑504-566-7006; www.westinneworleanscanalplace.com; 100 Iberville St; r from $290; 🅿✆❀@🖥🖥) At 29 stories high, the Westin has some of the city's best views of the Mississippi River. Watching the parade of freighters, tankers and barges in the wee hours beats TV. Rooms are large and modern, with Westin's signature 'heavenly beds', as well as sitting areas.

DAUPHINE ORLEANS   HOTEL $$$

Map p234 (☑504-586-1800; www.dauphineorleans.com; 415 Dauphine St; r from $300; 🅿✆❀🖥🖥) Through a lush courtyard are these bright-yellow Creole cottage-style rooms with exterior access (once part of a carriage house). Request one of these, or one with exposed cypress beams and brick across the road in the former home of merchant Herman Howard. Other rooms have less character, but similar appointments, including earthy color schemes and high-thread-count sheets. Prices include breakfast.

The bar was once an infamous brothel.

OMNI ROYAL ORLEANS   HOTEL $$$

Map p234 (☑504-529-5333; www.omnihotels.com; 621 St Louis St; r from $269; ✆❀@🖥🖥🖥) The Omni Royal is hard to miss; its massive structure was actually the center of a preservation battle during its construction. Everything here screams opulence and grandeur, including the marble-tiled lobby, the heated rooftop pool and the dignified rooms that combine historical furnishing with handsome frilliness. Pets are welcome.

INN ON URSULINES   HOTEL $$$

Map p234 (☑504-525-8509; www.frenchquarterguesthouses.com; 708 Ursulines Ave; r $368; 🖥🖥) This Spanish-era Creole cottage is one of the oldest buildings in the French Quarter. It's located in the laid-back Lower Quarter, and, despite its historical roots, has some tastefully modern rooms. Those located in front are a short step up from the sidewalk, perhaps too close to the neighborhood's stream of yammering late-night pedestrians. Those out back are much quieter.

Steep discounts are offered at certain times of year.

CORNSTALK HOTEL   HISTORIC HOTEL $$$

Map p234 (☑504-523-1515; www.cornstalkhotel.com; 915 Royal St; r $228-319; 🅿✆❀🖥) The Cornstalk is known as much for its exterior as its interior, which makes sense once you see its famous maize-bedecked gates. Pass through the cast-iron fence and into a plush, antiqued boutique hotel, where the serenity sweeps away the whirl of the busy streets outside. Rooms are all luxurious and clean. Limited parking. No breakfast is served.

SLEEPING FRENCH QUARTER

ASTOR CROWNE PLAZA HOTEL $$$

Map p234 (📞504-962-0500; www.as-torneworleans.com; 739 Canal St; r/ste from $253/426; 🚇❄️@🛜🏊) An $11-million renovation buys you some stylish design details. Look for stacked-silver-bubble lamps and tall, tufted headboards with pops of purple in a primarily neutral color scheme. Business is this hotel's primary pleasure, but tourists, too, will enjoy the grand lobby, pool terrace and Dickie Brennan's Seafood Bar.

HOTEL MAISON DE VILLE HISTORIC HOTEL $$$

Map p234 (📞504-324-4888; http://maisondeville.com; 727 Toulouse St; r $486; 🚇❄️🛜) A quintessential 10-room French Quarter property, dripping with tropical, historical accents and built around a lushly landscaped courtyard that feels plucked out of time. Bourbon St is just a quick stumble away. They usually require a two-night minimum stay, and guests must be 21 or older. Rates can be substantially lower at certain times of year.

ROYAL SONESTA HOTEL $$$

Map p234 (📞504-586-0300; www.sonesta.com/royalneworleans; 300 Bourbon St; r from $249; 🚇❄️🛜🏊) Don't the doormen look fancy in their blue royal-guard-look tux and tails? Most times of year this hotel exudes a gracious charm, but the location is ground zero for Bourbon St excesses (staff grease pillars to keep revelers from climbing to the balconies). Still, the 483 rooms provide classy retreats from the strip clubs and cover bands.

Book online for steep discounts.

🛏 Faubourg Marigny & Bywater

⭐BYWATER BED & BREAKFAST B&B $

Map p238 (📞504-944-8438; www.bywaterbnb.com; 1026 Clouet St; r without bath $100-150; 🛜) This is what happens when you fall through the rabbit hole and Wonderland is a B&B. This spot is homey and laid-back, but it's also bursting with wild New Orleans aesthetic touches. Expect to stay in what amounts to a folk-art gallery with a bit of historical heritage and a hallucinogenic vibe.

⭐DAUPHINE HOUSE B&B $

Map p238 (📞504-940-0943; www.dauphinehouse.com; 1830 Dauphine St; d $125; 🛜) The Dauphine only has two rooms, but it's actually a pretty big house, a classic Creole Esplanade Ridge–style mansion that's located

in Marigny. The place is quite plush and evocative of decadent good times. Which is pretty much what New Orleans is, right?

The owner is thoughtfully attentive and knows a ton about the city.

LOOKOUT INN OF NEW ORLEANS GUESTHOUSE $

Map p238 (📞504-947-8188; www.lookoutneworleans.com; 833 Poland Ave; d $99; 🛜🏊) This cozy little inn is located at the end of Bywater, a few blocks' walk from some excellent bars and restaurants. Four suites are individually appointed; your room may feature Elvis, dragons, a zebra-print sofa sleeper or Spanish-mission-style furnishings. There's a mini-pool and a hot tub if you need a soak. The property welcomes dogs.

BURGUNDY B&B $

(📞504-261-9477; www.theburgundy.com; 2513 Burgundy St; r $110-200; 🛜) This vibrant, red-and-white 1890s double-shotgun house is a fine B&B that's located on the quieter residential edge of Marigny. You're within a quick walk of local nightlife and the music scene on St Claude Ave. Four color-coded rooms (red, green, blue and coral) surround an attractive courtyard, parlor, library and sitting area.

LIONS INN B&B B&B $

Map p238 (📞504-945-2339; www.lionsinn.com; 2517 Chartres St; d $119-145; 🛜🏊) Situated on a quiet Marigny block, Lions Inn has nine simply furnished guest rooms that are painted in splashes of vibrant color. Jump into the swimming pool or Jacuzzi, or stroll five blocks to the edge of the Quarter. Solo travelers may wish to note that there is a single room with a twin bed and shared bathroom for $75.

CRESCENT CITY GUESTHOUSE B&B $

Map p238 (📞504-944-8722; www.crescentcitygh.com; 612 Marigny St; d $85-130; 🅿🛜) This laid-back B&B is a great choice for those who want peace and quiet but don't feel like surrendering the option of walking into the French Quarter, or onto Frenchmen St. The rooms are simple but cozy, and the owner is a treasure trove of New Orleans knowledge. The back garden is a great spot to chill with a book.

MELROSE MANSION BOUTIQUE HOTEL $$

Map p238 (📞504-944-2255; www.melrosemansion.com; 937 Esplanade Ave; d/ste $160-220/245-449; 🛜🏊) An exquisite 1884

Victorian mansion, Melrose stands out even among its stately neighbors. This is a retreat for the well-heeled and for honeymooners. Rooms are luxurious, airy spaces, with high ceilings and large French windows. Fastidiously polished furnishings strike a balance between modern simplicity and historical elegance.

PIERRE COULON
GUEST HOUSE
GUESTHOUSE **$$**

Map p238 (☑504-250-0965; www.pierrecoulonguesthouse.com; 714 Spain St; r 1-2 person $150, 3/4 person $225/300; ☏) This guesthouse is located in a gorgeous Creole cottage that feels like the home of an eclectic professor. The property manages to blend a sense of historic coziness with an eccentric edge, and is within walking distance of Marigny's finest bars and restaurants. A lovely outdoor courtyard is perfect for an afternoon of lazy reading.

AULD SWEET OLIVE
BED & BREAKFAST
B&B **$$**

Map p238 (☑504-947-4332; www.sweetolive.com; 2460 N Rampart St; r $145-160, ste $180-290; ☻☏) Tropical artwork and bohemian excess seem to infuse this B&B, which is filled with artifacts from New Orleans history. Individual rooms are suffused with decorative touches – faux wood and magnolia blooms. The outside courtyard has a shaded, relaxing patio, and the owners have worked at almost all levels of the local hospitality industry.

BALCONY GUEST HOUSE
GUESTHOUSE **$$**

Map p238 (☑504-810-8667; www.balconyguesthouse.com; 2483 Royal St; r $144-181; ☏) In a neighborhood full of adorable chintz, the Balcony is full of clean lines, understated decor and subtle prettiness. The four rooms all balance warm wooden accents and cool white bedding. The eponymous balcony overlooks one of the most charming intersections in the city, adjacent to good bars and coffee shops.

MAISON DE MACARTY
B&B **$$**

Map p238 (☑504-267-1564; www.maisonmacarty.com; 3820 Burgundy St; r/ste $150-200/225; ☏☒) This 19th-century ruby-red Bywater mansion conceals a surprising number of historical heritage rooms. The interior is stuffed with all kinds of cozy antiques; it's not as eccentric as the average Bywater property, but by no means dowdy

either. There's a pool out back, and you're a 10-minute bike ride from the Quarter.

LAMOTHE HOUSE
B&B **$$**

Map p238 (☑800-535-7815; www.frenchquarterguesthouses.com; 621 Esplanade Ave; d/ste $164-189/205-359; ℙ☏☒) Lovely, oak-shaded Esplanade Ave is a prime jumping-off point for prowling Frenchmen St and the Lower Quarter. Antiques lovers will appreciate the vintage furniture in the guest rooms, while those wanting to sleep off a big night can take advantage of the thick curtains. If you're determined to revive early, take a dip in the pool after your continental breakfast.

B&W COURTYARDS
B&B **$$**

Map p238 (☑504-324-0474; www.bandwcourtyards.com; 2425 Chartres St; r $145-165; ☏) The B&W is tastefully bohemian, but it also has the right amount of historical accents. There are six individualized rooms, all with bright, broad tropical color schemes. Service is friendly and unobtrusive.

FRENCHMEN HOTEL
HOTEL **$$**

Map p238 (☑504-945-5453; www.frenchmenhotel.com; 417 Frenchmen St; d/ste $119-179/179-289; ℙ☏☒) The three thoroughly refurbished 1850s houses that comprise this hotel are clustered around a courtyard with a swimming pool and a Jacuzzi. High ceilings, balconies and some rustic exposed brick are remnants from the buildings' more elegant past. Mix-and-match furnishings have limited antique appeal. The real selling point is the hotel's proximity to everything that Frenchmen St has to offer.

🛏 CBD & Warehouse District

LOFT 523
BOUTIQUE HOTEL **$$**

Map p242 (☑504-200-6523; www.loft523.com; 523 Gravier St; d $219-259, penthouse $679; ℙ@☏) If you've ever wondered what it would be like to sleep inside a piece of modern art, now's your chance. Top design magazines have recognized the industrial-minimalist style of this spot, where whirligig-shaped fans circle over low-lying Mondo beds. If you're looking for style, privacy and a freestanding half-egg tub – this is the place.

For drinks and posh lounging, guests have access to the mod, London-inspired Gravier Social Club beside the lobby. Since International House is a sister property, you share their fitness center. The front door is so hip it's invisible, but look close and you'll find it between the Omni and Lucky Dogs.

EMBASSY SUITES HOTEL
HOTEL **$$**

Map p242 (☏504-525-1993; www.embassyneworleans.com; 315 Julia St; incl breakfast d $189, ste $239-489; P 🅟 ✳ @ 🛜 🐾) Great for an annual group getaway, every room here is a large suite and no two are exactly the same. Most have balconies; higher floors have views of the city and the river. Adjoining historic loft-building rooms, in what was once a cotton warehouse, have tall ceilings and exposed-brick walls.

Beyond the rooms, the architecture astonishes with its vast size and a cacophony of angles, but the eccentric design grows on you. The soaring atrium is indeed impressive.

LA QUINTA INN
& SUITES DOWNTOWN
HOTEL **$$**

Map p242 (☏504-598-9977; www.laquintaneworleansdowntown.com; 301 Camp St; r/ste incl breakfast $189/229; P 🅟 ✳ @ 🛜 🐾) This shiny high-rise is not necessarily what you'd expect from the mid-level La Quinta hotel chain. Rooms are efficient but stylishly modern, with flat-screen TVs and over-size graphic art. An outdoor pool, laundry facilities and continental breakfast all add to the value – and it's just a few blocks from the Quarter.

MOXY HOTEL
NEW ORLEANS
BOUTIQUE HOTEL **$$**

Map p242 (☏504-525-6800; http://moxy-hotels.marriott.com; 210 O'Keefe Ave; d $199-239; P 🅟 ✳ 🛜 🐾) The Moxy is Marriott's bid for the youth hotel demographic, as evidenced by scads of graffiti murals, pop art accents, giant Jenga sets, and physical objects marked with hashtags. Rooms have an industrial-chic vibe, dark-leather headboards and low lighting.

ALOFT NEW ORLEANS
HOTEL **$$**

Map p242 (☏504-581-9225; www.aloftneworleansdowntown.com; 225 Baronne St; d $200; 🅟 ✳ 🛜 🐾) Effectively a total departure from the historical hotel model, the Aloft chain's New Orleans outpost has rooms rounded out by pop art and the brand's semifunky blue/violet color palette. This spot has a good rooftop pool, a ton of accommodations packages and the reliable amenities and service of a major hotel brand, plus a central location.

While there are many pet-friendly hotels in New Orleans, the Aloft is one of the few that will not charge extra to accommodate your furry friend (no animals above 40lb).

HOTEL MODERN
HOTEL **$$**

Map p242 (☏504-962-0900, reservations 800-684-9525; www.thehotelmodern.com; 936 St Charles Ave; d $129-159, ste $259-459; P 🅟 ✳ @ 🛜 🐾) The eye-catching Hotel Modern isn't exactly a 'hidden gem,' but if you want welcoming, reasonably priced accommodations near the Arts District and the National WWII Museum, this hip number is a great choice. Rooms are spartan and the smallest can feel cramped. Look for monochromatic accent walls, clean lines and an old book or two for whimsy.

LAFAYETTE HOTEL
HOTEL **$$**

Map p242 (☏504-524-4441; www.lafayettehotelneworleans.com; 600 St Charles Ave; r $183-207, ste $215-233; P 🅟 ✳ 🛜 🐾) Pleasant and small, this 1916 hotel is steps from Lafayette Sq and within easy walking distance of the Julia Row Arts District and the National WWII Museum. Surrounding blocks have a classic feel that's generally lacking in the modern CBD. The rooms are furnished with dark wood, antiques and king-size beds. Bathrooms are roomy and finished in marble.

There is a one-time, nonrefundable $65 fee for pets.

DRURY INN & SUITES
HOTEL **$$**

Map p242 (☏504-529-7800; www.druryhotels.com; 820 Poydras St; r incl breakfast $170-210, ste $220; P 🅟 ✳ @ 🛜 🐾) Come for the helpful tips and the local map given at check-in, stay for the way this outpost of the Drury embraces New Orleans' fun-loving, welcoming spirit. Rooms are stylish, comfy and come with 37in flat screens, pillow-top mattresses and a microwave and refrigerator.

Free drinks are served nightly at 5:30pm along with light fare such as hot dogs and baked potatoes. Hot breakfasts are included and there's a guest laundry. Check the online eSaver rate for the best price. Parking is $25 per night. Pet fee is $10 per day.

★ LE PAVILLON
HISTORIC HOTEL **$$$**

Map p242 (☏504-581-3111, reservations 844-656-8636; www.lepavillon.com; 833 Poydras Ave; r $233-260, ste $599-699; P 🅟 ✳ 🛜 🐾) Le Pavillon exudes an old-school joie de vivre that's easy to love. Fluted columns support the porte cochere off the alabaster facade, and the doorman wears white gloves and a top hat (and somehow doesn't look ridiculous). Both private and public spaces are redolent with historic portraits, magnificent chandeliers, marble floors and heavy drapery.

At the same time, Le Pavilion has a sense of fun, best exemplified by the nightly serving of peanut-butter-and-jelly sandwiches in the lobby at 10pm. It's worth noting that during slow periods, Le Pavillon offers some astounding deals. The breakfast buffet is famously good.

★ ROOSEVELT NEW ORLEANS   HOTEL $$$

Map p242 (📞504-648-1200; www.therooseveltneworleans.com; 123 Baronne St; r $259-309, ste $329-2000; 🅿 ➌ ✳ @ ☎ ☒) The majestic, block-long lobby harks back to the early 20th century, a golden age of opulent hotels and grand retreats. Swish rooms have classical details, but the spa, Domenica (p103), storied Sazerac Bar (p105) and swanky jazz lounge are at least half the reason to stay. The rooftop pool is pretty swell too. It's an easy walk to the French Quarter.

CATAHOULA HOTEL   BOUTIQUE HOTEL $$$

Map p242 (📞504-603-2442; www.catahoulahotel.com; 914 Union St; d $230-480, q $300; ➌ ✳ ☎) More than its many boutique competitors, the Catahoula does a good job of mixing up contemporary style with the historical vibe that is such a powerful New Orleans tourism draw. Clean lines and solid colors get the old exposed-brick and warm-wood accents, topped with a stylish roof lounge and slick murals.

Bunk rooms can accommodate four people if you're in a group.

INTERNATIONAL HOUSE   BOUTIQUE HOTEL $$$

Map p242 (📞504-313-4955; www.ihhotel.com; 221 Camp St; d $239-359, penthouses $379-1059; 🅿 ✳ @ ☎) Lavish rooms at this boutique crashpad offer an array of amenities, from marble desks to iHome stereos to two-headed showers. Should the budget allow, go for the penthouse rooms and their sweeping terraces. Be aware that 11th-floor 'Rockstar' rooms are windowless and may come with a pull-chain hatch that leads to the roof – or perhaps a parallel New Orleans?

The fashionable Loa (p107) bar sits amid soaring columns and plush, tufted ottomans. There's even an iMac for those who want to check their email.

ACE HOTEL   BOUTIQUE HOTEL $$$

Map p242 (📞front desk 504-900-1180, reservations 504-941-9191; www.acehotel.com/neworleans; 600 Carondelet St; d $300-360, ste $500-1100; ➌ ✳ ☎ ☒ ☒) The Ace is a chain that *really* wants to impart a boutique, local experience. The New Orleans result is a stylish hotel with Louisiana accents that still feels like most contemporary, minimalist-with-a-touch-of-swag, design-conscious boutique hotels the world over. It's exceedingly pretty, and popular with pretty people, and every austere accent is shareworthy on the social-media platform of your choice.

The on-site bar and rooftop lounge are a big hit with local hip kids. You can find significant discounts by booking online.

LOEWS NEW ORLEANS HOTEL   HOTEL $$$

Map p242 (📞504-595-3300; www.loewshotels.com; 300 Poydras St; r $244-324; 🅿 ➌ ✳ @ ☎ ☒ ☒) They say the enormous windows were installed so that steamship executives, who once occupied the building, could watch their ships on the Mississippi. Big views are just part of the fun at this snazzy hotel. The breeziness starts in the lobby with upbeat, eye-catching photos of New Orleans. The 285 elegantly modern rooms are larger than average.

All rooms on the 11th floor and above, many with superb river views. There's an indoor lap pool and health center, plus a noted spa. The Swizzle Stick Bar (p105) off the lobby regularly hosts live jazz. Loews is pet-friendly and charges a $100 pet cleaning fee, plus $25 per day. Parking is $39 per night.

NOPSI HOTEL   HOTEL $$$

Map p242 (📞844-439-1463; www.nopsihotel.com; 317 Baronne St; d $333-445; 🅿 ➌ ✳ ☒ ☒) A gorgeous grand dame of a lobby lifted from a Jazz Age fantasy, a twinkling rooftop pool and a handsome exterior contain a series of beigey rooms that aren't quite as exciting as their packaging. There's a spa on site and a staff that is helpful and eager to please.

What's in a name? The acronym is a callback to New Orleans Public Service Inc, a historical civic utility and transportation company.

WINDSOR COURT HOTEL   HOTEL $$$

Map p242 (📞504-523-6000; www.windsorcourthotel.com; 300 Gravier St; r $296, ste $398-555; 🅿 ➌ ✳ ☎ ☒) The sparkling lobby, with its portraits of noblemen and their Brittany spaniels, could double as a drawing room in the real Windsor Court. Guest rooms are decked out with elegant furniture and come with Italian-marble bathrooms, toile with aristocratic prints, butler's pantries and Frette linens. There's also a 4500ft spa.

🛏 Garden, Lower Garden & Central City

⭐ CREOLE GARDENS   B&B $

Map p246 (📞504-569-8700; http://creolegardens.com; 1415 Prytania St; d/ste $140/240; 🌐❄🛜🐕) Friendly, knowledgeable hosts, a rainbow-hued property with individualized rooms and plenty of New Orleans bordello-esque vibe, and they're cool with pets? Of any size? Hey, sign us up. This is a winning B&B that's dripping with character and out-of-the-box charm (one room is literally called Countess Willie Piazza's Hall of Splendors).

GARDEN DISTRICT B&B   B&B $

Map p246 (📞504-895-4302; www.gardendistrictbedandbreakfast.com; 2418 Magazine St; d $115-135; 🌐❄@) This inviting B&B is a great budget-to-midrange option for an extended stay. The private four-suite town house is like your own character-filled efficiency apartment. Each spacious room (most sleep three) has a separate entrance, kitchenette and table seating plus brick walls, tall ceilings and homey antiques such as a 1950s (nonworking) stove. Fresh-made breads and fruit are set out every morning.

The Patio Suite includes a wonderful little private courtyard. The innkeeper provides loads of local restaurant info, and respects guests' privacy. It's close to the Irish Channel neighborhood and within walking distance of good Magazine St shopping. Prices include breakfast.

FAIRCHILD HOUSE   B&B $

Map p246 (📞504-524-0154; www.fairchildhouse.com; 1518 Prytania St; d $89-119, ste $129; 🌐❄🛜) This B&B is attractively understated, which cuts against the grain of most properties of this type. The warm colors, scads of brick and hardwood floors (with the exception of some carpeted standard rooms) are appealingly simple. Standard rooms are a good price for private digs in this part of town.

ATLAS HOUSE   HOSTEL $

Map p246 (📞504-400-4851; www.theatlashouse.com; 1354 Magazine St; dm/d/tr/q $31/77/86/97; 🌐❄🛜) A clean, colorful hostel that provides that good old backpacker vibe, albeit a more laid-back version than you may expect in New Orleans. If you're older, look elsewhere (or book a private room); the dorms are only available to international or out-of-state travelers under the age of 33, or American students with a student ID.

PRYTANIA PARK   HOTEL $

Map p246 (📞504-524-0427; www.prytaniaparkhotel.com; 1525 Prytania St; r $89-139, ste $189-219; 🅿🌐❄🛜) It's rare to find a large, high-volume 'hotel' in this part of town, where B&Bs proliferate, but the Prytania Park is a good exception to this rule. There's a large variety of rooms, and not all are up to snuff, but many have brick walls, red pine floors and general historical beauty. Prices include breakfast.

Kids will get a kick out of the loft rooms that come with a spiral staircase. Complimentary parking is available in a guarded lot behind the property.

GREEN HOUSE INN   B&B $$

Map p246 (📞504-525-1333; www.thegreenhouseinn.com; 1212 Magazine St; r $179-199, ste $269; 🅿🌐❄🛜🖥🐕) The house's striking color – a tropical rubber-tree green – certainly stands out on a still-gentrifying section of Magazine St, near the Warehouse District. Things stay green within the landscaped pool and garden (clothing optional), which is surrounded by palms and exotic blooms. Though named after flowers, the guest rooms are far from delicate, with clean lines, hardwood floors and exposed brick.

TERRELL HOUSE   B&B $$

Map p246 (📞504-237-2076; www.terrellhouse.com; 1441 Magazine St; r $185-275; 🌐❄🛜) Southern hospitality is what impresses most at this stately 1858 Georgian Revival house with cast-iron galleries, a spacious courtyard and exquisite touches. Original art adds to the freshness of the simple but tasteful carriage-house rooms. Think high-thread-count linens, colorful spreads and clean-lined wooden or iron beds. Suites in the main house are more antique in nature, with period furnishings and Oriental rugs.

Common rooms are galleries filled with art, antiques and potted plants. Other amenities include in-room minifridges stocked with soda and bottled water. Breakfast is included, and the menu is divine. Owner Linda O'Brien is a warm host who's on top of the details. No children under 12.

PARISIAN COURTYARD   B&B $$

Map p246 (☑504-581-4540; www.theparisian-courtyardinn.com; 1726 Prytania St; d $172-220; ♺✳@🛜) This handsome B&B encompasses 10 individually appointed rooms that are all historically aglow with their hardwood floors and old-school furniture. Some rooms are a little plainer than others, but all come with private bathrooms and climate control – a nice touch in an older property.

HOTEL INDIGO   HOTEL $$

Map p246 (☑504-522-3650; www.hotelindigo.com; 2203 St Charles Ave; d $172-181, ste $216-604; 🅿♺✳@🛜✳) Hotel Indigo, we like your finger-popping style. In the guestrooms, New Orleans–themed photographic murals root you firmly in the city, while bright pillows and bold prints add an artsy sense of fun. The hotel is steps from the St Charles Avenue Streetcar line, and the big-windowed lobby overlooks Mardi Gras parades and the Rock 'n' Roll Marathon route.

Parking will cost you $23 a day, while pets are $50 per stay. We had no problems with free public parking along Jackson Ave.

THE QUEEN ANNE   B&B $$

Map p246 (☑504-524-0427; www.thequeenanne.com; 1625 Prytania St; d $129-179; ♺✳🛜) This B&B in a historical home, operated by the folks at nearby Prytania Park, is charming without being too overtly lace curtain. It's an 'adults only' property – guests must be over 25 – which presumably cuts down on the bad behavior folks tend to associate with New Orleans. All rooms have coffee makers, TVs and fridges.

HENRY HOWARD HOTEL   BOUTIQUE HOTEL $$$

Map p246 (☑504-313-1577; http://henryhoward-hotel.com; 2041 Prytania St; d $199-359; ♺✳🛜) In a neighborhood dripping with historical accommodations, the Henry Howard is... well, historical. But it's got a cool, contemporary design scheme, with deco-style accents, vintage and contemporary furniture, original art, hanging instruments and a general inviting airiness. A two-night minimum-stay rule is often enforced, and rates can wildly swing up or down depending on season.

🛏 Uptown & Riverbend

ALDER HOTEL   HOTEL $

Map p248 (☑504-207-4600; http://alder-hotel.com; 4545 Magnolia St; d from $109; 🅿♺✳🛜✳) Although it lacks the boutique chic of a B&B, the Alder is clean, comfy, quiet and very reasonable for the price. An added bonus is being just steps away from the fun of Freret St, with some other Uptown spots – like Gautreau's (p134) restaurant! – within walking distance, and the ambitious can even walk from here to the St Charles Ave trolley.

Rates include breakfast.

★ PARK VIEW HISTORIC HOTEL   HOTEL $$

Map p248 (☑504-861-7564; http://parkview-guesthouse.com; 7004 St Charles Ave; r $194-251; ♺@🛜) The breakfasts are amazing (oh, those cheese grits) at this well-appointed three-story inn, where everyone seems glad to see you. Beside Audubon Park, this ornate wooden masterpiece was built in 1884 to impress people attending the World Cotton Exchange Exposition. The rooms and guest lounge are heavy with antiques, and the verandah overlooking the park and St Charles Ave is lovely.

Tulane and Loyola Universities are just blocks away – many of the hotel's frequent guests are visiting parents. Complimentary wine is served in the afternoon and there's a computer for guest use. No surprise, it's listed in the National Historic Places registry. Rates include breakfast.

CHIMES   B&B $$

Map p248 (☑504-899-2621, 504-453-2183; www.chimesneworleans.com; 1146 Constantinople St; r $158-198; ♺@🛜) Five pleasant little rooms here each have outstanding individual touches, such as a floating staircase made from 4in-thick cypress slabs, or a sunken stone tub. Rooms surround a lovely patio and gardens, creating a courtyard community of sorts. Breakfast (included in rates) consists of fresh-baked goods and local Community Coffee. Eight namesake wind chimes hang on the front porch of the main house.

Chimes is located in a quiet residential neighborhood, but is quite close to Magazine St. Two- or three-night minimum stay required on weekends, depending on the season.

COLUMNS HOTEL   HISTORIC HOTEL $$

Map p248 (☑504-899-9308; www.thecolumns.com; 3811 St Charles Ave; r $165-288; ♺✳@🛜) This white-porched Southern manse, built in 1883, is a snapshot from the past. Fortunately that past doesn't take itself too seriously. A magnificent mahogany staircase climbs past a stained-glass window to the rooms, ranging from smallish doubles to the two-room Pretty Baby Suite (named for the 1970s Louis Malle film shot here). The environs aren't exactly posh, but they're well loved.

Elaborate marble fireplaces, richly carved armoires and claw-foot tubs are among the highlights. To absorb the late-night revelry, take a front room on the 2nd floor. A lavish hot breakfast is included. Guests enter through the columned front verandah and continue past two wood-paneled parlors that double as a bar-cafe.

🛏 Mid-City, Bayou St John & City Park

INDIA HOUSE HOSTEL   HOSTEL $

Map p252 (☑504-821-1904; www.indiahouse-hostel.com; 124 S Lopez St; dm $22-26, d/q $50/99; ⊛✿@🛜🏊) This colorful place is larger than it looks. Half a block off Canal St in Mid-City, the hostel is a minicomplex of subtropically themed good times. The grounds include an above-ground pool, a cabana-like patio and well-worn old houses used for sleeping. And the ambience? India House has a free-spirited party atmosphere that got you backpacking in the first place.

Bunk beds include linen and tax. Guests can use the washer and dryer. Children not permitted.

★THE DRIFTER HOTEL   HOTEL $$

Map p252 (☑504-605-4644; https://thedrifter-hotel.com; 3522 Tulane Ave; d $143-184, q $225; ⊛✿🛜🏊) Enormously popular with the hip New Orleans kids, the Drifter is a mid-century party that happened to get thrown on Tulane Ave. Sleek, rounded accoutrements and a *Mad Men*-esque furniture and design sensibility are enlivened by clean, modern rooms and a pool where frequent parties are thrown and pictures are hashtagged.

🛏 Tremé-Lafitte

★LA BELLE ESPLANADE   B&B $$

Map p254 (☑504-301-1424; www.labelleespla-nade.com; 2216 Esplanade Ave; r incl breakfast $190-230; ⊛✿🛜) A little quirky, a little saucy and the co-owner wears a jaunty fedora – a devil-may-care touch that ties the whole colorful shebang together. Furnishings in the five themed suites vary, but have chunky headboards, plush chairs, Gibson Girl portraits and claw-foot tubs. Bright, monochromatic walls keep it all pretension-free. Savor crawfish pie and other tasty Southern fare for breakfast.

DEGAS HOUSE   HISTORIC HOTEL $$

Map p254 (☑504-821-5009; www.degashouse.com; 2306 Esplanade Ave; r $189-250, ste from $300; 🅿⊛✿🛜) Edgar Degas, the famed French Impressionist, lived in this 1852 Italianate house when visiting his mother's family in the early 1870s. Rooms recall his time here through period furnishings and reproductions of his work. The suites have balconies and fireplaces, while the less expensive garret rooms are cramped top-floor quarters that once housed the Degas family's servants.

During his time here, Degas produced the city's most famous painting, *The Cotton Exchange in New Orleans*. Easels are available, *bien sûr*.

ASHTON'S BED & BREAKFAST   B&B $$

Map p254 (☑504-942-7048; www.ashtonsbb.com; 2023 Esplanade Ave; r incl breakfast $178-208; ⊛✿🛜) Looking at the detailed plaster ceilings, ornate stained glass and crisp paint and trim at this wonderful mansion, it's very hard to imagine it had a 60ft hole in the front of it after Hurricane Katrina. Nothing to worry about, though; the innkeepers meticulously restored this 1861 Greek Revival building. Luxe furnishings include half-tester canopy beds and claw-foot tubs.

A hot Creole breakfast and complimentary refreshments throughout the day are included. Ashton's is well situated if you're in town for Jazz Fest. Festive decorations – such as fancy pumps from the Muses parade – fill the home before Mardi Gras.

HH WHITNEY HOUSE   B&B $$

Map p254 (☑504-948-9448; www.hhwhitney-house.com; 1923 Esplanade Ave; incl breakfast r $125-185, ste $250-435; ⊛✿🛜) Common areas are not as spiffy as those in other B&Bs in the neighborhood, but this 19th-century Italianate house is a convenient choice if you're attending Jazz Fest. Each room has its own style, but all include vintage furniture and antique embellishments. The back garden is a nice spot in which to lounge under the shade of leafy oaks.

If you're a *Gone with the Wind* fan, there's an entire suite themed for Scarlett O'Hara, complete with a Vivien Leigh portrait.

Understand New Orleans

New Orleans Today

In 2018, New Orleans celebrated its 300th birthday, but the celebration was not as exuberant as one might expect in the city that gave the world Mardi Gras. This is a city that prides itself on its unchanging character, yet the defining characteristics of 21st-century New Orleans make the city, in some ways, unimaginable to its early settlers. This includes a commitment to the finer things like cuisine and music – the question is, can the majority of the city's residents enjoy those amenities.

Best on Film & TV

A Streetcar Named Desire (1951) Classic NOLA drama, with Marlon Brando and Vivien Leigh.
The Princess & the Frog (2009) Disney fable that captures the magic and wonder of the city and bayou.
Treme (2010–13) Life, love and music in post-Katrina New Orleans.
12 Years a Slave (2013) The most accurate cinematic portrayal of slavery in the American South.
True Detective, Season 1 (2014) A genre-bending police procedural that dabbles in supernatural horror.

Best in Print

Bienville's Dilemma (Richard Campanella; 2008) Definitive guide to the city's physical and cultural geography.
A Confederacy of Dunces (John Kennedy Toole; 1980) Quintessential New Orleans picaresque novel.
Nine Lives (Dan Baum; 2009) Nine oral histories form a cross-section of modern New Orleans.
The World That Made New Orleans (Ned Sublette; 2008) A deep and enjoyable dive into the city's history.
The Awakening (Kate Chopin; 1899) One of the first American novels written from a woman's perspective.
A.D. (Josh Neufeld; 2009) Graphic novel of the days leading to, and following, Hurricane Katrina.

A Changing Demographic

For most of the 20th century, New Orleans was, demographically speaking, considered a city of black and white – that is to say, African American and Caucasian. This dynamic has been changing for the past two decades, and has been exacerbated by Hurricane Katrina. While the metropolitan area lost some of its black population due to the storm, the population vacuum was not necessarily filled by white transplants. A significant amount of Asian and Hispanic 'new' New Orleanians arrived, adding to existing Honduran, Vietnamese, and Chinese American communities. Some wags have called this demographic trend the 'browning' of New Orleans.

We say 'metropolitan area' because many new arrivals are settling in the suburbs just outside of New Orleans. Williams Boulevard in Kenner – packed with South American, Central American and Asian restaurants – might be more cosmopolitan than any street in Orleans parish proper. The suburb of Metairie is now packed with international grocery stores selling tortillas and rice wine. A Latin American flea market sets up in Algiers every weekend, and Honduran and Mexican food trucks can be found outside any parking lot where migrant laborers converge. Within New Orleans, spots like Casa Borrega and stretches of New Orleans East are the center of local Hispanic and Asian gravity.

Louisiana Land Loss

All of the issues facing New Orleans are overshadowed by the fact that there may not *be* a New Orleans in a century. Louisiana is experiencing some of the fastest rate of land loss in the world. Since 2010, some 58 square miles of the state have been swept underwater.

The culprit? Coastal erosion, saltwater intrusion, decreased sediment deposits due to dams, canals and levees, oil and gas excavation that cause the land to lose structural integrity, and rising sea levels caused by climate change. At the end of the day, this state's economy is deeply tied to resource extraction, and resource extraction is linked to land loss. Some argue the fiscal wealth the energy sector creates can be invested in battling land loss, but increasingly, locals are wondering if those benefits fill state coffers.

Many legislators swear by Louisiana's Industrial Tax Exemption Program (ITEP), which ostensibly creates incentives, via tax breaks and other benefits, for businesses to stay in the state. There is mounting evidence that the ITEP's exemptions are so broad, the state is losing billions of dollars in lost taxes while businesses hire a bare minimum of local labor. The series 'No Strings Attached,' published by the Baton Rouge *Advocate*, is a comprehensive investigation into the fiscal fallout of the ITEP.

New Orleans skews to the political left, and land loss has become a major priority for her citizens. The situation has been primed for a showdown between the city and the state, and in a larger sense, Louisiana and the Gulf of Mexico.

The Night They Drove Old Dixie Down

One of the most heated battles of the current culture wars was fought in New Orleans in 2017. Following the Charleston church massacre by a white supremacist known for sporting Confederate flag regalia, then-mayor of New Orleans Mitch Landrieu called for the removal of four controversial New Orleans monuments. His decision was spurred by vigorous activism from groups like Take 'em Down NOLA.

Three were statues of Confederate slave holders – Robert E Lee, Jefferson Davis and PGT Beauregard. One was a monument to the 'battle' of Liberty Place, an 1874 paramilitary insurrection led by the Crescent City White League against the racially integrated Reconstruction-era Louisiana state government. The White League murdered black police officers, and the monument's inscription once read, in part, 'the national election of November 1876 recognized white supremacy in the South and gave us our state.'

That line spoke to the symbolism of the other statues, which were all erected long after the Civil War technically ceased in 1865. Landrieu argued – and historians agreed – that these statues were specifically raised in opposition to Reconstruction and integration. Later, they became rallying points for those opposed to Civil Rights.

The Liberty Place statue was removed on April 24, 2017 – Confederate Memorial Day in Mississippi and Alabama – amid threats of violence; one contractor who offered to remove the Lee statue found his car torched in a parking lot. The other three statues were removed in May of 2017 without incident, besides some angry protests. The statues will be moved to as-of-yet undetermined facilities, where they can be studied as artifacts of history, rather than venerated in a place of civic honor.

if New Orleans were 100 people

60 would be African American
30 would be white
3 would be Asian
2 would be mixed race

belief systems
(% of population)

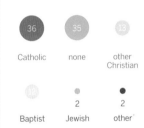

Catholic 36 | none 35 | other Christian 13

Baptist | Jewish 2 | other 2

population per sq mile

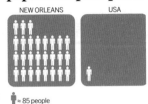

NEW ORLEANS | USA

= 85 people

History

New Orleans has ever been a place for exiles and seekers: French aristocrats and frontiers folk; rebel slaves, defeated slave owners and mixed-race children of uncertain status; American explorers, Spanish merchants and Jewish refugees; prostitutes and nuns; musicians, artists, homosexuals, those seeking to rebuild an almost-drowned city and, more recently, transplants drawn by the city's legendary funkiness.

Native Inhabitants

Louisiana was well settled and cultivated by the time of European arrival. Contrary to the myth of hunter-gatherers living in a state of harmony with the forest, local Native Americans significantly transformed their environment with roads, trade networks and substantial infrastructure. They were, however, susceptible to European diseases; the germs brought by early explorers wiped out thousands of Native Americans. Ironically, by the time the French arrived with the goal of colonization, the region had probably reverted to something like a state of nature due to the massive deaths caused by introduced diseases.

After 1700, Europeans documented numerous direct contacts with local tribes. A confederation known collectively as the Muskogeans lived north of Lake Pontchartrain and occasionally settled along the banks of the Mississippi River. The Houma nation thrived in isolated coastal bayous from Terrebonne to Lafourche up until the 1940s, when oil exploration began in southern Louisiana and disturbed their way of life. Today, the Houma are battling the impacts of coastal erosion, which threatens the physical integrity of their tribal homeland.

Early settlers planned a canal to link the Mississippi River to Bayou St John and, eventually, Lake Pontchartrain. The proposed canal was never built, but after the Louisiana Purchase its location – Canal St – became the border between the French Quarter and the American Sector, where Americans settled in what is now Uptown.

French & Spanish New Orleans

Europeans knew control of the mouth of the Mississippi equaled control of the interior of the continent, but the Mississippi eluded ships on the Gulf until 1699, when Canadian-born Pierre Le Moyne, Sieur d'Iberville, and his younger brother Jean-Baptiste Le Moyne, Sieur de Bienville, located the muddy outflow. They encamped 40 miles downriver from present-day

TIMELINE	Pre-European Contact	1600s	1690s
	Louisiana is populated by thousands of members of the First Nations, who live in villages and large towns in the Gulf Coast region and northern prairies.	European explorers search for the entrance to the Mississippi River. Control of this access point would provide command of the interior of the North American continent.	French fur traders establish small villages and forts in the south Louisiana bayous, paving the way for the eventual settlement of New Orleans.

New Orleans on the eve of Mardi Gras and, knowing their countrymen would be celebrating the pre-Lenten holiday, christened the small spit of land Pointe de Mardi Gras. With a Native American guide, Iberville and Bienville sailed upstream, noting the narrow portage to Lake Pontchartrain along Bayou St John in what would later become New Orleans.

Iberville died in 1706, but Bienville remained in Louisiana to found Nouvelle Orléans – named in honor of the Duc d'Orléans (Duke of Orléans) – in 1718. Bienville chose a patch of relatively high ground beside the Bayou St John, which connected the Mississippi to Lake Pontchartrain, thereby offering more direct access to the Gulf of Mexico. Factoring in the site's strategic position, Bienville's party decided to overlook the hazards of perennial flooding and mosquito-borne diseases. Engineer Adrien de Pauger's severe grid plan, drawn in 1722, still delineates the French Quarter today.

From the start, the objective was to populate Louisiana and make a productive commercial port, but Bienville's original group of 30 ex-convicts, six carpenters and four Canadians struggled against floods and yellow-fever epidemics. The colony, in the meantime, was promoted as heaven on earth to unsuspecting French, Germans and Swiss, who began arriving in New Orleans by the shipload. To augment these numbers, convicts and prostitutes were freed from French jails if they agreed to relocate to Louisiana.

In a secret treaty, one year before the Seven Years' War (1756–63) ended, France handed the unprofitable Louisiana Territory to King Charles III of Spain in return for being an ally in its war against England. But the 'Frenchness' of New Orleans was little affected for the duration of Spain's control. Spain sent only a small garrison and few financial resources. The main enduring impact left by the Spanish was the architecture of the Quarter. After fires decimated the French Quarter in 1788 and 1794, much of it was rebuilt by the Spanish. Consequently, the quaint Old Quarter with plastered facades that we know today is not French, as its name would suggest, but predominantly Spanish in style.

The Spanish sensed they might eventually have to fight the expansion-minded Americans to retain control of the lower Mississippi. So they jumped at Napoleon Bonaparte's offer to retake control of Louisiana in 1800.

A Demographic Gumbo

The Creoles could only loosely be defined as being of French descent. The progeny of unions between French Creoles and Native Americans or blacks also considered themselves Creole. Still, while the multicultural stew's constituent parts were not necessarily French, they

1718	1750s	1762	1788
Jean-Baptiste Le Moyne de Bienville founds Nouvelle Orléans, favoring the site for its strategic position controlling the mouth of the Mississippi River.	French Cajuns begin to arrive in southern Louisiana following the British conquest of Canada. The area they settle becomes known as (and is still referred to as) Acadiana.	France hands Louisiana Territory, which has proven to be unprofitable, over to Spain in exchange for an alliance in its wars in Europe.	On Good Friday, the Great New Orleans fire destroys 856 buildings, which are replaced with Spanish-style construction that characterizes the French Quarter to this day.

became French in character after exposure to the city. Early German immigrants, for example, frequently Gallicized their names and spoke French within a generation.

Ironically the group that did not assimilate to the French city was the French Acadians. The Acadians (forest-dwellers), former residents of Canada, were deported by the British from Nova Scotia in 1755 after refusing to pledge allegiance to England. Aboard unseaworthy ships they headed south, but the largely illiterate, Catholic peasants were unwanted in the American colonies. Francophile New Orleans seemed a natural home, but even here the citified Creoles regarded them as country trash. So the Acadians, now dubbing themselves Cajuns, fanned out into the upland prairies of western Louisiana, where they were able to resume their lifestyle of raising livestock.

Other former-French subjects arrived from St Domingue (now Haiti). The slave revolt there in 1791 established St Domingue as the second independent nation in the Americas and first black republic in the world. Following those revolts, thousands of slaveholders fled with their 'property' (slaves) to Louisiana, where slave and master bolstered French-speaking Creole traditions. Thousands of former slaves also relocated from St Domingue to New Orleans as free people of color. This influx doubled the city's population and injected an indelible trace of Caribbean culture that remains in evidence to this day. Their most obvious contribution was the practice of voodoo, which became popular in New Orleans during the 19th century.

As the Civil War approached, nearly half of the city's population was foreign born. Most were from Ireland, Germany or France. The Irish, in particular, took grueling, often hazardous work building levees and digging canals. They settled the low-rent sector between the Garden District and the docks, still known as the Irish Channel.

Despite the Napoleonic Code's mandate for Jewish expulsion, trade practices led to tolerance of Jewish merchants. Alsatian Jews augmented the small Jewish community in New Orleans, and by 1828 they had established a synagogue. Judah Touro, whose estate was valued at $4 million upon his death in 1854, funded orphanages and hospitals that would serve Jews and Christians alike.

Antebellum Prosperity

While Napoleon Bonaparte was waging war in Europe, the US was expanding westward into the Ohio River Valley. Napoleon needed cash to finance his wars, and US President Thomas Jefferson coveted control of the Mississippi. The deal seemed natural, but nevertheless the US minister in Paris, Robert Livingston, was astonished by Bonaparte's offer to

1791	1803	1811	1815
Following the slave revolution in Haiti, the arrival of French-speaking migrants, black and white, doubles New Orleans' population and adds a veneer of Caribbean culture.	Napoleon reclaims Louisiana, then sells the territory – which encompasses almost the entire drainage area of the Mississippi River – to the US for $15 million, doubling the nation's size.	The German Coast Uprising, the largest slave revolt in US history, occurs near New Orleans. Two white men and 95 slaves are killed during the fighting.	General Andrew Jackson defeats the British in Chalmette, just outside the city, at the battle of New Orleans. The battle occurs after the War of 1812 has technically ended.

sell Louisiana Territory – an act that would double the USA's national domain – at a price of $15 million.

Little cheer arose from the Creole community, who figured the Americans' Protestant beliefs, support for English common law and puritan work ethic jarred with the Catholic Creole way of life. In 1808 the territorial legislature sought to preserve Creole culture by adopting elements of Spanish and French law, a legacy that has uniquely persisted in Louisiana to this day, to the abiding frustration of many a Tulane law student.

New Orleans grew quickly under US control, becoming the fourth-wealthiest city in the world and the second-largest port in the USA by the 1830s. The city's population grew as well, and spilled beyond the borders of the French Quarter. Also in the 1830s, Samuel Jarvis Peters bought plantation land upriver from the French Quarter to build a distinctly American section.

The late 1850s saw the revival of Carnival. The old Creole tradition, now propelled by Americans who wanted to both appropriate and expand on the festival, hit the streets of New Orleans as a much grander affair than ever before. Americans also assumed control of the municipal government in 1852, further illustrating the erosion of Creole influence in New Orleans.

While the evidence is contested, the accepted wisdom in New Orleans is that the African musical traditions kept alive inside Congo Sq served as a base for jazz and later forms of homegrown black music.

Slavery and Free People of Color

From the beginning, people of African and Caribbean descent have been an important part of New Orleans' population and culture. Prior to the Civil War, enslaved people were part of many New Orleans households. Equally significant, though, was the city's considerable number of blacks who were free – though not given equal rights to whites – during the colonial and antebellum period.

Long before the Civil War, New Orleans had the South's largest population of free blacks. In Creole New Orleans they were known as *les gens de couleur libre*, or free people of color. Throughout the 18th and 19th centuries, it was not uncommon for slaves, or the children of enslaved people and slave owners, to be granted their freedom. Enslaved people who learned a trade were often allowed to hire themselves out and earn enough money to buy their freedom. In 1724, French Louisianans adopted the Code Noir (Black Code), a document that restricted the social position of blacks, but also addressed some of the needs of slaves (abused slaves could legally sue their masters) and accorded certain privileges to free persons of color. The Code Noir permitted free blacks to own property and conduct business.

Free blacks often identified with Creole culture, speaking French and attending Mass. Orchestras of free black musicians regularly

1820s	1828	1830s	1840
New Orleans becomes the second-largest immigrant hub in the USA. Many immigrants come from Germany and Ireland; those from Ireland often settle in the area now known as the 'Irish Channel.'	The first synagogue in the city opens for services. New Orleans Jews are a mixture of Spanish, Alsatian and Germanic groups, giving the community a unique cultural makeup.	Marie Laveau markets herself as the Voodoo Queen of New Orleans, popularizing the religion among the upper class and linking it to the city's public identity.	Antoine's opens for business. It is still open today, the oldest family restaurant in America, and its kitchen is supposedly responsible for dishes such as oysters Rockefeller.

performed at opulent Creole balls. Free blacks in New Orleans were often well educated, and some owned land and slaves of their own. But they didn't share all the rights and privileges of white Creoles and Americans: they could not vote or serve in juries, and while going about their business were sometimes required to show identification in order to prove that they were free.

Subtle gradations of color led to a complex class structure in which those with the least African blood tended to enjoy the greatest privileges (octoroons, for instance, who were in theory one-eighth black, rated higher than quadroons, who were one-quarter black).

Read the above and you might think that blacks in Creole Louisiana were better off than those in other parts of the United States. To a degree, this was true, but a more brutal reality persisted: New Orleans was built on slavery.

The French brought some 1300 African slaves to New Orleans in the city's first decade. Although the import of slaves became illegal in the USA in 1808, slavery itself remained legal, and thanks to smugglers like Jean Lafitte, New Orleans had become the largest slave-trading center in the country by the mid-19th century.

The reason? Enslaved people could still be traded within the USA. Sitting at the mouth of the Mississippi, New Orleans became the capital of the domestic slave trade, which was seminal to the local economy. Riverboats were designed to accommodate a maximal amount of human cargo. Insurance policies were created to cover slaves. Slave traders were considered integral to the city's financial sector, and became the wealthiest men in the South. Newspapers of the day were filled with classifieds that listed slaves for sale or sought escapees.

At no point was that trade humane, although, at least for a period, enslaved people in French and Spanish Louisiana were allowed to retain more of their African culture than slaves in other parts of the USA. Drumming and dancing were permitted during nonworking hours, and free blacks and slaves were allowed to congregate at Congo Sq, initially called Place des Negres. Immense crowds, including tourists from the East Coast and Europe, showed up to witness complicated polyrhythmic drumming and dances.

Still, enslaved people were ultimately considered less than human. Even a 'kind' master would split up an enslaved family with the same ease as selling livestock. The industry was a point of pride for New Orleanians; the slave market held in the gorgeous rotunda of the St Louis Hotel was even considered an attraction. Postcards were sold showing the St Louis' lobby with the slave auction operating at a full clip. In 1960, the Omni Royal Orleans was built on the former site of the St Louis Hotel.

Alliances between escaped African slaves and Native Americans were not uncommon. Early French settlers also sometimes married Native American women. Today, most of the thousands of Louisianans who identify as Native American are culturally and racially mixed.

1853	1857	1860s	1862
A yellow-fever epidemic claims the lives of almost 8000 citizens, or 10% of the city's population. Eventually the outbreak is traced to mosquito-borne transmission.	The Mistick Krewe of Comus launches modern Mardi Gras with a torch-lit night parade. Eventually, hundreds of other 'krewes' will add their imprint to the celebration.	French instruction in New Orleans schools is abolished in 1862. A statewide ban on French education is implemented in 1868, limiting French cultural influence.	New Orleans is occupied by the Union for the duration of the Civil War. Many citizens resent the Northern presence, setting the stage for a difficult postwar reconstruction period.

Union Occupation

As cosmopolitan as New Orleans was, it was also a slave city in a slave state, and it was over this very issue that the nation hurtled toward civil war. On January 26, 1861, Louisiana became the sixth state to secede from the Union, and on March 21 the state joined the Confederacy – but not for long. The Union captured New Orleans in April 1862 and held it till the end of the war.

Major Benjamin Butler, nicknamed 'Beast,' oversaw a strict occupation, but is also credited with giving the Quarter a much-needed cleanup, building orphanages, improving the school system and putting thousands of unemployed – both white and black – to work. But he didn't stay in New Orleans long enough to implement Abraham Lincoln's plans for 'reconstructing' the city. Those plans, blueprints for the Reconstruction of the South that followed the war, went into effect in December 1863, a year after Butler returned to the North.

Reconstruction

The 'Free State of Louisiana,' which included only occupied parts of the state, was re-admitted to the Union in 1862. Slavery was abolished and the right to vote was extended to select blacks. But the move to extend suffrage to all black men, in 1863, sparked a bloody riot that ended with 36 casualties. All but two were black.

At the war's end, Louisiana's state constitution was redrawn. Full suffrage was granted to blacks, but denied to former Confederate soldiers and rebel sympathizers. Blacks used the vote to challenge discrimination laws, such as those forbidding them from riding 'white' streetcars, and racial skirmishes regularly flared up around town.

In the 1870s, the White League was formed with the twin purposes of ousting what it considered to be an 'Africanized' government (elected in part by new black voters) and ridding the state government of Northerners and Reconstructionists. By all appearances, the White League was arming itself for an all-out war. Police attempted to block a shipment of guns in 1874, and after an ensuing 'battle' – in reality, a lynching of black police officers by a White League militia – the Reconstructionist governor William Pitt Kellogg was ousted from office for five days. Federal troops entered the city to restore order, but the 'Battle of Liberty Place,' as the lynchers called it, had already been mythologized by supremacists.

Although Reconstruction officially ended in 1877, New Orleans remained at war with itself for many decades afterwards. Many of the civil liberties that blacks gained after the Civil War were reversed by

'Beast' Butler decreed that any woman who insulted a Union officer would be treated as a 'woman of the town plying her avocation' – ie a prostitute. Toilet bowls around New Orleans were soon imprinted with Butler's visage.

1870s	1880s	1895–1905	1896
The 'White League' is formed in post–Civil War years as an often-violent backlash against the election of black politicians and the presence of Northern government officials.	Mardi Gras 'Indians' appear – black New Orleanians dressed in stylized Native American costume, a supposedly respectful nod to Indian tribes that resisted white conquest.	Buddy Bolden, who will eventually go insane and die in relative obscurity, reigns as the first 'King of Jazz.' His music influences generations of performers.	Homer Plessy, an octoroon (one-eighth black), challenges New Orleans' segregation laws. Subsequently, discrimination remains legal under the 'separate but equal' clause.

what became known as Jim Crow law, which reinforced and increased segregation and inequality between blacks and whites.

At the turn of the 19th century, monuments to the Confederacy began to be built around the city. They were a message, literally wrought in stone, to the city's black residents: the white power structure of the city had returned, and had no intention of relinquishing its grip.

White-supremacist groups appeared throughout the South following Reconstruction. In New Orleans, organizations called the Knights of the White Camellia and the Crescent City Democratic Club initiated a reign of terror that targeted blacks and claimed several hundred lives during a particularly bloody few weeks in 1874. Worryingly, a spike of contemporary white nationalist groups and militias were seen protesting the removal of the city's Confederate statues in 2017.

Into the 20th Century

As the 20th century dawned, manufacturing, shipping, trade and banking all resumed, but New Orleans did not enjoy the prosperity of its antebellum period. Nonetheless, the era was a formative period: this was when the city morphed from an industrial port into a cultural beacon.

A new musical style was brewing in the city. Called 'jass' and later jazz, the music wed black Creole musicianship to African American rhythms. It also benefited from a proliferation of brass and wind instruments that accompanied the emergence of marching bands during the war years. As jazz spread worldwide, the music became a signature of New Orleans, much as impressionist painting had become synonymous with Paris.

In the 1930s oil companies began dredging canals and laying a massive pipe infrastructure throughout the bayou region to the southwest of New Orleans. The project brought a new source of wealth to New Orleans' CBD, where national oil companies opened their offices, but not without significant environmental impact.

Changing Demographics

The demographics of the city were changing. During the 'white flight' years, chiefly after WWII, black residents moved out of the rural South and into the cities of the North as well as Southern cities such as New Orleans. Desegregation laws finally brought an end to Jim Crow legislation, but traditions shaped by racism were not so easily reversed. In 1960, as schools were desegregated, federal marshals had to escort black schoolchildren to their classrooms to protect them from white protestors.

Most whites responded to integration by relocating to suburbs such as Metairie and the Northshore (Slidell, Mandeville, Covington and other towns). Their children were plucked from public schools and enrolled in private academies; the tragic irony is that formerly all-white public schools became nearly all black.

New Orleans' cityscape also changed during the postwar years. A new elevated freeway was constructed above Claiborne Ave and ran through black neighborhoods, largely so white citizens who fled town after desegregation could commute to work easily. The side effect of placing a highway through a major African American commercial

1897	1901	1917	1927
Storyville, New Orleans' infamous red-light district, is established. The music played in the best 'clubs' helps popularize jazz with out-of-town visitors (ie customers).	Louis Armstrong is born on August 4. He will go on to reform school and a storied career, becoming one of New Orleans' most famous musical icons.	The Department of the Navy shuts down Storyville – the red-light district – despite the protests of Mayor Martin Behrman.	During the Great Mississippi Flood, the levee is dynamited in St Bernard Parish, flooding poorer residents' homes to divert water and protect the wealthy in New Orleans.

district was not hard to predict: businesses shuttered, the economy suffered, and the income gap widened and deepened.

That doesn't mean development was placed on hold during the 1970s. High-rise office buildings and hotels shot up around the CBD, and in the mid-1970s the Louisiana Superdome opened.

In 1978 New Orleans elected its first black mayor, Ernest 'Dutch' Morial. Morial, a Democrat, appointed blacks and women to many city posts during his two terms in office, and was both loved and hated for his abrasive fights with the City Council. His tenure ended in 1986, and in 1994 his son, Marc Morial, was elected mayor and then re-elected in 1998. In 2001, the younger Morial attempted to pass a referendum permitting him to run for a third term, but the city electorate turned him down. Another African American, businessman Ray Nagin, became mayor in 2002, serving until 2010.

Katrina

Occupying a low-lying, drained swamp that sits on a hurricane-prone coast, New Orleans has long lived in fear of the one powerful storm that could wipe out the city. On the morning of Saturday August 28, 2005, Hurricane Katrina prepared to lay claim to that title. The storm had just cut a path of destruction across Florida – killing seven people – when it spilled into the warm Gulf of Mexico. It quickly recharged from its trip across land, and morphed from a dangerous Category Three storm into a Category Five monster, the deadliest designation on the Saffir-Simpson Scale of hurricane strength. Computer models predicted a direct hit on New Orleans.

Mayor Ray Nagin ordered a mandatory evacuation, the first in the city's history. Four out of five residents left the greater New Orleans area. Nearly 200,000 stayed behind. The holdouts included those who could not find transportation, people who thought the predictions too dire, and those who wanted to protect their homes and stores from looters.

The storm weakened to a Category Three before making landfall near the Louisiana–Mississippi line just before midnight. As the sun rose Monday morning, it was clear Katrina's winds had caused extensive damage – blowing out windows, tearing large sections of the Superdome's roof, and knocking over trees and telephone poles. Yet a sense that it could have been much worse prevailed.

Voodoo is an authentic part of New Orleans life, but isn't the touristy version of the religion hawked in so many tourism brochures. If you want to visit an authentic spell shop, stop by F&F Botanica in Mid-City.

Storm Surge

But while house-flattening winds are the most reported feature of hurricanes, in this case the most deadly aspect was the storm surge, the rising tide of water driven inland by the gales. Katrina's winds pushed

1936	1960	1965	1970
Vieux Carré Commission is founded to regulate changes to French Quarter exteriors. The Quarter is now one of the oldest preserved neighborhoods in the USA.	Federal marshals escort black children into desegregated schools. In the following years, 'white flight' into the suburbs will leave city schools with few white students.	Hurricane Betsy, the billion-dollar hurricane, batters the Big Easy. Improvements to the levee system made following the disaster fail to protect the city in 2005.	Jazz Fest is held for the first time, beginning its long history as a gathering of a few hundred fans celebrating the city's unique musical heritage.

water from the Gulf of Mexico up the Mississippi River, into Lake Pontchartrain and through the canals that lace the city. The levees built to protect the city did not hold. A torrent of water from the Industrial Canal washed away the Lower Ninth Ward; in neighborhoods such as Lakeview and Gentilly, houses were submerged when the 17th St and London Ave Canals gave way.

In all, four-fifths of the city was submerged in a toxic soup of salt and fresh water, gasoline, chemicals, human waste and floating bodies. The massive pumps that clear the city after rainy days couldn't process the volume of water, which rose as high as 15ft in parts of the city, and remained for weeks. Stranded residents found little time to escape. They moved from the 1st floor to the 2nd floor, then the attic. Some drowned there; those lucky enough to find tools to hack through the roof got out, or used cans of paint to dash out crude appeals for help.

Oh, When the Saints...

Pundits, geophysicists and even then–House Speaker Dennis Hastert (who claimed that rebuilding a city that lies below sea level 'doesn't make sense to me,' before backtracking) seriously debated writing off New Orleans as a lost cause. The city, they said, was – by dint of its geography – not worth rebuilding.

Yet millions of Americans and thousands of New Orleanians rose to the challenge. They waded into basements in 100°F-plus weather and slopped out trash, rubble and corpses; they mowed lawns, planted gardens and fixed each other's roofs, sometimes using discarded pieces of swept-away flooring. They celebrated small victories with what beer they could scrape together, and these impromptu parties became their own building blocks of reconstruction, the cultural component of rebirth in a city where enjoying life is as integral as cement.

By 2010, new restaurants and bars were popping up with happy frequency, and the arts scene in particular has turned the town into something of a Southern Left Bank for the 21st century. Young entrepreneurs, attracted by low rents and the city's undeniable culture, are flooding into the city. When the Saints, the local NFL franchise, won the Superbowl in 2010 during Carnival season, the city collectively lost its mind. There was no happier place on Earth.

Rebuild, Reform, Relocate

Determination to reconstruct, a flourishing in the food and arts worlds, and the winning of the Superbowl is the bright side of the rebuilding story. The other perspective? Well, that requires some background on the relationship between New Orleans and the state of Louisiana. The

Best Historical Reads

Bienville's Dilemma (Richard Campanella)

Rising Tide: The Great Mississippi Flood of 1927 and How It Changed America (John M Barry)

Storyville (Al Rose)

The Free People of Color of New Orleans (Mary Gehman)

New Orleans: An Illustrated History (John R Kemp)

Breach of Faith (Jed Horne)

1978	2002	2005	Feb–Mar 2010
New Orleans' first black mayor, Ernest 'Dutch' Morial, is elected. Despite lingering racial tensions, a dynasty is established: his son, Marc Morial, is elected mayor in 1994 and '98.	Long-shot Ray Nagin becomes mayor of New Orleans. Nagin vows to clean up the city, but his term in office has its share of scandals.	The storm surge following Hurricane Katrina floods 80% of New Orleans. The city is evacuated, although thousands who could not or did not leave linger in the city for days.	The Saints win the Superbowl, Mardi Gras happens and Mitch Landrieu is elected mayor, the first white mayor to win a broad portion of the black vote.

former, since the 1970s, has been largely African American and liberal; the latter, in terms of politics, increasingly conservative.

Many New Orleanian institutions were lost post-Katrina, but of particular note are Charity Hospital, a public teaching hospital, and the city's public school system.

Charity Hospital was replaced by the modern, multi-block LSU Health Center New Orleans. The public school system has already been shuttered; former Orleans Parish public schools have been replaced by a charter school system (charter schools receive public funding but operate independently of a local school board). A lottery system determines placement in local charters. Teachers were replaced by young, often white individuals enrolled in programs like Teach for America.

Many felt all of the above was an attack on the city's black population, a way of using a weather-related disaster to further the political goal of stomping out public schools and hospitals. The opposing view was that the above institutions were seriously compromised even before Katrina and in serious need of reform. How one feels on these issues can spark some very contentious debate in New Orleans; while it is true that the public schools, for example, had enormous performance issues, was this attributable to teaching quality or centuries of structural inequality or a combination of both factors? Either way, Charity and the school system were largely staffed by (and served) African Americans, and the loss of these two institutions gutted the local African American middle class.

New Orleans is one of the worst cities for income inequality in the country – a Bloomberg study named it the second most fiscally unequal city in the USA. The mansions of St Charles Ave truly feel a universe removed from blocks in St Roch and New Orleans East where children grow into Post-Traumatic Stress Syndrome while lacking basic literacy skills. This fundamental chasm in living standards remains a baked-in obstacle to civic optimism, even in a city known for celebration. The situation is exacerbated by infrastructure that still, a decade after Katrina, floods in the event of heavy rain.

And yet: New Orleans parties on. In a sense, it has to. New York has to do business. Washington DC must do politics. Los Angeles lives by entertainment. New Orleans finds ways to enjoy itself, and make you enjoy life. And there is some holdout for hope. The city celebrates its 300th birthday in 2018, and some believe a round number is in and of itself an impetus for change. Indeed, in 2017, the monuments of white Confederate slave holders – those unambiguous statements of white supremacy erected in the public sphere – were finally (and literally) taken off of their pedestals. Not long after, Latoya Cantrell, a city council member who began her political career as a Broadmoor neighborhood activist, was elected the first female mayor of New Orleans.

Apr–Sept 2010	2011	2014–15	2017
The Deepwater Horizon oil spill pumps 4.9 million barrels of oil into the Gulf of Mexico, becoming the largest, costliest environmental disaster in American history.	The census reveals the population of New Orleans has shrunk by 29% since 2000. A corresponding increase in population is noted in some suburbs.	The city of New Orleans begins enforcing a noise ordinance and passes a smoking ban; both moves create considerable outcry on either side of the issue.	A year before its 300th anniversary, New Orleans takes down four prominent Confederate monuments and elects Latoya Cantrell as its first female mayor.

People of New Orleans

Ask someone to describe the demographics of New Orleans, and the 'gumbo analogy' – that is to say, a bunch of different ingredients simmered together into something greater than their individual parts – is often invoked. And while we are wary of repeating clichés, that gumbo diagram works (it helps that allusions to food pretty much always go down well in this city). French, Spanish, Africans, Caribbeans, Germans, Jews, Irish, Vietnamese, Hondurans – and, perhaps most exotic of all, Americans – all come here and turn out New Orleanian.

The Quality of Creole

The term 'Creole' refers to people of mixed ancestry in most of the post–French Colonial world. The implication is often that a Creole is mixed race, but this isn't necessarily the case in Louisiana, although it can be. Long story short: Louisiana Creole usually refers to the descendants of the original European colonists who settled this area. Because of the shifting political status of the Louisiana colony (French, then Spanish, then French again), those Europeans were most often from France and Spain.

After the Louisiana Purchase in 1803, New Orleans was absorbed into the USA. Unsurprisingly, there was tension between the largely Protestant Anglo Americans and Catholic Creole New Orleanians. The latter found the former uncouth and boring; the former considered Louisianans feckless and indolent, proving tired regional clichés stretch back centuries.

New Orleans has a habit of digesting its settlers and turning them into its own, though. Successive waves of immigration into New Orleans added layers to the city's demographic, but the original Creole city teased something quintessentially New Orleanian – ie commitment to fun, food and music – out of each new slice of the population pie.

Take the Italians, who suffused local foodways and musicality with muffuletta sandwiches and crooners like Louis Prima. In a similar vein, the Vietnamese have brought both food and a penchant for festivals; the Vietnamese New Year (Tet) is now a major celebration point for New Orleanians of all creeds and colors. Creole implies mixture, and mixing is something this town excels at, even if it doesn't always do so easily.

The most recent addition to the demographic pot are Hondurans; it is estimated the New Orleans metropolitan area has the largest Honduran American community in the USA (a little over 100,000 souls). However, a good chunk of these Hondurans have been here longer than many European-descended Americans. The first waves of Honduran migration came in the late 19th century when fruit companies with Central American plantations moved their corporate operations to New Orleans. Others arrived as part of the construction boom that followed Hurricane Katrina.

Yat-itude

Native New Orleanians are affectionately deemed 'Yats' for their accents; their way of saying hello is the stereotypical, 'Where yat?'

It's an accent that feels closer to Brooklyn than the American South, one formed by a Creole population living in isolation from the rest of North America for decades. Sadly, the Yat brogue is, like many regional accents in the USA, a fading thing. It's also a white thing; local African Americans have their own accent, a syrup-y slow drawl that is distinctive from other iterations of African American English. You may hear someone speaking Yat in New Orleans, but it's easier to hear the dialect in neighboring St Bernard Parish, which has absorbed much of the city's working-class white population.

Other Yat terms:

Awrite	Alright
Berl	Boil
Bra	A man with whom you are friends, or, a male sibling
Catlick	A Christian denomination led by the Pope
Da, Dat, Dis, Dem	The, That, This, Them
Dawlin'	A woman
Earl	Makes your car run
Ersta	A bivalve mollusk
Laginiappe	Pronounced 'lan-yap.' A little extra, like when the baker throws in another cookie.
Mirliton	Pronounced 'mel-ee-tawn.' A squash, also known as a chayote, that's pretty great when stuffed with seafood.
Praline	That delicious, sugary baked good? It's a prah-leen.
Turlet	Where one goes to the bathroom
YaMomInEm	Your family

Voodoo & Louisiana

If you're a Christian, imagine if the majority of the world discussed your faith through these terms: 'They believe a dead man was brought back to life, and if you drink his blood and eat his body, you can live forever.' The description is technically accurate, but it misses so much context, background and lived experience that it becomes insulting. It reduces a complex belief system to a sensationalistic cliché.

Such is the struggle practitioners of voodoo endure on a daily basis. To a voodoo follower, theirs is a religion like any other. The traditions and source of their faith may seem outlandish to a nonbeliever, but what religion doesn't sound a little weird to someone who doesn't practice it? And even as their religion is stereotyped as a source of witchcraft and sorcery, it is simultaneously commercialized, forming the marketing slogan of dozens of tours, T-shirts and store fronts.

Voodoo as a faith comes from West Africa. It is a belief system that stresses ancestor worship and the presence of the divine via a pantheon of spirits and deities. Slaves from Africa and the Caribbean brought voodoo to Louisiana, where it melded with Roman Catholicism. One faith stressed saints and angels, the other ancestor spirits and supernatural forces; all eventually fell under the rubric of voodoo. Hoodoo are the magical implements popularly associated with voodoo, but how much magic they provide and their import to daily worship is often exaggerated (to use the same Christian comparison, many would find it insulting to call a rosary or crucifix a magic talisman).

The most well-known voodoo practitioner was Marie Laveau, a 19th-century mixed race woman who married a Haitian free person of color. The legends surrounding Laveau are legion, but she is popularly associated with leading voodoo rituals near Bayou St John and providing magic spells for high-class New Orleans women. It's a fair bet much of this folklore was sensationalized by the popular press of the time; stories of magic brown-skinned women performing devilish rituals sold newspapers and magazines, at least more so than a sober recording of a religion that mixed Western Christianity and African ancestor worship.

The Cajuns

While many people feel the terms Cajun and Creole are interchangeable, they refer to two very different populations. The Creoles are the largely urbanized descendants of 18th-century French and Spanish colonists. The Cajuns descend from Francophone refugees who fled the maritime provinces of Canada after it was conquered by Britain during the Seven Years'/French and Indian War. This exile was known as *Le Grand Dérangement.*

The maritime provinces (New Brunswick, Prince Edward Island and Nova Scotia) were, under French rule, known as *Acadie,* and the refugees deemed themselves Acadians. A homeless population of Acadians searched for decades for a place to settle until seven boatloads of exiles arrived in New Orleans in 1785. The settlers spread out into the Louisiana countryside and mixed with early German peasant farmers, Isleños (Canary Islanders) and Americans. By the early 19th century some 3000 to 4000 Acadians, or Cajuns as they became known, lived in southern Louisiana. Some occupied the swamplands, where they eked out a living based on fishing and trapping, while others farmed rice.

Cajun culture is distinct within Louisiana. Older Cajuns still speak a distinct dialect of French, and the Cajun Mardi Gras, or *Courir de Mardi Gras,* is its own celebration, a ritual that involves medieval costuming and a drunken scrum over a runaway chicken (see the documentary *Dance for a Chicken* for more background).

Architecture

New Orleans has the most distinctive cityscape in the USA. This sense of place is directly attributable to its great quantity of historic homes, and the cohesion of so many of its neighborhoods. The French Quarter and Garden District have long been considered exemplars of New Orleans architecture, but send the Tremé, the Marigny or the Irish Channel to another city, and they would stand out as treasure troves of history and heritage.

Cross-section of a City

There are 171 sites in Orleans Parish listed on the National Register of Historic Places. While we stress that there's more to the city's architecture than the French Quarter and Garden District, those neighborhoods *do* nicely illustrate the pronounced difference between the two 'sectors' of New Orleans: Creole and American. It's worth noting that

Above: Presbytère museum (p53), French Quarter

there is no perfect split between the two sides of the city; Creole cottages can be found Uptown, and shotgun houses pack Bywater and the Marigny.

The Quarter and Creole 'faubourgs' (Marigny, Bywater and the Tremé) downriver from Canal St are densely packed with stuccoed brick structures built in various architectural styles and housing types that are rarely found in other US cities. This is where you'll find a glut of candy-colored Euro-Caribbean buildings that seem transplanted into North America.

Cross Canal St and you'll find the wide lots and luxuriant houses of the Garden District more closely resemble upscale homes found throughout the South. This is big mansion territory, but you'll also find thousands of shotgun houses lining these blocks. As one heads up the river into the heart of the Garden District and Uptown, the displays of wealth intensify to the point of near-gaudiness, although the effect scales back a little closer to Tulane and Loyola Universities.

It is worth noting that for all of the city's preservation credentials, fire, rot, hurricanes and redevelopment have all taken their toll on the city's historical building stock. Currently, roughly 25 buildings only survive intact from the French and Spanish Colonial age; good examples include the Ursuline Convent, Presbytère and Cabildo.

French Colonial Houses

Surviving structures from the French period are rare. New Orleans was a French colony only from 1718 until the Spanish takeover in 1762, and twice during the Spanish period fires destroyed much of the town. Only one French Quarter building, the Ursuline Convent (p56), remains from the French period. The convent was built for the climate of French Canada, but the French recognized Caribbean design was more appropriate in New Orleans.

Madame John's Legacy, at 628 Dumaine St, is a good example of a French Caribbean home. Marked by a steep hipped roof, casement windows and batten shutters, it possesses galleries – covered porches – that help keep the house cool in summer. These galleries served to shade rooms from direct light and rainfall.

Out on Bayou St John, the Pitot House, home of the city's first mayor, is another signature French Colonial compound. A huge 2nd-floor wraparound balcony essentially served as the house's living space during the summer months. Furniture would be moved outdoors (even the beds), and residents would take advantage of the breeze to cool themselves off from the summer swelter. This practice of moving a living space into the outdoors (to say nothing of a focus on gardens and fountains) has roots in North Africa, from where the idea spread to Spain, and later this French Spanish colony.

If you head outside of the city, the Laura Plantation, located an hour west of New Orleans, is an excellent example of a French Creole plantation. The raised main house (along with much of the rest of the compound) was built by highly skilled slaves who undoubtedly imported some West African building techniques into the design.

Spanish Colonial Houses

During the Spanish period, adjacent buildings were designed to rub shoulders, with no space between, which created the continuous facade of the French Quarter. While some cottages were built during this time, the signature home of the period is the two-story town house, with commercial space on the ground floor and residential quarters upstairs. While properties were adjacent on the street, there was usually

Briquette-entrepoteaux, where brick fills the spaces between vertical and diagonal posts, was common to French Colonial houses. This style endured during the Spanish period. It is visible where stucco was cleared to expose the exterior walls of Lafitte's Blacksmith Shop in the French Quarter.

Laura Plantation (p162)

an open area behind the lot, and this space was converted into a well-shaded, private courtyard, used like a family room. Arches, tiled roofs and balconies with ornate wrought-iron railings became common.

Creole Town Houses

Very few buildings survive from the Spanish Colonial period, and not all the survivors reflect the Spanish style. But the Creoles of New Orleans appreciated Spanish architecture and regularly applied its key elements (especially the courtyard, carriageway and loggia) to French Quarter town houses. Most surviving examples date from the American period. An especially elaborate three-story example of the Creole town house, with key Spanish elements, is Napoleon House (p67).

Creole town houses are most common by far within the French Quarter, where they make up much of the area's residential and commercial stock. A few survive within the CBD and Warehouse District, although many of these have been rebuilt or renovated in such a manner that they are no longer true examples of the style.

Perhaps the most distinctive element of a Creole town house, particularly those within the French Quarter, is the balcony. Made from wrought iron, and often wrapped around corners, balconies were valuable slices of living space during the intense heat of the summer months. Residents would spend so much time on their balconies, dividers would be built between adjoining balconies. In some places, you may see 'Romeo Spikes' – wickedly sharp points meant to prevent potential suitors from shimmying up a balcony pole to a waiting paramour.

Creole and Spanish town houses share many similarities, and many of the Quarter homes built after the fires of 1788 and 1794 share elements of both styles.

The French Quarter is also called the Maghreb Quarter. Packed town houses are built Spanish-style, with outdoor space reserved for private courtyards and public balconies. This in turn is a North African tradition, inherited from the Muslim conquest of Spain. In Morocco, houses built in this style are called *riads*.

Double-shotgun house, Faubourg Marigny

Creole Cottages

The most basic historical structure in New Orleans is also one of its most iconic, and particularly obvious as you head downriver from Canal St. The largest concentration of freestanding Creole cottages are found throughout the French Quarter, the Tremé, Faubourg Marigny and Bywater.

Essentially, a Creole cottage is a square, divided into four smaller squares; while this is the simplest version of the structure, it is one that can be found across the city, but in very few other places in the USA, barring a few other Gulf of Mexico communities.

True Creole cottages are one-and-a-half-story buildings. They feature high-gabled, sharply sloping roofs and, sometimes, full covered front porches (airy spaces that are crucial during the summer months). With that said, urban Creole cottages, which you are likely to encounter within the French Quarter, Tremé and Faubourg Marigny, generally lack a porch. Either way, Creole cottages lack hallways or corridors and are generally built to the edge of the property line – in other words, they lack anything like a front yard.

The front of the house usually has two casement doors, sometimes four. These openings are often shuttered to shield the interior space from sidewalk traffic, which can be passing within inches away. The airy floor plan has four interconnected chambers, each with an opening (a door or window) to the side of the house. These openings allow for a degree of air flow, providing another cooling mechanism against the heat.

Shotgun Houses

During the latter half of the 19th century, the inexpensive shotgun became a popular single-family dwelling. The name supposedly derives from the legend that a bullet could be fired from front to back through the open doorways of all of the rooms, but in truth only the most basic shotguns have doors lined up so perfectly. It's also worth noting that some historians believe the name may derive from a West African word. The shotgun style is not unique to New Orleans, and similar homes can be found throughout much of the Caribbean, especially Haiti, lending credence to some kind of African diaspora origin.

The standard 'single-shotgun' house is a row of rooms with doors leading from one to the next. As there is no hall, you pass through each room to traverse the house. Shotguns are freestanding, with narrow spaces along either side. Windows on both sides and high ceilings encourage cross-ventilation and keep the rooms cool. The narrow style of home is a good fit for an urban space; while shotguns are detached housing, they can be clustered together in high density.

'Double-shotguns' are duplexes, with mirror-image halves traditionally forming two homes. Many double-shotguns have been converted into large single homes; it's a New Orleanian real-estate cliché for someone to buy a double-shotgun, rent out one half, and then knock down the center wall and create a large single home once they're ready to start a family.

Other variations upon the simple shotgun formula include 'camel-backs,' which have a 2nd floor above the back of the house, and 'sidehall' homes, with a corridor appended to the stacked squares of the shotgun.

Gallier Hall, once the City Hall building for New Orleans, marks the epitome of Greek Revival pomp and circumstance. It overlooks Lafayette Sq and is used for civic functions today.

ARCHITECTURE GREEK REVIVAL

Greek Revival

Perhaps no style symbolizes the wealth and showiness of mid-19th-century America than Greek Revival architecture. The genre, readily recognizable for its tall columns, was inspired by classics such as the Parthenon. Greek Revival houses can be found along St Charles Ave in Uptown and in the Garden District. A nice example is the raised villa at 2127 Prytania St.

Five-Bay Center Hall Houses

The one-and-a-half-story center hall house became common with the arrival of more Anglo-Americans to New Orleans after the Louisiana Purchase in 1803. The raised center hall house, found in the Garden District and Uptown, became the most usual type; it stands on a pier foundation 2ft to 8ft above ground, and its columned front gallery spans the entire width of the house.

Double Gallery Houses

Double gallery houses were built throughout the 19th century (most commonly between 1820 and 1850) on Esplanade Ridge and the upriver side of Canal, primarily in Uptown and the Lower Garden and Garden Districts. All of these neighborhoods were considered 'suburbs' at the time; double gallery homes were built by those seeking space. These two-story houses are set back from the property line and feature a two-story gallery, or porch, framed and supported by columns. The front door is usually set to one side.

Today, many double gallery homes are split into multiple units, with the owners occupying one floor and renters another (usually with separate entrances). Other double gallery residences have been split into separate condo units.

Italianate Style

The Italianate style, inspired by Tuscan villas, gained popularity after the Civil War. Segmental arches, frequently used over doors and windows, and the decorative box-like parapets over galleries are commonly identified as Italianate features.

Music

New Orleans without music is like Washington without politics: inconceivable. In this city of appetites, music feeds the soul. The city's history can be traced in its music. The French and their Creole descendants gave the city two opera companies before any other US city had one. Meanwhile, slaves and free persons of color preserved African music in Congo Sq. These influences came together when French-speaking black Creoles livened up European dance tunes by adding African rhythms. From there, jazz was an inevitability.

The Rise & Fall (& Rise) of Jazz

A proliferation of brass instruments after the Civil War led to a brass-instrument craze that spread throughout the South and the Midwest. Many of the musicians, white and black, learned to play music without learning to read it. Instead they operated by ear and by memory. Improvisation became the default baseline for playing music.

One of the most problematic figures in jazz history is Charles 'Buddy' Bolden, New Orleans' first 'King of Jazz.' Some said Bolden 'broke his heart' when he performed, while others mused that he would 'blow his brains out' by playing so loudly.

Successors to Bolden included Joe 'King' Oliver, whose Creole Jazz Band found a receptive audience in Chicago. Oliver was soon overshadowed by his protégé, Louis Armstrong; working together, Oliver and Armstrong made many seminal jazz recordings, including 'Dipper-mouth Blues.'

Although jazz went into decline for several decades, the genre has experienced a renaissance since the 1980s. In 1982, then 19-year-old Wynton Marsalis stormed onto the scene followed by his older brother Branford. Other musicians, who were studying with Wynton and Branford's father, Ellis Marsalis, at the New Orleans Center for Creative Arts, formed the nucleus of a New Orleans jazz revival.

Brass music is distinct from jazz; it's less improvisational and far more danceable. With that said, many brass bands still play traditional music inspired by marching band arrangements of the 19th century. Others, like the streetwise Rebirth, fuse styles from trad jazz to funk, R&B and modern jazz. Rapping trombone player Trombone Shorty jumps between genres like a frog, sometimes bouncing into hip-hop, R&B and even indie rock.

R&B & Funk

New Orleans owes its reputation as a breeding ground for piano players to Henry Roeland Byrd – also known as Professor Longhair. His rhythmic rumba and boogie-woogie style of playing propelled him to success with tunes such as 'Tipitina' (for which the legendary nightclub is named) and 'Go to the Mardi Gras.'

In the 1960s, R&B and New Orleans fell under the spell of Allen Toussaint, a talented producer who molded songs to suit the talents of New

Orleans' artists. The formula worked for Ernie K-Doe, who hit pay dirt with the disgruntled and catchy 'Mother-In-Law,' in 1961.

Aaron Neville, whose soulful falsetto is one of the most instantly recognizable voices in pop music, began working with Toussaint in 1960, when his first hit single, the menacing but pretty 'Over You' was recorded. The association later yielded the gorgeous 'Let's Live.' But 'Tell It Like It Is' (1967), recorded without Toussaint, was the biggest national hit of Neville's career.

Art Neville, a piano player from the Professor Longhair school, heads up the Meters, whose sound molded modern New Orleans funk.

Today, New Orleans funk is undergoing both reinvention and renaissance. Contemporary bands like Tank & the Bangas blend hip-hop, trippy arrangements, razor-sharp lyrics and deft instrumentals into full-on musical feasts for the soul. Jon Cleary, a New Orleans piano-man who came to the city by way of Kent, in the UK, won the Grammy Award for Best Regional Roots Music Album in 2016 via his album *Go-Go Juice.*

Bounce

While outfits such as No Limit Records and Partners-N-Crime, and artists like Lil' Wayne and Dee-1 represent New Orleans in the hip-hop world, bounce is the defining sound of young black New Orleans. It's a high-speed genre distinct to the city that involves drum-machine-driven beats, call-and-response, sexualized lyrics and extremely raunchy dancing. Shows are led by DJs, who play a role similar to a selector at a Jamaican dancehall concert.

The genre was invented in the early 1990s, when bounce became the default dance music in many New Orleans clubs, with DJs calling out over the hyperquick 'Triggerman' rhythm that has been sampled into a thousand-and-one tracks. Then and now, dancers get freaky on the floor and call out wards (subdivisions of the city) and projects (subsidized housing tracts). Pioneers include Juvenile, Soulja Slim, Mia X and DJ Jubilee, whose track 'Get Ready, Ready' is a good introduction to the genre.

External media has dubbed the music of transgender bounce artists including Katey Red, Sissy Nobby and Big Freedia 'sissy bounce' ('sissy' is local slang for gay African American people who grew up in poor neighborhoods); while the label has stuck, Katey Red has said she simply considers herself a transgender bounce artist.

The best radio stations in New Orleans are WTUL, 91.5 FM, and WWOZ, 90.7 FM. The former is Tulane University's radio station and plays an eclectic mix of generally high-quality tunes. 'O-Z,' as it's called, plays local New Orleans music and is a backbone of the city's musical community.

Zydeco

Cajun music is the music of white Cajuns, while zydeco is the music of French-speaking African Americans who share the region. They have plenty in common, but the differences are distinct.

Zydeco ensembles originally comprised a fiddle, diatonic button accordion, guitar and triangle (the metal percussion instrument common to symphony orchestras and kindergarten music classes); the rhythm section usually included a *frottoir,* a metal washboard-like instrument that's worn like armor and played with spoons. The end result is a genre of music that is made for dance accompaniment; the Thursday-night zydeco party at Rock 'N' Bowl (p136) is not to be missed.

Zydeco, it should be noted, is not a static form of music restricted to country dance halls. Innovators from Clifton Chenier, the father of zydeco, to Beau Joques, Buckwheat Zydeco, Terrance Simien and Keith Frank have incorporated the blues, R&B, funk and soul into the zydeco sound. Baton Rouge rapper Lil Boosie uses zydeco music to propel his lyrics on the appropriately named track 'Zydeco' on the mixtape *225/504.*

Rock And (Almost) Everything Else

Between jazz, brass and hip-hop, you'd be forgiven for missing the impact of rock on the New Orleans music scene. And to be fair, maybe New Orleans has had more influence on rock than the other way around. Folks like Robert Plant will occasionally show up in town just to jam with local guitarists, and the entire genre of rock 'n' roll owes its existence to New Orleans rhythms.

Plus, there are so many genres of rock, it's hard to properly categorize. Straight-up Americana rock has emerged via '90s darlings like Better Than Ezra and Cowboy Mouth. And did you know NOLA has a fierce homegrown metal scene? 'Sludge metal' emerges like a howling muck of distortion and rough vocals, best epitomized by Louisiana bands like Acid Bath and Crowbar.

On the softer side, New Orleans is now a home base for Arcade Fire and local indie darlings like Alexis & the Samurai and Hurray for the Riff Raff. Blurring the lines of many genres are bands like Debauche, which blend zydeco, klezmer, punk and Russian folk music into exuberant live performances that are a highlight of many a New Orleans night out.

Voodoo (Voodoo Fest; www.voodoofestival.com; City Park; ⊗ last weekend of Oct) is the highest-profile rock festival in New Orleans, but it now contends with **BUKU** (www.thebukuproject.com; Blaine Kern's Mardi Gras World, 1380 Port of New Orleans Pl; ⊗ Mar) for both name recognition and Electronic Dance Music (EDM) cred. EDM, house and techno experience hills and valleys of popularity in this town; excellent shows often pop off at Republic (p108) and the Dragon's Den (p92), and there's a hybrid scene that draws on local EDM fans – some of who have been DJing for decades – and students from Tulane and Loyola.

Even classical music has a piece of the pie in New Orleans. The local symphony orchestras are lovely, but the big draw is the small outfits that make the most of the city's famed instrumental talent – check out the **Birdfoot Festival** (http://birdfootfestival.org; ⊗ late May) if you want to get schooled in New Orleans' small chamber-music scene.

Environment

New Orleans is shaped by its environment more than most American cities. Consider: while outsiders bemoan the foolishness of placing a city in a low-lying river basin, it was founded precisely here so it could command the mouth of the Mississippi. Nevertheless, the local dance between humans and nature has generally been an uneasy one: do nothing and the land is uninhabitable; impact the land too much and the waters will flood elsewhere.

The Lay of the Watery Land

The first important factor to consider is that New Orleans is surrounded by water. It stands between the Mississippi River, which curls like a devilish snake around much of the city, and Lake Pontchartrain, a large saltwater body connected to the Gulf of Mexico. Swamps and marshes cover much of the remaining area around the city.

The land the city stands on has been wrested from the Mississippi's natural floodplain. The oldest parts of town adhere to the high ground, which is, in fact, made up of natural levees created by the Mississippi depositing soil there during floods. The high ground in New Orleans is just a few feet above sea level. Much of the rest of the city is below sea level, forming a bowl that obviously remains vulnerable to flooding, despite human-made levees. The city's elevation averages 2ft below sea level. And it is sinking.

Mean Old Levee

The US Army Corps of Engineers built and maintains miles of levees that have kept the Mississippi River on a fixed course for more than a century. You'll see the levee from Jackson Sq, in the French Quarter, as it rises like an evenly graded hill and hides the river from view. That's right: as you walk uphill in New Orleans, you're coming *closer* to the water.

Compounding the difficult geography is the weather. New Orleans sits within the Atlantic hurricane zone, and hurricane season lasts approximately half a year here, from early summer to late fall. Hurricanes cause floods by pushing in water from the Gulf (not, as many assume, the Mississippi). Surging gulf waters run through town via the canal system and can be far more difficult to predict than rising river tides. Storm surges rise like tsunamis, lunging upward as they squeeze through narrow canal passageways. River floods, by contrast, can be observed far upstream, often weeks in advance.

The levee system was extensively updated, repaired and built out after Hurricane Katrina. Hopefully it will stand up to the next storm, but the final test will be whenever a big storm hits.

In the meantime, smaller rains are meant to be dealt with by the city's pump system, which is administered by the archaic Sewerage & Water Board. In 2017, heavy rains – but no hurricane or tropical storm – caused severe flooding in parts of the city. There were famously parts of Claiborne Ave that looked more soaked than they did during Katrina. This waterlogged state of affairs was partly down to a full 14 pumps

Hurricane Katrina hit during the particularly brutal 2005 hurricane season, when a record 27 tropical storms spawned 15 hurricanes. Of the five to make landfall, two (Katrina and Rita) slammed southern Louisiana within a three-week period. Katrina was by far the most destructive, but Rita was actually stronger.

being inoperational in the midst of the storm. As was the case during Katrina, human error exacerbated rough natural conditions, and the resulting outcome was an avoidable disaster.

The Vanishing Coast

Louisiana's coastal parishes lost 2006 square miles of land from 1932 to 2016. Erosion is further enhanced by the extensive canal network that's dredged for oil production; Louisiana is one of the top oil and natural gars producing states in the country. Oil pipes and rigs are also subject to leaks and spills. In addition, the wakes of shipping traffic wear away the delicate edges of the canals.

Miles of bird refuges – home to more than half of North America's bird species, as well as freshwater homes to Louisiana's treasured crawfish – are disappearing. For New Orleans, the loss of these wetlands makes the city more vulnerable to hurricanes, as the diminishing land buffer enables hurricanes to maintain full strength nearer to the city. For similar reasons, New Orleans will become more vulnerable to storm surges like the one that followed Katrina.

Schoolchildren in Louisiana grow up learning that their state is shaped like a boot, but given the amount of land loss experienced in the last few decades, journalist Brett Anderson has proposed a new map be drawn of the state, one where the iconic boot looks as if it has been slashed with a pair of garden shears. See his story 'Louisiana Loses Its Boot,' on medium.com.

We want to finish on an upbeat note, but the loss of Louisiana's coast has not only continued unabated in recent years – it's gotten worse. Environmental regulation is contentious in Louisiana, especially when the affected industries are oil and shipping. Those industries have a considerable political voice in Louisiana – the energy sector has provided employment for thousands of residents and helped lift the Cajuns, formerly one of the poorest demographics in the country, out of poverty.

We advise you to see the Louisiana wetlands south of New Orleans now. They may well be underwater in a generation.

In the travelogue *Bayou Farewell* (2003), author and journalist Mike Tidwell documents the culture, folkways and natural environment of the vast, yet shrinking, Louisiana wetlands. It's one of the better nonfiction literary insights into Cajun culture.

The BP Oil Spill

On April 20, 2010, the Deepwater Horizon, an offshore drilling rig owned by Transocean and leased to BP operating in the Gulf of Mexico, exploded after highly pressurized gas expanded into the rig and ignited. Eleven men were killed. Two days later, oil from the underwater Macondo Prospect was spotted seeping into the ocean.

In all, 4.9 million barrels of oil were spilled into the Gulf as a result of the Deepwater disaster, the most expensive in US environmental history. The tourism industry of the Gulf states took a significant hit. Wildlife did worse: oil-slicked animal corpses were found (and continue to be found) on beaches in Grad Isle, south of New Orleans, while reports of lesions, missing eyes and other mutations have been attributed to the chemical dispersants used by BP to clear away oil.

The Gulf of Mexico's tourism and seafood industry seem to have recovered from the spill (helped along by the $7.8 billion settlement BP paid to those who lost livelihoods as a result of the spill), but the long-term impacts remain to be seen. Oil has entered the food chain via zooplankton, which could have biological impacts five or 10 years (or more) down the road. Disturbingly, scientists say they have discovered a 10-million-gallon 'bath mat' of oil that has adhered to the floor of the Gulf of Mexico. How this impacts the ecology of the region has yet to be determined, but one imagines 10 million gallons of oil does not make for a healthy environment.

Survival Guide

Transportation

ARRIVING IN NEW ORLEANS

The majority of travelers to New Orleans will arrive by air, landing in **Louis Armstrong New Orleans International Airport** (MSY; ☑504-303-7500; www.flymsy. com; 900 Airline Hwy, Kenner, LA; ☎). The airport was originally named for aviator John Moisant and was known as Moisant Stock Yards, hence the airport code.

Another option is to fly into Baton Rouge (BTR), 89 miles north of the city; or **Gulfport-Biloxi** (GPT; ☑228-863-5951; www.flygpt. com) (GPT), Mississippi, 77 miles east. Neither of these options is as convenient as a direct flight to New Orleans, but they may be cheaper during big events such as Mardi Gras or Jazz Fest.

Many travelers drive or bus to New Orleans, which is located at the crossroads of several major highways. Train travel to New Orleans is easy; the city is served by three Amtrak lines.

Louis Armstrong New Orleans International Airport (MSY)

Located 13 miles west of New Orleans. A taxi to the CBD costs $36, or $15 per passenger for three or more passengers. Shuttles to the CBD cost $24/44 per person one way/return. The E2 bus takes you to Carrollton and Tulane Ave in Mid-City for $2. It's about a five-minute walk to the airport rental-car facility from the main terminal.

Amtrak and **Greyhound** are located adjacent to each other downtown on Loyola Ave. You can walk to the CBD or French Quarter, but don't do so at night, or with heavy luggage. A taxi from here to the French Quarter should cost around $10; further afield you'll be unlikely to spend more than $20.

GETTING THERE & AWAY

Air

New Orleans' **airport** is located in the suburb of Kenner, 13 miles west of the city along I-10; the drive takes about 30 minutes. It's not a major hub, so you'll likely connect here through Atlanta, Houston, Dallas, Chicago or Charlotte. International service now connects New Orleans directly to London.

Transport Options

BUS

If your baggage is not too unwieldy and you're in no hurry, **Jefferson Transit** (www.jeffersontransit. org) offers the cheapest ride downtown aboard its E2 Airport Downtown Express ($2). The ride to New Orleans follows city streets and stops approximately every two blocks. On weekdays, until 6:52pm, the bus goes all the way to Tulane and Loyola Ave, at the edge of downtown and the French Quarter; on weekends it will only get you as far as the corner of Tulane St and Carrollton Ave. From there it's a cheap cab ride to the French Quarter, or you can transfer to a **Regional Transit Authority bus** (www. norta.com). Bus 27 will get you to St Charles Ave in the Garden District; bus 39 follows Tulane Ave to Canal St, just outside the French Quarter. Check the RTA website (www.norta.com/getting-around/getting-to-the-airport.aspx) for more details about public transit to and from the airport and downtown New Orleans.

CAR

Rental agencies and cars are housed at a new facility within walking distance of the terminals. Exit at the West Terminal baggage claim. The quickest drive between the airport and downtown is on I-10. Coming from downtown on I-10, take exit 223 for the airport; going to downtown, take exit 234 as the Louisiana Superdome looms before you. Traffic can get very congested near the Huey Long Bridge.

CLIMATE CHANGE & TRAVEL

Every form of transport that relies on carbon-based fuel generates CO_2, the main cause of human-induced climate change. Modern travel is dependent on airplanes, which might use less fuel per kilometer per person than most cars but travel much greater distances. The altitude at which aircraft emit gases (including CO_2) and particles also contributes to their climate change impact. Many websites offer 'carbon calculators' that allow people to estimate the carbon emissions generated by their journey and, for those who wish to do so, to offset the impact of the greenhouse gases emitted with contributions to portfolios of climate-friendly initiatives throughout the world. Lonely Planet offsets the carbon footprint of all staff and author travel.

SHUTTLE

Most visitors take the **Airport Shuttle** (☑504-522-3500; www.airportshuttleneworleans. com; one way/return $24/44) to and from the airport. It offers frequent service between the airport and downtown hotels, although it can be time-consuming, especially if your hotel is the last stop. At the airport, buy tickets from agencies in the baggage-claim area. For your return to the airport, call a day ahead to arrange for a pickup, which you should schedule at least two hours prior to your flight's departure.

TAXI

A taxi ride downtown costs a flat rate of $36 for one or two passengers, or $15 per person for three or more passengers.

Other Airports

It's worth checking out the following airports if you plan to rent a car, but probably not otherwise. **Baton Rouge Metropolitan Airport** (BTR; ☑225-355-0333; www.flybtr. com; 9430 Jackie Cochran Dr) is 89 miles (and minutes) north of town; the **Tiger Airport Shuttle** (www. tigerairportshuttle.com; BTR to downtown New Orleans day/ night $175/205) provides direct service to downtown New Orleans, the rate fluctuating based on the time of day. **Gulfport-Biloxi International Airport** (GPT; ☑228-863-5951; www. flygpt.com) is about 77 miles (80 minutes) east of New Orleans; there are rental-car agencies on-site.

Bus

Greyhound (www.greyhound. com) buses stop at the **New Orleans Union Passenger Terminal** (☑Amtrak 800-872-7245, Greyhound ☑504-525-6075; 1001 Loyola Ave), which is also known as Union Station. It's seven blocks upriver from Canal St. Greyhound regularly connects to Lafayette, Opelousas and Baton Rouge, plus Clarksdale, MS, and Memphis, TN, en route to essentially every city in the continental USA.

Train

Three Amtrak (☑800-872-7245; www.amtrak.com) trains serve New Orleans at the New Orleans Union Passenger Terminal. The *City of New Orleans* train runs to Memphis, TN; Jackson, MS; and Chicago, IL. Alternatively, the *Crescent Route* serves Birmingham, AL; Atlanta, GA; Washington, DC; and New York City. The *Sunset Limited* connects Los Angeles, CA, with Tucson, AZ, and New Orleans.

GETTING AROUND

Streetcar New Orleans' streetcars are charming, but the service only covers a relatively small part of the city. One-way fares cost $1.25, and multitrip passes are available.

Bus Services are OK, but try not to time your trip around them. Fares won't run more than $2.

Walk If you're just exploring the French Quarter, your feet will serve just fine.

Bicycle Flat New Orleans is easy to cycle – you can cross the entirety of town in 45 minutes.

Car This is the easiest way to access outer neighborhoods such as Mid-City. Parking is problematic in the French Quarter and CBD.

Bicycle

Cyclists will find New Orleans flat and relatively compact; however, heavy traffic, potholes, narrow roads and unsafe neighborhoods present some negatives to cycling, and fat tires are a near necessity. Oppressive summer heat and humidity also discourage a lot of cyclists.

All ferries offer free transportation for bicycles. Buses are now equipped with bike racks. Only folding bicycles are permitted on streetcars.

The city operates a fleet of **blue bikes** (☑504-608-0603; http://nola.socialbicycles. com; per hr $8) for rent. You can also find private bicycle-rental outfits across New Orleans.

A Bicycle Named Desire (☑504-345-8966; http:// abicyclenameddesire.com; 632 Elysian Fields Ave;

4hr/8hr/24hr $20/25/35, per additional day $25; ⊙10am-5pm Wed-Mon)

Alex's Bikes (☑504-327-9248; www.alexsbikes.com; 607 Marigny St; per hr/day $5/30; ⊙10am-6pm Tue-Fri, to 5pm Sat, noon-5pm Sun)

American Bicycle Rental Co (☑504-324-8257; www.amebrc.com; 318 N Rampart St; per 4hr/8hr/24hr $25/30/40; ⊙9am-5pm)

Bicycle Michael's (☑504-945-9505; www.bicyclemichaels. com; 622 Frenchmen St; per day from $35; ⊙10am-4:30pm Sun-Tue & Thu, to 6:30pm Fri & Sat)

Dashing Bicycles (☑504-264-3343; www.dashingnola. com; 1234 N Broad St; per half day/7hr/day $15/25/35; ⊙10am-7pm Mon-Fri, 9am-6pm Sat, 10am-5pm Sun)

Boat

The cheapest way to cruise the Mississippi River is aboard the **Canal Street Ferry** (☑504-376-8233; www. norta.com/Maps-Schedules/New-Orleans-Ferry; per person $2; ⊙6am-9:45pm Mon-Thu, to 11:45pm Fri, 10:30am-11:45pm Sat, 10:30am-9:45pm Sun), which operates between Canal St and the West Bank community of Algiers. The ferry is open to pedestrians and cyclists (no cars). Have exact change for the fare. Change will not be given, and you cannot pay in advance for the return trip.

Bus

The Regional Transit Authority offers bus and streetcar services. Service is decent, but we wouldn't recommend relying solely on public transport during a New Orleans visit, especially if you're staying longer than a few days. Fare is $1.25 plus 25¢ per transfer.

No buses run through the heart of the French Quarter, so most visitors only use them when venturing Uptown or out to City Park.

Car & Motorcycle

Having your own car or renting one in New Orleans can make it much easier to fully experience the entire city, from Faubourg Marigny up to Riverbend, and out along Esplanade Ave. If you are planning to spend most of your time in the French Quarter, though, don't bother. You'll just end up wasting money on parking.

Many city streets, even in posh Uptown, are in an atrocious state, and tires have accordingly short life spans. Navigating tricky left turns through very common four-way intersections can be a hazard. Crossing St Charles Ave, while watching for the streetcar, adds another level of adventure. Although stop signs are set out in residential areas, not everyone obeys them. New Orleanian friendliness can be annoying if people stop their cars in the middle of a narrow street to chat with someone – every New Orleans driver has a story about this incident. Local drivers also have a reputation for not turning on their headlights in the event of rain or fog.

Visitors from abroad may find it wise to back up their national driver's license with an International Driving Permit, available from their local automobile club.

Parking

Downtown on-street parking is typically for short-term use only. In some parts of town, look for solar-powered parking meters. One meter often serves an entire block, so don't assume parking is free just because there's no meter on the curb immediately beside where you park. There are also all

kinds of restrictions to do with street cleaning that limit when you can park on certain streets. Be sure to read all parking signs before leaving your car. Enforcement is particularly efficient in the French Quarter, the CBD and the Warehouse District.

Vehicles parked illegally are sometimes towed; 'sometimes' becomes 'often' during major events like Jazz Fest. Towable offenses include parking your car in a driveway, within 20ft of a corner or crosswalk, within 15ft of a fire hydrant or in restricted areas on a street-sweeping day. Towed cars are brought to the Claiborne Auto Pound (400 N Claiborne Ave), where you'll have to pay anywhere from $75 to $150 (or more) to spring your vehicle.

Free street parking is available on many blocks in the Lower Quarter and along Esplanade Ave. Otherwise, there are plenty of commercial lots scattered through downtown and the French Quarter; expect to pay around $25 to $40 per day, and keep in mind that rates skyrocket at night.

Outside the Quarter and downtown, parking is a cinch. There's plenty of street parking and not many restrictions, although you will find parking meters along much of Magazine St. Again, be careful of street parking during Mardi Gras and Jazz Fest, when police are liable to ticket or tow you for even very minor infractions.

For more details about parking enforcement, visit www.nola.gov/dpw/parking.

Rental

Most big car-rental companies like Avis, Budget and Hertz can be found in New Orleans. At Louis Armstrong Airport, rental agencies and cars are now within walking distance of the terminals. Typically to rent a car you must be at least 25 years of age and hold a major credit card, as well as a valid driver's license.

Rates go up and availability lessens during special events or large conventions. US citizens who already have auto insurance are probably covered, but should check with their insurance company first.

Streetcar

Streetcars (aka trolleys or trams) have made a comeback in New Orleans, with four lines serving key routes in the city. They are run by the Regional Transit Authority (www.norta.com). Fares cost $1.25 – have exact change – or purchase a Jazzy Pass (one-/three-/five-/31-day unlimited rides $3/9/15/55), which is also good on buses. Jazzy Passes can be purchased from streetcar conductors, bus drivers, in Walgreens drugstores and from ticketing machines at RTA shelters along Canal St. Streetcars run about every 15 to 20 minutes, leaning toward every 30 minutes later at night.

Canal Streetcar Lines

Two slightly different lines follow Canal St to Mid-City. Both run from Harrah's Casino up Canal St. The Cemeteries line goes to City Park

Ave, where it crosses the entrance to the Greenwood Cemetery (24 hours). More useful for tourists is the City Park line (6am to midnight), which heads up a spur on N Carrollton Ave, ending up at the Esplanade Ave entrance to City Park.

Riverfront Streetcar Line

This 2-mile route (operating from about 5:30am to 11:30pm) runs between the French Market, in the lower end of the French Quarter near Esplanade Ave, and the upriver Convention Center, crossing Canal St on the way.

St Charles Avenue Streetcar Line

When the St Charles Ave route opened as the New Orleans & Carrollton Railroad in 1835, it was the nation's second horse-drawn streetcar line. Now it is one of the few streetcars in the US to have survived the automobile era. It runs 24 hours from Carrollton and Claiborne, down Carrollton to St Charles, then via St Charles Ave to Canal & Carondelet.

Rampart–St Claude Streetcar Line

The newest streetcar line in the city runs from around 6am to midnight. It connects

the Union Passenger Terminal (☑Amtrak 800-872-7245, Greyhound 504-525-6075; 1001 Loyola Ave) to Canal St via Rampart St, then rolls up Rampart, skirting the edge of the French Quarter, before turning onto St Claude Ave. The line follows St Claude for a few blocks before terminating at Elysian Fields Ave, right in front of Gene's (☑504-943-3861; 1040 Elysian Fields Ave; po'boys $8; ⊘24hr), a giant pink po'boy shop that sells a mean daiquiri.

Taxi

If you're traveling alone or at night, taxis are recommended. **United Cabs** (%504-522-9771) is the biggest and most reliable company in New Orleans. You might have to call for a pickup, unless you are in a central part of the French Quarter, where it is relatively easy to flag down a passing cab.

Fares within the city start with a $3.50 flag-fall charge for one passenger (plus $1 for each additional passenger). From there it's $2 per mile. New Orleans is small, so don't expect fares to top $20. Don't forget to tip your driver about 15%.

Popular ridesharing apps are also available in New Orleans.

Directory A–Z

Accessible Travel

New Orleans is somewhat lax in this department. Sidewalk curbs rarely have ramps, and many historic public buildings and hotels are not equipped to meet the needs of wheel-chair-users. Modern hotels adhere to standards established by the federal Americans with Disabilities Act by providing ramps, elevators and accessible bathrooms.

Red streetcars on the Canal St, Rampart Riverfront and Loyola–UPT Streetcar lines are accessible to riders with disabilities. The green streetcars that run along St Charles Ave are protected by the National Register of Historic Places and have not been made accessible (www.norta.com/Accessibility.aspx). Regional Transit Authority buses offer a lift service; for information about paratransit service (alternative transportation for those who can't ride regular buses), call **RTA Paratransit** (☑504-827-7433; www.norta.com/Accessibility/Paratransit).

Customs Regulations

US Customs and Border Protection (www.cbp.gov) allows a person to bring into the US up to 200 cigarettes duty-free, and each person over the age of 21 years to bring in 1L of liquor. Non-US citizens are allowed to enter the USA with $100-worth of gifts from abroad. There are restrictions on bringing fresh fruit and flowers into the country, and there is a strict quarantine on animals. If you are carrying $10,000 or more in US and foreign cash, traveler's checks, money orders or the like, you need to declare the excess amount. There is no legal restriction on the amount that may be imported, but undeclared sums in excess of $10,000 may be subject to confiscation.

Discount Cards

The New Orleans pass (adult/child from $69/49) is a discount card that scores you either free or discounted admission at over 25 sights and tours, including the New Orleans Museum of Art, the Audubon Aquarium and Mardi Gras World. The pass can be purchased and downloaded online (www.neworleanspass.com).

Electricity

The electrical current in the USA is 110V to 115V, 60Hz AC. Outlets may be suited to flat two-prong (not grounded) or three-prong (grounded) plugs. If your appliance is made for another electrical system, you will need a transformer or adapter; if you didn't bring one along, buy one at any consumer-electronics store around town.

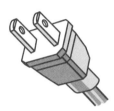

Type A
120V/60Hz

Type B
120V/60Hz

Emergency

Ambulance (☏911)
Fire (☏911)
**National Sexual Assault
Hotline** (☏800-656-4673)
Police (emergency) (☏911)
Police (nonemergency)
(☏504-821-2222)

Health

Excellent medical care is
readily available, but the
need for medical insurance
when visiting anywhere in
the USA cannot be over-
emphasized. Doctors often
expect payment on the spot
for services rendered, after
which your insurance com-
pany may reimburse you.
US citizens should check
with their insurer before
leaving home to see what
conditions are covered in
their policy.

If you need immediate
medical attention and you
are in your hotel, your first
call should be to the front
desk. Some of the larger
hotels have agreements
with on-call doctors who
can make house calls if
necessary. In really urgent
situations, you can call an
ambulance (911), which will
deliver you to a hospital
emergency room.

If you can get to an emergency room, your best bet
is the **Tulane University
Medical Center** (☏504-
988-5263; https://tulane-
healthcare.com; 1415 Tulane
Ave; ◷24hr) or LSU's **University Medical Center**
(☏emergency 504-702-2138,
main switchboard 504-702-
3000; www.umcno.org; 2000
Canal St; ◷24hr), both located in or adjacent to the CBD.
If your kids need emergency
medical attention, the best
bet is **Children's Hospital** (☏504-899-9511; www.
chnola.org; 200 Henry Clay Ave;
◷24hr), located Uptown.

PRACTICALITIES

Smoking

Indoor smoking is banned in New Orleans bars, but is
still permitted in most outdoor gathering areas, including patios, courtyards and balconies.

Newspapers

Gambit (www.bestofneworleans.com) Weekly publica-
tion that covers arts, culture and music.

The Times-Picayune (www.nola.com) Broadsheet
news and arts coverage three times a week.

The Advocate (www.theadvocate.com/new_orleans)
More broadsheet news and culture writing.

New Orleans Magazine (www.myneworleans.com/
new-orleans-magazine) Monthly focus on city society.

The Lens (http://thelensnola.org) Investigative jour-
nalism and culture coverage; online only.

Radio

88.3 WRBH Reading radio for the blind.

89.9 WWNO NPR (National Public Radio).

90.7 WWOZ Louisiana music and community radio.

91.5 WTUL Tulane radio.

93.3 WQUE Hip-hop and R&B.

96.3 Classic hip-hop and R&B.

102.3 WHIV Music and community radio with an activist
bent.

Insurance

Foreign travelers may want
to purchase health insurance
before visiting the USA, as
the cost of healthcare can be
prohibitive (a single hospital
visit can run to thousands
of dollars). Other forms of
insurance can cover the cost
of changing tickets in the
event of unforeseen developments during your trip.

Worldwide travel insur-
ance is available at www.
lonelyplanet.com/travel-
insurance. You can buy,
extend and claim online any-
time – even if you're already
on the road.

Internet Access

Many hotels offer wi-fi and
cable internet access. Wi-fi
is available in almost every

coffee shop in town, and all
branches of the New Orleans
Public Library (www.ne-
worleanspubliclibrary.org).

Legal Matters

Although it may seem that
anything goes, New Orleans
has its limits. Common tour-
ist-related offenses include
underage drinking, drinking
outdoors from a bottle rather
than from a plastic go cup,
teen curfew violations and
(most commonly) flaunting
of private parts.

For people aged 21 years
or more, the legal blood-
alcohol limit for driving in
Louisiana is 0.08%, however
you can be cited for driving
while impaired even when
your blood-alcohol content
is lower. For those under 21,
the legal limit is 0.02%.

The legal drinking age is 21. Curfew laws are strict – if you are under 17, you cannot drive from 11pm to 5am unless accompanied by a licensed parent, guardian or adult who is at least 21.

Most bars will offer your drink in a plastic cup, so accept it if you're going to wander off with your drink. Bourbon St flashers rarely get in serious trouble for flashing their private parts, but repeatedly doing so in front of the cops is asking for trouble. Don't grope flashers. That's a no-no and, we hope, rather obvious.

The legal age for gambling is 21 and businesses with gaming devices (usually video poker machines) out in the open are closed to minors. Even cafes with gaming devices are off-limits to minors, unless the games are contained within private rooms or booths.

Traffic cameras are becoming increasingly commonplace in New Orleans, especially around schools. If they catch you speeding, you'll be sent a letter with a fine. The city is ruthlessly persistent about this enforcement.

During big tourism events like Jazz Fest and Mardi Gras, the city's parking enforcement officers get pretty aggressive. At most times of year, parking too close to a stop sign or intersection might get you a fine or warning; during season in New Orleans, your car is likely to get towed.

Money

ATMs are widely available.

Credit & Debit Cards

Major credit cards are widely accepted by car-rental agencies and most hotels, restaurants, gas stations, shops and larger grocery stores. Many smaller restaurants and bars accept cash only. Many recreational and tourist activities can also be paid for by credit card. The most commonly accepted cards are Visa, MasterCard and American Express.

Tipping

Hotels A dollar or two per bag carried to your room.

Restaurants Not optional! Standard 18% for good service, 20% for exceptional service.

Cafes A tip jar is often left out by the register, but tipping isn't expected.

Music It's good manners to kick in a few bucks when the band passes around a bucket or hat.

Bars A good rule of thumb is to leave a dollar every time you order – more, if it's a complicated drink or large round.

Taxi Tip 10% or round up the fare.

Opening Hours

New Orleans maintains business hours similar to much of the rest of the USA, except when it comes to bars.

Banks 9am to 5pm Monday to Thursday, 10am to 5:30pm Friday. Some branches are open 9am to noon Saturday.

Bars Usually 5pm until around 2am on weekdays and 3am or 4am on weekends. Many bars stay open indefinitely, but on the flip side, they'll often close if business is slow.

Post offices 8:30am to 4:30pm Monday to Friday and 8:30am to noon Saturday.

Restaurants 10am or 11am to 11pm (sometimes with a break from 2pm to 5pm); usually closed Sunday and/or Monday.

Stores 10am to 7pm or 8pm.

Post

New Orleans' main post office is near City Hall at 701 Loyola Ave. There are smaller branches throughout the city, including in the CBD at Lafayette Sq (9am to 1pm and 2pm to 5pm Monday to Friday) and Uptown Station at 2000 Louisiana Ave (8am to 4:30pm Monday to Friday and 8am to noon Saturday).

There are lots of independent postal shops as well, such as Fedex and the French Quarter Postal Emporium. These shops will send letters and packages at the same rates as the post office.

Public Holidays

Note that when national holidays fall on a weekend, they are often celebrated on the nearest Friday or Monday so that everyone enjoys a three-day weekend. The following are all national holidays:

New Year's Day January 1

Martin Luther King Jr Day Third Monday in January

Presidents' Day Third Monday in February

Memorial Day Last Monday in May

Independence Day July 4

Labor Day First Monday in September

Columbus Day Second Monday in October

Veterans' Day November 11

Thanksgiving Fourth Thursday in November

Christmas Day December 25

Safe Travel

New Orleans has a high crime rate, but the majority of violent crime occurs between parties that already know each other.

➜ Muggings do occur. Solo travelers are targeted more often; avoid entering secluded areas alone.

➜ The French Quarter is a secure around-the-clock realm for the visitor.

→ The CBD and Warehouse District are busy on weekdays, but relatively deserted at night and on weekends.

→ The B&Bs along Esplanade Ridge are close enough to troubled neighborhoods to require caution at night.

→ Some areas of Central City can feel lonely after dark. At night, park close to your destination on a well-traveled street.

→ Be wary before entering an intersection: local drivers are notorious for running yellow and even red lights.

→ Drink spikings do occur.

Taxes & Refunds

New Orleans' 10% sales tax is tacked onto virtually everything, including meals, groceries and car rentals. For accommodations, room and occupancy taxes, add an additional 13% to your bill plus $1 to $3 per person, depending on the size of the hotel.

For foreign visitors, some merchants in Louisiana participate in a program called Louisiana Tax Free Shopping (www.louisianataxfree.com). Look for the snazzy red-and-blue 'Tax Free' logo in the window or on the sign of the store. Usually these stores specialize in the kinds of impulse purchases people are likely to make while on vacation. In these stores, present a passport to verify you are not a US citizen, and request a voucher as you make your purchase. Reimbursement centers are located in the **Downtown Refund Center** (☎504-568-3605; The Outlet Collection at Riverwalk, 500 Port of New Orleans Place; ☺10am-6pm Mon-Sat, 11am-5pm Sun) and the **Airport Refund Center** (☎504-467-0723; ☺8am-5pm Mon-Fri, 9am-3pm Sat & Sun) in the main ticket lobby in Terminal C at the airport.

Telephone
Area Codes
The area code in New Orleans is ☎504. In Thibodaux and Houma it's ☎985; Baton Rouge and surrounds ☎225; and Shreveport and the northern part of the state ☎318.

When dialing a number with a different area code from your own, you must dial ☎1 before the area code. For example, to call a Baton Rouge number from New Orleans, begin by dialing ☎1-225. Note that hotel telephones often have heavy surcharges.

International Codes
If you're calling from abroad, the international country code for the USA (and Canada) is ☎1.

To make an international call from New Orleans, dial ☎011 + country code + area code (dropping the leading 0) + number. For calls to Canada, there's no need to dial the international access code ☎011. For international operator assistance, dial ☎00.

Time
New Orleans Standard Time is six hours behind GMT/UTC. In US terms, that puts it one hour behind the East Coast and two hours ahead of the West Coast. In early March, clocks move ahead one hour for Daylight Saving Time; clocks move back one hour in early November.

Toilets
A recording by Benny Grunch, 'Ain't No Place to Pee on Mardi Gras Day,' summarizes the situation in the French Quarter. While tour guides delight in describing the unsanitary waste-disposal practices of the old Creole days, the stench arising from back alleys is actually more recent in origin.

Public rest rooms can be found in the Jackson Brewery mall and in the French Market. Larger hotels often have accessible rest rooms off the lobby, usually near the elevators and pay phones.

Tourist Information
Right next to popular Jackson Sq in the heart of the French Quarter, the **New Orleans Welcome Center** (☎504-568-5661; www.crt.state.la.us/tourism; 529 St Ann St; ☺8:30am-5pm) in the lower Pontalba Building offers maps, listings of upcoming events and a variety of brochures for sights, restaurants and hotels. The helpful staff can help you find accommodations in a pinch, answer questions and offer advice about New Orleans.

Information kiosks scattered through main tourist areas offer most of the same brochures as the Welcome Center, but their staff tend to be less knowledgeable.

Order or download a Louisiana-wide travel guide online from the **Louisiana Office of Tourism** (www.louisianatravel.com).

In the Tremé, you can pick up a New Orleans map and look at displays about city attractions at the **Basin St Visitors Center** (☎504-293-2600; www.basinststation.com; 501 Basin St; ☺9am-5pm) inside Basin St Station.

Otherwise, **New Orleans Convention & Visitors Bureau** (CVB; ☎504-566-5011; www.neworleans.com; 2020 St Charles Ave; ☺8:30am-5pm) has plenty of free maps and helpful information.

Visas

Visas are required for most foreign visitors unless eligible for the Visa Waiver Program (VWP). If you're staying for 90 days or less, you may qualify for the VWP; citizens of roughly three-dozen countries are eligible. Note that nationals of waiver countries who have traveled in Iran, Iraq, Libya, Somalia, Sudan, Syria or Yemen after March 1, 2011, are no longer eligible for the VWP. In addition, nationals of VWP countries who are also nationals of Iran, Iraq, Sudan or Syria no longer qualify for a waiver.

Apart from most Canadian citizens and those entering under the VWP, a passport with an official visa is required for most visitors to the USA; contact the US embassy or consulate in your home country for more information about specific requirements. Most applicants have to be interviewed before a visa is granted and all applicants must pay a fee. You'll also have to prove you're not trying to stay in the USA permanently. The US Department of State has useful and up-to-date visa information online at http://travel.state.gov/content/visas/english/visit.html.

Volunteering

Literally hundreds of volunteer organizations descended upon New Orleans after Hurricane Katrina. Some did fantastic work; some acted with arrogance and left a sour taste. Almost everyone agrees that **Common Ground Relief** (☏504-312-1729; www.commonground relief.org; 1800 Deslonde St) is one of the better organizations in New Orleans – it works with locals, is committed to best practices and has a good track record in town.

Women Travelers

Drunk men in the French Quarter and along parade routes often catcall or make lewd comments to passing women. This occurs on any Friday or Saturday night, not just during Mardi Gras.

The New Orleans branch of Planned Parenthood (www.plannedparenthood.org/health-center/louisiana/new-orleans) provides health-care services for women, including walk-in pregnancy testing and emergency contraception.

Glossary

banh mi – Vietnamese sandwiches of sliced pork, cucumber, cilantro and other lovelies; locally called a Vietnamese po'boy

beignet – a flat square of dough flash-fried to golden, puffy glory, dusted with powdered sugar and served scorching hot

boudin – a tasty Cajun sausage made with pork, pork liver, cooked rice and spices

bousillage – mud- and straw-filled walls supported by cypress timbers

briquette entre poteaux – a style of architecture common to French-colonial houses, where brick fills the spaces between vertical and diagonal posts

Cajun (cuisine) – the rustic cuisine of the countryside

calliope – an organ-like musical instrument fitted with steam whistles; historically played on showboats and in traveling fairs

Creole (cuisine) – the rich, refined cuisine of the city

étouffée – a Cajun or Creole stew of shellfish or chicken served over rice

Fais do do – a Cajun dance party

faubourgs – literally 'suburbs,' although neighborhoods is a more accurate translation in spirit

frottoir – a metal washboard-like instrument that's worn like armor and played with spoons

go cup – a plastic cup given to patrons in bars so they can take their drink with them when they leave

gris-gris – amulets or spell bags

jambalaya – hearty, rice-based dish with any combination of fowl, shellfish or meat (but usually includes ham)

krewes – a deliberate misspelling of 'crews'; organizations or groups of people that create floats and stage festivities during Mardi Gras

migas – scrambled eggs mixed with fried tortilla strips

mudbug – a term for crawfish

muffuletta – a round sesame-crusted loaf spread with a salty olive salad and layered with cheeses and deli meats

plaçage – a cultural institution whereby white men 'kept' light-skinned black women as their mistresses

po'boy – a large sandwich made on French bread and overstuffed with a variety of fillings

Santeria – a Puerto Rican religion related to voodoo

Sazerac – a potent whiskey drink that uses rye as its primary ingredient, with aromatic bitters (including the locally produced Peychaud's), a bit of sugar and a swish of absinthe

snowballs – shaved ice in a paper cup doused liberally with flavored syrup

tasso – a cured, smoked piece of ham

Vieux Carré – alternate term for French Quarter; literally 'Old Square'

zydeco – a style of local music that combines French tunes with Caribbean music and blues

Behind the Scenes

SEND US YOUR FEEDBACK

We love to hear from travelers – your comments keep us on our toes and help make our books better. Our well-traveled team reads every word on what you loved or loathed about this book. Although we cannot reply individually to your submissions, we always guarantee that your feedback goes straight to the appropriate authors, in time for the next edition. Each person who sends us information is thanked in the next edition – the most useful submissions are rewarded with a selection of digital PDF chapters.

Visit **lonelyplanet.com/contact** to submit your updates and suggestions or to ask for help. Our award-winning website also features inspirational travel stories, news and discussions.

Note: We may edit, reproduce and incorporate your comments in Lonely Planet products such as guidebooks, websites and digital products, so let us know if you don't want your comments reproduced or your name acknowledged. For a copy of our privacy policy visit lonelyplanet.com/privacy.

WRITER THANKS

Adam Karlin

Thanks to Trisha Ping, for putting me on this assignment this time around, and to Jennye Garibaldi for putting me on it the first time. Thanks also to the ever-expanding NOLA family: Dan; Bobby; Dorothy; Trish; Jonah, Mel and Lincoln; Molly, Travis and Sylvie; AJ, Halle, Hugo and Sadie; Adrian, Darcy and Seb; Mike, Nora, David and Dash; and all the crew at UNO. My thanks to Mom and Dad for everything. Finally, thanks to Rachel and Sanda for being the greatest exploration team ever assembled, and to 'Gus', an oncoming explorer in his own right.

Ray Bartlett

Thanks first and always to my family for making this possible, and for putting up with me. Thanks to Trisha Ping, my awesome editor, and to my fine coauthor Adam Karlin. Hugs to everyone who showed me around their amazing city: Gimena and Miles; Lindsey and Nick; Barrett, Shemsi, Ilana, Nancy, Henny, Angel and Lexi, to name just a few. And a shout out to all the other incredible NOLA denizens who made researching this such an awesome voyage. I can't wait to come back.

ACKNOWLEDGEMENTS

Cover photograph: Canal Streetcar, French Quarter, Jason Langley/Alamy ©

THIS BOOK

This 8th edition of Lonely Planet's *New Orleans* guidebook was researched and written by Adam Karlin and Ray Bartlett, and curated by Adam. The previous two editions were written by Amy C Balfour and Adam. This guidebook was produced by the following:

Destination Editor Trisha Ping
Senior Product Editor Vicky Smith
Product Editor Ronan Abayawickrema
Senior Cartographer Alison Lyall
Cartographer James Leversha
Book Designer Gwen Cotter

Assisting Editors James Bainbridge, Jacqueline Danam, Melanie Dankel, Carly Hall, Alexander Knights
Cover Researcher Naomi Parker
Thanks to Victoria Harrison, Lesya Hrycenko, Aslihan Karatas, Kate Kiely, Jessica Ryan, Angela Tinson, Sam Wheeler

Index

EATING

⚲ DRINKING & NIGHTLIFE

New Orleans Maps

Sights

- Beach
- Bird Sanctuary
- Buddhist
- Castle/Palace
- Christian
- Confucian
- Hindu
- Islamic
- Jain
- Jewish
- Monument
- Museum/Gallery/Historic Building
- Ruin
- Shinto
- Sikh
- Taoist
- Winery/Vineyard
- Zoo/Wildlife Sanctuary
- Other Sight

Activities, Courses & Tours

- Bodysurfing
- Diving
- Canoeing/Kayaking
- Course/Tour
- Sento Hot Baths/Onsen
- Skiing
- Snorkeling
- Surfing
- Swimming/Pool
- Walking
- Windsurfing
- Other Activity

Sleeping

- Sleeping
- Camping

Eating

- Eating

Drinking & Nightlife

- Drinking & Nightlife
- Cafe

Entertainment

- Entertainment

Shopping

- Shopping

Information

- Bank
- Embassy/Consulate
- Hospital/Medical
- Internet
- Police
- Post Office
- Telephone
- Toilet
- Tourist Information
- Other Information

Geographic

- Beach
- Gate
- Hut/Shelter
- Lighthouse
- Lookout
- Mountain/Volcano
- Oasis
- Park
- Pass
- Picnic Area
- Waterfall

Population

- Capital (National)
- Capital (State/Province)
- City/Large Town
- Town/Village

Transport

- Airport
- BART station
- Border crossing
- Boston T station
- Bus
- Cable car/Funicular
- Cycling
- Ferry
- Metro/Muni station
- Monorail
- Parking
- Petrol station
- Subway/SkyTrain station
- Taxi
- Train station/Railway
- Tram
- Underground station
- Other Transport

Note: Not all symbols displayed above appear on the maps in this book

Routes

- Tollway
- Freeway
- Primary
- Secondary
- Tertiary
- Lane
- Unsealed road
- Road under construction
- Plaza/Mall
- Steps
- Tunnel
- Pedestrian overpass
- Walking Tour
- Walking Tour detour
- Path/Walking Trail

Boundaries

- International
- State/Province
- Disputed
- Regional/Suburb
- Marine Park
- Cliff
- Wall

Hydrography

- River, Creek
- Intermittent River
- Canal
- Water
- Dry/Salt/Intermittent Lake
- Reef

Areas

- Airport/Runway
- Beach/Desert
- Cemetery (Christian)
- Cemetery (Other)
- Glacier
- Mudflat
- Park/Forest
- Sight (Building)
- Sportsground
- Swamp/Mangrove

MAP INDEX

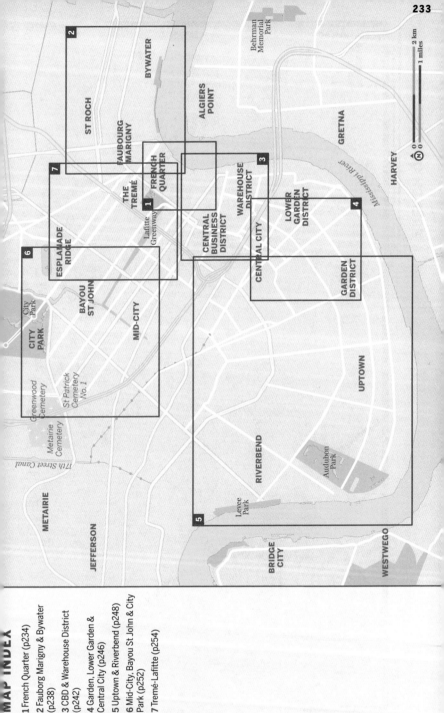

FRENCH QUARTER

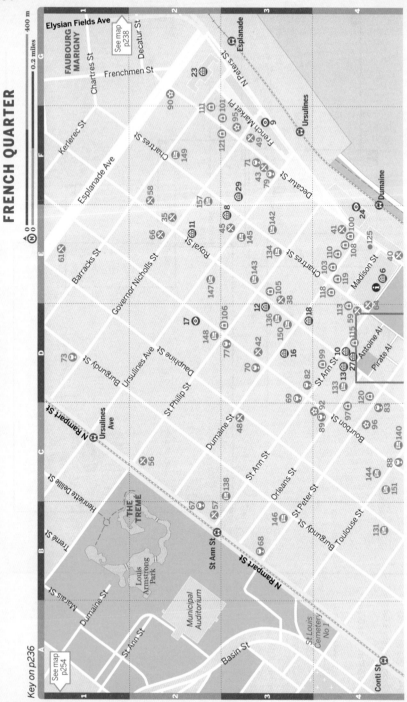

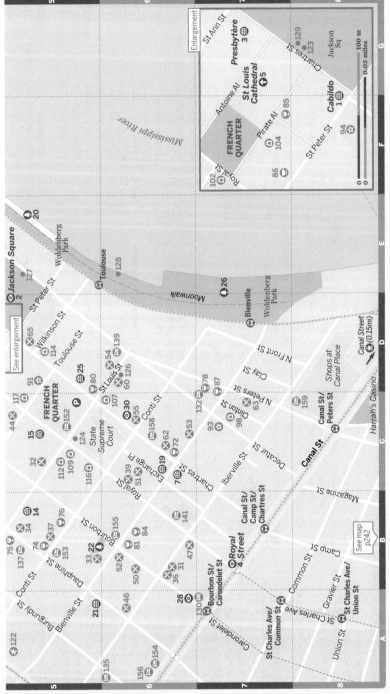

FRENCH QUARTER

FAUBOURG MARIGNY & BYWATER

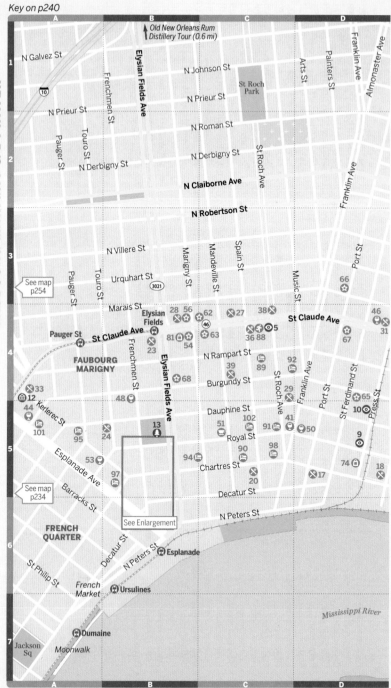

Old New Orleans Rum
Distillery Tour (0.6 mi)

N Galvez St

N Johnson St

St Roch
Park

Arts St

Painters St

Franklin Ave

Almonaster Ave

N Prieur St

Frenchmen St

N Prieur St

N Roman St

Elysian Fields Ave

Pauger St

Touro St

N Derbigny St

N Derbigny St

St Roch Ave

N Claiborne Ave

Franklin Ave

N Robertson St

N Villere St

Touro St

Pauger St

Urquhart St

Marigny St

Mandeville St

Spain St

Music St

Port St

See map
p254

3021

66

Marais St

Elysian
Fields

28 56

62

27

38

St Claude Ave

46

31

Pauger St

St Claude Ave

81

54

63

36 88

5

67

23

FAUBOURG
MARIGNY

Frenchmen St

N Rampart St

39

89

92

Port St

St Ferdinand St

Press St

68

Burgundy St

St Roch Ave

Franklin Ave

33

Elysian Fields Ave

48

Dauphine St

102

41

65

12

44

Kerlerec St

101

95

24

13

51

91

29

50

10

9

Royal St

90

98

53

94

Chartres St

74

18

97

20

17

See map
p234

Barracks St

Decatur St

See Enlargement

N Peters St

FRENCH
QUARTER

Decatur St

N Peters St

Esplanade

St Philip St

French
Market

Ursulines

Mississippi River

Dumaine

Jackson
Sq

Moonwalk

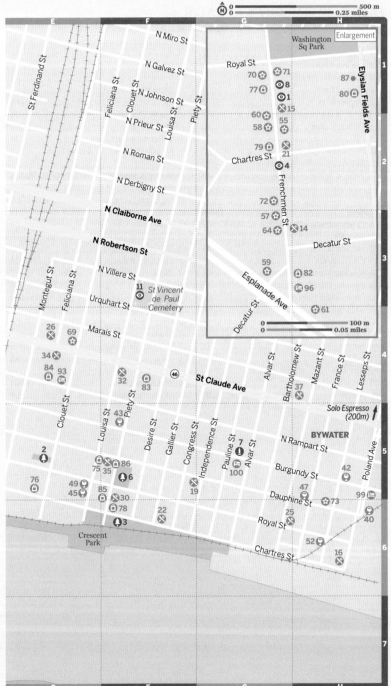

N Miro St
N Galvez St
St Ferdinand St
Feliciana St
Clouet St
N Johnson St
Louisa St
Piety St
N Prieur St
N Roman St
N Derbigny St
N Claiborne Ave
N Robertson St
Montegut St
Feliciana St
N Villere St
Urquhart St
Marais St
St Vincent de Paul Cemetery

Royal St
Washington Sq Park
Enlargement
70 ✪71
77 ◉ ✪8
◉ ✪1
87 ●
80 ⊡
60 ✪ ✪15
58 ✪ 55 ✪
79 ⊡ ✪21
Chartres St
◉4
72 ✪
57 ✪
64 ⊡ ✪14
Decatur St
59 ✪
⊡82
⊡96
✪61
Esplanade Ave
Decatur St

Elysian Fields Ave

0 —— 100 m
0 —— 0.05 miles

26 ✪
69 ✪
34 ✪
84 ⊡ 93 ⊡
32 ✪ ⊡83
46

Alvar St
Bartholomew St
Mazant St
France St
Lesseps St

St Claude Ave
37 ✪

Solo Espresso (200m) ↑

Clouet St
Louisa St
Piety St
43 ⊡
Desire St
Gallier St
Congress St
Independence St
Pauline St
7 ⓘ
Alvar St
N Rampart St
BYWATER

42 ⊡
Burgundy St
2 ⚲
75 35 ✪ ⊡86
⚲6
76 ⊡
49 ⚲ 85 ⊡
45 ⊡ ✪30
100
19 ✪
47 ⊡
Dauphine St
25 ✪
73 ✪
99 ⊡
40
78 ⊡
22 ✪
3 ⚲
52 ✪
16 ✪
Crescent Park
Royal St
Chartres St
Poland Ave

FAUBOURG MARIGNY & BYWATER *Map on p238*

Key on p244

CBD & WAREHOUSE DISTRICT

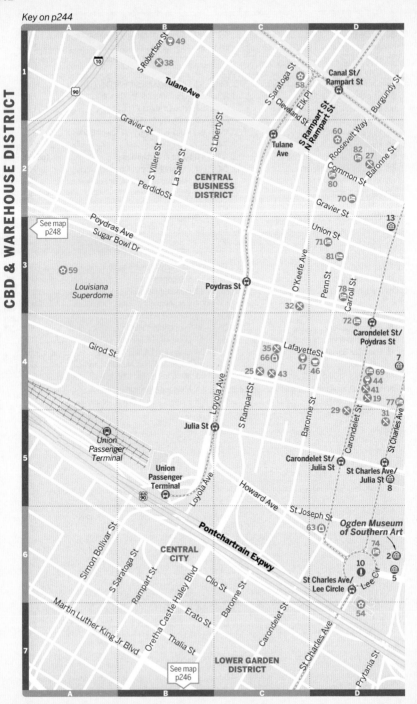

S Robertson St
49
38
Tulane Ave

10
90

Gravier St

S Villere St
La Salle St
S Liberty St
Perdido St

CENTRAL
BUSINESS
DISTRICT

S Saratoga St
S Cleveland St
Elk Pl
58
Canal St/
Rampart St

Tulane
Ave
S Rampart St
N Rampart St

Roosevelt Way
60
82
27
Common St
80
70

Burgundy St
Baronne St

See map
p248

Poydras Ave
Sugar Bowl Dr

59

Louisiana
Superdome

Poydras St

Gravier St

Union St
71
81

O'Keefe Ave
Penn St
78
Carroll St

13

Girod St

Poydras St
32

35
66
25
43
LafayetteSt
47
46

Carondelet St/
Poydras St

72

7
69
44
41
19

29
31

77

Loyola Ave
S Rampart St

Baronne St
Carondelet St
St Charles Ave

Julia St

Union
Passenger
Terminal

Union
Passenger
Terminal
90

Loyola Ave

Howard Ave

St Joseph St
63

Carondelet St/
Julia St

St Charles Ave/
Julia St
8

Ogden Museum
of Southern Art

74
2
5

10

Simon Bolivar St
S Saratoga St
Rampart St
Oretha Castle Haley Blvd
Clio St
Baronne St

CENTRAL
CITY

Pontchartrain Expwy

St Charles Ave/
Lee Circle

Lee Cir

54

Martin Luther King Jr Blvd
Erato St
Thalia St

Carondelet St

St Charles Ave

Prytania St

LOWER GARDEN
DISTRICT

See map
p246

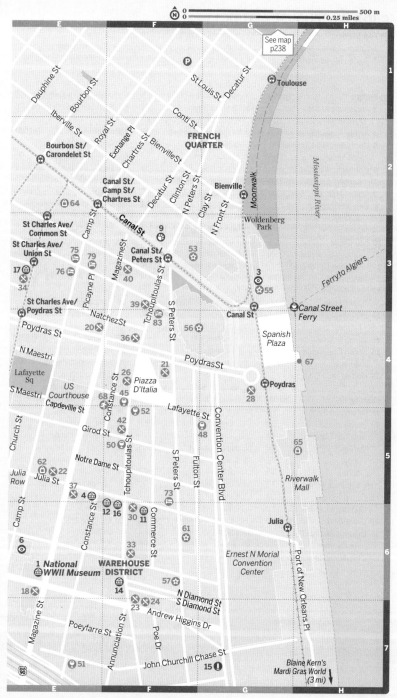

0 — 500 m
0 — 0.25 miles

See map
p238

**FRENCH
QUARTER**

St Louis St
Decatur St

Toulouse

Dauphine St
Bourbon St
Iberville St
Royal St
Conti St

Exchange Pl
Chartres St
Bienville St

**Bourbon St/
Carondelet St**

Decatur St
Clinton St
N Peters St
Clay St
N Front St

Bienville

Moonwalk

**Canal St/
Camp St/
Chartres St**

Canal St

Woldenberg
Park

64

Mississippi River

**St Charles Ave/
Common St**

9

**St Charles Ave/
Union St**

75
79
76
40

Magazine St

**Canal St/
Peters St**

53

3
55

17
34

**St Charles Ave/
Poydras St**

39
83

Tchoupitoulas St
S Peters St

Canal St

Ferry to Algiers

**Canal Street
Ferry**

Poydras St
Natchez St
20
36

56

Spanish
Plaza

67

Poydras St

21

Lafayette
Sq

26
45
68
Constance St
Piazza
D'Italia

Poydras

28

S Maestri
N Maestri
US
Courthouse

Capdeville St

52
42
Girod St
50

Lafayette St
48

Convention Center Blvd

65

Church St

62
22
Julia St

Notre Dame St

Julia
Row

37
4
Tchoupitoulas St

73

Riverwalk
Mall

12 16
30 11
Commerce St
S Peters St
Fulton St

Julia

Camp St

6

33

61

1 National
WWII Museum

**WAREHOUSE
DISTRICT**

14

57

Ernest N Morial
Convention
Center

18

Magazine St

N Diamond St
S Diamond St

Port of New Orleans Pl

23
24

Andrew Higgins Dr

Poeyfarre St
Annunciation St
Poe Dr

BUS
90

51

John Churchill Chase St

15

Blaine Kern's
Mardi Gras World
(3 mi)

CBD & WAREHOUSE DISTRICT *Map on p242*

GARDEN, LOWER GARDEN & CENTRAL CITY Map on p246

GARDEN, LOWER GARDEN & CENTRAL CITY

Key on p245

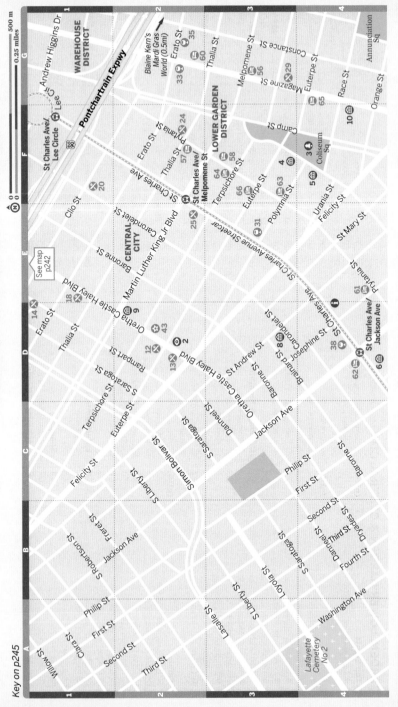

See map p242

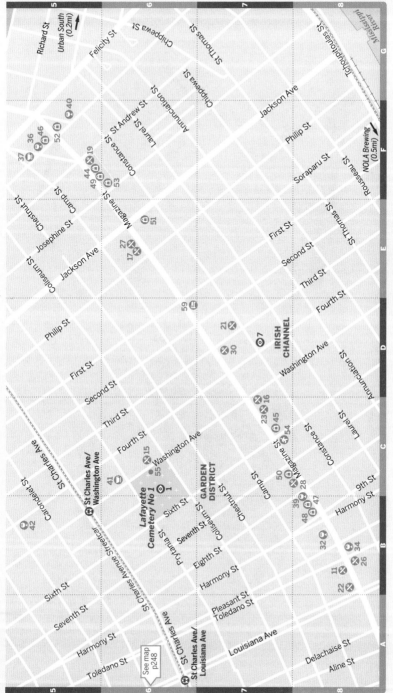

Key on p250

UPTOWN & RIVERBEND

A **B** **C** **D**

S Carrolton Ave/
S Claiborne Ave

Rock 'N' Bowl
(0.5mi)

1

Eagle St
21
Monroe St
16
Leonidas St
Joliet St
Cambronne St

Neron St
Sycamore St
Panola St
Spruce St
Cohn St
St Mary
Cemetery
S Carrollton Ave

S Versailles Blvd
90

Dante St
32
27 Dublin St
57
51 52
15
Short St
Hickory St
Green St
Birch St
Carrollton
Cemetery

Audubon Blvd

S Claiborne Ave

2

7
Levee
Park

23 62
70
40
17
46

St Carrollton Ave/
Oak St

RIVERBEND

St-Jeannette St
Fern St
Willow St
Plum St
Oak St
53

Lowerline St
Pine St
Broadway St

Ursuline
College &
Convent

S Carrollton Ave/
St Charles Ave

41
13

Burdette St
Adams St
Hillary St
Zimple St
Burthe St

9

Calhoun St

Palmer Ave
State St

Clara St
Magnolia St
S Robertson St

Hampson St
Maple St

St Charles Ave

3

Pearl St
Dominican St
Benjamin St

Cherokee St
Millaudon St
Lowerline St
Pine St

St Charles Ave/
Broadway St

Newcomb Blvd

6

Freret St

11

Nashville Ave
Joseph St
Octavia St
Loyola St
Jefferson Ave

Hurst St
Garfield St
Pitt St

Broadway St
Audubon St
Walnut St

73
56

Tulane
University

8

3

4

Mississippi River

Mississippi River Trail

Leake Ave

St Charles Ave/
Tulane University

Audubon Park
Golf Course

Exposition Blvd

St Charles Ave/
Calhoun St

St Charles Avenue Streetcar

St Charles Ave/
Nashville Ave

Benjamin St
Hurst St
Garfield St
Pitt St
Prytania St

Eleonore St
Nashville Ave
Arabella St
Joseph St
Octavia St

St Charles Ave/
Jefferson Ave

5

Audubon Park Trail

4

Henry Clay Ave
Webster St
State St

Perrier St
Coliseum St
Chestnut St
Camp St

58

6

Walnut St

Zoo Ave
5

1
Audubon Zoo

East Dr

Magazine St
50
Constance St
Patton St

12
64
44
54
68

29

Riverview Dr

River Dr

Laurel St
37
Annunciation St
19
Tchoupitoulas St

Eleonore St
Nashville Ave
Arabella St
Joseph St
Octavia St

Leontine St
Valmont St
Bellecastle St

26

7

Orleans Parish
Jefferson Parish

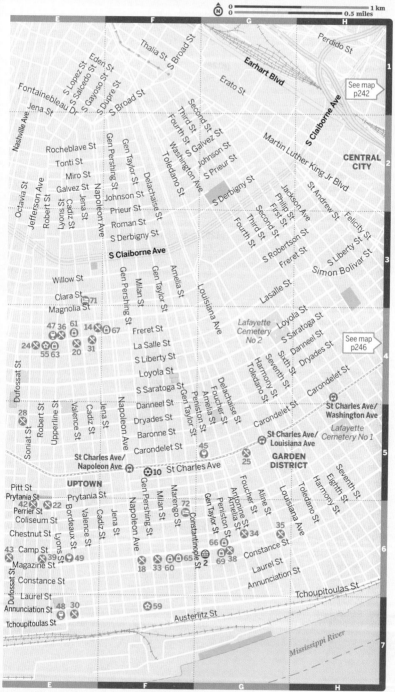

0   1 km
0   0.5 miles

Perdido St

Thalia St

S Broad St

Earhart Blvd

Erato St

See map
p242

S Claiborne Ave

CENTRAL
CITY

Fontainebleau Dr

Jena St

S Lopez St
S Salcedo St
S Gayoso St
S Dupre St
S Broad St
Eden St

Nashville Ave

Rocheblave St

Tonti St

Miro St

Galvez St

Octavia St

Jefferson Ave

Robert St

Lyons St

Cadiz St

Jena St

Napoleon Ave

Gen Pershing St

Johnson St

Prieur St

Roman St

S Derbigny St

Delachaise St

Second St
Third St
Fourth St
Washington Ave
Toledano St

S Galvez St

Johnson St

S Prieur St

S Derbigny St

Martin Luther King Jr Blvd

Jackson Ave
Philip St
First St
Second St
Third St
Fourth St

St Andrew St

S Robertson St

Freret St

S Liberty St

Felicity St

S Bolivar St

S Claiborne Ave

Willow St

Clara St

Magnolia St

Gen Pershing St

Milan St

Gen Taylor St

Amelia St

Louisiana Ave

Lasalle St

Simon Bolivar St

Loyola St

S Saratoga St

Danneel St

Dryades St

Lafayette
Cemetery
No 2

See map
p246

47 36 61

24

55 63

14

20

67

31

Freret St

La Salle St

S Liberty St

Loyola St

S Saratoga St

Danneel St

Dryades St

Baronne St

Carondelet St

Delachaise St

Foucher St

Amelia St

Gen Taylor St

Peniston St

Sixth St
Seventh St
Harmony St
Toledano St

Carondelet St

Carondelet St

St Charles Ave/
Washington Ave

Dufossat St

28

Soniat St

Robert St

Upperline St

Valence St

Cadiz St

Jena St

Napoleon Ave

St Charles Ave/
Napoleon Ave

45

10

25

St Charles Ave

St Charles Ave/
Louisiana Ave

Lafayette
Cemetery
No 1

GARDEN
DISTRICT

UPTOWN

Pitt St

Prytania St

42

22

Perrier St

Coliseum St

Chestnut St

43

Camp St

39

49

Magazine St

Constance St

Laurel St

Annunciation St

Dufossat St

48

30

Tchoupitoulas St

Prytania St

Bordeaux St

Valence St

Cadiz St

Jena St

Napoleon Ave

Lyons St

Gen Pershing St

Milan St

Marengo St

Constantinople St

Gen Taylor St

Peniston St

Amelia St

72

66

18 33 60

65

2

69 38

Foucher St

Antonine St

Aline St

34

35

Constance St

Laurel St

Annunciation St

Louisiana Ave

Toledano St

Harmony St

Eighth St

Seventh St

59

Austerlitz St

Tchoupitoulas St

Mississippi River

UPTOWN & RIVERBEND *Map on p248*

MID-CITY, BAYOU ST JOHN & CITY PARK *Map on p252*

MID-CITY, BAYOU ST JOHN & CITY PARK

MID-CITY, BAYOU ST JOHN & CITY PARK

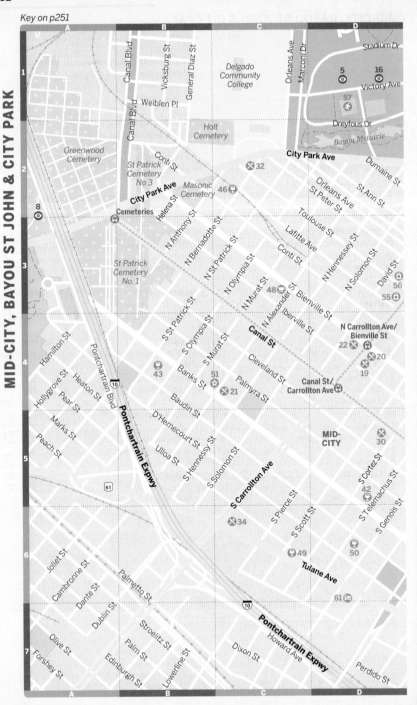

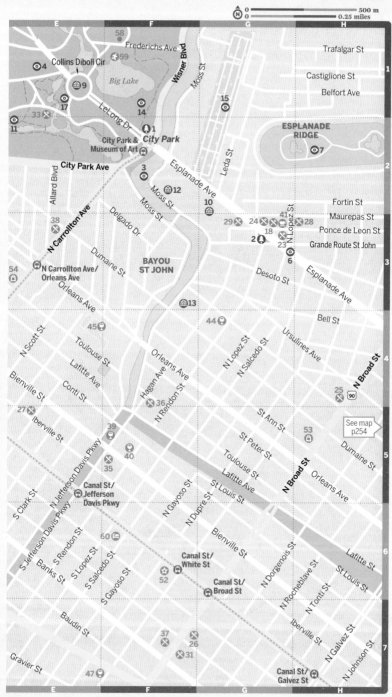

0   500 m
0   0.25 miles

58
Frederichs Ave
59
4
Collins Diboll Cir
9
Big Lake
Wisner Blvd
Trafalgar St
Castiglione St
Belfort Ave

Moss St

LeLong Dr
17
14
33
15

11
1
City Park
City Park & City Park
Museum of Art

ESPLANADE
RIDGE
7

City Park Ave

Allard Blvd

N Carrollton Ave

3
Esplanade Ave
Leda St

Moss St
12
10
38
Delgado Dr
Moss St

Fortin St
29
24
41
28
Maurepas St
18
Ponce de Leon St
2
23
Grande Route St John
6

N Lopez St

Dumaine St
54
N Carrollton Ave/
Orleans Ave

BAYOU
ST JOHN
Desoto St
Esplanade Ave

Orleans Ave
13

Bell St

45
44
Ursulines Ave

N Scott St
Toulouse St
N Lopez St
N Salcedo St

Orleans Ave

N Broad St

Lafitte Ave
Conti St
Bienville St

27
Iberville St
Hagan Ave
N Rendon St
36
St Ann St

25
90

39
St Peter St
53
See map
p254

40
35
Toulouse St

N Gayoso St
N Dupre St
Lafitte Ave
St Louis St

N Broad St
Orleans Ave
Dumaine St

Canal St/
Jefferson
Davis Pkwy

N Jefferson Davis Pkwy

60
Bienville St

Lafitte St

S Clark St
S Rendon St
S Lopez St
S Salcedo St
S Gayoso St
Banks St

Canal St/
White St

52

Canal St/
Broad St

N Dorgenois St
N Rocheblave St
N Tonti St
St Louis St

Baudin St
37
26
31
Iberville St
N Galvez St
N Johnson St

Gravier St
47
Canal St/
Galvez St

TREMÉ-LAFITTE

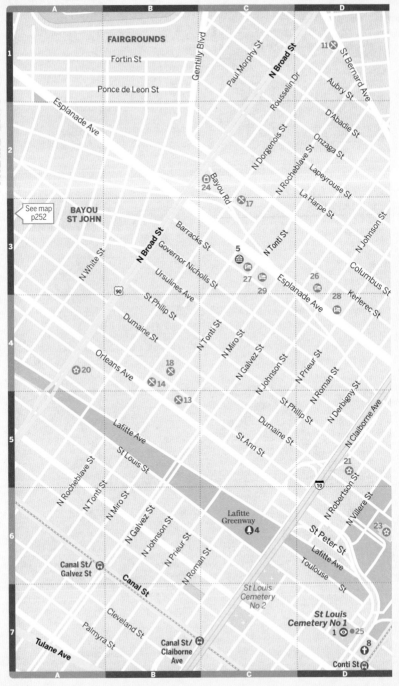

FAIRGROUNDS

Fortin St

Ponce de Leon St

Gentilly Blvd

Paul Morphy St

N Broad St

Rousselin Dr

Aubry St

11 ✕

St Bernard Ave

D'Abadie St

Onzaga St

N Dorgenois St

N Rocheblave St

Lapeyrouse St

La Harpe St

Esplanade Ave

N Johnson St

Columbus St

24 🏠 Bayou Rd

17 ✕

Barracks St

N Tonti St

See map p252

BAYOU ST JOHN

N White St

N Broad St

Governor Nicholls St

5
27 🛏
29 📮

26 🛏

28 🛏

Kerlerec St

Esplanade Ave

Ursulines Ave

St Philip St

90

Dumaine St

N Tonti St

N Miro St

N Galvez St

N Johnson St

N Prieur St

N Roman St

N Derbigny St

N Claiborne Ave

Orleans Ave

20 ✪

18 ✕

14 ✕

13 ✕

St Philip St

Dumaine St

St Ann St

Lafitte Ave

St Louis St

N Rocheblave St

N Tonti St

N Miro St

N Galvez St

N Johnson St

N Prieur St

N Roman St

I-10

21 ✪

N Robertson St

N Villere St

23 ✪

Lafitte Greenway
4 ❶

St Peter St

Lafitte Ave

Toulouse St

Canal St/ Galvez St 🚋

Canal St

St Louis Cemetery No 2

St Louis Cemetery No 1

1 ◉ 25

Cleveland St

Palmyra St

Tulane Ave

Canal St/ Claiborne Ave 🚋

8 ℹ

Conti St 🚋

0 500 m
0 0.25 miles

Our Story

A beat-up old car, a few dollars in the pocket and a sense of adventure. In 1972 that's all Tony and Maureen Wheeler needed for the trip of a lifetime – across Europe and Asia overland to Australia. It took several months, and at the end – broke but inspired – they sat at their kitchen table writing and stapling together their first travel guide, *Across Asia on the Cheap*. Within a week they'd sold 1500 copies. Lonely Planet was born.

Today, Lonely Planet has offices in Franklin, London, Melbourne, Oakland, Dublin, Beijing and Delhi, with more than 600 staff and writers. We share Tony's belief that 'a great guidebook should do three things: inform, educate and amuse'.

Our Writers

Adam Karlin

Faubourg Marigny & Bywater; CBD & Warehouse District; Garden, Lower Garden & Central City; Mid-City, Bayou St John & City Park; Tremé-Lafitte

Adam has contributed to dozens of Lonely Planet guidebooks, covering an alphabetical spread that ranges from the Andaman Islands to the Zimbabwe border. As a journalist, he has written on travel, crime, politics, archeology and the Sri Lankan Civil War, among other topics. He has sent dispatches from every continent barring Antarctica (one day!), and his essays and articles have featured in the BBC, NPR and multiple non-fiction anthologies. He is based out of New Orleans, which helps explain his love of wetlands, food and good music. Learn more at http://walkonfine.com or follow on Instagram @ adamwalkonfine. Adam also wrote the Plan Your Trip, Understand New Orleans and Survival Guide sections.

Ray Bartlett

French Quarter, Uptown & Riverbend, Day Trips from New Orleans

Ray has been travel writing for nearly two decades, bringing Japan, Korea, Mexico and many parts of the United States to life in rich detail for top publishers, newspapers and magazines. His acclaimed debut novel, *Sunsets of Tulum*, set in Yucatán, was a *Midwest Book Review* 2016 Fiction pick. Among other pursuits, he surfs regularly and is an accomplished Argentine tango dancer. Follow him on Facebook, Twitter and Instagram or contact him via www.kaisora.com, his website. Ray currently divides his time between homes in the USA, Japan and Mexico.

Published by Lonely Planet Global Limited
CRN 554153
8th edition – Nov 2018
ISBN 978 1 78657 179 3
© Lonely Planet 2018   Photographs © as indicated 2018
10 9 8 7 6 5 4 3 2 1
Printed in China